AMERICA'S COOKING FOR TWO COOKBOOK 2021

The New Complete Guide With 750 Quick and Delicious Recipes Perfectly Adapted to Serve Just Two. Test Your Kitchen Skills in 30 Minutes or Less!

The Kookerz

© Copyright The Kookerz 2021 - All rights reserved.

The content contained within this book may not be reproduced, duplicated or transmitted without direct written permission from the author or the publisher.

Under no circumstances will any blame or legal responsibility be held against the publisher, or author, for any damages, reparation, or monetary loss due to the information contained within this book. Either directly or indirectly.

Legal Notice:

This book is copyright protected. This book is only for personal use. You cannot amend, distribute, sell, use, quote or paraphrase any part, or the content within this book, without the consent of the author or publisher.

Disclaimer Notice:

By reading this document, the reader agrees that under no circumstances is the author responsible for any losses, direct or indirect, which are incurred as a result of the use of information contained within this document, including, but not limited to, — errors, omissions, or inaccuracies.

Table of Contents

Introduction 1

Chapter 1: Breakfast 2

1. THAI STYLE OMELETTE 2
2. BREAKFAST SANDWICH 2
3. APPLE-CINNAMON EMPANADAS 2
4. ZUCCHINIS IN TOMATO JUICE 3
5. BLACKBERRY SMOOTHIE 3
6. CARROT AND AVOCADO HASH 3
7. WESTERN BROCCOLI HASH 4
8. ZUCCHINI CASSEROLE 4
9. TOFU WAFFLES 4
10. CAULIFLOWER AND SPINACH SALAD 4
11. COUSCOUS AND CHICKPEAS BOWLS 5
12. ZUCCHINI AND QUINOA PAN 5
13. COCONUT CINNAMON OATMEAL 5
14. BRUSSELS SPROUTS WITH NUT 6
15. CINNAMON BANANA BUCKWHEAT PORRIDGE 6
16. SPINACH AND MUSHROOM FRITTATA 6
17. CREAMY WALNUT GRITS 6
18. HEALTHY WHEAT PORRIDGE 7
19. QUINOA PUMPKIN PORRIDGE 7
20. BLUEBERRY OATMEAL 7
21. CHEESY MUSHROOM OATS 8
22. MAPLE AND VANILLA QUINOA BOWL 8
23. ONION, TOMATO, AND SWEET POTATO FRITTATA 8
24. MEAT-LOADED QUICHE 8
25. HONEY OATMEAL 9
26. EGG AND RICE PORRIDGE 9
27. TASTY HERBED POTATOES 9
28. MAC AND CHEESE 9
29. BROCCOLI EGG CASSEROLE 10
30. PINE NUT SPINACH POCKETS 10
31. BISCUITS CASSEROLE 10
32. TURKEY BURRITO 11
33. MUSHROOM OATMEAL 11
34. WALNUTS AND PEAR OATMEAL 11
35. FRENCH TOAST DELIGHT 11
36. MILKY SEMOLINA CUTLETS 12
37. LIGHT BLUEBERRY MUFFINS 12
38. CREAMY POTATO MASH 12
39. CHOCO BERRY SMOOTHIE 13
40. RAISIN FARRO BREAKFAST 13
41. EGG AND ASPARAGUS FRITTATA 13
42. HARD BOILED EGG LOAF 14
43. TURKEY SAUSAGE FRITTATA 14
44. CABBAGE WITH TURKEY SAUSAGES BREAKFAST 14
45. COCONUT FLAKE CEREALS PORRIDGE 15
46. TOMATO, PEPPER, AND SAUSAGE BREAKFAST 15
47. COCONUT BLUEBERRY OATMEAL 15
48. HEARTY POLENTA PORRIDGE 15
49. PEACH OATMEAL 16
50. BRUSSELS SPROUTS WITH NUT 16
51. CREAMY BUTTER POLENTA 16
52. ORZO AND VEGGIE BOWLS 17
53. LEMON PEAS QUINOA MIX 17
54. BANANA BREAD 17
55. CHIA SMOOTHIE 18
56. COCONUT PANCAKES 18
57. MIXED VEGGIE HASH 18
58. AVOCADO SMOOTHIE 18
59. ZUCCHINI HASH 19
60. BAKED EGGS 19
61. CORN KERNEL FRITTERS 19
62. APPLE OAT SUNRISE FRITTERS 19
63. BLANC LEEKS FRITTATA 20
64. HAM AND CHEESE PIE 20
65. CINNAMON VANILLA TOAST 20
66. PAPRIKA EGG SCRAMBLE 21
67. CHERRY RICE PUDDING 21
68. BROCCOLI ASPARAGUS BURRITOS 21
69. ONION POTATO HASH 21
70. EGGPLANT BOWLS 22
71. BANANA OATMEAL 22
72. CHEDDAR EGGS 22
73. SPINACH FRITTATA 22
74. MUSHROOM OATMEAL 23
75. STRAWBERRY BOWLS 23
76. SWEET POTATO MIX 23
77. WALNUT AND BERRIES BOWLS 23
78. CHIVES AVOCADO QUINOA 24
79. BALSAMIC AVOCADO AND TOMATO SALAD 24
80. APPLE SALAD 24
81. PESTO ZUCCHINI RAMEKINS 24
82. CHICKPEAS BREAKFAST SPREAD 25
83. LEMON EGGS 25
84. OREGANO SCRAMBLE 25
85. BACON AND RADISH SCRAMBLE 25
86. BRUSSELS SPROUTS SALAD 26
87. SEEDS PORRIDGE 26

88. Cinnamon Eggs 26
89. Swiss Eggs 26
90. Salmon Sandwich 27
91. Beetroot Carrot Smoothie 27
92. Cheesy Broccoli Soup 27
93. Breakfast Sausage Patties 28
94. BLTs with Overnight Bacon 28
95. Pork Knuckles 28
96. Pork Belly Sliders 29
97. Chinatown Braised Pork 29
98. Sausage and Pepper Sandwiches 29
99. Brown Rice Salad 29
100. Walnuts Yogurt Mix 30
101. Tahini Pine Nuts Toast 30
102. Cheesy Olives Bread 30
103. Sweet Potato Tart 30
104. Stuffed Pita Breads 31
105. Blueberries Quinoa 31
106. Endives, Fennel and Orange Salad ... 31
107. Banana and Strawberry Shake 32
108. Basil Avocado Mix 32
109. Baked Avocado with Tofu 32
110. Chicken and Eggs 32
111. Lime and Chia Eggs 33
112. Broccoli Eggs 33
113. Ginger Tomatoes Eggs 33
114. Cheesy Vegan Mix 33
115. Crunchy Blueberry Bread Bites 34
116. Corn Kernel Fritters 34
117. Lemony Raspberries Bowls 34
118. Spaghetti Squash Fritters 34
119. Mushrooms and Cheese Spread 35
120. Breakfast Egg Tomato 35
121. Mushroom Leek Frittata 35
122. Perfect Breakfast Frittata 35
123. Tuna and Spring Onions Salad 36
124. Cinnamon Pudding 36
125. Tomatoes and Swiss Chard Bake 36
126. Indian Cauliflower 36
127. Creamy Garlic Potato Mash 37
128. Coconut Almond Breakfast Risotto 37
129. Sausage and Cauliflower Mash 37
130. Pumpkin Oatmeal 38
131. Ground Pork with Eggs Frittata 38
132. Italian Turkey Sausage Muffins 38
133. Mustard Eggs and Avocado Mash 39
134. Apple Cinnamon Oatmeal 39
135. Classic Apple Oats 39
136. Roasted Potatoes 40
137. Zucchini Salad 40
138. Egg, Bacon and Cheese Roll Ups 40
139. Crispy Ham Egg Cups 41
140. Olives and Kale 41
141. Stuffed Poblanos 41
142. Raspberries Oatmeal 42
143. Bell Pepper Eggs 42
144. Apple Oat Sunrise Fritters 42
145. Simple Egg Soufflé 42
146. Vegetable Egg Soufflé 43
147. Cinnamon and Cream Cheese Oats 43
148. Cherries Risotto 43
149. Rice, Almonds and Raisins Pudding 44

Chapter 2: Lunch 45

150. Beef and cabbage 45
151. Lamb Shanks 45
152. Lamb Ribs 46
153. Mediterranean lamb 46
154. Coriander Potatoes 46
155. Creamy Green Beans and Tomatoes 47
156. Buttery Artichokes 47
157. Sweet Potato and Eggplant Mix 47
158. Turkey and Mushroom Stew 47
159. Okra Casserole 48
160. Tomato and Avocado 48
161. Tuscan Soup 48
162. Creamed New York Strip 48
163. Ground Beef, Cheese and Bean Bowl 49
164. Basil Beef with Yams 49
165. Authentic Mississippi Pork 50
166. Pork with Spicy Red Sauce 50
167. Sriracha Lemon Pork Chops 50
168. Rosemary Lemon Pork Chops 51
169. Instant BBQ Baby Back Ribs 51
170. Beef Stroganoff 51
171. Duck and Veggies Recipe 52
172. Pork Stew 52
173. Chicken Stew 52
174. Lamb and Raisins 53
175. Sour Cream Lamb Mix 53
176. Garlic Lamb and Peppers 53
177. Lamb and Cauliflower Mix 53
178. Allspice Pork Mix 54
179. Cauliflower Cream 54
180. Easy Cilantro Rice 54
181. Special Chorizo Pinto Beans 55
182. Yummy Coconut Rice 55
183. Easy Bean Mustard Curry 55
184. Mexican Rice 55
185. Lentil Risotto 56
186. Instant Fennel Risotto 56
187. Flavorful Onion Rice 56

#	Recipe	Page
188.	Black Bean Rice	57
189.	Easy Baked Beans	57
190.	Braised Soybeans with Sesame Seeds	57
191.	Pork & Pinto Bean Casserole	58
192.	Rosemary Navy Beans with Mushrooms & Spinach	58
193.	Italian Bean Chowder with Crispy Prosciutto	58
194.	Moroccan Chickpea Curry	59
195.	Bean & Fennel Tempeh Chops	59
196.	Spicy Kidney Bean Dip	60
197.	Cheesy Bean Spread	60
198.	White Beans and Orange Soup	60
199.	Basil Zucchini Soup	61
200.	Chicken and Leeks Soup	61
201.	Lemony Lamb Soup	61
202.	Sausage and Beans Soup	61
203.	Fish Soup	62
204.	Chickpeas Soup	62
205.	Tomato Soup	62
206.	Oyster Stew	63
207.	Potatoes and Lentils Stew	63
208.	Lamb and Potatoes Stew	63
209.	Ground Pork and Tomatoes Soup	64
210.	Peas Soup	64
211.	Minty Lamb Stew	64
212.	Peas and Orzo Soup	65
213.	Turmeric Chard Soup	65
214.	Turmeric Shrimp Mix	65
215.	Whiskey Infused Apples	65
216.	Blueberry Lime Compote	66
217.	Apricot Dates Compote	66
218.	Tropical Pineapple	66
219.	Stuffed Apples	66
220.	Infused Pineapple with Sorbet	67
221.	Vanilla Poached Peaches	67
222.	Plums in Red Wine	68
223.	Orange Compote	68
224.	Lime Artichokes	68
225.	Basil Green Beans	68
226.	Buttery Leeks	69
227.	Green Beans and Capers	69
228.	Balsamic Tomatoes	69
229.	Mustard Asparagus	69
230.	Green Beans and Corn	70
231.	Balsamic Radishes	70
232.	Parsley Artichokes	70
233.	Balsamic Zucchini Mix	70
234.	Garlic Brussels Sprouts	70
235.	Creamy Bell Peppers	71
236.	Cayenne Broccoli	71
237.	Nutmeg Brussels Sprouts	71
238.	Garlic Kale	71
239.	Chives Radish	72
240.	Dill Tomatoes	72
241.	Green Beans Sauté	72
242.	Garlic Spinach	72
243.	Creamy Zucchini	72
244.	Chicken and Coconut Casserole	73
245.	Italian Style Eggplant Sandwich	73
246.	Beef Stew	73
247.	Stuffed Meatballs	74
248.	Air Fryer Bacon Pudding	74
249.	Chicken Zucchini Lunch	74
250.	Special Pancake Mix	75
251.	Turkish Style Koftas Mix	75
252.	Chicken Wings Recipe	75
253.	Summer Squash Fritters Mix	76
254.	Fresh Style Chicken Recipe	76
255.	Asian Chicken Recipe	76
256.	Lamb Ragout	77
257.	Lamb and Barley Dish	77
258.	Lamb and White Beans	77
259.	Mexican-Style Lamb	77
260.	Cacciatore Chicken	78
261.	Honey Barbecue Chicken Wings	78
262.	Sweet and Tangy Chicken	78
263.	Turkey Chili	79
264.	Chicken Romano	79
265.	Filipino Chicken	79
266.	Chicken in Tomatillo Sauce	80
267.	Beer Coated Duck Breast	80
268.	Duck Breast with Figs	80
269.	Herbed Duck Legs	81
270.	Chicken Wings with Prawn Paste	81
271.	Spicy Green Crusted Chicken	81
272.	Creamy Chicken Tenders	82
273.	Chicken Breasts with Chimichurri	82
274.	Fried Chicken Thighs	82
275.	Sweet Sriracha Turkey Legs	83
276.	Gyro Seasoned Chicken	83
277.	Chicken Curry	83
278.	Chicken with Yogurt and Mustard	84
279.	Almond Chicken	84
280.	Mushroom Chicken	84
281.	Braised Duck and Potatoes	84
282.	Goat with Roasted Tomatoes	85
283.	Goat and Potatoes	85
284.	Apple Cider Pork	85
285.	Pork Chops and Onion	86
286.	Creamy pork chops	86
287.	Beef and Barley Soup	87

288. Beef stew 87
289. Glazed Chicken and Apples 87
290. Lemon Chicken and Asparagus 88
291. Turkey with Fig Sauce 88
292. Simple Garlic and Lemon Chicken 88
293. Tarragon Chicken Breasts 88
294. Chicken and Pear Sauce 89
295. Honey Chicken and Dates 89
296. Chicken and Leeks 89
297. Chicken and Yogurt Mix 89
298. Air Fried Chicken Wings 90
299. Tomato Duck Breast 90
300. Turkey, Mushrooms and Peas Casserole 90
301. Duck Breast with Fig Sauce Recipe 90
302. Chicken Thighs and Baby Potatoes 91
303. Cream-Poached Pork Loin 91
304. Hoisin Glazed Pork Tenderloin 91
305. Beef and Tomato Mix 92
306. Lentils and Quinoa Stew 92
307. Chickpeas Stew 92
308. Chickpeas Bowls 92
309. Broccoli Salad 93
310. Herbed Mushrooms 93
311. Balsamic Sprouts 93
312. Mushroom Cream 93
313. Lentils Cakes 94
314. Coconut and Lime Sweet Potatoes 94
315. Lemony Cauliflower Soup 94
316. Spinach Bowls 95
317. Black Bean Patties 95
318. Rice and Avocado Bowls 95
319. Pesto Mushroom Bowls 95
320. Veggie and Pasta Soup 96
321. Avocado Salad 96
322. Peppers Stew 96
323. Potato Stew 96
324. Green Beans Salad 97
325. The Simplest No-Sear Sous Vide Chicken Breast 97
326. Delicious Rosemary Salmon Meal 97
327. Slightly Spicy Garam Masala Encrusted Lamb Rack 98
328. Honey Drizzled Dijon Lamb Rack 98
329. Interesting Salmon with Hollandaise . 98
330. Blackberry Hibiscus Delight 99
331. Smoked Sausage & Cabbage Potatoes 99
332. Boneless Pork Ribs 100
333. Coffee-Chili Pork Porterhouse 100
334. Balsamic Glazed Pork Rib Chop 101
335. Siu-Style Chinese Baby Back Ribs 101
336. Lamb and Cucumber Mix 101
337. Ground Lamb and Carrots Mix 102
338. Pork with Tomatoes and Potatoes 102
339. Lamb and Savoy Cabbage Mix 102
340. Beef with Carrots and Cabbage 102
341. Orange Lamb 103
342. Ginger Pork 103
343. Beef and Swiss Chard 103
344. Nutmeg Pork Roast 103
345. Lamb with Ginger Artichokes 104
346. Chicken and Apricot Sauce Recipe 104
347. Creamy Chicken Casserole Recipe 104
348. Chicken and Garlic Sauce Recipe 105
349. Pork in Creamy Sauce 105
350. Salsa Verde Pork with Velveeta Cheese 105
351. Pork Chops with Caramelized Apples ... 106
352. Broccoli & Cabbage Pork Ramen 106
353. Tuscan Pork Chops 107
354. Balsamic Beef Roast 107
355. Lamb with Tomatoes and Zucchini 107
356. Mushroom Beef Ribs 107
357. Steak Salad with Feta Cheese 108
358. Rustic Beef Brisket with Vegetables ... 108
359. Pork Bean Dip 108
360. Beef with Wontons and Cream Cheese 109
361. Minty Balsamic Lamb 109
362. Tasty Lamb Ribs 110
363. Cinnamon and Coriander Lamb 110
364. Lamb and Plums Mix 110
365. Rosemary Lamb 110
366. Lemony Lamb and Potatoes 111
367. Lamb and Feta Artichokes 111
368. Lamb and Mango Sauce 111
369. Pork Chops with Sweet Peppers and Cabbage 111
370. Greek Lamb and Eggplant 112
371. Roasted Baby Potatoes 112
372. Indian Peppers with Coconut Flour Naan 112
373. Tofu with Zhoug Sauce 113
374. Classic Vegan Cauliflower Soup 113
375. Thai Cream of Celery Soup 114
376. Cauliflower Tikka Masala 114
377. Barbecue Jackfruit 115
378. Green Beans with Scallions and Mushrooms 115
379. Ranch Broccoli Dip 115
380. Pork Bowls 116
381. Shrimp and Sweet Potato Bowls 116
382. Chicken and Eggplants 116
383. Turkey Hash 117

384. Eggplant Stew 117
385. Chicken and Rice Soup 117
386. Chicken and Carrots Soup 117
387. Roasted Peppers Soup 118
388. Lentils Soup 118
389. White Bean Soup 118
390. Veggie Soup 119
391. Seafood Gumbo 119
392. Chicken and Orzo Soup 119
393. Lentils Soup 120
394. Zucchini Soup 120
395. Spanish-Style Carrot Dip 120
396. Cauliflower Risotto 121
397. Spicy Chickpea Curry 121
398. Tasty Mushroom Stroganoff 121
399. Chinese-Style Bok Choy 122
400. Spanish Salmorejo with Pepitas 122
401. Pork Kebabs 122
402. Cilantro Pork and Olives 123
403. Pork and Parsley Sauce 123
404. Pork Tenderloin and Dill Sauce 123
405. Lamb and Couscous 124
406. Pork Meatloaf 124
407. Marjoram Pork 124
408. Simple Fish Chowder 124
409. Pulled Pork 125
410. Pork Roast with Fennel 125
411. Chinese Barbecue Pork 126

Chapter 3: Dinner 127

412. Shrimp and Dill Sauce 127
413. Lemon Rainbow Trout 127
414. Trout and Peppers Mix 128
415. Cod and Cabbage 128
416. Mediterranean Mussels 128
417. Mussels Bowls 128
418. Calamari and Dill Sauce 129
419. Chili Calamari and Veggie Mix 129
420. Cheesy Crab and Lime Spread . 129
421. Horseradish Cheesy Salmon Mix 129
422. Greek Trout Spread 130
423. Scallions and Salmon Tartar 130
424. Salmon and Green Beans 130
425. Cayenne Cod and Tomatoes 130
426. Salmon and Watermelon Gazpacho 131
427. Shrimp and Dill Mix 131
428. Minty Sardines Salad 131
429. Salmon and Zucchini Rolls 132
430. Wrapped Scallops 132
431. Chorizo Shrimp and Salmon Mix 132
432. Garlic Scallops and Peas Mix .. 132
433. Kale, Beets, and Cod Mix 133
434. Salmon, Calamari, and Mango Mix 133
435. Squid and Cucumber Mix 133
436. Octopus and Radish Salad 134
437. Shrimp and Mushrooms Mix ... 134
438. Scallops and Carrots Mix 134
439. Shrimp and Potato 134
440. Parsley Cod 135
441. Cod, Olives, and Zucchinis 135
442. Creamy Salmon Mix 135
443. Trout and Capers Mix 136
444. Balsamic Sea Bass 136
445. Creole Calamari 136
446. Clams and Wine Sauce 136
447. Tarragon Trout 137
448. Shrimp, Corn, and Tomato Bowls 137
449. Shrimp, Crab, and Avocado Bowls 137
450. Salmon and Kale 137
451. Fried Chicken 138
452. Sticky Duck Wings 138
453. Cauliflower soup 138
454. Turkey and Cranberry Sauce ... 139
455. Sage Turkey Mix 139
456. Turkey and Asparagus Mix 139
457. Herbed Almond Turkey 139
458. Thyme Chicken and Potatoes .. 140
459. Lemony Turkey and Pine Nuts 140
460. Yogurt Chicken and Red Onion Mix 140
461. Chicken and Mint Sauce 141
462. Turkey and sweet potato soup .. 141
463. Chicken meatball soup 141
464. Shrimp Creole 142
465. Teriyaki Shrimp 142
466. Rice Flour Coated Shrimp 142
467. Shrimp Kebabs 142
468. Garlic Parmesan Shrimp 143
469. Prawn Burgers 143
470. Buttered Scallops 143
471. Scallops with Capers Sauce 144
472. Bulgur and Avocado Mix 144
473. Lettuce and Tomato Mix 144
474. Avocado and Cucumber Mix ... 145
475. Delicious Shrimp Risotto 145
476. Lentils and Beets Salad 145
477. Corn and Peas Salad 145
478. Cucumber and Carrot Salad 146
479. Carrot Soup 146
480. Tomato and Spinach Soup 146
481. Salmon Burger 147
482. Crunchy Coconut Shrimps 147
483. Salmon Cakes 147

#	Title	Page
484.	Crispy Catfish Fingers	147
485.	Chicken with Asparagus & Jasmine Rice	148
486.	Chicken with Rotini, Mushrooms & Spinach	148
487.	Lemon Butter chicken	148
488.	Instant Pot Turkey Breast	149
489.	Thai Chicken Curry Rice	149
490.	Rich Louisiana Chicken with Quinoa	149
491.	Creamy Peanut Butter Chicken	150
492.	BBQ Pulled Chicken	150
493.	Buffalo Chicken Breasts	150
494.	Green Chicken	151
495.	Cheesy Chicken Stuffed Peppers	151
496.	Holiday BBQ Chicken	151
497.	Spicy Chicken Manchurian	152
498.	Maple Balsamic & Thyme Chicken	152
499.	Sweet & Saucy Chicken	152
500.	Sausage & Red Kidney Stew	153
501.	Classic Beef Stew	153
502.	Moroccan Beef Stew with Couscous	154
503.	Tomato Soup	154
504.	Healthy Vegetable Soup	154
505.	Curried Lentil Stew	155
506.	Carrot Broccoli Soup	155
507.	Squid Potato Stew	155
508.	Trout Radish Stew	156
509.	Lamb & Mushroom Stew	156
510.	Tunisian Lamb Stew	156
511.	Easy Beef Stew	157
512.	Green Bean and Turkey Soup	157
513.	Homemade German Soup	157
514.	Pumpkin-Ginger Soup	158
515.	Mango Salad	158
516.	Crispy Scallops	158
517.	Scallops with Spinach	159
518.	Bacon Wrapped Scallops	159
519.	Glazed Calamari	159
520.	Buttered Crab Shells	160
521.	Crab Cakes	160
522.	Spicy Shrimp and Rice	160
523.	Shrimp Scampi	161
524.	Fish and shrimp	161
525.	Shrimp with Risotto and Herbs	161
526.	Celery soup	162
527.	Chestnut soup	162
528.	Fennel soup	162
529.	Curry Sea Bass	163
530.	Calamari and Mushrooms	163
531.	Curry Trout and Green Beans	163
532.	Coriander Shrimp Mix	163
533.	Shrimp and Mustard Sauce	164
534.	Vegetable Soup	164
535.	Chicken Chili Soup	164
536.	Simple Cracker Mix	165
537.	Simple Char Mix	165
538.	Coriander Char Strips	165
539.	Kipper and Jasmine Rice	165
540.	Kipper and Carrots	165
541.	Tasty Cod	166
542.	Italian Barramundi Fillets	166
543.	Endive Risotto	166
544.	Eggplant Ratatouille	167
545.	Eggplant Marinara	167
546.	Babaganoush	167
547.	Eggplant Surprise	167
548.	Braised Fennel	168
549.	Fennel Risotto	168
550.	Kale with Garlic and Lemon	168
551.	Braised Kale	169
552.	Kale and Bacon	169
553.	Baked Trout and Fennel	169
554.	Seafood Noodles	170
555.	Caramel Shrimp Chili	170
556.	Mediterranean Tilapia Stew	170
557.	Tomatoes Stuffed with Tuna	170
558.	Walnut Coated Halibut	171
559.	Poached Halibut	171
560.	Eggplant Cream	171
561.	Hot Peppers and Garlic Soup	172
562.	Broccoli Soup	172
563.	Onion and Mushroom Soup	172
564.	Corn Soup	173
565.	Green Onions Soup	173
566.	Spinach Soup	173
567.	Garlic Coconut and Avocado Soup	173
568.	Cabbage Soup	174
569.	Quinoa Salad	174
570.	Cream of Butter Squash	174
571.	Beef Stew with Potatoes & Mushrooms	174
572.	Beef & Butternut Squash Stew	175
573.	Turkey with Tomatoes and Red Beans	175
574.	Orange and Cranberry Turkey Wings	175
575.	Chicken Cacciatore with Kale, Rice & Mushrooms	176
576.	Hot Chicken Dirty Rice	176
577.	Spicy Mango-Glazed Chicken	177
578.	Chicken Gruyere with Bell Peppers	177
579.	Onion Chicken with Salsa Verde	178
580.	Lime Squid and Capers Mix	178
581.	Leeks and Calamari Mix	178

- 582. Cod and Brussels Sprouts 178
- 583. Cajun Shrimp 179
- 584. Quick & Easy Shrimp 179
- 585. Rosemary-Flavored Salmon 179
- 586. Tuna Steaks with Capers & Lemon 179
- 587. Tuna Noodle One-Pot 180
- 588. Halibut & Butternut Squash Soup 180
- 589. Fried Snapper in Orange-Ginger Sauce 181
- 590. Tangy Shrimp Asparagus 181
- 591. Garlic Lemon Shrimp 181
- 592. Shrimp Creole 182
- 593. Crab Cakes 182
- 594. Simple Broccoli Mackerel 182
- 595. Classic Shrimp Tomato Meal 182
- 596. Hot Lemony Instant Pot Tilapia with Asparagus 183
- 597. Instant Pot Thai Seafood Boil 183
- 598. Cheesy Shrimp Grits 184
- 599. Healthy Salmon Chowder 184
- 600. Shrimp with Sausage 184
- 601. Nutritious Salmon 184
- 602. Tarragon Trout and Beets 185
- 603. Ginger Trout and Eggplant 185
- 604. Octopus Stew 185
- 605. Greek Octopus 186
- 606. Stuffed Squid 186
- 607. Squid Masala 186
- 608. Braised Squid 187
- 609. Squid Roast 187
- 610. Lemongrass Chicken 187
- 611. Salsa Chicken 188
- 612. Chicken and potatoes 188
- 613. Chicken Sandwiches 188
- 614. Moroccan Chicken 189

Chapter 4: Snacks And Desserts 190

- 615. Lemon Cake 190
- 616. Greek Creamy Vanilla Cake 190
- 617. Eggy Vanilla Bread 190
- 618. Sugary Zucchini Bread 191
- 619. Citrus Cake 191
- 620. Cinnamon Apples 191
- 621. Yogurt Pine Carrot Cake 191
- 622. Ale Graham Cheesecake 192
- 623. Chinese Beef Bites 192
- 624. Shrimp Meatballs 192
- 625. Sausage Bites 192
- 626. Vanilla and Apple Brownies 193
- 627. Chocolate Zucchini Bundt Cake ... 193
- 628. Molten Brownie Pudding 193
- 629. Nutella Lava Cakes 194
- 630. Chocolate Peppermint Pudding 194
- 631. Coconut Pudding 195
- 632. Orange Cake 195
- 633. Keto Orange Semolina Cake 195
- 634. Banana Bread in a Jar 196
- 635. Easy Cherry Cobbler 196
- 636. Crack Chicken 196
- 637. Summer Pineapple Cake 197
- 638. Favorite Almond Cheesecake 197
- 639. Fancy Buckwheat Pudding with Figs .. 198
- 640. Vanilla cake with meringues 198
- 641. Sweet Rice Pudding 198
- 642. Coconut, Cranberry, And Quinoa Crockpot Breakfast 199
- 643. Caramel and Pear Pudding 199
- 644. Cardamom and Banana Tapioca Pudding 199
- 645. Carrot Almond Cake 199
- 646. Indian Rice Pudding 200
- 647. Raspberry Parfait 200
- 648. Greek Hosafi (Stewed Dried Fruits) 201
- 649. Nut Butter Brownies 201
- 650. Hot Mulled Apple Cider 201
- 651. Hungarian Golden Dumpling Cake 202
- 652. Walnut Cream 202
- 653. Chocolate Cream 202
- 654. Skinny Blueberry Lemon Loaf or Muffins 202
- 655. Banana Cake 203
- 656. Chia Pudding 203
- 657. Coconut Mousse 203
- 658. Mango Coconut Pudding 203
- 659. Rhubarb and Berries Pie 204
- 660. Banana Salad 204
- 661. Lemon Berries 204
- 662. Orange Compote 204
- 663. Vanilla Yolk Ice Cream 205
- 664. Rum Bananas 205
- 665. Pistachio Almond Milk Ice Cream 205
- 666. Citrus Confit 205
- 667. Raspberry Compote 206
- 668. Strawberry Jam 206
- 669. Peach and Orange Jam 206
- 670. Blueberry Jam 206
- 671. Coconut and Date Pudding 206
- 672. Chocolate Mousse 207
- 673. Chocolate Chip Oat Cookies 207
- 674. Banana Chocolate Chip Muffins 207
- 675. Simple Vanilla Egg Custard 208
- 676. Chocolate Fondue 208
- 677. Pressure Cooked Brownies 208

- 678. ALMOND TAPIOCA PUDDING ... 208
- 679. SPICED RUM APPLE CIDER ... 209
- 680. FANCY CREAMED FRUIT SALAD ... 209
- 681. PERFECT STRAWBERRY SOUFFLE ... 209
- 682. FUDGY BROWNIE POTS ... 210
- 683. PEANUT BUTTER COOKIES ... 210
- 684. CHEWY BROWNIES ... 210
- 685. LEMON LB. CAKE ... 210
- 686. PERFECT LIMONCELLO ... 211
- 687. LIME-GINGER GIN TONIC ... 211
- 688. "BARREL-AGED" NEGRONI ... 211
- 689. LEMON CUPCAKES ... 212
- 690. APPLE CRISP ... 212
- 691. MOIST CHOCOLATE CAKE ... 212
- 692. KEY LIME PIE ... 213
- 693. LEMON BROCCOLI ... 213
- 694. BAKED POTATO ... 213
- 695. CAJUN SPICED PECANS ... 213
- 696. EASY INSTANT POT CHEESECAKE ... 214
- 697. APPLE STREUSEL DESSERT ... 214
- 698. HOT FUDGE SUNDAE CAKE ... 214
- 699. AMERICAN-STYLE CHEESECAKE ... 215
- 700. LEMON AND BLUEBERRY MOUSSE ... 215
- 701. GRANDMA'S STUFFED APPLES ... 215
- 702. CINNAMON CHERRY CRUMBLE ... 216
- 703. CRANBERRY SWEET RISOTTO ... 216
- 704. BROWN RICE PUDDING ... 216
- 705. CRANBERRY STUFFED APPLES ... 217
- 706. GINGERBREAD PUDDING CAKE ... 217
- 707. TOM COLLINS COCKTAIL ... 217
- 708. CHERRY MANHATTAN ... 218
- 709. CARAMEL MACCHIATO CAKE ... 218
- 710. APPLE PEACH COBBLER ... 218
- 711. CHEESY ASPARAGUS ... 218
- 712. OREGANO BLACK BEAN ... 219
- 713. COCONUT PUDDING ... 219
- 714. SRIRACHA TURKEY BITES ... 220
- 715. BEET SALSA ... 220
- 716. BALSAMIC SALMON BITES ... 220
- 717. LEMON GELATIN CREAM ... 220
- 718. CARAMEL CREAM ... 221
- 719. CHOCOLATE PUDDING ... 221
- 720. VANILLA SOUFFLÉ ... 221
- 721. CHOCOLATE SOUFFLÉ ... 222
- 722. CHILI CAKE CHOCOLATE ... 222
- 723. CHIP COOKIES CHOCOLATE ... 223
- 724. MOUSSE STRAWBERRY ... 223
- 725. CREME CHOCOLATE DE POTS ... 223
- 726. COOKIE CARAMEL DOUGH ... 224
- 727. RICE PUDDING ... 224
- 728. BANOFFEE SWEETEN PIE ... 224
- 729. FROZEN YOGURT SPICED ... 224
- 730. VANILLA BROWNIES ... 225
- 731. POMEGRANATE FUDGE ... 225
- 732. DATES AND ALMONDS CAKE ... 225
- 733. GRAPE CREAM ... 226
- 734. LIME PARFAIT ... 226
- 735. PEACH PIE ... 226
- 736. COCONUT AND COCOA BROWNIES ... 226
- 737. MANGO AND CRANBERRIES TART ... 227
- 738. AVOCADO CAKE ... 227
- 739. BLUEBERRY PANCAKES ... 227
- 740. AVOCADO FUDGE ... 227
- 741. ORANGE CAKE ... 228
- 742. WATERMELON MINT VODKA INFUSION ... 228
- 743. RUMMY EGGNOG ... 228
- 744. CARAMEL SAUCE ... 228
- 745. COCONUT MILK CARDAMOM ... 229
- 746. VANILLA CAKE WITH CHOCOLATE TOPPING 229
- 747. VANILLA CARAMEL ICE CREAM ... 229
- 748. CREAMY EGGY BERRY BLEND ... 229
- 749. MILKY CACAO BROWNIES ... 230
- 750. YOGURT AND CREAM CHEESECAKE ... 230

Conclusion ... 231

Introduction

Food is a big part of any relationship. Eating meals is one of the best ways to spend time with your loved one and talk about things that are going on in your lives. However, going out can be a struggle, especially if you are a person who is conscious about the amount you pay on food and your overall health. Instead of going out and spending money on food that are served in small portions, why not cook a meal for yourself and your partner? Good food creates a feeling of happiness and contentedness. Cooking together would also create a bond that could further deepen your relationship, as you both experience new flavors together.

Our food choices are so important in this day of age as more people are exposed to unhealthy foods all around us. They surround us through fast food chains, salty snacks in the grocery store, and restaurant meals that contain high amounts of overall calories. There has been a rising rate of obesity, diabetes, cancer, skin conditions and many more, and this alarming rate should encourage us to take better care of the body we were born in. There are also times when we may not know what the ingredients are of a certain food item which can lead to dangerous allergic reactions.

Home-cooked meals are the safer route. There are many benefits of cooking at home. It has been found that home-cooked meals contribute to a healthier and happier lifestyle as you are ingesting less sugar and processed foods. It can also lead to higher energy levels, as well as better mental health. It offers many benefits as you can have a much healthier diet through home-cooked meals. Cooking at home also allows you to control the size of your portions, the amount of sweetness or saltiness that you would prefer in each dish, and you are also able to handpick your own ingredients, so you know the quality and safety of your dish.

Cooking meals is a great bonding experience for you and your partner as you try cooking various recipes together. In this recipe book, I have included 750 recipes that have been carefully selected to satisfy both you and your partner's nutritional needs and cravings. The ingredients that have been chosen for every recipe can be easily found in any store. I chose these ingredients so that it would not be a struggle to create these recipes. I wanted recipes that could be cooked with ingredients that you would normally have in your own pantry. These recipes are supposed to be fun and simple to recreate with your loved one. Each recipe has been tested and tried, and trust me, they are definitely yummy!

This book contains recipes that would be suitable for every person's taste due to the wide variation to choose from. Some recipes may include meat such as pork, poultry, or lamb, while others could contain vegetables, seafoods, or dairy. The recipes also vary in cultural taste as I considered every individual's backgrounds. The information that can be found in this book will prove useful, especially in days when you cannot decide what to cook. I hope that this book will help you enjoy easily made healthy, delicious, and tasty recipes at home.

This book also contains a step-by-step method to guide you in your cooking process, as well as preparation and cook times that are mentioned in every recipe. The nutritional benefits of every recipe are also stated. There are definitely numerous ways to eat healthy, and I am sure that the recipes you find in this book is one of those ways.

The recipes provided in this book ranges from breakfast foods, lunch, dinner, dessert, and even healthy snacks. I have gathered a tasty collection of whole food diet recipes that are hearty and would help you improve your cooking skills. There are recipes that are very easy and does not require actual cooking, while there are also some that are more challenging to help you master cooking. Each recipe can vary from 10 minutes that could be made instantly if you are in a hurry, to an hour of cooking time. However, every minute would be worth it in the end as I am sure that the food you make will come out delicious. Happy cooking!

Chapter 1: Breakfast

1. Thai Style Omelette

Preparation: 5 minutes | **Cooking time:** 10 minutes | **Servings:** 2

Ingredients:
- 3 ½ oz minced Pancetta
- 1 cup onion, diced
- 2 Eggs
- 1 tablespoon fish salt

Directions:
Beat the eggs until it is light and fluffy. Preheat the Air fryer to 280°F.
In a bowl, add together all the ingredients. Pour the mixture into the air fryer tray.
Remove after 10 minutes or once omelet is golden brown. Cut and serve.

Nutrition:
Calories: 113, Fat: 8.2 g, Carbs: 0.3 g, Sugar: 0.2 g, Protein: 5.4 g, Cholesterol: 18 mg

2. Breakfast Sandwich

Preparation: 5 minutes | **Cooking time:** 7 minutes | **Servings:** 2

Ingredients:
- 2 Bacon Slices
- 1 Egg
- 1 English muffin Salt and Pepper to taste

Directions:
Beat the egg into a soufflé cup and add salt and pepper to taste.
Heat the air fryer to 390°F and place the soufflé cup, English muffin and bacon into the tray.
Cook all the ingredients for 6-10 minutes. Assemble sandwich and enjoy.

Nutrition:
Calories: 113, Fat: 8.2 g, Carbs: 0.3 g, Sugar: 0.2 g, Protein: 5.4 g, Cholesterol: 18 mg

3. Apple-Cinnamon Empanadas

Preparation: 15 minutes | **Cooking time:** 30 minutes | **Servings:** 2

Ingredients:
- 2-3 baking apples, peeled & diced
- ¼ cup white sugar
- 2 tsps. of cinnamon
- 1 tablespoon brown sugar

1 tablespoon of water
¼ tsp. of vanilla extract
4 pre-made empanada dough shells (Goya)
½ tablespoon cornstarch
2 tbsps.. of margarine or margarine

Directions:
In a bowl, add together white sugar, brown sugar, cornstarch and cinnamon, set aside. Put the diced apples in a pot and place on a stovetop. Add the combined dry ingredients to the apples, then add the water, vanilla extract, and margarine, stirring well to mix.
Cover pot and cook on high heat. Once it starts boiling, lower heat and simmer, until the apples are soft. Remove from the heat and cool.
Lay the empanada shells on a clean counter. Ladle the apple mixture into each of the shells, being careful to prevent spillage over the edges. Fold shells to fully cover apple mixture, seal edges with water, pressing down to secure with a fork.
Cover the air fryer basket with tin foil but leave the edges uncovered so that air can circulate through the basket. Place the empanadas shells in the foil lined air fryer basket, set temperature at 350°F and timer for 15 minutes.
Halfway through, slide the frying basket out and flip the empanadas using a spatula. Remove when golden and serve directly from the basket onto plates.

Nutrition:
Calories: 113, Fat: 8.2 g, Carbs: 0.3 g, Sugar: 0.2 g, Protein: 5.4 g, Cholesterol: 18 mg

4. Zucchinis in Tomato Juice

Preparation time: 10 minutes | **Cooking time:** 15 minutes | **Servings:** 2

Ingredients:
1 teaspoon garlic, diced
½ lb. zucchinis, roughly sliced
1 shallot, diced
1 teaspoon chili flakes
1 teaspoon chives, chopped
1 cup tomato juice
1 teaspoon salt
1 teaspoon coconut oil

Directions:
Heat up a pan with the oil over medium heat, add the shallot and chili flakes and cook for 3 minutes.
Add the zucchinis and the other ingredients, toss, cook for 12 minutes more, divide into bowls and serve.

Nutrition:
Calories: 287, Fat: 5.5 g, Fiber: 4.3 g, Carbs: 4 g, Protein: 6.2 g

5. Blackberry Smoothie

Preparation time: 5 minutes | **Cooking time:** 0 minutes | **Servings:** 2

Ingredients:
1 banana, peeled, frozen
½ cup blackberries, frozen
1 avocado, peeled, pitted and chopped
1 teaspoon stevia
½ cup of coconut milk

Directions:
In a blender, mix the berries with the avocado and the other ingredients, blend and serve.

Nutrition:
Calories: 231, Fat: 8.4 g, Fiber: 11.1 g, Carbs: 9.3 g, Protein: 8.5 g

6. Carrot and Avocado Hash

Preparation time: 10 minutes | **Cooking time:** 20 minutes | **Servings:** 2

Ingredients:
½-lb. carrots, peeled and roughly cubed
½ white onion, chopped
1 teaspoon oregano, dried
1 cup crushed tomatoes
½ teaspoon ground black pepper
½ teaspoon dried thyme
2 avocados, peeled, pitted and cubed
1 tablespoon olive oil
1 teaspoon coriander, ground
½ teaspoon salt
½ teaspoon ground paprika

Directions:
Heat up a pan with the oil over medium heat, add the onion and carrots and cook for 10 minutes stirring often.
Add the rest of the ingredients, toss, cook for another 10 minutes, divide into bowls and serve.

Nutrition:
Calories: 176, Fat: 9.1 g, Fiber: 2.1 g, Carbs: 6.9 g, Protein: 7.2 g

7. Western Broccoli Hash

Preparation time: 10 minutes | **Cooking time:** 20 minutes | **Servings:** 2

Ingredients:
- 1-lb. broccoli florets, chopped
- 1 teaspoon oregano, dried
- 1 tablespoon chives, chopped
- 1 tablespoon olive oil
- 2 tomatoes, chopped
- 1 teaspoon turmeric powder
- 1 red onion, sliced
- 1 shallot, diced
- 1 teaspoon salt
- ½ teaspoon white pepper

Directions:
Heat up a pan with the oil over medium heat, add shallot and onion and cook for 5 minutes.
Add the broccoli and the other ingredients, toss, cook over medium heat for 15 minutes, divide into bowls and serve.

Nutrition:
Calories: 240, Fat: 8.6 g, Fiber: 4.9 g, Carbs: 3.5 g, Protein: 4.9 g

8. Zucchini Casserole

Preparation time: 15 minutes | **Cooking time:** 40 minutes | **Servings:** 2

Ingredients:
- 1-lb. zucchinis, sliced
- 1 teaspoon garam masala
- 3 tablespoons coconut cream
- 1 teaspoon ground nutmeg
- 4 spring onions, chopped
- 1 teaspoon curry powder
- 1 teaspoon salt
- 3 oz tofu, crumbled
- 1 teaspoon dried parsley
- 1 teaspoon olive oil

Directions:
Grease a baking pan with the oil and combine the zucchinis with the other ingredients except the tofu.
Sprinkle the tofu on top, cover the pan with tin foil and cook at 365 °F for 40 minutes.
Divide between plates and serve.

Nutrition:
Calories: 254, Fat: 8.6 g, Fiber: 2.2 g, Carbs: 9.7 g, Protein: 7.8 g

9. Tofu Waffles

Preparation time: 20 minutes | **Cooking time:** 10 minutes | **Servings:** 2

Ingredients:
- 2 tablespoons flax meal mixed with 4 tablespoons water
- ½ cup coconut cream
- ½ teaspoon onion powder
- ½ teaspoon salt
- 1 cup tofu, crumbled
- 1 teaspoon chive, chopped
- 2 tablespoons almond flour
- 1 teaspoon olive oil

Directions:
In a bowl, mix the tofu with coconut cream and the other ingredients except the oil.
Stir the mixture until you get the smooth waffle batter.
Then preheat the waffle iron until it is hot and brush with olive oil.
Pour the small amount of the waffle batter in the waffle iron and flatten it.
Cook it for 1 minute from each side.

Nutrition:
Calories: 120, Fat: 9.3 g, Fiber: 2 g, Carbs: 6.3 g, Protein: 4.7 g

10. Cauliflower and Spinach Salad

Preparation time: 15 minutes | **Cooking time:** 0 minutes | **Servings:** 2

Ingredients:
- 2 cups cauliflower florets, steamed
- 1 cup baby spinach

½ cup cucumber, cubed
1 teaspoon chili powder
1 tablespoon olive oil
¼ onion, diced
½ teaspoon ground black pepper
½ cup black olives, pitted and halved
Juice of 1 lime
1 tablespoon balsamic vinegar
A pinch of salt

Directions:
In a bowl, mix the cauliflower with the spinach, cucumber and the other ingredients, toss and serve for breakfast.

Nutrition:
Calories: 219, Fat: 7.8 g, Fiber: 3.6 g, Carbs: 2.2 g, Protein: 6.2 g

11. Couscous and Chickpeas Bowls

Preparation time: 10 minutes | **Cooking time:** 6 minutes | **Servings:** 2

Ingredients:

¾ cup whole wheat couscous
1 tablespoon olive oil
2 garlic cloves, minced
A pinch of salt and black pepper
14 oz. canned artichokes, drained and chopped
½ teaspoon oregano, dried
1 yellow onion, chopped
1 cup water
15 oz. canned chickpeas, drained and rinsed
15 oz. canned tomatoes, chopped
½ cup Greek olives, pitted and chopped
1 tablespoon lemon juice

Directions:
Put the water in a pot, bring to a boil over medium heat, add the couscous, stir, take off the heat, cover the pan, leave aside for 10 minutes and fluff with a fork.
Heat up a pan with the oil over medium-high heat, add the onion and sauté for 2 minutes.
Add the rest of the ingredients, toss and cook for 4 minutes more.
Add the couscous, toss, divide into bowls and serve for breakfast.

Nutrition:
Calories: 340, Fat: 10 g, Fiber: 9 g, Carbs: 51 g, Protein: 11 g

12. Zucchini and Quinoa Pan

Preparation time: 10 minutes | **Cooking time:** 20 minutes | **Servings:** 2

Ingredients:

1 tablespoon olive oil
1 cup quinoa
2 tablespoons basil, chopped
1 tomato, cubed
2 cups water
A pinch of salt and black pepper
2 garlic cloves, minced
1 zucchini, roughly cubed
¼ cup green olives, pitted and chopped
½ cup feta cheese, crumbled
1 cup canned garbanzo beans, drained and rinsed

Directions:
Heat up a pan with the oil over medium-high heat, add the garlic and quinoa and brown for 3 minutes.
Add the water, zucchinis, salt and pepper, toss, bring to a simmer and cook for 15 minutes.
Add the rest of the ingredients, toss, divide everything between plates and serve for breakfast.

Nutrition:
Calories: 310, Fat: 11 g, Fiber: 6 g, Carbs: 42 g, Protein: 11 g

13. Coconut Cinnamon Oatmeal PC

Preparation time: 8 minutes | **Cooking time:** 4 minutes | **Servings:** 2

Ingredients:

2 cups steel cut oats
4 cups unsweetened coconut milk
½ tsp ground cinnamon
¼ tsp vanilla
2 tbsp coconut sugar
¼ salt

Directions:
Add all ingredients into the instant pot and stir well.

Seal pot with lid and cook on high pressure for 4 minutes.
Allow to release pressure naturally. Open the lid carefully.
Stir well and serve.

Nutrition:
Calories: 504, Carbs: 33.8 g, Protein: 7.6 g, Fat: 39.9 g, Sugar: 5.6 g, Sodium: 47 mg

14. Brussels sprouts with Nut

Preparation time: 5 minutes | **Cooking time:** 3 minutes | **Servings:** 2

Ingredients:
- 1 lb. Brussels sprouts
- 1 cup water
- Pepper
- 4 tbsp pine nuts
- ½ tbsp olive oil
- Salt

Directions:
Pour water into the instant pot.
Add Brussels sprouts in steamer basket and place basket in the pot.
Seal pot with lid and cook on manual high pressure for 3 minutes.
Release pressure using quick release method. Open the lid carefully.
Season with pepper and salt. Drizzle with olive oil.
Sprinkle pine nuts and serve.

Nutrition:
Calories: 122, Carbs: 11.5 g, Protein: 5.1 g, Fat: 8 g, Sugar: 2.8 g, Sodium: 69 mg

15. Cinnamon Banana Buckwheat Porridge

Preparation time: 5 minutes | **Cooking time:** 5 minutes | **Servings:** 2

Ingredients:
- ½ cup buckwheat groats, rinse
- ½ banana, sliced
- ¼ tsp vanilla
- 2 tbsp raisins
- 1 ½ cups almond milk
- ½ tsp cinnamon

Directions:
Add all ingredients into the instant pot and stir well to combine.
Seal pot with lid and cook on high pressure for 5 minutes.

Allow to release pressure naturally then open the lid.
Stir and serve.

Nutrition:
Calories: 571, Carbs: 45.6 g, Protein: 8.5 g, Fat: 44 g, Sugar: 15.8 g, Sodium: 32 mg

16. Spinach and Mushroom Frittata

Preparation time: 10 minutes | **Cooking time:** 7 minutes | **Servings:** 2

Ingredients:
- 1 cup fresh baby spinach
- 6 bacon slices, diced
- 1 cup water
- 8 large eggs
- Pinch of salt, pepper

Directions:
Press "Sauté" on Instant Pot. Add diced bacon. Cook until brown. Set aside. Turn off "Sauté" function.
In a large bowl, add eggs, spinach, bacon, salt, pepper. Stir until combined.
Grease 4 individual ramekins with nonstick cooking spray. Divide egg mixture evenly between ramekins. Cover with aluminum foil.
Add 1 cup water, and trivet to Instant Pot. Place ramekins on top.
Lock, seal lid. Press "Manual" button. Cook on HIGH 5 minutes.
When done, naturally release pressure 10 minutes, remove lid. Serve.

Nutrition:
Calories 293, Fat: 20.9g, Carbs: 3.2g, Dietary Fiber: 1.3, Protein: 23.3g

17. Creamy Walnut Grits

Preparation time: 10 minutes | **Cooking time:** 4 minutes | **Servings:** 2

Ingredients:
- 2 cups instant cook grits
- ¼ cup maple syrup
- 2 tsp cinnamon
- 1 cup milk
- 2 tbsp butter
- ½ cup walnuts, chopped
- 1 tsp vanilla
- ½ cup brown sugar
- 2 cups of water
- Pinch of salt

Directions:
Add butter into the instant pot and set the pot on sauté mode.
Once butter is melted then add grits and cook for 2 minutes.
Add water and salt and stir well.
Seal pot with lid and cook on manual high pressure for 2 minutes.
Once done then release pressure using quick-release method than open the lid.
Add remaining ingredients and stir everything well.
Serve and enjoy.

Nutrition:
Calories: 235, Fat: 11 g, Carbs: 31.8 g, Sugar: 21.6 g, Protein: 4.7 g, Cholesterol: 14 mg

18. Healthy Wheat Porridge

Preparation time: 10 minutes | **Cooking time:** 13 minutes | **Servings:** 2

Ingredients:
- 1 cup cracked wheat
- 1 tbsp raisins
- 1 tsp ground cardamom
- 3 ½ cups almond milk
- 1 tbsp coconut oil
- 2 tbsp almonds, chopped
- ¼ cup sugar

Directions:
Add coconut oil into the instant pot and set the pot on sauté mode.
Add cracked wheat to the pot and cook for 2-3 minutes.
Add 2 ½ cups almond milk, almonds, raisins, and cardamom and stir well.
Add sugar and stir well. Seal pot with lid and cook on high pressure for 10 minutes.
Once done then allow to release pressure naturally then open the lid.
Add remaining milk and stir well.
Serve and enjoy.

Nutrition:
Calories: 403, Fat: 36.9 g, Carbs: 20.4 g, Sugar: 14 g, Protein: 4.2 g

19. Quinoa Pumpkin Porridge

Preparation time: 10 minutes | **Cooking time:** 11 minutes | **Servings:** 2

Ingredients:
- 1 cup quinoa, uncooked
- ¾ cup coconut milk
- ⅓ cup brown sugar
- ½ cup pumpkin puree
- 1 tsp vanilla
- ¾ cup water
- 1 tsp pumpkin pie spice
- ¼ tsp salt

Directions:
Add quinoa, vanilla, coconut milk, water, sugar, pumpkin pie spice, pumpkin puree, and salt into the instant pot and stir well.
Seal pot with lid and cook on manual high pressure for 1 minute.
Once done then allow to release pressure naturally then open the lid.
Stir well and serve with milk.

Nutrition:
Calories: 428, Fat: 17.9 g, Carbs: 59.4 g, Sugar: 19.2 g, Protein: 9.9 g

20. Blueberry Oatmeal

Preparation time: 10 minutes | **Cooking time:** 13 minutes | **Servings:** 2

Ingredients:
- 1 cup steel-cut oats
- ½ cup blueberries
- 1 ½ cups milk
- 2 tbsp sugar
- Pinch of salt
- 1 tbsp chia seeds
- 1 ½ cups water
- 1 tsp vanilla
- 1 tbsp coconut oil

Directions:
Add oil into the instant pot and set the pot on sauté mode.
Add oats to the pot and toast for 2-3 minutes.
Add remaining
Ingredients except for blueberries and stir well. Seal pot with lid and cook on high pressure for 10 minutes.
Once done then allow to release pressure naturally for 10 minutes then release using quick-release method. Open the lid.
Add blueberries and stir well.
Serve and enjoy.

Nutrition:
Calories: 223, Fat: 8.8 g, Carbs: 30.1 g, Sugar: 12.3 g, Protein: 7 g, Cholesterol: 8 mg

21. Cheesy Mushroom Oats

Preparation time: 5 minutes | **Cooking time:** 30 minutes | **Servings:** 2

Ingredients:

- 1 tbsp Butter
- ¼ Onion, diced
- 1 Thyme Sprig
- ¼ cup grated Cheddar Cheese
- ½ cups Water
- 6 oz. sliced Mushrooms
- ½ cup Steel-Cut Oats
- 1 tsp minced Garlic
- 7 oz. Chicken Broth

Directions:
Melt the butter in the IP on SAUTE.
Add the onions and mushrooms and cook for 3-4 minutes.
Add the garlic and cook for one more minute.
Place the oats inside and cook for an additional minute.
Pour the water and broth over and give it a good stir.
Place the thyme sprig inside and close the lid.
Cook on HIGH for 12 minutes.
Do a natural pressure release. Serve and enjoy!

Nutrition:
Calories: 266, Fats: 12 g, Carbs: 31 g, Protein: 9 g, Fiber: 3 g

22. Maple and Vanilla Quinoa Bowl

Preparation time: 5 Minutes | **Cooking time:** 20 Minutes | **Servings:** 2

Ingredients:

- 1 cup Quinoa, uncooked
- 1 tsp Vanilla Extract
- 1 ½ cups Water
- 2 tbsp Maple Syrup
- 2 tbsp Coconut Flakes

Directions:
Dump all the ingredients in your Instant Pot.
Stir well to combine.
Close and seal the lid and set the IP to MANUAL.
Cook the mixture for 5-8 minutes on HIGH.
Let the pressure come down on its own.
Serve and enjoy!

Nutrition:
Calories: 372, Fats: 2.5 g, Carbs: 35.7 g, Protein: 6 g, Fiber: 3 g

23. Onion, Tomato, and Sweet Potato Frittata

Preparation time: 5 minutes | **Cooking time:** 15 minutes | **Servings:** 2

Ingredients:

- 3 Large Eggs, beaten
- 1 tbsp Coconut Flour
- 1 Tomato, chopped
- 2 tbsp Milk
- 1 tbsp Olive Oil
- ½ Onion, diced
- 4 oz. Sweet Potato, shredded
- 1 ½ cups Water

Directions:
Pour the water into your IP and lower the trivet.
Whisk the oil, eggs, and milk in one large bowl.
Fold in the flour and veggies.
Pour the mixture into a greased baking dish.
Place the dish on the trivet and close the lid of the IP.
Set the Instant Pot to MANUAL and cook on HIGH for 16 minutes.
Do a quick pressure release.
Serve and enjoy!

Nutrition:
Calories: 202, Fats: 11.6 g, Carbs: 14 g, Protein: 11 g, Fiber: 2 g

24. Meat-Loaded Quiche

Preparation time: 5 minutes | **Cooking time:** 40 minutes | **Servings:** 2

Ingredients:

- 2 Ham Slices, diced
- 2 Bacon Slices, cooked and crumbled
- 3 Eggs, beaten
- 1 Green Onion, sliced
- 1 ½ cups Water
- ½ cup cooked and crumbled Sausage
- ½ cup grated Cheddar Cheese
- ¼ cup Milk
- Salt and Pepper, to taste

Directions:
Pour the water into your IP and lower the trivet.
Combine all the ingredients in a bowl.

Pour the mixture into a baking dish.
Cover the dish with aluminum foil and place on the trivet.
Close the lid and cook on HIGH for 22 minutes.
Press CANCEL and wait 10 minutes before releasing the pressure quickly.
Serve and enjoy!

Nutrition:
Calories: 660, Fats: 40 g, Carbs: 8 g, Protein: 40 g, Fiber: 0.3 g

25. Honey Oatmeal *PC*

Preparation time: 5 minutes | **Cooking time:** 10 minutes | **Servings:** 2

Ingredients:
- ½ cup Steel-Cut Oats
- 3 tbsp Honey
- Pinch of Salt
- ½ cup warm Milk
- Pinch of Cinnamon
- 2 cups Water

Directions:
Pour 1 cup of the water into the Instant Pot and lower the trivet.
In a heatproof bowl, place the oats and the remaining water.
Close the lid and cook on HIGH for 6 minutes.
Do a quick pressure release.
Stir in the honey, cinnamon, salt, and milk.
Serve and enjoy!

Nutrition:
Calories: 155, Fats: 2 g, Carbs: 28 g, Protein: 4 g, Fiber: 2.3 g

26. Egg and Rice Porridge *PC*

Preparation time: 5 minutes | **Cooking time:** 40 minutes | **Servings:** 2

Ingredients:
- ¼ cup Rice
- 1 cup Water
- 2 Scallions, chopped
- 1 tbsp Olive Oil
- ¼ tsp Salt
- 2 Eggs
- 1 cup Chicken Broth
- ½ tbsp Sugar
- 1 tsp Soy Sauce
- ¼ tsp Pepper

Directions:
Combine the rice, water, broth, salt, and sugar, in the Instant Pot.
Close the lid and set the IP to PORRIDGE.
Cook for 30 minutes.
Do a quick pressure release and transfer to a bowl.
Wipe the IP clean and add the olive oil.
Cook the scallions on SAUTE for about a minute.
Add the remaining
Ingredients and cook until the eggs are set.
Stir the mixture into the rice. Serve and enjoy!

Nutrition:
Calories: 214, Fats: 2 g, Carbs: 24 g, Protein: 10 g, Fiber: 2.3 g

27. Tasty Herbed Potatoes *PC*

Preparation time: 10 minutes | **Cooking time:** 20 minutes | **Servings:** 2

Ingredients:
- 1 ½ lbs. baby potatoes
- 5 tbsp olive oil
- 3 garlic cloves
- Salt
- 1 rosemary spring
- 1 cup water
- Pepper

Directions:
Add oil in instant pot and set the pot on sauté mode.
Add potatoes, rosemary, and garlic and sauté for 10 minutes.
Add water and stir well. Seal pot with lid and cook on high pressure for 10 minutes.
Release pressure using quick release method than open lid carefully.
Season potatoes with pepper and salt.
Serve and enjoy.

Nutrition:
Calories: 252, Carbs: 21.9 g, Protein: 4.5 g, Fat: 17.7 g, Sodium: 58 mg

28. Mac and Cheese *PC*

Preparation time: 10 minutes | **Cooking time:** 7 minutes | **Servings:** 2

Ingredients:
- 2 cups noodles, gluten-free
- 1 cup chicken stock
- 2 cups cheddar cheese, shredded
- Salt
- 1 cup heavy cream
- 4 tbsp butter
- Pepper

Directions:
Add cream, noodles, and stock in an instant pot.
Seal pot with lid and cook for 7 minutes.
Release pressure using quick release method than open lid carefully.
Add butter, cheese, and stir until melted.
Season with pepper and salt.
Serve and enjoy.

Nutrition:
Calories: 546, Carbs: 21.9 g, Protein: 18.6 g, Fat: 43.1 g, Sugar: 0.8 g, Sodium: 678 mg

29. Broccoli Egg Casserole AF

Preparation time: 10 minutes | **Cooking time:** 30 Minutes | **Servings:** 2

Ingredients:

1 Broccoli head, florets separated and steamed	1 Tomato, chopped
1 tsp Thyme, chopped	3 Carrots, chopped and steamed
2 oz. Cheddar cheese, grated	2 oz. Milk
1 tsp. Parsley, chopped	2 Eggs
Salt and black pepper to taste	

Directions:
Whisk eggs with parsley, milk, thyme, pepper, and salt in a bowl.
Toss in the broccoli, tomato, and carrots.
Spread these vegetables in the air fryer basket.
Top them with cheddar cheese and seal the air fryer.
Cook them for 20 minutes at 350°F.
Enjoy.

Nutrition:
Calories: 214, Fat: 4 g, Fiber: 7 g, Carbs: 12 g, Protein: 3 g

30. Pine Nut Spinach Pockets AF

Preparation time: 10 minutes | **Cooking time:** 14 minutes | **Servings:** 2

Ingredients:

1 lb. Baby spinach leaves, roughly chopped	4 sheets Filo pastry
½ lb. Ricotta cheese	2 tbsp Pine nuts
1 Egg, whisked	Zest from 1 lemon, grated
Greek yogurt for serving	Salt and black pepper to taste

Directions:
Mix cheese, lemon zest, egg, salt, pepper, pine nuts, and spinach in a bowl.
Spread the filo sheets on the working surface and divide the spinach mixture over them.
Fold each sheet diagonally and seal the parcels.
Place these parcels in the air fryer basket and seal the fryer.
Cook them for 4 minutes at the air fryer mode at 400°F.
Serve.

Nutrition:
Calories: 182, Fat: 4 g, Fiber: 8 g, Carbs: 9 g, Protein: 5 g

31. Biscuits Casserole AF

Preparation time: 10 minutes | **Cooking time:** 15 minutes | **Servings:** 2

Ingredients:

12 oz. biscuits, quartered	3 tbsps. flour
½ lb. sausage, diced	A pinch of salt and black pepper
2 ½ cups milk	Cooking spray

Directions:
Grease your air fryer with cooking spray and heat it over 350°F.
Add biscuits on the bottom and mix with sausage.
Add flour, milk, salt and pepper, toss a bit and cook for 15 minutes.
Divide among plates and serve for breakfast.

Nutrition:
Calories: 113, Fat: 8.2 g, Carbs: 0.3 g, Sugar: 0.2 g, Protein: 5.4 g, Cholesterol: 18 mg

32. Turkey Burrito AF

Preparation time: 10 minutes | **Cooking time:** 10 minutes | **Servings:** 2

Ingredients:
- 4 slices turkey breast already cooked
- 2 eggs
- 2 tbsps. salsa
- ⅛ cup mozzarella cheese, grated
- ½ red bell pepper, sliced
- 1 small avocado, peeled, pitted and sliced
- Salt and black pepper to the taste
- Tortillas for serving

Directions:
In a bowl, whisk eggs with salt and pepper to the taste, pour them in a pan and place it in the air fryer's basket.
Cook at 400°F for 5 minutes, take pan out of the fryer and transfer eggs to a plate.
Arrange tortillas on a working surface, divide eggs on them, also divide turkey meat, bell pepper, cheese, salsa and avocado.
Roll your burritos and place them in your air fryer after you've lined it with some tin foil.
Heat up the burritos at 300°F for 3 minutes, divide them on plates and serve.

Nutrition:
Calories: 113, Fat: 8.2 g, Carbs: 0.3 g, Sugar: 0.2 g, Protein: 5.4 g, Cholesterol: 18 mg

33. Mushroom Oatmeal

Preparation time: 10 minutes | **Cooking time:** 20 minutes | **Servings:** 2

Ingredients:
- 1 small yellow onion, chopped
- 2 garlic cloves, minced
- ½ cup water
- 3 thyme springs, chopped
- ½ cup gouda cheese, grated
- Salt and black pepper to the taste
- 1 cup steel cut oats
- 2 tbsps. margarine
- 14 oz. canned chicken stock
- 2 tbsps. extra virgin olive oil
- 8 oz. mushroom, sliced

Directions:
Heat up a pan that fits your air fryer with the margarine over medium heat, add onions and garlic, stir and cook for 4 minutes.
Add oats, water, salt, pepper, stock and thyme, stir, introduce in your air fryer and cook at 360°F for 16 minutes.
Meanwhile, heat up a pan with the olive oil over medium heat, add mushrooms, cook them for 3 minutes, add to oatmeal and cheese, stir, divide into bowls and serve for breakfast.

Nutrition:
Calories: 113, Fat: 8.2 g, Carbs: 0.3 g, Sugar: 0.2 g

34. Walnuts and Pear Oatmeal AF

Preparation time: 5 minutes | **Cooking time:** 12 minutes | **Servings:** 2

Ingredients:
- 1 cup water
- ¼ cups brown sugar
- 1 cup rolled oats
- 2 cups pear, peeled and chopped
- 1 tablespoon margarine, soft
- ½ tsp. cinnamon powder
- ½ cup walnuts, chopped
- ½ cup raisins

Directions:
In a heat proof dish that fits your air fryer, mix milk with sugar, margarine, oats, cinnamon, raisins, pears and walnuts, stir, introduce in your fryer and cook at 360°F for 12 minutes. Divide into bowls and serve.

Nutrition:
Calories: 113, Fat: 8.2 g, Carbs: 0.3 g, Sugar: 0.2 g, Protein: 5.4 g, Cholesterol: 18 mg

35. French Toast Delight

Preparation time: 5 minutes | **Cooking time:** 6 minutes | **Servings:** 2

Ingredients:
- 4 bread slices
- ½ tsp. cinnamon
- Pinch salt
- Pinch Nutmeg Icing sugar and maple syrup, to serve
- 2 tbsps. margarine
- 2 Eggs
- Pinch ground cloves

Directions:

Preheat Air Fryer to 350°F. Whisk together eggs, cloves, cinnamon, nutmeg, cloves and salt in a bowl. Margarine sides of each bread slice and cut into strips. Soak the bread strips in the egg mixture one after the other and arrange in the tray. Cook in two batches, if necessary.

Cook 2 minutes and then remove the strips. Lightly coat bread strips with cooking spray on both sides. Place back the tray into the air fryer and cook another 4 minutes, checking to ensure they are cooking evenly.

Remove bread from Air Fryer once it's golden brown. Sprinkle with icing sugar and drizzle with maple syrup.

Nutrition:
Calories: 113, Fat: 8.2 g, Carbs: 0.3 g, Sugar: 0.2 g, Protein: 5.4 g, Cholesterol: 18 mg

36. Milky Semolina Cutlets

Preparation time: 45 minutes | **Cooking time:** 15 minutes | **Servings:** 2

Ingredients:

3 tbsps. of vegetable oil	1 cup of semolina
12 oz. of mixed vegetables (any of your choice), chopped	2 ½ lbs. of milk
½ tsp. salt	½ tsp. black pepper, ground

Directions:

Pour the milk into a saucepan and heat. Add the mixed vegetables and allow it to cook until they are soft for about 3 minutes.

Add the pepper and salt and then the semolina. Cook until the mixture thickens, this will take about 10 minutes.

Grease a flat plate with oil, spread the semolina mixture on it. Refrigerate for about 4 hours until it is firm.

Heat the air fryer to 350°F.

Remove from the refrigerator and cut into flat round shapes. Brush the cutlets with oil and place them into the air fryer.

Cook for 10 minutes. Serve while hot with any sauce of your choice.

Nutrition:
Calories: 113, Fat: 8.2 g, Carbs: 0.3 g, Sugar: 0.2 g, Protein: 5.4 g, Cholesterol: 18 mg

37. Light Blueberry Muffins

Preparation time: 15 minutes | **Cooking time:** 15 minutes | **Servings:** 2

Ingredients:

1 cup of fresh, ripe blueberries, rinsed	1½ cups all-purpose flour
½ cup of white sugar	2 tsps. of baking powder
⅓ cup of vegetable oil	1 medium-sized egg
½ tsp. of salt	¼ cup unsweetened yogurt
1 tablespoon brown sugar	2 tsps. vanilla extract.

Directions:

Lightly coat the blueberries with flour, shake, and set aside. Combine the baking powder, sugar, flour, and salt in a large bowl, stirring well to evenly combine.

In a smaller bowl, whisk together the egg, oil, yogurt, and vanilla extract until evenly combined. Pour it into the larger bowl containing the dry ingredients and mix well with a whisk or fork.

Add the blueberries, using a wooden spoon or spatula to gently fold in. Arrange muffin cups on the baking tin and place on the air fryer basket, (do two batches). Spoon the batter into the muffin tins, filling up about ¾ of the way.

Now sprinkle brown sugar onto them. Set to 350°F for 10 minutes. Remove.

Muffins are ready when an. inserted toothpick in the center comes out dry. Otherwise, return basket and reset the air fryer to 320°F and 2 minutes Cooking time

Let your muffins cool for a while then enjoy!

Nutrition:
Calories: 113, Fat: 8.2 g, Carbs: 0.3 g, Sugar: 0.2 g

38. Creamy Potato Mash

Preparation time: 10 minutes | **Cooking time:** 8 minutes | **Servings:** 2

Ingredients:

3 lbs. potatoes, clean and diced	4 tbsp half and half
2 tbsp butter	1 cup chicken stock
¼ tsp pepper	¾ tsp salt

Directions:
Place steamer rack in the instant pot then pour chicken stock.
Add potatoes and seal pot with lid.
Cook on manual high pressure for 8 minutes.
Release pressure using quick release method than open lid carefully.
Transfer potatoes in large bowl and mash with masher.
Add half and half, butter, pepper, and salt. Stir to combine.
Serve and enjoy.

Nutrition:
Calories: 205, Carbs: 36.2 g, Protein: 4.3 g, Fat: 5.3 g, Sugar: 2.8 g, Sodium: 463 mg

39. Choco Berry Smoothie

Preparation time: 5-8 minutes | **Cooking time:** 0 minutes | **Servings:** 2

Ingredients:

2 bananas, peeled	1 avocado, pitted and sliced
2 cups almond or coconut milk	½ cup raspberries or strawberries
2 tablespoons cocoa powder, unsweetened	Ice cubes, optional

Directions:
In a blender, add the almond milk and other ingredients. Add ice cubes, if desired.
Blend well to make a smooth mix. Serve chilled in a tall glass.

Nutrition:
Calories 263, Fat 14 g, Carbs 36 g, Fiber 11 g, Sodium 168 mg, Protein 5 g

40. Raisin Farro Breakfast

Preparation time: 5 minutes | **Cooking time:** 5 minutes | **Servings:** 2

Ingredients:
2 cups water
¼ cup brown sugar
1 cup farro
2 tablespoons vegetable oil
1 teaspoon vanilla extract
¼ teaspoon ground cinnamon
¼ cup raisins
¼ teaspoon salt
chopped nuts of your choice

Directions:
Rinse the farro in a colander.
Take Instant Pot and carefully arrange it over a clean, dry kitchen platform. Turn on the appliance.
Find and press "Sauté" cooking function.
In the cooking pot area, add the oil and farro in the pot. Cook until turn fragrant. Add remainder of ingredients and stir again.
Close the pot lid and seal the valve to avoid any leakage. Find and press "Manual" cooking setting and set cooking time to 5 minutes.
Allow the recipe ingredients to cook for the set time, and after that, the timer reads "zero". Press "Cancel" and press "QPR" setting for quick pressure release.
Open the pot and arrange the cooked recipe in serving plates. Serve immediately topped with nuts and/or extra sugar.

Nutrition:
Calories: 203, Fat: 7 g, Carbs: 33 g, Fiber: 2 g, Protein: 4.5 g

41. Egg and Asparagus Frittata

Preparation time: 10 minutes | **Cooking time:** 23 minutes | **Servings:** 2

Ingredients:

6 large eggs	½ cup of unsweetened almond milk or unsweetened coconut milk
Pinch of salt, pepper	2 Tablespoons fresh chives, chopped
1 cup fresh asparagus, stemmed, cut into bite-sized pieces	

Directions:
Grease an eight-inch cake pan with nonstick cooking spray.

In a bowl, mix eggs, milk, salt, pepper, chives, asparagus. Stir.
Pour mixture in cake pan. Cover with foil.
Add 1 cup water, and trivet to Instant Pot.
Place cake pan on trivet. Lock, seal lid. Press "Manual." Cook on HIGH 23 minutes.
When done, naturally release pressure 10 minutes, then quick release. Remove lid.
Remove pan. Allow to set 5 minutes before slicing. Serve.

Nutrition:
Calories: 170, Fat: 13.8 g, Carbs: 3.4 g, Fiber: 1.4 g, Protein: 9.7 g

42. Hard Boiled Egg Loaf

Preparation time: 5 minutes | **Cooking time:** 10 minutes | **Servings:** 2

Ingredients:
- 12 large eggs
- Pinch of salt, pepper

Directions:
Grease a baking dish that will fit your Instant Pot with nonstick cooking spray.
Crack eggs into baking dish. Season with salt, pepper. Don't stir.
Add 1 cup water, and steamer rack to Instant Po. Place baking dish on rack.
Close, seal lid. Press "Manual" button. Cook on HIGH 5 minutes.
When done, naturally release pressure 5 minutes, then quick release remaining pressure.
Remove lid. Allow pan to settle 5 minutes.
Transfer egg loaf to a cutting board. Slice. Serve.

Nutrition:
Calories: 63, Fat: 4.4 g, Carbs: 0.3 g, Fiber: 0 g, Protein: 5.5 g

43. Turkey Sausage Frittata

Preparation time: 5 minutes | **Cooking time:** 23 minutes | **Servings:** 2

Ingredients:
- 1 ½ cups ground turkey breakfast sausage
- 12 large eggs, beaten
- 1 Tablespoon of olive oil
- 1 cup of unsweetened coconut milk or unsweetened almond milk
- 1 teaspoon of salt
- 1 teaspoon of freshly cracked black pepper

Directions:
Press "Sauté" function on Instant Pot. Add olive oil.
Add breakfast turkey to Instant Pot. Cook until brown, stirring occasionally. Turn off "Sauté" function and set aside.
Grease a spring form pan with nonstick cooking spray. Add cooked turkey.
In a bowl, add eggs, milk, salt, pepper. Stir until combined. Pour over turkey.
Add 2 cups water, and trivet to Instant Pot. Place spring form pan on top of trivet.
Lock the lid, seal valve. Press "Manual" button. Cook on HIGH, 7 minutes.
When cooking is done, naturally release pressure. Remove the lid.
Remove pan. Allow to settle 5 minutes, then slice.
Serve.

Nutrition:
Calories: 471, Fat: 31.7 g, Carbs: 4.3 g, Fiber: 1.3 g, Protein: 42.9 g

44. Cabbage with Turkey Sausages Breakfast

Preparation time: 8 minutes | **Cooking time:** 12 minutes | **Servings:** 2

Ingredients:
- 1 lb. Turkey Sausage sliced
- 1 head cabbage sliced
- 4 cloves minced garlic
- 2 Tbsp olive oil
- 1 onion diced
- 3 tsp vine vinegar or to taste

Directions:
Place the oil and sliced sausages in your Instant Pot.
Press SAUTÉ button on your Instant Pot and sauté sausages about 10-12 minutes.
Add sliced cabbage, onion and garlic and sauté for 10 minutes, stirring frequently.
Press CANCEL button and transfer the sausages and cabbage mixture to serving plate.
Sprinkle with wine vinegar and serve.

Nutrition:
Calories: 641, Fat: 15 g, Carbs: 16.4 g, Fiber: 6 g, Protein: 14.43 g

45. Coconut Flake Cereals Porridge

Preparation time: 3 minutes | **Cooking time:** 12 minutes | **Servings:** 2

Ingredients:

6 tbsps. organic unsweetened shredded coconut	1 ½ Tbsp raw whole golden flaxseed
1 cup unsweetened coconut milk, preferably additive free	½ tsp. vanilla extract

For Toppings:

Liquid stevia drops	Ground cinnamon or cardamom, to taste

Directions:
Press SAUTÉ button on your Instant Pot.
When the word "hot" appears on the display, pour the milk and cook for 2 minutes, stirring frequently.
Add organic unsweetened shredded coconut, raw whole golden flaxseed, and vanilla extract, stir well for 2 - 3 minutes.
Lock lid into place and set on the MANUAL setting for 6 -7 minutes.
When the timer beeps, press "Cancel" and carefully flip the Quick Release valve to let the pressure out.
Serve hot with liquid stevia to taste and sprinkle with ground cinnamon or cardamom, to taste.

Nutrition:
Calories: 281.93, Fat: 29.14 g, Carbs: 6.76 g, Fiber: 2.04 g, Protein: 2.83 g

46. Tomato, Pepper, and Sausage Breakfast

Preparation time: 5 minutes | **Cooking time:** 40 minutes | **Servings:** 2

Ingredients:

2 Green Bell Peppers, chopped	4 Italian Sausage Links
14 oz. diced Tomatoes	1 Garlic Clove, minced
1 tsp Italian Seasoning	1 ½ cups Water

Directions:
Pour the water into the Instant Pot and lower the trivet.
Grease a baking dish with some cooking spray and dump all the ingredients in it.
Stir to combine well.
Place the dish in the trivet and close the lid.
Set the IP to MANUAL and cook on HIGH for 22 minutes.
Release the pressure naturally.
Serve and enjoy!

Nutrition:
Calories: 400, Fats: 30 g, Carbs: 9 g, Protein: 20 g, Fiber: 0.8 g

47. Coconut Blueberry Oatmeal

Preparation time: 10 minutes | **Cooking time:** 30 minutes | **Servings:** 2

Ingredients:

2 ¼ cups oats	1 cup blueberries
¼ cup gluten-free flour	½ tsp vanilla
3 cups of water	14 oz coconut milk
6 tbsp brown sugar	⅛ tsp salt

Directions:
Add all ingredients into the instant pot and stir well.
Seal pot with lid and cook on manual mode for 30 minutes.
Once done then release pressure using the quick-release method than open the lid.
Stir well and serve.

Nutrition:
Calories: 337, Fat: 18.1 g, Carbs: 40.3 g, Sugar: 13.7 g, Protein: 6.4 g

48. Hearty Polenta Porridge

Preparation time: 10 minutes | **Cooking time:** 9 minutes | **Servings:** 2

Ingredients:

½ cup polenta	1 cup of water
½ tsp vanilla	3 tbsp maple syrup

2 cups almond milk   3 tbsp milk

Directions:
Spray oven-safe dish with cooking spray.
Add polenta, vanilla, maple syrup, and 2 cups almond milk into the prepared dish and stir well.
Pour water into the instant pot then place trivet into the pot.
Place dish on top of the trivet.
Seal pot with lid and cook on manual high pressure for 9 minutes.
Once done then allow to release pressure naturally then open the lid.
Carefully remove the dish from the pot. Add 3 tbsp milk into the polenta mixture and whisk polenta until creamy.
Serve and enjoy.

Nutrition:
Calories: 392, Fat: 29 g, Carbs: 32.6 g, Sugar: 13.7 g, Protein: 4.6 g, Cholesterol: 1 mg

49.   Peach Oatmeal

Preparation time: 10 minutes | **Cooking time:** 6 minutes | **Servings:** 2

Ingredients:
- 4 cups rolled oats
- ⅓ cup sugar
- 3 ½ cups milk
- Pinch of salt
- 2 cups peaches
- ½ tsp cinnamon
- 2 ½ cups water

Directions:
Add all ingredients into the instant pot and stir well.
Seal pot with lid and cook on manual high pressure for 6 minutes.
Once done then allow to release pressure naturally then open the lid.
Stir well and serve with milk.

Nutrition:
Calories: 255, Fat: 5 g, Carbs: 44.9 g, Sugar: 17.1 g, Protein: 9.2 g, Cholesterol: 9 mg

50.   Brussels sprouts with Nut

Preparation time: 10 minutes | **Cooking time:** 3 minutes | **Servings:** 2

Ingredients:
- 1 lb. Brussels sprouts
- 1 cup water
- 4 tbsp pine nuts
- ½ tbsp olive oil
- Pepper
- Salt

Directions:
Pour water into the instant pot.
Add Brussels sprouts in steamer basket and place basket in the pot.
Seal pot with lid and cook on manual high pressure for 3 minutes.
Release pressure using quick release method. Open the lid carefully.
Season with pepper and salt. Drizzle with olive oil.
Sprinkle pine nuts and serve.

Nutrition:
Calories: 122, Carbs: 11.5 g, Protein: 5.1 g, Fat: 8 g, Sugar: 2.8 g, Sodium: 69 mg

51.   Creamy Butter Polenta

Preparation time: 10 minutes | **Cooking time:** 5 minutes | **Servings:** 2

Ingredients:
- ½ cup dry polenta, gluten-free
- ½ tbsp butter
- ¼ tsp salt
- 1 cup almond milk
- 1 cup water

Directions:
Add almond milk, water, and salt in instant pot. Stir well. Set instant pot on saute mode.
When almond milk mixture begins to boil then add polenta slowly and stir well to combine.
Seal pot with lid and cook on manual high pressure for 5 minutes.
Allow to release pressure naturally. Open the lid carefully.
Set pot on sauté mode and cook until all liquid absorbed.
Stir and serve.

Nutrition:
Calories: 293, Carbs: 24.7 g, Protein: 3.8 g, Fat: 21.2 g, Sugar: 2.9 g, Sodium: 223 mg

52. Orzo and Veggie Bowls

Preparation time: 10 minutes
Cooking time: 0 minutes
Servings: 2

Ingredients:

- 2 ½ cups whole-wheat orzo, cooked
- 1 yellow bell pepper, cubed
- A pinch of salt and black pepper
- 1 red onion, chopped
- 2 cups feta cheese, crumbled
- ¼ cup lemon juice
- 1 cucumber, cubed
- 3 garlic cloves, minced
- 14 oz. canned cannellini beans, drained and rinsed
- 1 green bell pepper, cubed
- 3 tomatoes, cubed
- 1 cup mint, chopped
- 2 tablespoons olive oil
- 1 tablespoon lemon zest, grated
- 1 ¼ cup kalamata olives, pitted and sliced

Directions:
In a salad bowl, combine the orzo with the beans, bell peppers and the rest of the ingredients, toss, divide the mix between plates and serve for breakfast.

Nutrition:
Calories: 411, Fat: 17 g, Fiber: 13 g, Carbs: 51 g, Protein: 14 g

53. Lemon Peas Quinoa Mix

Preparation time: 10 minutes | **Cooking time:** 20 minutes | **Servings:** 2

Ingredients:

- 1 and ½ cups quinoa, rinsed
- 3 cups water
- 2 tablespoons lemon juice
- ½ lb. sugar snap peas, steamed
- A pinch of salt and black pepper
- 1 lb. asparagus, steamed and chopped
- 2 tablespoons parsley, chopped
- 1 teaspoon lemon zest, grated
- ½ lb. green beans, trimmed and halved
- 3 tablespoons pumpkin seeds
- 1 cup cherry tomatoes, halved
- 2 tablespoons olive oil

Directions:
Put the water in a pot, bring to a boil over medium heat, add the quinoa, stir and simmer for 20 minutes.
Stir the quinoa, add the parsley, lemon juice and the rest of the ingredients, toss, divide between plates and serve for breakfast.

Nutrition:
Calories: 417, Fat: 15 g, Fiber: 9 g, Carbs: 58 g, Protein: 16 g

54. Banana Bread

Preparation time: 25 minutes | **Cooking time:** 60 minutes | **Servings:** 2

Ingredients:

- 1 cup mashed ripe banana
- ½ cup sugar
- ½ cup unsalted butter
- 2 teaspoons vanilla
- ½ teaspoon baking soda
- 1 teaspoon cinnamon powder
- ¼ teaspoon salt
- 1 egg
- ¼ cup brown sugar
- 2 cups all-purpose flour
- 2 teaspoons baking powder
- 3 tablespoons buttermilk
- 2 tablespoons powdered sugar

Directions:
Whip butter, sugar and brown sugar together till it becomes light and fluffy. Add egg, vanilla to this mixture and beat well.
Take a mixing bowl. Sift the dry ingredients like all-purpose flour, baking powder, cinnamon, baking powder, baking soda and salt. Mix all these dry ingredients well.
Take another mixing bowl. In this, mix banana with buttermilk.
Take the butter mixture. Add the small amount of dry ingredients and banana mixture alternately with continuous stirring. It should form a uniform and smooth batter.
Set the sous vide machine to 195°F.
Take the above dough in the sous vide bag.
In a small bowl, combine cinnamon powder and the powdered sugar.

Sprinkle this sugar cinnamon mixture over the batter.
Seal the bag by removing all the air and place the bag in sous vide and cook for 45 minutes.
Remove the bread from the bag and allow it to cool and serve.

Nutrition:
Calories: 158

55. Chia Smoothie

Preparation time: 10 minutes | **Cooking time:** 0 minutes | **Servings:** 2

Ingredients:
- 2 tablespoons chia seeds
- 1 cup almond milk
- 1 banana, peeled and cubed
- ½ cup strawberries, halved
- 1 teaspoon flax meal

Directions:
In a blender, mix the chia seeds with the strawberries and the other ingredients, blend and serve.

Nutrition:
Calories: 234, Fat: 4.7 g, Fiber: 5.2 g, Carbs: 5.8 g, Protein: 8 g

56. Coconut Pancakes

Preparation time: 10 minutes | **Cooking time:** 15 minutes | **Servings:** 2

Ingredients:
- ½ cup of coconut milk
- 1 teaspoon vanilla extract
- 1 teaspoon lemon juice
- 1 tablespoon stevia
- 1 tablespoon flax meal mixed with 2 tablespoons water
- 1 teaspoon baking soda
- 1 cup coconut flour

Directions:
In a bowl, mix the coconut milk with flax meal and the other ingredients and stir.
Preheat the non-stick skillet well.
Then pour the pancake batter in the hot skillet with the help of the ladle (1 ladle = 1 pancake).
Cook the pancake for 1 minute and flip it on another side. Cook it for 30 seconds more or until the pancake is light brown.
Repeat the same steps with all remaining batter.

Nutrition:
Calories: 127, Fat: 8.6 g, Fiber: 1 g, Carbs: 2.6 g, Protein: 3.4 g

57. Mixed Veggie Hash

Preparation time: 5 minutes | **Cooking time:** 10 minutes | **Servings:** 2

Ingredients:
- 1 yellow onion, chopped
- 1 cup cherry tomatoes, halved
- 1 leek, sliced
- ½ teaspoon ground black pepper
- 1 sweet pepper, chopped
- 1 tablespoon avocado oil
- 1 avocado, peeled, pitted and cubed
- 2 sweet potatoes, peeled and cubed
- ½ teaspoon salt

Directions:
Preheat the skillet well with the oil over medium heat.
Add the onion and cook for 2 minutes.
Add the rest of the ingredients, toss, cook for 8 minutes more, divide between plates and serve.

Nutrition:
Calories: 274, Fat: 15 g, Fiber: 2.1 g, Carbs: 10.6 g, Protein: 6.7 g

58. Avocado Smoothie

Preparation time: 5 minutes | **Cooking time:** 0 minutes | **Servings:** 2

Ingredients:
- 2 oz blueberries, frozen
- ½ cup of coconut milk
- 2 avocados, peeled, pitted and cubed
- 1 teaspoon stevia

Directions:
Put the frozen blueberries in the blender.
Add the rest of the ingredients.
Pulse for a couple of minutes.
Pour the cooked smoothies in the glass.

Nutrition:
Calories: 206, Fat: 4.9 g, Fiber: 5.2 g, Carbs: 5.5 g, Protein: 5.6 g

59. Zucchini Hash

Preparation time: 15 minutes | **Cooking time:** 10 minutes | **Servings:** 2

Ingredients:

- 1 sweet potato, peeled
- 1 cup tomatoes, crushed
- ½ teaspoon salt
- 2 tablespoons chives, chopped
- 3 zucchinis, roughly cubed
- 1 tablespoon olive oil
- 1 teaspoon chili flakes

Directions:
Then heat up the skillet with the oil over medium heat.
Add zucchinis, tomatoes and the other ingredients, toss, cook for 10 minutes, divide between plates and serve.

Nutrition:
Calories: 129, Fat: 3.2 g, Fiber: 4 g, Carbs: 5.2 g, Protein: 4.4 g

60. Baked Eggs

Preparation: 2 minutes | **Cooking time:** 15-20 minutes | **Servings:** 2

Ingredients:

- 7 Oz. leg ham
- 4 tsps. Full cream milk
- 1 lb. baby spinach
- Salt and Pepper to taste
- 4 eggs
- Margarine
- 1 tablespoon olive oil

Directions:
Preheat the Air Fryer to 350°F. Layer four ramekins with margarine.
Equally divide the spinach and ham into the four ramekins. Break 1 egg into each and add a tsp. of milk. Spice with salt and pepper.
Place into Air Fryer for about 15-20 minutes. For a runny yolk, cook for 15 minutes, for fully cooked, 20 minutes.

Nutrition:
Calories: 113, Fat: 8.2 g, Carbs: 0.3 g, Sugar: 0.2 g, Protein: 5.4 g, Cholesterol: 18 mg

61. Corn Kernel Fritters

Preparation: 5 minutes | **Cooking time:** 5 minutes | **Servings:** 2

Ingredients:

- 1 Egg
- ¾ cup milk
- 1 ½ tsps. Baking powder
- ¼ tsps. Pepper
- 1 cup corn kernels
- 1 cup flour
- ½ tsps. Salt
- 2 tbsps. margarine, melted

Directions:
Preheat Air fryer to 375°F. In a bowl, combine flour, baking powder, salt and pepper.
In another bowl, whisk together egg, milk, and margarine and add to the dry ingredients, stirring well. Fold in the corn and leave for 5 minutes to allow the batter sit well.
Now, form batter into small, rounded fritters. Place the fritters on a tray and let it freeze for 5 minutes to retain the shape.
Finally, place the fritters into the Air fryer tray, set timer for 4-5 minutes. Serve and enjoy with yoghurt or salsa dip.

Nutrition:
Calories: 113, Fat: 8.2 g, Carbs: 0.3 g, Sugar: 0.2 g, Protein: 5.4 g, Cholesterol: 18 mg

62. Apple Oat Sunrise Fritters

Preparation: 10 minutes | **Cooking time:** 5 minutes | **Servings:** 2

Ingredients:

- 2 Apples, peeled, cored & sliced into rings
- 1 ½ tsps. ground cinnamon, divided
- 2 tbsps. cornstarch
- ½ cup club soda
- 1 Egg
- ½ cup + 2 tbsps. sugar
- ½ cup rice flour
- 1 tsp. baking powder
- 1 cup oats
- ¾ tsp. kosher salt

Directions:

Combine cinnamon and sugar in a shallow bowl, whisking well. Next, preheat the Air Fryer to 350°F.

In a food processor, pulse the oats to a coarse powder. Remove to a large bowl and add in the rice flour, baking powder, cornstarch, salt, cinnamon and the rest of the sugar, whisking well.

Add in the egg and club soda, whisking in more soda, a little at a time, until the mixture is like pancake batter.

Dip the apple rings into the batter then place into the Air fryer tray, one set at a time. Cook until golden brown and crisp for about 4 minutes.

Serve fritters sprinkled with the reserved cinnamon sugar.

Nutrition:

Calories: 113, Fat: 8.2 g, Carbs: 0.3 g

63. Blanc Leeks Frittata

Preparation: 10 minutes | **Cooking time:** 28 minutes | **Servings:** 2

Ingredients:

- 2 Gold potatoes, boiled, peeled and chopped-
- 10 Eggs, whisked
- 2 tbsp. Butter
- Salt and black pepper to taste
- ¼ cup Whole milk
- 5 oz. From-age blanc, crumble
- 2 Leeks, sliced

Directions:

Heat a medium-sized pan suitable to fit in the air fryer.

Add butter and leeks, saute for 4 minutes.

Stir in potatoes, milk, cheese, eggs, salt and pepper, cook for 1 minute.

Place the pan in the air fryer and cook the potatoes for 13 minutes on Air fryer mode at 350°F.

Slice and serve to devour.

Nutrition:

Calories: 271, Fat: 6 g, Fiber: 8 g, Carbs: 12 g, Protein: 6 g

64. Ham and Cheese Pie

Preparation: 10 minutes | **Cooking time:** 35 minutes | **Servings:** 2

Ingredients:

- 16 oz. Crescent rolls dough
- 2 cups Ham, cooked and chopped
- 2 cups Cheddar cheese, grated
- Cooking spray
- 1 tbsp. Parmesan, grated
- 2 Eggs, whisked
- Salt and black pepper to taste

Directions:

Grease the air fryer's container with cooking oil and spread the half of the crescent rolls at the bottom of the air fryer.

Whisk eggs with parmesan, salt, pepper, and cheddar cheese in a bowl.

Pour this mixture over the dough and top it with the ham.

Add the remaining strips of dough over the ham. Place the ham over the dough and seal the air fryer.

Cook it for 25 minutes at 300°F on Air fryer mode.

Slice this pie and serve.

Nutrition:

Calories: 400, Fat: 27 g, Fiber: 7 g, Carbs: 22 g, Protein: 16 g

65. Cinnamon Vanilla Toast

Preparation: 10 minutes | **Cooking time:** 15 minutes | **Servings:** 2

Ingredients:

- 1 stick Butter, soft
- 1 ½ tsp Vanilla extract
- ½ cup Sugar
- 12 Bread slices
- 1 ½ tsp Cinnamon powder

Directions:

Whisk butter with cinnamon, vanilla and sugar in a bowl.

Spread the bread slices in the air fryer.

Pour the butter mixture over the bread slices evenly.

Seal the fryer and cook the bread for 5 minutes at 400°F on Air fryer mode.

Enjoy.

Nutrition:
Calories: 221, Fat: 4 g, Fiber: 7 g, Carbs: 12 g, Protein: 8 g

66. Paprika Egg Scramble

Preparation: 10 minutes | **Cooking time:** 20 minutes | **Servings:** 2

Ingredients:
- 2 Eggs
- 1 Red bell pepper, chopped
- A pinch of Sweet paprika
- 2 tbsp Butter
- Salt and black pepper to taste

Directions:
Whisk eggs with paprika, salt, pepper, and red bell pepper in a bowl.
Add butter to the air fryer container and preheat the fryer at 140°F.
Add eggs mixture and secure the fryer.
Cook them for 10 minutes at the same temperature on Air fryer mode.
Stir well.
Enjoy.

Nutrition:
Calories: 200, Fat: 4 g, Fiber: 7 g, Carbs: 10 g, Protein: 3 g

67. Cherry Rice Pudding

Preparation: 10 minutes | **Cooking time:** 22 minutes | **Servings:** 2

Ingredients:
- 1 ½ cups Arborio rice
- 1 cup Apple juice
- ½ cup Cherries, dried
- A pinch of Salt
- 2 Apples, cored and sliced
- 1 ½ tsp Cinnamon powder
- 3 cups Milk
- ⅓ cup Brown sugar
- 2 tbsp Butter

Directions:
Add butter to a pan suitable to fit the air fryer.
Place it over medium heat and add rice to it.
Stir cook for 5 minutes then add apples, sugar, apple juice, cinnamon, cherries, and milk.
Toss well then place the pan in the air fryer.
Seal the air fryer and cook the rice for 8 minutes at 350°F.
Serve in the bowls and enjoy.

Nutrition:
Calories: 162, Fat: 12 g, Fiber: 6 g, Carbs: 23 g, Protein: 8 g

68. Broccoli Asparagus Burritos

Preparation: 10 minutes | **Cooking time:** 20 minutes | **Servings:** 2

Ingredients:
- ½ cup Sweet potatoes, steamed and cubed
- 2 tbsp Cashew butter
- 2 tbsp Water
- 4 Rice papers
- 8 Roasted red peppers, chopped
- ½ Small broccoli head, florets separated and steamed
- 2 tbsp Tamari
- 2 tbsp Liquid smoke
- 7 Asparagus stalks
- A handful of Kale, chopped

Directions:
Mix cashew butter with tamari, water and liquid smoke in a bowl.
Place the rice papers on a working surface and wet them with water.
Divide the broccoli, sweet potatoes, red peppers, asparagus, and kale onto the rice papers.
Wrap the rice papers to make burritos then dip them in the cashew mix.
Place the burritos in the air fryer basket and seal the fryer.
Cook them for 10 minutes at 350°F.
Serve.

Nutrition:
Calories: 172, Fat: 4 g, Fiber: 7 g, Carbs: 8 g, Protein: 3 g

69. Onion Potato Hash

Preparation: 10 minutes | **Cooking time:** 35 minutes | **Servings:** 2

Ingredients:
- 1 ½ Potatoes, cubed
- 2 tsp Olive oil
- ½ tsp Thyme, dried
- Salt and black pepper to taste
- 1 Yellow onion, chopped
- 2 Eggs
- 1 Green bell pepper, chopped

Directions:
Let your air fryer preheat at 350°F.
Add oil, onion, bell pepper, salt, black pepper, thyme, eggs and potatoes to the air fryer container.
Seal the fryer and cook the potatoes for 20 minutes at 360°F.
Serve.

Nutrition:
Calories: 241, Fat: 4 g, Fiber: 7 g, Carbs: 12 g, Protein: 7 g

70. Eggplant Bowls

Preparation time: 10 minutes | **Cooking time:** 25 minutes | **Servings:** 2

Ingredients:
- 2 spring onions, chopped
- 8 eggs, whisked
- ½ teaspoon basil, dried
- A pinch of salt and black pepper
- 1 lb. eggplants, cubed
- 1 cup baby spinach
- 1 tablespoon oregano, chopped
- 1 tablespoon chives, chopped

Directions:
In a bowl mix the eggs with the basil, oregano and the other ingredients, whisk and pour into a Ziplock bag.
Seal the bag, submerge in the water oven and cook at 170°F for 25 minutes.
Divide into bowls and serve.

Nutrition:
Calories: 223, Fat: 12 g, Fiber: 5 g, Carbs: 15 g, Protein: 5 g

71. Banana Oatmeal

Preparation time: 10 minutes | **Cooking time:** 25 minutes | **Servings:** 2

Ingredients:
- 1 cup old fashioned oats
- 2 bananas, peeled and mashed
- ½ teaspoon nutmeg, ground
- 2 cups almond milk
- ½ teaspoon vanilla extract

Directions:
In a sous vide bag, mix the oats with the milk and the other ingredients, whisk, seal the bag, submerge in the water oven and cook at 167 °F for 25 minutes.
Divide the oatmeal into bowls and serve.

Nutrition:
Calories: 371, Fat: 12 g, Fiber: 2 g, Carbs: 5 g, Protein: 5 g

72. Cheddar Eggs

Preparation time: 10 minutes | **Cooking time:** 30 minutes | **Servings:** 2

Ingredients:
- 8 eggs, whisked
- ½ cup cheddar cheese, shredded
- ½ teaspoon sweet paprika
- 2 tablespoons chives, chopped
- ½ cup almond milk
- 2 spring onions, chopped
- A pinch of salt and black pepper

Directions:
In a bowl, mix the eggs with the milk and the other ingredients, whisk and divide into 4 ramekins.
Put the ramekins in the water oven and cook at 165 °F for 25 minutes.
Serve for breakfast.

Nutrition:
Calories: 367, Fat: 13 g, Fiber: 3 g, Carbs: 15 g, Protein: 12 g

73. Spinach Frittata

Preparation time: 5 minutes | **Cooking time:** 30 minutes | **Servings:** 2

Ingredients:
- 8 eggs, whisked
- 2 spring onions, chopped
- A pinch of salt and black pepper
- 1 cup baby spinach
- ½ teaspoon sweet paprika
- ½ cup heavy cream

Directions:
In a bowl, mix the eggs with the spinach and the other ingredients, whisk and pour into a Ziplock bag.

Seal the bag, submerge in the water oven and cook at 168 °F for 30 minutes.
Serve for breakfast.

Nutrition:
Calories: 253, Fat: 9 g, Fiber: 2 g, Carbs: 4 g, Protein: 6 g

74. Mushroom Oatmeal

Preparation time: 10 minutes | **Cooking time:** 30 minutes | **Servings:** 2

Ingredients:
- ½ lb. mushrooms, sliced
- 2 cups coconut milk
- 1 red chili, minced
- 1 carrot, peeled and grated
- 1 cup steel cut oats
- ½ teaspoon cumin, ground
- A pinch of salt and black pepper

Directions:
In a Ziplock bag, mix the oats with the mushrooms and the other ingredients, whisk and seal the bag.
Submerge in the water oven and cook at 170 °F for 30 minutes.
Divide into bowls and serve.

Nutrition:
Calories: 342, Fat: 12 g, Fiber: 5 g, Carbs: 16 g, Protein: 15 g

75. Strawberry Bowls

Preparation time: 10 minutes | **Cooking time:** 25 minutes | **Servings:** 2

Ingredients:
- 1 cup strawberries
- ¼ teaspoon raw honey
- 2 teaspoons vanilla extract
- 1 cup coconut milk
- ½ tablespoon lime juice

Directions:
In a sous vide bag, mix the berries with the honey and the other ingredients, toss gently, seal the bag and cook in the water oven for 25 minutes at 117 °F.
Divide into bowls and serve for breakfast.

Nutrition:
Calories: 197, Fat: 2 g, Fiber: 3 g, Carbs: 36 g, Protein: 6 g

76. Sweet Potato Mix

Preparation time: 10 minutes | **Cooking time:** 30 minutes | **Servings:** 2

Ingredients:
- ½ lb. sweet potatoes, peeled, and cubed
- ½ teaspoon sweet paprika
- 3 tablespoons Greek yogurt
- 1 tablespoon chives, chopped
- 4 eggs, whisked
- A pinch of salt and black pepper
- 1 teaspoon oregano, dried

Directions:
In a bowl, mix the sweet potatoes with the eggs and the other ingredients, whisk and pour everything into a Ziplock bag.
Seal the bag, submerge in the water oven and cook at 165 °F for 30 minutes.
Divide the mix into bowls and serve.

Nutrition:
Calories: 438, Fat: 13 g, Fiber: 9 g, Carbs: 64 g, Protein: 26 g

77. Walnut and Berries Bowls

Preparation time: 10 minutes | **Cooking time:** 30 minutes | **Servings:** 2

Ingredients:
- 1 cup walnuts, chopped
- 1 cup blackberries
- 1 tablespoon raisins
- ½ cup old fashioned oats
- 1 cup coconut cream
- ½ teaspoon vanilla extract

Directions:
In a sous vide bag, mix the walnuts with the berries and the other ingredients, toss, seal the bag and cook in the water oven at 160 °F for 30 minutes.
Divide into bowls and serve.

Nutrition:
Calories: 224, Fat: 12 g, Fiber: 5 g, Carbs: 15 g, Protein: 5 g

78. Chives Avocado Quinoa

Preparation time: 10 minutes | **Cooking time:** 30 minutes | **Servings:** 2

Ingredients:

- 1 cup quinoa
- 1 avocado, peeled, pitted and cubed
- ½ teaspoon coriander, ground
- A pinch of salt and black pepper
- ½ teaspoon sweet paprika
- 2 cups veggie stock
- 1 tablespoon chives, chopped
- ½ teaspoon chili powder
- 1 teaspoon chili powder

Directions:

In a Ziplock bag, mix the quinoa with the stock and the other ingredients, toss, seal the bag, submerge in the water oven and cook at 165°F for 30 minutes.
Divide into bowls and serve for breakfast.

Nutrition:

Calories: 300, Fat: 12 g, Fiber: 6 g, Carbs: 16 g, Protein: 6 g

79. Balsamic Avocado and Tomato Salad

Preparation time: 10 minutes | **Cooking time:** 15 minutes | **Servings:** 2

Ingredients:

- ½ lb. cherry tomatoes, halved
- ½ teaspoon rosemary, dried
- 1 avocado, peeled, pitted and cubed
- 1 tablespoon balsamic vinegar
- 1 tablespoon chives, chopped
- 1 tablespoon avocado oil
- ½ teaspoon chili powder
- 2 cucumbers, cubed
- A pinch of salt and black pepper

Directions:

In a sous vide bag, mix the tomatoes with the avocado oil, avocado and the other ingredients, toss, seal the bag and cook at 165 °F for 15 minutes.
Divide into bowls and serve for breakfast.

Nutrition:

Calories: 424, Fat: 23 g, Fiber: 12 g, Carbs: 42 g, Protein: 15 g

80. Apple Salad

Preparation time: 5 minutes | **Cooking time:** 20 minutes | **Servings:** 2

Ingredients:

- ½ lb. apples, cored and cut into wedges
- 1 teaspoon cinnamon powder
- 1 teaspoon vanilla extract
- ¼ cup almond milk
- 2 teaspoons raw honey

Directions:

In a sous vide bag, mix the apples with the milk and the other ingredients, toss, seal the bag, submerge in the water oven and cook at 165 °F for 20 minutes.
Divide the salad into bowls and serve for breakfast.

Nutrition:

Calories: 305, Fat: 19 g, Fiber: 5 g, Carbs: 29 g, Protein: 8 g

81. Pesto Zucchini Ramekins

Preparation time: 10 minutes | **Cooking time:** 30 minutes | **Servings:** 2

Ingredients:

- Cooking spray
- 2 tablespoons basil pesto
- 2 garlic cloves, minced
- ½ teaspoon oregano, dried
- A pinch of salt and black pepper
- 2 spring onions, chopped
- ½ lb. zucchinis, cubed
- 8 eggs, whisked
- ½ teaspoon chili powder
- 1 tablespoon dill, chopped

Directions:

In a bowl, mix the eggs with the zucchinis and the other ingredients except the cooking spray and whisk well.
Grease 4 ramekins with the cooking spray, divide the zucchini mix, put the ramekins in the water oven and cook at 170 °F for 30 minutes.

Serve the mix for breakfast.

Nutrition:
Calories: 356, Fat: 29 g, Fiber: 2 g, Carbs: 3 g, Protein: 18 g

82. Chickpeas Breakfast Spread

Preparation time: 10 minutes | **Cooking time:** 20 minutes | **Servings:** 2

Ingredients:
- 2 cups canned chickpeas, drained and rinsed
- 2 spring onions, chopped
- 1 tablespoon lemon juice
- 1 tablespoon tahini paste
- A pinch of salt and black pepper
- 1 cup heavy cream
- 1 tablespoon avocado oil
- 1 tablespoon lemon zest, grated
- ¼ teaspoon sweet paprika
- 1 tablespoon chives, chopped

Directions:
In a sous vide bag, mix the chickpeas with the cream, spring onions and the other ingredients except the oil and the tahini paste, seal the bag, submerge in the water oven and cook at 165°F for 20 minutes.
Transfer the mix to a blender, add the remaining ingredients, pulse well, divide into bowls and serve for breakfast.

Nutrition:
Calories: 203, Fat: 12 g, Fiber: 4 g, Carbs: 15 g, Protein: 4 g

83. Lemon Eggs

Preparation time: 10 minutes | **Cooking time:** 20 minutes | **Servings:** 2

Ingredients:
- ½ cup chives, chopped
- Salt and black pepper to the taste
- 2 teaspoons lemon thyme, chopped
- Juice of 1 lemon
- 4 eggs, whisked

Directions:
In a sous vide bag, mix the eggs with the lemon thyme, chives and the other ingredients, whisk and seal the bag.
Submerge the bag into the water oven and cook at 167°F for 20 minutes.
Divide between plates and serve for breakfast.

Nutrition:
Calories: 203, Fat: 7 g, Fiber: 2 g, Carbs: 11 g, Protein: 8 g

84. Oregano Scramble

Preparation time: 10 minutes | **Cooking time:** 20 minutes | **Servings:** 2

Ingredients:
- 8 eggs, whisked
- 2 tablespoons butter, melted
- ½ teaspoon sweet paprika
- ½ cup heavy cream
- 1 tablespoon oregano, chopped
- 2 tablespoons parmesan cheese, grated
- Salt and black pepper to the taste

Directions:
In a bowl, mix the eggs with the oregano, butter and the other ingredients, whisk well, pour into a Ziplock bag, introduce in your sous vide machine in the water oven and cook at 167°F for 20 minutes.
Divide the mix between plates and serve.

Nutrition:
Calories: 160, Fat: 3 g, Fiber: 2 g, Carbs: 6 g, Protein: 10 g

85. Bacon and Radish Scramble

Preparation time: 10 minutes | **Cooking time:** 30 minutes | **Servings:** 2

Ingredients:
- ½ cup bacon, chopped
- 8 eggs, whisked
- 1 yellow onion, chopped
- ½ cup radish, chopped
- Salt and black pepper to the taste
- 1 tablespoon chives, chopped

Directions:
In a bowl, mix the eggs with the radishes and the other ingredients, whisk, pour into a Ziplock bag, seal, introduce in your sous vide machine and cook at 170°F for 30 minutes.
Divide everything between plates and serve.

Nutrition:
Calories: 240, Fat: 7 g, Fiber: 3 g, Carbs: 12 g, Protein: 8 g

86. Brussels Sprouts Salad

Preparation time: 10 minutes | **Cooking time:** 30 minutes | **Servings:** 2

Ingredients:
- Salt and black pepper to the taste
- 1 cup cherry tomatoes, halved
- 2 shallots, minced
- 2 oz. bacon, cooked and chopped
- 1 tablespoon olive oil
- ½ cup black olives, pitted and halved
- 12 oz. Brussels sprouts, halved
- 1 tablespoon balsamic vinegar

Directions:
In a sous vide bag, mix the sprouts with the tomatoes and the other ingredients, toss, seal, introduce in your sous vide machine and cook at 170°F for 30 minutes.
Divide into bowls and serve for breakfast.

Nutrition:
Calories: 240, Fat: 7 g, Fiber: 4 g, Carbs: 12 g, Protein: 12 g

87. Seeds Porridge

Preparation time: 3 minutes | **Cooking time:** 1 hour | **Servings:** 2

Ingredients:
- 1 cup almond milk
- 1 tablespoon sunflower seeds
- ½ teaspoon cinnamon powder
- ¾ teaspoon vanilla extract
- 2 tablespoons flax seeds
- ½ cup heavy cream
- 1 tablespoon sugar

Directions:
In a sous vide bag, mix the almond milk with the seeds and the other ingredients, seal the bag, introduce in your sous vide machine and cook at 180°F for 1 hour Divide the porridge into bowls and serve for breakfast.

Nutrition:
Calories: 230, Fat: 12 g, Fiber: 7 g, Carbs: 12 g, Protein: 13 g

88. Cinnamon Eggs

Preparation time: 10 minutes | **Cooking time:** 30 minutes | **Servings:** 2

Ingredients:
- 4 eggs, whisked
- 2 tablespoons sugar
- ½ teaspoon cinnamon powder
- 1 teaspoon ginger powder
- ⅓ cup heavy cream

Directions:
In a sous vide bag, combine the eggs with the sugar and the other ingredients, seal, introduce in your sous vide machine and cook at 167°F for 30 minutes.
Divide into bowls and serve.

Nutrition:
Calories: 240, Fat: 12 g, Fiber: 6 g, Carbs: 12 g, Protein: 14 g

89. Swiss Eggs

Preparation time: 15 minutes | **Cooking time:** 45 minutes | **Servings:** 2

Ingredients:
- 1 lb. pork sausage
- 2 cups shredded Swiss cheese
- ½ cup light cream
- 12 eggs
- 2 tablespoons mustard
- ⅛ teaspoon pepper

Directions:
Take a saucepan. Break the meat using a fork and cook it on a medium flame till it turns brown.
Grease the baking dish with butter or cooking spray. Fill this cooked sausage in this baking dish and spread shredded cheese over it.

Take a small mixing bowl. Mix the pepper, mustard and cream thoroughly to make a smooth paste.
Add this smooth paste over the sausage and cheese.
Take another mixing bowl and beat eggs in it till it becomes frothy. Pour these eggs in the baking dish over the cream mixture. Add some butter on the frothy eggs.
Set the sous vide machine to 195°F.
Take the above mixture is a glass vessel. Remove the air and seal.
Place the vessel in sous vide and cook for 40 minutes.
Cut it into square pieces and serve.

Nutrition:
Calories: 380

90. Salmon Sandwich

Preparation time: 10 minutes | **Cooking time:** 20 minutes | **Servings:** 2

Ingredients:
- 16 Brown bread slices
- 2/3 cup low-fat mayonnaise
- 3 tablespoons honey mustard
- 1 red bell pepper
- 1/2 teaspoon marjoram
- 5-6 oz. salmon fillets
- 1/3 cup grated Parmesan cheese
- 1 orange bell pepper
- 3 stalks celery
- Salt and pepper to taste

Directions:
Cut the salmon into small pieces.
Chop the bell peppers and celery stalks.
Take a large mixing bowl. Add mayonnaise, cheese, honey mustard, and mix well.
Set the sous vide machine to 175°F.
Take the salmon fillets in the Ziplock bags, sprinkle some salt and pepper. Seal the bag to remove the air.
Place the bag in sous vide and cook for 20 minutes.
Add these cooked salmon pieces and chopped vegetables and mix.
Add the marjoram, salt and pepper and toss to mix evenly.
Chill the sandwich spread.
Apply the spread on the bread and serve.

Nutrition:
Calories: 290

91. Beetroot Carrot Smoothie

Preparation time: 10 minutes | **Cooking time:** 15 minutes | **Servings:** 2

Ingredients:
- 1 sliced beetroot
- 1/2 cup red grapes
- 1 tablespoon sugar
- 1/2 cup ice
- 1 sliced carrot
- 1 peeled Clementine
- 1 slice ginger

Directions:
Set the sous vide machine to 135°F.
Take the slices of carrot and beetroot in a Ziplock bag and seal the bag.
Place them in the water bath for 15 minutes.
Then, put all the ingredients in a blender.
Blend it to form a smooth mixture.
Add ice and blend it once again.
Serve the cold smoothie in an attractive glass.

Nutrition:
Calories: 120

92. Cheesy Broccoli Soup

Preparation time: 15 minutes | **Cooking time:** 30 minutes | **Servings:** 2

Ingredients:
- 5 tablespoons butter
- 1 cup chopped celery
- 1/4 cup flour
- 5 cup broccoli florets
- 3 cups shredded cheddar cheese
- 1 chopped onion
- 3 minced garlic cloves
- 8 cup vegetable broth
- 1 chopped carrot
- Salt and pepper

Directions:
In a cooking bowl, melt butter and cook the onion and garlic.
Add broth, salt, pepper and boil until thicken.
Set the sous vide machine to 175°F.
Take the broccoli florets and chopped cabbage in the Ziplock bag and vacuum seal it.
Place the bag in sous vide and cook for 20 minutes.
Add the cooked broccoli and cook for 2 minutes.
Make a puree of this mixture.

Take this puree in a bowl, add cheese and heat for 1 minute.
Serve hot.

Nutrition:
Calories: 200, Fat: 3 g, Carbs: 3 g, Protein: 4 g

93. Breakfast Sausage Patties

Preparation time: 20 minutes | **Cooking time:** 20 hours and 20 minutes | **Servings:** 2

Ingredients:

1-lb. ground pork	1 teaspoon salt
½ teaspoon pepper	1 clove garlic, minced
½ onion, minced	½ teaspoon dried thyme
½ teaspoon dried rosemary	½ teaspoon dried sage
½ teaspoon dried parsley	1 egg
1 tablespoon olive oil	

Directions:
Preheat the water bath to 140°F.
Mash together all ingredients in a bowl. Place in bag and press to fill all corners in a flat patty. Seal bag, place in the water bath, and cook 2 hours.
When pork is cooked, cut off the bag. Cut patty into squares.
Immediately before serving, heat oil in a pan. Sear patties in oil until brown on both sides. Serve.

Nutrition:
Calories: 407, Fat: 239 g, Carb: 14 g, Fiber: 4 g, Protein: 364 g

94. BLTs with Overnight Bacon

Preparation time: 20 minutes | **Cooking time:** 4 hours and 20 minutes | **Servings:** 2

Ingredients:

1 package thick-cut bacon in original vacuum-sealed packaging	6 slices bread, toasted
6 slices tomato	3 leaves lettuce
3 tablespoons mayonnaise	

Directions:
Preheat the water bath to 140°F.
Place sealed bacon in the water bath. Cook at least 4 hours or overnight.
After at least 4 hours, remove bacon from pan. Brown in the hot pan on both sides. Drain on paper towel.
Spread mayonnaise on bread. Assemble sandwiches with tomato and lettuce. Serve.

Nutrition:
Calories: 812, Fat: 707 g, Carb: 256 g, Fiber: 6 g, Protein: 274 g

95. Pork Knuckles

Preparation time: 20 minutes | **Cooking time:** 24 hours | **Servings:** 2

Ingredients:

2 10 oz. pork knuckles	Salt and pepper, to taste
4 cloves garlic, chopped	½ cup mustard
½ cup raw apple cider vinegar	2 ¾ cups apple juice
½ cup brown sugar	4 sprigs thyme
1 bay leaf	

Directions:
Preheat Sous Vide cooker to 158°F.
Generously season pork knuckles with salt and pepper.
Heat some oil in a large skillet. Sear pork 2 minutes per side. Remove from the skillet.
Toss the remaining ingredients into a skillet and cook until reduced by half. Place aside to cool.
Place the pork knuckles in Sous Vide bag along with the prepared sauce.
Vacuum seal the bag. Submerge bag in a water bath.
Cook 24 hours.
Remove shanks from the bag and place aside. Strain cooking juices into a saucepan.
Simmer over medium heat until thickened.
Pour the sauce over shanks and serve.

Nutrition:
Calories: 358, Fat: 6 g, Carb: 42 g, Fiber: 3 g, Protein: 29 g

96. Pork Belly Sliders

Preparation time: 30 minutes | **Cooking time:** 10 hours | **Servings:** 2

Ingredients:

- 2 lb. pork belly
- ½ cup + 1 tablespoon brown sugar
- 2 cloves garlic, mashed into the paste
- 1 dozen slider buns, or large dinner rolls, split
- ½ cup low-sodium soy sauce
- ½ cup dry sherry
- 1-inch piece of ginger, mashed into the paste
- Lettuce (optional)

Directions:

Preheat the water bath to 170°F.

Mix soy sauce, ½ cup sugar, sherry, garlic, and ginger. Rub all over pork belly. Seal pork into bag and place into the water bath. Cook for 10 hours.

When pork is cooked, pour cooking liquids into the pan, add 1 tablespoon sugar, and reduce into a syrupy sauce.

Cut pork into 1-inch-thick chunks. Place in buns and top with the reduced sauce and a leaf of lettuce, if using.

Nutrition:

Calories: 556, Fat: 45 g, Carb: 303 g, Fiber: 1 g, Protein: 18 g

97. Chinatown Braised Pork

Preparation time: 30 minutes | **Cooking time:** 8 hours 20 minutes | **Servings:** 2

Ingredients:

- 2 lb. boneless pork shoulder
- ¼ teaspoon cinnamon
- ¼ teaspoon pepper
- ¼ cup hoisin sauce
- ¼ cup soy sauce
- ¼ cup sesame oil
- 1-inch peeled ginger
- 1 tablespoon olive oil
- 2 teaspoons salt
- ¼ teaspoon cloves
- ¼ teaspoon ground fennel
- ¼ cup honey
- ¼ cup dry sherry
- 2 whole star anise
- 2 cloves garlic
- Cooked white rice for serving

Directions:

Preheat the water bath to 140°F.

Rub pork with salt, cinnamon, cloves, pepper, and fennel.

Combine hoisin sauce, honey, soy sauce, dry sherry, and sesame oil. Spread over meat.

Seal pork into bags with star anise, ginger, and garlic. Place in water bath and cook 8 hours.

When pork is cooked, heat 1 tablespoon oil in a pan. Sear pork on all sides.

Slice across the grain and serve with white rice.

Nutrition:

Calories: 554, Fat: 305 g, Carb: 351 g, Fiber: 1 g, Protein: 495 g

98. Sausage and Pepper Sandwiches

Preparation time: 20 minutes | **Cooking time:** 3 hours | **Servings:** 2

Ingredients:

- 4 Italian sausage links
- 1 onion, sliced
- ½ can 14 oz. whole tomatoes, crushed
- 4 sausage rolls
- 2 bell peppers, sliced into strips
- 1 clove garlic, minced
- ¼ cup fresh basil, chopped

Directions:

Preheat the water bath to 140°F.

Seal sausages into the bag with peppers, onions, garlic, and tomatoes. Place in water bath and cook 3 hours.

When sausages are finished, place one on each roll and top with the sauce. Garnish with fresh basil.

Nutrition:

Calories: 285, Fat: 99 g, Carb: 369 g, Fiber: 2 g, Protein: 189 g

99. Brown Rice Salad

Preparation time: 10 minutes | **Cooking time:** 0 minutes | **Servings:** 2

Ingredients:

- 9 oz. brown rice, cooked
- 7 cups baby arugula

15 oz. canned garbanzo beans, drained and rinsed
¾ cup basil, chopped
2 tablespoons lemon juice
¼ cup olive oil
4 oz. feta cheese, crumbled
A pinch of salt and black pepper
¼ teaspoon lemon zest, grated

Directions:
In a salad bowl, combine the brown rice with the arugula, the beans and the rest of the ingredients, toss and serve cold for breakfast.

Nutrition:
Calories: 473, Fat: 22 g, Fiber: 7 g, Carbs: 53 g, Protein: 13 g

100. Walnuts Yogurt Mix

Preparation time: 10 minutes | **Cooking time:** 0 minutes | **Servings:** 2

Ingredients:
2 ½ cups Greek yogurt
1 teaspoon vanilla extract
2 teaspoons cinnamon powder
1 ½ cups walnuts, chopped
¾ cup honey

Directions:
In a bowl, combine the yogurt with the walnuts and the rest of the ingredients, toss, divide into smaller bowls and keep in the fridge for 10 minutes before serving for breakfast.

Nutrition:
Calories: 388, Fat: 24.6 g, Fiber: 2.9 g, Carbs: 39.1 g, Protein: 10.2 g

101. Tahini Pine Nuts Toast

Preparation time: 5 minutes | **Cooking time:** 0 minutes | **Servings:** 2

Ingredients:
2 whole wheat bread slices, toasted
1 tablespoon tahini paste
Juice of ½ lemon
1 teaspoon water
2 teaspoons feta cheese, crumbled
2 teaspoons pine nuts
A pinch of black pepper

Directions:
In a bowl, mix the tahini with the water and the lemon juice, whisk well and spread over the toasted bread slices.
Top each serving with the remaining ingredients and serve for breakfast.

Nutrition:
Calories: 142, Fat: 7.6 g, Fiber: 2.7 g, Carbs: 13.7 g, Protein: 5.8 g

102. Cheesy Olives Bread

Preparation time: 1 hour and 40 minutes | **Cooking time:** 30 minutes | **Servings:** 2

Ingredients:
4 cups whole-wheat flour
2 teaspoons dry yeast
1 ½ cups black olives, pitted and sliced
½ cup feta cheese, crumbled
3 tablespoons oregano, chopped
¼ cup olive oil
1 cup water

Directions:
In a bowl, mix the flour with the water, the yeast and the oil, stir and knead your dough very well. Put the dough in a bowl, cover with plastic wrap and keep in a warm place for 1 hour.
Divide the dough into 2 bowls and stretch each ball well.
Add the rest of the ingredients on each ball and tuck them inside well kneading the dough again. Flatten the balls a bit and leave them aside for 40 minutes more.
Transfer the balls to a baking sheet lined with parchment paper, make a small slit in each and bake at 425°F for 30 minutes.
Serve the bread as a Mediterranean breakfast.

Nutrition:
Calories: 251, Fat: 7.3 g, Fiber: 2.1 g, Carbs: 39.7 g, Protein: 6.7 g

103. Sweet Potato Tart

Preparation time: 10 minutes | **Cooking time:** 1 hour and 10 minutes | **Servings:** 2

Ingredients:

- 2 lbs. sweet potatoes, peeled and cubed
- 7 oz. feta cheese, crumbled
- 2 eggs, whisked
- 1 tablespoon herbs de Provence
- 6 phyllo sheets
- ¼ cup olive oil + a drizzle
- 1 yellow onion, chopped
- ¼ cup almond milk
- A pinch of salt and black pepper
- 1 tablespoon parmesan, grated

Directions:

In a bowl, combine the potatoes with half of the oil, salt and pepper, toss, spread on a baking sheet lined with parchment paper and roast at 400°F for 25 minutes.

Meanwhile, heat up a pan with half of the remaining oil over medium heat, add the onion and sauté for 5 minutes.

In a bowl, combine the eggs with the milk, feta, herbs, salt, pepper, the onion, sweet potatoes and the rest of the oil and toss.

Arrange the phyllo sheets in a tart pan and brush them with a drizzle of oil.

Add the sweet potato mix and spread it well into the pan.

Sprinkle the parmesan on top and bake covered with tin foil at 350°F for 20 minutes.

Remove the tin foil, bake the tart for 20 minutes more, cool it down, slice and serve for breakfast.

Nutrition:
Calories: 476, Fat: 16.8 g, Fiber: 10.2 g, Carbs: 68.8 g, Protein: 13.9 g

104. Stuffed Pita Breads

Preparation time: 5 minutes | **Cooking time:** 15 minutes | **Servings:** 2

Ingredients:

- 1 ½ tablespoons olive oil
- 1 garlic clove, minced
- ¼ cup parsley, chopped
- ¼ cup lemon juice
- 4 whole wheat pita bread pockets
- 1 tomato, cubed
- 1 red onion, chopped
- 15 oz. canned fava beans, drained and rinsed
- Salt and black pepper to the taste

Directions:

Heat up a pan with the oil over medium heat, add the onion, stir and sauté for 5 minutes.

Add the rest of the ingredients, stir and cook for 10 minutes more

Stuff the pita pockets with this mix and serve for breakfast.

Nutrition:
Calories: 382, Fat: 1.8 g, Fiber: 27.6 g, Carbs: 66 g, Protein: 28.5 g

105. Blueberries Quinoa

Preparation time: 5 minutes | **Cooking time:** 0 minutes | **Servings:** 2

Ingredients:

- 2 cups almond milk
- ½ teaspoon cinnamon powder
- 1 cup blueberries
- 2 cups quinoa, already cooked
- 1 tablespoon honey
- ¼ cup walnuts, chopped

Directions:

In a bowl, mix the quinoa with the milk and the rest of the ingredients, toss, divide into smaller bowls and serve for breakfast.

Nutrition:
Calories: 284, Fat: 14.3 g, Fiber: 3.2 g, Carbs: 15.4 g, Protein: 4.4 g

106. Endives, Fennel and Orange Salad

Preparation time: 5 minutes | **Cooking time:** 0 minutes | **Servings:** 2

Ingredients:

- 1 tablespoon balsamic vinegar
- 1 teaspoon Dijon mustard
- 1 tablespoon lemon juice
- ½ cup black olives, pitted and chopped
- 7 cups baby spinach
- 3 medium navel oranges, peeled and cut into segments
- 2 garlic cloves, minced
- 2 tablespoons olive oil
- Sea salt and black pepper to the taste
- 1 tablespoon parsley, chopped
- 2 endives, shredded
- 2 bulbs fennel, shredded

Directions:
In a salad bowl, combine the spinach with the endives, oranges, fennel and the rest of the ingredients, toss and serve for breakfast.

Nutrition:
Calories: 97, Fat: 9.1 g, Fiber: 1.8 g, Carbs: 3.7 g, Protein: 1.9 g

107. Banana and Strawberry Shake

Preparation time: 5 minutes | **Cooking time:** 0 minutes | **Servings:** 2

Ingredients:
- 4 bananas, peeled
- 1 cup of coconut milk
- ½ teaspoon vanilla extract
- 1 cup strawberries, halved
- 3 teaspoons Erythritol
- ½ teaspoon ground cinnamon

Directions:
Put all ingredients in the blender and blend the liquid until it is smooth.
Then pour the cooked banana shake in the serving glass.

Nutrition:
Calories: 327, Fat: 19.6 g, Fiber: 6.1 g, Carbs: 40.8 g, Protein: 3.6 g

108. Basil Avocado Mix

Preparation time: 10 minutes | **Cooking time:** 0 minutes | **Servings:** 2

Ingredients:
- ¼ cup fresh basil, chopped
- 1 cup cucumber, cubed
- 1 tablespoon balsamic vinegar
- 1 teaspoon coconut shred
- ½ teaspoon black pepper
- 2 avocados, peeled, pitted and cubed
- Juice of ½ lemon
- 2 tomatoes, chopped
- ½ teaspoon salt

Directions:
In a bowl, mix the avocados with the basil, cucumber and the other ingredients, toss, divide into smaller bowls and serve.

Nutrition:
Calories: 4.9, Fiber: 3.9 g, Carbs: 3.2 g, Protein: 6.2 g

109. Baked Avocado with Tofu

Preparation time: 10 minutes | **Cooking time:** 10 minutes | **Servings:** 2

Ingredients:
- 1 avocado, pitted, halved
- 1 tablespoon chive, chopped
- ¼ teaspoon salt
- ½ cup tofu, crumbled
- ½ teaspoon chili flakes
- 1 teaspoon olive oil

Directions:
Scoop the small amount of the avocado meat to make the wholes with the help of the scooper.
Stuff each avocado half with tofu mixed with the other ingredients.
Preheat the oven to 365°F.
Put the avocado halves in the tray and bake them for 10 minutes.

Nutrition:
Calories: 289, Fat: 26.3 g, Fiber: 6.7 g, Carbs: 9 g, Protein: 7.5 g

110. Chicken and Eggs

Preparation time: 10 minutes | **Cooking time:** 30 minutes | **Servings:** 2

Ingredients:
- 1 cup rotisserie chicken, cooked and shredded
- 1 tomato, chopped
- 1 avocado, peeled, pitted and cubed
- ½ cup black olives, pitted and halved
- 4 eggs, whisked
- Salt and black pepper to the taste

Directions:
In a sous vide bag, combine the meat with the eggs and the other ingredients, toss, seal the bag, introduce in your sous vide machine and cook at 170 °F for 30 minutes.
Divide between plates and serve.

Nutrition:
Calories: 260, Fat: 6 g, Fiber: 6 g, Carbs: 12 g, Protein: 25 g

111. Lime and Chia Eggs

Preparation time: 10 minutes | **Cooking time:** 20 minutes | **Servings:** 2

Ingredients:
- 4 eggs, whisked
- 1 tablespoon lime juice
- 1 teaspoon sweet paprika
- 1 tablespoon chia seeds
- ½ cup heavy cream
- Salt and black pepper to the taste

Directions:
In a sous vide bag, combine the eggs with the chia seeds and the other ingredients, toss, seal, introduce in your sous vide machine and cook in the water oven at 167°F for 20 minutes.
Divide the mix between plates and serve.

Nutrition:
Calories: 260, Fat: 12 g, Fiber: 6 g, Carbs: 14 g, Protein: 14 g

112. Broccoli Eggs

Preparation time: 10 minutes | **Cooking time:** 30 minutes | **Servings:** 2

Ingredients:
- 1 cup broccoli florets
- ½ teaspoon coriander, ground
- 4 eggs, whisked
- 1 tablespoon chives, chopped
- ½ teaspoon sweet paprika
- Salt and black pepper to the taste
- 2 garlic cloves, minced
- ½ cup heavy cream

Directions:
In a sous vide bag, combine the eggs with the broccoli, paprika and the other ingredients, toss, seal, introduce in your sous vide machine and cook at 175°F for 30 minutes.
Divide everything between plates and serve for breakfast.

Nutrition:
Calories: 230, Fat: 3 g, Fiber: 3 g, Carbs: 6 g, Protein: 10 g

113. Ginger Tomatoes Eggs

Preparation time: 10 minutes | **Cooking time:** 40 minutes | **Servings:** 2

Ingredients:
- 1 cup cherry tomatoes, cubed
- 4 eggs, whisked
- 1 red onion, chopped
- A pinch of red pepper, crushed
- 1 tablespoon chives, chopped
- 1 tablespoon ginger, grated
- A drizzle of olive oil
- Salt and black pepper to the taste
- 1 garlic clove, minced

Directions:
Heat up a pan with the oil over medium heat, add the ginger, onion and the other ingredients except the eggs, stir and cook for 10 minutes.
In a bowl, combine the eggs with the ginger mix, stir, pour this into a sous vide bag, seal, submerge in the water oven and cook at 170°F for 30 minutes.
Divide everything between plates and serve for breakfast.

Nutrition:
Calories: 210, Fat: 6 g, Fiber: 4 g, Carbs: 15 g, Protein: 12 g

114. Cheesy Vegan Mix

Preparation time: 10 minutes | **Cooking time:** 35 minutes | **Servings:** 2

Ingredients:
- 1 Yellow onion, sliced
- 1 Gold potato, chopped
- 8 Eggs
- 3 cups Milk
- 12 oz. Sourdough bread, cubed
- Salt and black pepper to taste
- 1 Red bell pepper, chopped
- 2 tbsp Olive oil
- 2 tbsp Mustard
- 8 oz. Brie, trimmed and cubed
- 4 oz. Parmesan, grated

Directions:
Let your air fryer preheat at 350°F.
Saute onion, potato, and bell pepper with oil in a pan for 5 minutes.

Whisk eggs with salt, pepper, milk, and mustard in a bowl.
Place the brie and bread in the Air fryer pot. Add eggs mixture, vegetables and parmesan. Seal the fryer and cook them for 20 minutes at 350°F.

Nutrition:
Calories: 231, Fat: 5 g, Fiber: 10 g, Carbs: 20 g, Protein: 12 g

115. Crunchy Blueberry Bread Bites

Preparation time: 10 minutes | **Cooking time:** 18 minutes | **Servings:** 2

Ingredients:
- ⅓ cup Milk
- ¼ tsp Nutmeg, ground
- 1 ½ cups Corn flakes, crumbled
- 2 Eggs, whisked
- 4 tbsp Cream cheese, whipped
- ¼ cup Blueberries
- 3 tsp Sugar
- 5 Bread slices

Directions:
Whisk eggs with milk, nutmeg, and sugar in a bowl.
Mix cream cheese with blueberries in a bowl.
Spread corn flakes in a separate bowl.
Top the bread slices with cream cheese mixture then dip them in the eggs.
Coat the slices with the corn flakes and place them in the air fryer basket,
Seal the fryer, and Air fry them for 8 minutes at 400°F.
Enjoy.

Nutrition:
Calories: 300, Fat: 5 g, Fiber: 7 g, Carbs: 16 g, Protein: 4 g

116. Corn Kernel Fritters

Preparation time: 5 minutes | **Cooking time:** 5 minutes | **Servings:** 2

Ingredients
- 1 Egg
- ¾ cup milk
- 1½ tsps. Baking powder
- 1 cup corn kernels
- 1 cup flour
- ½ tsps. Salt
- ¼ tsps. Pepper
- 2 tbsps. margarine, melted

Directions:
Preheat Air Fryer to 375°F. In a bowl, combine flour, baking powder, salt and pepper.
In another bowl, whisk together egg, milk, and margarine and add to the dry ingredients, stirring well. Fold in the corn and leave for 5 minutes to allow the batter sit well.
Now, form batter into small, rounded fritters. Place the fritters on a tray and let it freeze for 5 minutes to retain the shape.
Finally, place the fritters into the Air Fryer tray, set timer for 4-5 minutes. Serve and enjoy with yoghurt or salsa dip.

Nutrition:
Calories: 113, Fat: 8.2 g, Carbs: 0.3 g, Sugar: 0.2 g, Protein: 5.4 g, Cholesterol: 18 mg

117. Lemony Raspberries Bowls

Preparation time: 17 minutes | **Cooking time:** 30 minutes | **Servings:** 2

Ingredients:
- 1 cup raspberries
- 2 tbsp. lemon juice
- 2 tbsp. butter
- 1 tsp. cinnamon powder

Directions:
In your air fryer, mix all the ingredients, toss, cover, cook at 350°F for 12 minutes, divide into bowls and serve for breakfast

Nutrition:
Calories: 208, Fat: 6 g, Fiber: 9 g, Carbs: 14 g, Protein: 3 g

118. Spaghetti Squash Fritters

Preparation time: 23 minutes | **Cooking time:** 30 minutes | **Servings:** 2

Ingredients:
- 2 cups cooked spaghetti squash
- 1 large egg.
- 2 tbsp. unsalted butter, softened.
- 1 tsp. dried parsley.
- 2 stalks green onion, sliced
- ¼ cup blanched finely ground almond flour.
- ½ tsp. garlic powder.

Directions:
Remove excess moisture from the squash using a cheesecloth or kitchen towel.
Mix all ingredients in a large bowl. Form into four patties
Cut a piece of parchment to fit your air fryer basket. Place each patty on the parchment and place into the air fryer basket
Adjust the temperature to 400°F and set the timer for 8 minutes. Flip the patties halfway through the cooking time. Serve warm.

Nutrition:
Calories: 131, Protein: 3.8 g, Fiber: 2.0 g, Fat: 10.1 g, Carbs: 7.1 g

119. Mushrooms and Cheese Spread

Preparation time: 25 minutes | **Cooking time:** 30 minutes | **Servings:** 2

Ingredients:
- ¼ cup mozzarella, shredded
- 1 cup white mushrooms
- Cooking spray
- ½ cup coconut cream
- A pinch of salt and black pepper

Directions:
Put the mushrooms in your air fryer's basket, grease with cooking spray and cook at 370°F for 20 minutes.
Transfer to a blender, add the remaining ingredients, pulse well, divide into bowls and serve as a spread

Nutrition:
Calories: 202, Fat: 12 g, Fiber: 2 g, Carbs: 5 g, Protein: 7 g

120. Breakfast Egg Tomato

Preparation time: 10 minutes | **Cooking time:** 24 minutes | **Servings:** 2

Ingredients:
- 2 eggs
- 1 tsp fresh parsley
- Salt
- 2 large fresh tomatoes
- Pepper

Directions:
Preheat the air fryer to 325°F.
Cut off the top of a tomato and spoon out the tomato innards.
Break the egg in each tomato and place in air fryer basket and cook for 24 minutes.
Season with parsley, pepper, and salt.
Serve and enjoy.

Nutrition:
Calories: 95, Fat: 5 g, Carbs: 7.5 g, Sugar: 5.1 g, Protein: 7 g, Cholesterol: 164 mg

121. Mushroom Leek Frittata

Preparation time: 10 minutes | **Cooking time:** 32 minutes | **Servings:** 2

Ingredients:
- 6 eggs
- 1 cup leeks, sliced
- 6 oz mushrooms, sliced
- Salt

Directions:
Preheat the air fryer to 325°F.
Spray air fryer baking dish with cooking spray and set aside.
Heat another pan over medium heat. Spray pan with cooking spray.
Add mushrooms, leeks, and salt in a pan sauté for 6 minutes.
Break eggs in a bowl and whisk well.
Transfer sautéed mushroom and leek mixture into the prepared baking dish.
Pour egg over mushroom mixture.
Place dish in the air fryer and cook for 32 minutes.
Serve and enjoy.

Nutrition:
Calories: 116, Fat: 7 g, Carbs: 5.1 g, Sugar: 2.1 g, Protein: 10 g, Cholesterol: 245 mg

122. Perfect Breakfast Frittata

Preparation time: 10 minutes | **Cooking time:** 32 minutes | **Servings:** 2

Ingredients:
- 3 eggs
- 2 tbsp sour cream
- ¼ cup onion, chopped
- 2 tbsp parmesan cheese, grated
- ½ cup bell pepper, chopped
- ½ tsp pepper

½ tsp salt

Directions:
Add eggs in a mixing bowl and whisk with remaining ingredients.
Spray air fryer baking dish with cooking spray. Pour egg mixture into the prepared dish and place in the air fryer and cook at 350°F for 5 minutes.
Serve and enjoy.

Nutrition:
Calories: 227, Fat: 15.2 g, Carbs: 6 g, Sugar: 2.6 g, Protein: 18.2 g, Cholesterol: 271 mg

123. Tuna and Spring Onions Salad

Preparation time: 20 minutes | **Cooking time:** 30 minutes | **Servings:** 2

Ingredients:
- 14 oz. canned tuna, drained and flaked
- 1 cup arugula
- A pinch of salt and black pepper
- 2 spring onions, chopped.
- 1 tbsp. olive oil

Directions:
In a bowl, all the ingredients except the oil and the arugula and whisk.
Preheat the Air Fryer over 360°F, add the oil and grease it. Pour the tuna mix, stir well and cook for 15 minutes
In a salad bowl, combine the arugula with the tuna mix, toss and serve.

Nutrition:
Calories: 212, Fat: 8 g, Fiber: 3 g, Carbs: 5 g, Protein: 8 g

124. Cinnamon Pudding

Preparation time: 16 minutes | **Cooking time:** 30 minutes | **Servings:** 2

Ingredients:
- 4 eggs, whisked
- 2 tbsp. heavy cream
- ¼ tsp. allspice, ground
- 4 tbsp. erythritol
- ½ tsp. cinnamon powder
- Cooking spray

Directions:
Take a bowl and mix all the ingredients except the cooking spray, whisk well and pour into a ramekin greased with cooking spray
Add the basket to your Air Fryer, put the ramekin inside and cook at 400°F for 12 minutes. Divide into bowls and serve for breakfast.

Nutrition:
Calories: 201, Fat: 11 g, Fiber: 2 g, Carbs: 4 g, Protein: 6 g

125. Tomatoes and Swiss Chard Bake

Preparation time: 20 minutes | **Cooking time:** 30 minutes | **Servings:** 2

Ingredients:
- 4 eggs, whisked
- 1 cup tomatoes, cubed
- Salt and black pepper to taste.
- 3 oz. Swiss chard, chopped.
- 1 tsp. olive oil

Directions:
Take a bowl and mix the eggs with the rest of the ingredients except the oil and whisk well.
Grease a pan that fits the fryer with the oil, pour the swish chard mix and cook at 359°F for 15 minutes.
Divide between plates and serve for breakfast

Nutrition:
Calories: 202, Fat: 14 g, Fiber: 3 g, Carbs: 5 g, Protein: 12 g

126. Indian Cauliflower

Preparation time: 10 minutes | **Cooking time:** 20 minutes | **Servings:** 2

Ingredients:
- 3 cups cauliflower florets
- 2 tsp fresh lemon juice
- 1 tsp chili powder
- ½ cup vegetable stock
- Salt
- 2 tbsp water
- ½ tbsp ginger paste
- ¼ tsp turmeric
- Pepper

Directions:
Add all ingredients into the air fryer baking dish and mix well.
Place dish in the air fryer and cook at 400°F for 10 minutes.
Stir well and cook at 360°F for 10 minutes more. Stir well and serve.

Nutrition:
Calories: 49, Fat: 0.5 g, Carbs: 9 g, Sugar: 3 g, Protein: 3 g

127. Creamy Garlic Potato Mash

Preparation time: 8 minutes | **Cooking time:** 4 minutes | **Servings:** 2

Ingredients:
- 4 russet potatoes, peeled and diced
- 1 cup vegetable stock
- ½ cup coconut milk
- Salt
- 5 garlic cloves, chopped
- 4 tbsp parsley, chopped
- Pepper

Directions:
Add garlic, potatoes, and stock in an instant pot.
Seal pot with lid and cook on high pressure for 4 minutes.
Release pressure using quick release method than open lid carefully.
Transfer potatoes in a large bowl and add coconut milk.
Mash potatoes using potato masher until smooth.
Add parsley and salt. Mix well.
Serve and enjoy.

Nutrition:
Calories: 226, Carbs: 37.1 g, Protein: 4.6 g, Fat: 7.9 g, Sugar: 4 g, Sodium: 239 mg

128. Coconut Almond Breakfast Risotto

Preparation time: 8 minutes | **Cooking time:** 5 minutes | **Servings:** 2

Ingredients:
- 1 cup Arborio rice
- ⅓ cup coconut sugar
- 2 tbsp almonds, sliced and toasted
- 1 tsp vanilla
- 1 cup coconut milk
- 2 tbsp coconut flakes, sliced and toasted
- 2 cups almond milk

Directions:
Add coconut milk and almond milk in instant pot and set the pot on saute mode.
When milk mixture begins to boil then add rice and stir well.
Seal pot with lid and cook on high for 5 minutes.
Allow to release pressure naturally then open the lid.
Add remaining ingredients and stir well to combine.
Serve and enjoy.

Nutrition:
Calories: 366, Carbs: 44.8 g, Protein: 5.8 g, Fat: 18.6 g, Sugar: 2.4 g, Sodium: 106 mg

129. Sausage and Cauliflower Mash

Preparation time: 3 minutes | **Cooking time:** 5 minutes | **Servings:** 2

Ingredients:
- 1 large head cauliflower, cut into florets
- ½ cup unsweetened coconut milk or unsweetened almond milk
- 1 teaspoon organic mustard powder
- 1 Tablespoon arrowroot powder
- ½ cup vegetable broth
- 2 Tablespoons of olive oil
- 1 Tablespoon non-dairy butter or ghee, melted
- Pinch of sea salt, pepper
- 2 cups ground sausage mild, spicy – your choice
- 1 ½ cups water

Directions:
Add 1 cup water, and trivet to Instant Pot. Place cauliflower on top of trivet.
Lock lid ensure valve is sealed. Press "Manual" button. Cook on HIGH 4 minutes.
When done, quick release pressure, remove the lid. Remove cauliflower, and trivet. Discard water. Transfer cauliflower to oven-proof dish, keep warm at 200°F.
In a large bowl, combine cauliflower, milk, ghee, mustard powder, salt, pepper. Use a potato masher to mash the cauliflower until broken apart. Set aside.

Press "Sauté" on Instant Pot. Heat olive oil. Brown ground sausage.
Add vegetable broth, ½ cup water. Stir.
Close, seal lid. Press "Manual" button. Cook on HIGH 8 minutes.
When done, quick release pressure, remove lid.
Press "Sauté" on Instant Pot. Sprinkle arrowroot flour over ingredients. Allow to thicken, stirring occasionally.
Transfer cauliflower rice to serving dish. Spoon sausage, sauce over cauliflower. Serve.

Nutrition:
Calories 618, Fat: 47.2 g, Carbs: 31.2 g, Fiber: 11.8 g, Protein: 17. 3 g

130. Pumpkin Oatmeal

Preparation time: 10 minutes | **Cooking time:** 10 minutes | **Servings:** 2

Ingredients:
- 1 cup steel cut oats
- ¼ cup pumpkin
- 1 tbsp brown sugar
- 1 ¼ cups water
- ½ tsp salt
- 2 tbsp maple syrup
- ¼ tsp cinnamon
- 1 tsp vanilla
- 14 oz can coconut milk

Directions:
Add oats, vanilla, water, coconut milk, and salt into the instant pot and stir well.
Seal pot with lid and select manual high pressure for 10 minutes.
Release pressure using quick release method than open the lid.
Stir in cinnamon, brown sugar, maple syrup, and pumpkin.
Serve and enjoy.

Nutrition:
Calorie: 187, Carbs: 25.9 g, Protein: 4.5 g, Fat: 7.2 g, Sugar: 10.6 g, Sodium: 303 mg

131. Ground Pork with Eggs Frittata

Preparation time: 7 minutes | **Cooking time:** 13 minutes | **Servings:** 2

Ingredients:
- 2 tbsp ghee
- 1 onion, finely chopped
- 1 lb. ground pork grass-fed
- 2 Tbsp fresh cilantro, roughly chopped
- 1 cup water for Instant Pot
- 6 free-range eggs
- Salt and ground black pepper to taste

Directions:
Press SAUTÉ button on your Instant Pot.
When the word "hot" appears on the display, heat ghee and sauté the onions about 3 - 4 minutes.
Add the ground pork and sauté with a pinch of salt for 2 minutes.
Sprinkle fresh cilantro, stir and press the Stop button.
Whisk the eggs in a bowl with a pinch of salt and pepper.
Pour eggs in your Instant Pot and stir.
Lock lid into place and set on the MANUAL setting for 5 minutes.
Use Quick Release - turn the valve from sealing to venting to release the pressure.
Serve hot.

Nutrition:
Calories: 253, Fat: 11.03 g, Carbs: 0.93 g, Fiber: 0.17 g, Protein: 34.95 g

132. Italian Turkey Sausage Muffins

Preparation time: 5 minutes | **Cooking time:** 15 minutes | **Servings:** 2

Ingredients:
- 1 lb. Turkey Italian sausage
- 6 pastured eggs
- 2 cloves garlic
- 2 Tbsp dried minced onion
- 1 cup water for Instant Pot
- 2 cups chopped kale
- ¼ cup Extra Virgin Olive oil
- 2 Tbsp Italian seasoning
- Sea salt and ground black pepper to taste

Directions:
Place the kale leaves, eggs, olive oil, garlic, Italian seasoning, onion, salt, and pepper in your blender and pulse/ blend for about 1 minute, or until thoroughly mixed.

Transfer to a large bowl and stir in the sausage until well mixed.
Fill the muffin tins to just beneath the rim.
Pour water into the inner stainless-steel pot in the Instant Pot and place the trivets inside steam rack or a steamer basket.
Place a muffin tins on a trivet.
Lock lid into place and set on the MANUAL setting for 10 minutes.
When the beep sounds, quick release the pressure by pressing Cancel, and twisting the steam handle to the Venting position.
Serve hot or cold.

Nutrition:
Calories: 349.23, Fat: 28.77 g, Carbs: 5.27g, Fiber: 0.72 g, Protein: 18.61 g

133. Mustard Eggs and Avocado Mash

Preparation time: 5 minutes | **Cooking time:** 10 minutes | **Servings:** 2

Ingredients:
- 2 cups water for Instant Pot
- ½ cup stone ground mustard
- 1 tsp of lemon juice, freshly squeezed
- Salt and pepper, to taste
- 6 free-range eggs
- 1 avocado, chopped
- 1 Tbsp fresh chopped parsley optional

Directions:
Pour water into the inner stainless-steel pot in the Instant Pot and place the steamer basket.
Lock lid into place and set on the MANUAL setting for 5 minutes.
It will take the cooker approximately 5 minutes to build to pressure and then 5 minutes to cook.
Use Quick Release - turn the valve from sealing to venting to release the pressure.
Place the eggs in cold water and peel. Cut the eggs into small pieces and season with the salt and pepper.
Wash, peel and clean avocado.
Mash avocado with the fork, and sprinkle with the salt and pepper.
Combine the eggs, mustard, mashed avocado, lemon juice and fresh parsley.
Refrigerate for one hour and serve.

Nutrition:
Calories: 161, Fat: 12.05 g, Carbs: 4.97 g, Fiber: 3.24 g, Protein: 9.35 g

134. Apple Cinnamon Oatmeal

Preparation time: 10 minutes | **Cooking time:** 4 minutes | **Servings:** 2

Ingredients:
- 2 cups steel-cut oats
- 1 ½ tsp cinnamon
- 4 ½ cups water
- ¼ tsp nutmeg
- 2 apples, diced

Directions:
Add all ingredients into the instant pot and stir well.
Seal pot with lid and cook on manual high pressure for 4 minutes.
Once done then allow to release pressure naturally for 10 minutes then release using quick-release method. Open the lid.
Stir well and serve.

Nutrition:
Calories: 216, Fat: 2.9 g, Carbs: 43.9 g, Sugar: 12.1 g, Protein: 5.7 g

135. Classic Apple Oats

Preparation time: 5 minutes | **Cooking time:** 5 minutes | **Servings:** 2

Ingredients:
- ½ teaspoon cinnamon
- 2 apples, make half-inch chunks
- 1 ½ cups water
- Pinch of salt
- Pinch of nutmeg
- ¼ teaspoon ginger
- ½ cup oats, steel cut
- Maple syrup, as needed
- Pinch of clove

Directions:
Take Instant Pot and carefully arrange it over a clean, dry kitchen platform. Turn on the appliance.
In the cooking pot area, add the water, oats, cinnamon, ginger, clove, nutmeg, apple and salt. Stir the ingredients gently.
Close the pot lid and seal the valve to avoid any leakage. Find and press "Manual" cooking setting and set cooking time to 5 minutes.

Allow the recipe ingredients to cook for the set time, and after that, the timer reads "zero".
Press "Cancel" and press "NPR" setting for natural pressure release. It takes 8-10 times for all inside pressure to release.
Open the pot and arrange the cooked recipe in serving plates.
Sweeten as needed with maple or agave syrup and serve immediately. Top with some chopped nuts, optional.

Nutrition:
Calories: 248, Fat: 5.5 g, Carbs: 52 g, Fiber: 13 g, Protein: 7 g

136. Roasted Potatoes

Preparation time: 5 minutes | **Cooking time:** 12 minutes | **Servings:** 2

Ingredients:

1 ½ lbs. russet potatoes, cut into wedges	1 cup chicken stock
½ tsp onion powder	4 tbsp olive oil
¼ tsp paprika	1 tsp garlic powder
¼ tsp pepper	1 tsp sea salt

Directions:
Add oil in instant pot and select sauté.
Add potatoes in the pot and sauté for 5-6 minutes.
Add remaining ingredients into the pot and stir well.
Seal pot with lid and cook on high pressure for 6 minutes.
Release pressure using quick release method than open lid carefully.
Stir well and serve.

Nutrition:
Calories: 244, Carbs: 27.8 g, Protein: 3.2 g, Fat: 14.3 g, Sugar: 2.4 g, Sodium: 670 mg

137. Zucchini Salad

Preparation time: 10 minutes | **Cooking time:** 25 minutes | **Servings:** 2

Ingredients:

1 lb. zucchini, cut into slices	2 tbsp tomato paste
½ tbsp tarragon, chopped	1 yellow squash, diced
½ lb. carrots, peeled and diced	1 tbsp olive oil
Pepper	Salt

Directions:
In air fryer baking dish mix zucchini, tomato paste, tarragon, squash, carrots, pepper, and salt. Drizzle with olive oil.
Place in the air fryer and cook at 400°F for 25 minutes. Stir halfway through.
Serve and enjoy.

Nutrition:
Calories: 79, Fat: 3 g, Carbs: 11 g, Sugar: 5 g, Protein: 2 g

138. Egg, Bacon and Cheese Roll Ups

Preparation time: 30 minutes | **Cooking time:** 30 minutes | **Servings:** 2

Ingredients:

12 slices sugar-free bacon.	½ medium green bell pepper, seeded and chopped
6 large eggs.	¼ cup chopped onion
1 cup shredded sharp Cheddar cheese.	½ cup mild salsa, for dipping
2 tbsp. unsalted butter.	

Directions:
In a medium skillet over medium heat, melt butter. Add onion and pepper to the skillet and sauté until fragrant and onions are translucent, about 3 minutes
Whisk eggs in a small bowl and pour into skillet. Scramble eggs with onions and peppers until fluffy and fully cooked, about 5 minutes. Remove from heat and set aside
On work surface, place three slices of bacon side by side, overlapping about ¼-inch. Place ¼ cup scrambled eggs in a heap on the side closest to you and sprinkle ¼ cup cheese on top of the eggs. Tightly roll the bacon around the eggs and secure the seam with a toothpick if necessary. Place each roll into the air fryer basket
Adjust the temperature to 350°F and set the timer for 15 minutes. Rotate the rolls halfway

through the cooking time. Bacon will be brown and crispy when completely cooked. Serve immediately with salsa for dipping.

Nutrition:
Calories: 460, Protein: 28.2 g, Fiber: 0.8 g, Fat: 31.7 g, Carbs: 6.1 g

139. Crispy Ham Egg Cups

Preparation time: 17 minutes | **Cooking time:** 30 minutes | **Servings:** 2

Ingredients:
- 4 large eggs.
- ½ cup shredded medium Cheddar cheese.
- 2 tbsp. diced red bell pepper.
- 2 tbsp. full-fat sour cream.
- 4: 1-oz. slices deli ham
- ¼ cup diced green bell pepper.
- 2 tbsp. diced white onion.

Directions:
Place one slice of ham on the bottom of four baking cups.
Take a large bowl, whisk eggs with sour cream. Stir in green pepper, red pepper and onion
Pour the egg mixture into ham-lined baking cups. Top with Cheddar. Place cups into the air fryer basket. Adjust the temperature to 320°F and set the timer for 12 minutes or until the tops are browned. Serve warm.

Nutrition:
Calories: 382, Protein: 29.4 g, Fiber: 1.4 g, Fat: 23.6 g, Carbs: 6.0 g

140. Olives and Kale

Preparation time: 25 minutes | **Cooking time:** 30 minutes | **Servings:** 2

Ingredients:
- 4 eggs, whisked
- ½ cup black olives, pitted and sliced
- Cooking spray
- 1 cup kale, chopped.
- 2 tbsp. cheddar, grated
- A pinch of salt and black pepper

Directions:
Take a bowl and mix the eggs with the rest of the ingredients except the cooking spray and whisk well.
Now, take a pan that fits in your air fryer and grease it with the cooking spray, pour the olives mixture inside, spread
Put the pan into the machine and cook at 360°F for 20 minutes. Serve for breakfast hot.

Nutrition:
Calories: 220, Fat: 13 g, Fiber: 4 g, Carbs: 6 g, Protein: 12 g

141. Stuffed Poblanos

Preparation time: 30 minutes | **Cooking time:** 30 minutes | **Servings:** 2

Ingredients:
- ½ lb. spicy ground pork breakfast sausage
- 4 large eggs.
- 4 oz. full-fat cream cheese, softened.
- 8 tbsp. shredded pepper jack cheese
- 4 large poblano peppers
- ½ cup full-fat sour cream.
- ¼ cup canned diced tomatoes and green chiles, drained

Directions:
In a medium skillet over medium heat, crumble and brown the ground sausage until no pink remains. Remove sausage and drain the fat from the pan. Crack eggs into the pan, scramble and cook until no longer runny
Place cooked sausage in a large bowl and fold in cream cheese. Mix in diced tomatoes and chiles. Gently fold in eggs
Cut a 4"–5" slit in the top of each poblano, removing the seeds and white membrane with a small knife. Separate the filling into four and spoon carefully into each pepper. Top each with 2 tbsp. pepper jack cheese
Place each pepper into the air fryer basket. Adjust the temperature to 350°F and set the timer for 15 minutes.
Peppers will be soft, and cheese will be browned when ready. Serve immediately with sour cream on top.

Nutrition:
Calories: 489, Protein: 22.8 g, Fiber: 3.8 g, Fat: 35.6 g, Carbs: 12.6 g

142. Raspberries Oatmeal

Preparation time: 20 minutes | **Cooking time:** 30 minutes | **Servings:** 2

Ingredients:

- 1 ½ cups coconut, shredded
- 2 cups almond milk
- 2 tsp. stevia
- Cooking spray
- ½ cups raspberries
- ¼ tsp. nutmeg, ground
- ½ tsp. cinnamon powder

Directions:
Grease the air fryer's pan with cooking spray, mix all the ingredients inside, cover and cook at 360°F for 15 minutes. Divide into bowls and serve

Nutrition:
Calories: 172, Fat: 5 g, Fiber: 2 g, Carbs: 4 g, Protein: 6 g

143. Bell Pepper Eggs

Preparation time: 25 minutes | **Cooking time:** 30 minutes | **Servings:** 2

Ingredients:

- 4 medium green bell peppers
- 3 oz. cooked ham, chopped
- 1 cup mild Cheddar cheese
- ¼ medium onion, peeled and chopped
- 8 large eggs.

Directions:
Cut the tops off each bell pepper. Remove the seeds and the white membranes with a small knife. Place ham and onion into each pepper Crack 2 eggs into each pepper. Top with ¼ cup cheese per pepper. Place into the air fryer basket Adjust the temperature to 390 °F and set the timer for 15 minutes. When fully cooked, peppers will be tender, and eggs will be firm. Serve immediately.

Nutrition:
Calories: 314, Protein: 24.9 g, Fiber: 1.7 g, Fat: 18.6 g, Carbs: 6.3 g

144. Apple Oat Sunrise Fritters

Preparation time: 10 minutes | **Cooking time:** 5 minutes | **Servings:** 2

Ingredients:

- 2 Apples, peeled, cored & sliced into rings
- 1½ tsps. Ground cinnamon, divided
- 2 tbsps. cornstarch
- ½ cup club soda
- Egg
- ½ cup + 2 tbsps. sugar
- ½ cup rice flour
- 1 tsp. baking powder
- 1 cup oats
- ¾ tsp. kosher salt

Directions:
Combine 1 tsp. of cinnamon and ½ cup sugar in a shallow bowl, whisking well. Next, preheat the Air Fryer to 350°F.
In a food processor, pulse the oats to a coarse powder. Remove to a large bowl and add in the rice flour, baking powder, cornstarch, salt, cinnamon and the rest of the sugar, whisking well.
Add in the egg and club soda, whisking in more soda, a little at a time, until the mixture is like pancake batter.
Dip the apple rings into the batter then place into the Air Fryer tray, one set at a time. Cook until golden brown and crisp for about 4 minutes.
Serve fritters sprinkled with the reserved cinnamon sugar.

Nutrition:
Calories: 113, Fat: 8.2 g, Carbs: 0.3 g, Sugar: 0.2 g, Protein: 5.4 g, Cholesterol: 18 mg

145. Simple Egg Soufflé

Preparation time: 5 minutes | **Cooking time:** 8 minutes
Serving: 2

Ingredients:

- 2 eggs
- ¼ tsp chili pepper 2 tbsp heavy cream ¼ tsp pepper

1 tbsp parsley, chopped Salt

Directions:
In a bowl, whisk eggs with remaining gradients.
Spray two ramekins with cooking spray.
Pour egg mixture into the prepared ramekins and place into the air fryer basket.
Cook soufflé at 390°F for 8 minutes.
Serve and enjoy.

Nutrition:
Calories: 116, Fat: 10 g, Carbs: 1.1 g, Sugar: 0.4 g, Protein: 6 g, Cholesterol: 184 mg

146. Vegetable Egg Soufflé

Preparation time: 10 minutes | **Cooking time:** 20 minutes | **Servings:** 2

Ingredients:
- 4 large eggs
- 1 tsp red pepper, crushed
- 1 tsp onion powder 1 tsp garlic powder
- ½ cup broccoli florets, chopped ½ cup mushrooms, chopped

Directions:
Spray four ramekins with cooking spray and set aside.
In a bowl, whisk eggs with onion powder, garlic powder, and red pepper.
Add mushrooms and broccoli and stir well.
Pour egg mixture into the prepared ramekins and place ramekins into the air fryer basket.
Cook at 350°F for 15 minutes. Make sure souffle is cooked if souffle is not cooked then cook for 5 minutes more.
Serve and enjoy.

Nutrition:
Calories: 91, Fat: 5.1 g, Carbs: 4.7 g, Sugar: 2.6 g, Protein: 7.4 g, Cholesterol: 186 mg

147. Cinnamon and Cream Cheese Oats

Preparation time: 10 minutes | **Cooking time:** 25 minutes | **Servings:** 2

Ingredients:
- 1 cup steel oats
- 3 cups milk
- 1 tablespoon margarine
- 1 tsp. cinnamon powder
- 2 tbsps. white sugar
- ¾ cup raisins
- ¼ cup brown sugar
- 2 oz. cream cheese, soft

Directions:
Heat up a pan that fits your air fryer with the margarine over medium heat, add oats, stir and toast them for 3 minutes.
Add milk and raisins, stir, introduce in your air fryer and cook at 350°F for 20 minutes.
Meanwhile, in a bowl, mix cinnamon with brown sugar and stir.
In a second bowl, mix white sugar with cream cheese and whisk.
Divide oats into bowls and top each with cinnamon and cream cheese.

Nutrition:
Calories: 90, Fat: 5.1 g, Carbs: 3.7 g, Sugar: 2.6 g, Protein: 7.4 g, Cholesterol: 186 mg

148. Cherries Risotto

Preparation time: 10 minutes | **Cooking time:** 12 minutes | **Servings:** 2

Ingredients:
- 1 ½ cups Arborio rice
- ⅓ cup brown sugar
- 2 tbsps. margarine
- 1 cup apple juice
- ½ cup cherries, dried
- 1 ½ tsps. Cinnamon powder
- A pinch of salt
- 2 apples, cored and sliced
- 3 cups milk

Directions:
Heat up a pan that fist your air fryer with the margarine over medium heat, add rice, stir and cook for 4-5 minutes.
Add sugar, apples, apple juice, milk, cinnamon and cherries, stir, introduce in your air fryer and cook at 350°F for 8 minutes.
Divide into bowls and serve for breakfast.

Nutrition:
Calories: 113, Fat: 8.2 g, Carbs: 0.3 g, Sugar: 0.2 g, Protein: 5.4 g, Cholesterol: 18 mg

149. Rice, Almonds and Raisins Pudding

Preparation time: 5 minutes | **Cooking time:** 8 minutes | **Servings:** 2

Ingredients:
- 1 cup brown rice
- 1 cup milk
- ½ cup maple syrup
- ¼ cup almonds
- ½ cup coconut chips
- 2 cups water
- ¼ cup raisins
- A pinch of cinnamon powder

Directions:
Put the rice in a pan that fits your air fryer, add the water, heat up on the stove over medium high heat, cook until rice is soft and drain.
Add milk, coconut chips, almonds, raisins, cinnamon and maple syrup, stir well, introduce in your air fryer and cook at 360°F for 8 minutes.
Divide rice pudding in bowls and serve.

Nutrition:
Calories: 113, Fat: 8.2 g, Carbs: 0.3 g, Sugar: 0.2 g, Protein: 5.4 g, Cholesterol: 18 mg

Chapter 2: Lunch

150. Beef and cabbage

Preparation time: 10 minutes | **Cooking time:** 1 hour and 20 minutes | **Servings:** 2

Ingredients:
- 2 bay leaves
- 4 carrots, peeled and chopped
- 4 cups water
- 3 turnips, cut into quarters
- 1 cabbage head, cut into
- 6 potatoes, cut into quarters
- 3 garlic cloves, peeled and chopped
- 2 ½ lbs. beef brisket
- Salt and ground black pepper, to taste
- Horseradish sauce, for serving
- 6 wedges

Directions:
Place the chicken breast and water in the Instant Pot, add salt, pepper, garlic and bay leaf, cover the Instant Pot and cook the meat / stew for 1 hour and 15 minutes.
Release the pressure, uncover the Instant Pot, add the carrots, cabbage, potatoes and turnips, mix, cover the Instant Pot and cook in the Manual setting for 6 minutes.
Release the pressure naturally, uncover the Instant Pot, share the dishes and serve with horseradish sauce on top.

Nutrition:
Calories: 340, Fat: 24 g, Fiber: 1 g, Carbs: 14 g, Proteins: 26 g

151. Lamb Shanks

Preparation time: 10 minutes | **Cooking time:** 45 minutes | **Servings:** 2

Ingredients:
- 4 lamb shanks
- 3 carrots, peeled and chopped
- 2 tablespoons white flour
- 2 tablespoons tomato paste
- 2 tablespoons water
- 1 yellow onion, peeled and diced
- 2 tablespoons extra virgin olive oil
- 2 garlic cloves, peeled and minced
- 1 tomato, cored and chopped
- 1 teaspoon dried oregano

Salt and ground black pepper, to taste
4 oz. red wine
1 beef bouillon cube

Directions:

In a bowl, mix the flour with salt and pepper. Add the lamb shank and mix well. Put the instant pot in the sauté mode, add the oil and heat.

Add the lamb, brown on all sides and transfer to a bowl. Add the onion, oregano, carrot and garlic to the Instant Pot, stir and cook for 5 minutes.

Add tomatoes, tomato paste, water, wine and cube stock, mix and bring to a boil. Return the lamb to the pan, stir, cover and cook manually for 25 minutes.

Release the pressure, uncover the Instant Pot, divide the lamb between the plates, pour the sauce and serve.

Nutrition:

Calories: 430, Fat: 17 g, Fiber: 2.5 g, Carbs: 11.3 g, Proteins: 50 g

152. Lamb Ribs

Preparation time: 15 minutes | **Cooking time:** 20 minutes | **Servings:** 2

Ingredients:

8 lamb ribs
4 rosemary sprigs
2 carrots, peeled and chopped
Salt and ground black pepper, to taste
13 oz. veggie stock
4 garlic cloves, peeled and minced
2 tablespoons extra virgin olive oil
3 tablespoons white flour

Directions:

Put the instant pot in the sauté mode, add the oil and heat. Add the lamb, garlic, salt and pepper and brown them on all sides.

Add the flour, stock, rosemary and carrot, mix well, cover the instant pot and cook in the Meat / Stew setting for 20 minutes.

Release the pressure, uncover the instant pot, discard the rosemary, divide the lamb into the dishes and serve with the cooking liquid spread over it.

Nutrition:

Calories: 234, Fats: 8.4 g, Fiber: 1 g, Carbs: 3 g, Proteins: 35 g

153. Mediterranean lamb

Preparation time: 15 minutes | **Cooking time:** 60 minutes | **Servings:** 2

Ingredients:

6 lb. lamb leg, boneless
2 tablespoons extra virgin olive oil
1 bay leaf
3 garlic cloves, peeled and minced
1 teaspoon dried sage
3 tablespoons arrowroot powder, mixed with
3 lbs. potatoes, chopped
1 teaspoon marjoram
Salt and ground black pepper, to taste
1 teaspoon ginger, grated
1 teaspoon dried thyme
2 cups vegetable stock
⅓ cup water

Directions:

Put the instant pot in the sauté mode, add the oil and heat. Add the leg of lamb and brown on all sides.

Add salt, pepper, bay leaf, marjoram, sage, ginger, garlic, thyme and broth, mix, cover the instant pot and cook in the Meat / Stew setting for 50 minutes. Relieve the pressure, add the potatoes, arrowroot mixture, more salt and pepper, if necessary, stir, cover the Instant Pot and cook in the manual for 10 minutes.

Relieve the pressure, uncover the Instant Pot, divide the lamb between the plates and serve.

Nutrition:

Calories: 238, Fat: 5 g, Fiber: 4 g, Carbs: 17 g, Proteins: 7.3 g

154. Coriander Potatoes

Preparation time: 10 minutes | **Cooking time:** 25 minutes | **Servings:** 2

Ingredients:

1 lb. gold potatoes, peeled and cut into wedges
1 tablespoon tomato sauce
½ teaspoon garlic powder
Salt and black pepper to the taste
2 tablespoons coriander, chopped
1 teaspoon chili powder

1 tablespoon olive oil

Directions:

In a bowl, combine the potatoes with the tomato sauce and the other **Ingredients:**, toss, and transfer to the air fryer's basket.
Cook at 370 °F for 25 minutes, divide between plates and serve as a side dish.

Nutrition:
Calories: 210, Fat: 5 g, Fiber: 7 g, Carbs: 12 g, Protein: 5 g

155. Creamy Green Beans and Tomatoes

Preparation time: 10 minutes | **Cooking time:** 20 minutes | **Servings:** 2

Ingredients:

1 lb. green beans, trimmed and halved	½ lb. cherry tomatoes, halved
2 tablespoons olive oil	1 teaspoon oregano, dried
1 teaspoon basil, dried	Salt and black pepper to the taste
1 cup heavy cream	½ tablespoon cilantro, chopped

Directions:

In your air fryer's pan, combine the green beans with the tomatoes and the other **Ingredients:**, toss and cook at 360°F for 20 minutes.
Divide the mix between plates and serve.

Nutrition:
Calories: 174, Fat: 5 g, Fiber: 7 g, Carbs: 11 g, Protein: 4 g

156. Buttery Artichokes

Preparation time: 10 minutes | **Cooking time:** 20 minutes | **Servings:** 2

Ingredients:

4 artichokes, trimmed and halved	3 garlic cloves, minced
1 tablespoon olive oil	Salt and black pepper to the taste
4 tablespoons butter, melted	¼ teaspoon cumin, ground

1 tablespoon lemon zest, grated

Directions:

In a bowl, combine the artichokes with the oil, garlic and the other **Ingredients:**, toss well and transfer them to the air fryer's basket.
Cook for 20 minutes at 370 °F, divide between plates and serve as a side dish.

Nutrition:
Calories: 214, Fat: 5 g, Fiber: 8 g, Carbs: 12 g, Protein: 5 g

157. Sweet Potato and Eggplant Mix

Preparation time: 10 minutes | **Cooking time:** 20 minutes | **Servings:** 2

Ingredients:

2 sweet potatoes, peeled and cut into medium wedges	2 eggplants, roughly cubed
1 tablespoon avocado oil	Juice of 1 lemon
4 garlic cloves, minced	1 teaspoon nutmeg, ground
Salt and black pepper to the taste	1 tablespoon rosemary, chopped

Directions:

In your air fryer, combine the potatoes with the eggplants and the other ingredients. Toss and cook at 370°F for 20 minutes.
Divide the mix between plates and serve as a side dish.

Nutrition:
Calories: 182, Fat: 6 g, Fiber: 3 g, Carbs: 11 g, Protein: 5 g

158. Turkey and Mushroom Stew

Preparation time: 30 minutes | **Servings:** 2

Ingredients:

½ lb. brown mushrooms, sliced	1 turkey breast, skinless, boneless, cubed and browned
¼ cup tomato sauce	1 tbsp. parsley, chopped.

Salt and black pepper to taste.

Directions:
In a pan that fits your air fryer, mix the turkey with the mushrooms, salt, pepper and tomato sauce, toss, introduce in the fryer and cook at 350°F for 25 minutes
Divide into bowls and serve for lunch with parsley sprinkled on top.

Nutrition:
Calories: 220, Fat: 12 g, Fiber: 2 g, Carbs: 5 g, Protein: 12 g

159. Okra Casserole

Preparation time: 25 minutes | **Servings:** 2

Ingredients:

2 red bell peppers, cubed	2 tomatoes, chopped.
3 garlic cloves, minced	3 cups okra
½ cup cheddar, shredded	¼ cup tomato puree
1 tbsp. cilantro, chopped.	1 tsp. olive oil
2 tsp. coriander, ground	Salt and black pepper to taste.

Directions:
Grease a heat proof dish that fits your air fryer with the oil, add all the ingredients except the cilantro and the cheese and toss them gently
Sprinkle the cheese and the cilantro on top, introduce the dish in the fryer and cook at 390°F for 20 minutes.
Divide between plates and serve for lunch.

Nutrition:
Calories: 221, Fat: 7 g, Fiber: 2 g, Carbs: 4 g, Protein: 9 g

160. Tomato and Avocado

Preparation time: 8 minutes | **Servings:** 2

Ingredients:

½ lb. cherry tomatoes, halved	2 avocados, pitted, peeled and cubed
1 ¼ cup lettuce, torn	⅓ cup coconut cream

A pinch of salt and black pepper | Cooking spray

Directions:
Grease the air fryer with cooking spray, combine the tomatoes with avocados, salt, pepper and the cream and cook at 350°F for 5 minutes shaking once
In a salad bowl, mix the lettuce with the tomatoes and avocado mix, toss and serve.

Nutrition:
Calories: 226, Fat: 12 g, Fiber: 2 g, Carbs: 4 g, Protein: 8 g

161. Tuscan Soup

Preparation time: 10 minutes | **Cooking time:** 15 minutes | **Servings:** 2

Ingredients:

1 yellow onion, chopped	4 garlic cloves, minced
2 tablespoons olive oil	½ cup celery, chopped
½ cup carrots, chopped	15 oz. canned tomatoes, chopped
1 zucchini, chopped	6 cups veggie stock
2 tablespoons tomato paste	15 oz. canned white beans, drained and rinsed
2 handfuls baby spinach	1 tablespoon basil, chopped
Salt and black pepper to the taste	

Directions:
Heat up a pot with the oil over medium heat, add the garlic and the onion and sauté for 5 minutes. Add the rest of the ingredients, stir, bring the soup to a simmer and cook for 10 minutes.
Ladle the soup into bowls and serve right away.

Nutrition:
Calories: 471, Fat: 8.2 g, Fiber: 19.4 g, Carbs: 76.5 g, Protein: 27.6 g

162. Creamed New York Strip

Preparation time: 30 minutes | **Cooking time:** 20 minutes | **Servings:** 2

Ingredients:

- 2 lbs. New York strip, sliced into thin strips
- 2 carrots, sliced
- 1 small leek, sliced
- 1 tablespoon tamari sauce
- 2 tablespoons sesame oil
- ½ cup heavy cream
- 1 cup cream of mushroom soup
- 2 cloves garlic, sliced
- ½ cup dry red wine
- Kosher salt and ground black pepper, to taste

Directions:

Press the "Sauté" button to preheat your Instant Pot. Heat the sesame oil until sizzling. Once hot, brown the beef strips in batches.

Add wine to deglaze the pan. Stir in the remaining ingredients, except for the heavy cream.

Secure the lid. Choose the "Manual" mode and cook for 20 minutes at High pressure. Once cooking is complete, use a quick pressure release, carefully remove the lid.

Remove the beef from the cooking liquid. Mash the vegetables using a potato masher.

Press the "Sauté" button one more time. Now, bring the liquid to a boil. Heat off and stir in the heavy cream.

Spoon the sauce over the New York strip and serve immediately.

Enjoy!

Nutrition:
Calories: 439, Fat: 21.9 g, Carbs: 9.8 g, Protein: 50 g, Sugars: 2.3 g

163. Ground Beef, Cheese and Bean Bowl

Preparation time: 20 minutes | **Cooking time:** 20 minutes | **Servings:** 2

Ingredients:

- 1 ½ lbs. lean ground chuck
- 1 15-oz. can black beans, drained and rinsed
- 1 onion, chopped
- 1 cup tomato puree
- 1 ½ cups Monterey-Jack cheese, shredded
- 1 cup vegetable broth
- 2 garlic cloves, minced
- 1 tablespoon chipotle paste
- 1 1-oz. packet taco seasoning mix
- 1 teaspoon olive oil
- 1 green bell pepper, deseeded and sliced
- 2 tablespoons fresh cilantro leaves, chopped
- 1 red bell pepper, deseeded and sliced

Directions:

Press the "Sauté" button to preheat your Instant Pot. Heat the oil and cook the ground chuck for 2 to 3 minutes or until mostly brown.

Next, add the taco seasoning mix, broth, onion, garlic, and peppers.

Secure the lid. Choose the "Manual" mode and cook for 10 minutes at High pressure. Once cooking is complete, use a natural pressure release, carefully remove the lid.

Divide the meat mixture between four serving bowls. Add the tomato puree, chipotle paste, and black beans, gently stir to combine.

Top with the cheese and serve garnished with fresh cilantro leaves. Enjoy!

Nutrition:
Calories: 535, Fat: 31.2 g, Carbs: 16.9 g, Protein: 48.1 g, Sugars: 6.7 g

164. Basil Beef with Yams

Preparation time: 5 minutes | **Cooking time:** 45 minutes | **Servings:** 2

Ingredients:

- 2 Yams, peeled and chopped
- 3 Garlic Cloves, minced
- 1 Bell Pepper, chopped
- ½ tbsp dried Basil
- 1 tbsp Olive Oil
- 1 ½ cups Homemade Bone Broth
- 2 ½ lbs. Beef, cut into cubes
- 1 Onion, diced
- 3 tbsp Tomato Paste

Directions:

Heat the olive oil in the Instant Pot on SAUTE.

Add the onions and peppers and cook for 3 minutes.

Add the garlic and cook for one more.

Place the beef inside and cook it until it becomes browned.

Stir in the remaining ingredients and close the lid.

Set the IP to MANUAL and cook on HIGH for 30 minutes.
Do a quick pressure release.
Serve and enjoy!

Nutrition:
Calories: 390, Fats: 28 g, Carbs: 2 g, Protein: 43 g, Fiber: 1 g

165. Authentic Mississippi Pork

Preparation time: 5 minutes | **Cooking time:** 50 minutes | **Servings:** 2

Ingredients:

1 lb. pork shoulder	1 pack ranch dressing mix
16 oz deli sliced pepperoncini peppers with ½ cup juices	Salt and black pepper to taste

Directions:
Combine pork, ranch dressing mix, and pepperoncini with juices in inner pot. Seal the lid, select Manual/Pressure Cook mode on High, and set cooking time to 30 minutes.
After cooking, perform a natural pressure release for 10 minutes, then a quick pressure release until remaining steam is out, and unlock the lid. Using two forks, shred meat into small strands, adjust taste with salt and black pepper, and dish. Serve warm over rice or with potatoes.

Nutrition:
Calories: 479, Carbs: 5 g, Fat: 28 g, Protein: 51 g

166. Pork with Spicy Red Sauce

Preparation time: 5 minutes | **Cooking time:** 35 minutes | **Servings:** 2

Ingredients:

1 lb. ground pork	2 tbsp chili powder
Salt and black pepper to taste	½ tsp dried oregano
2 tsp garlic, minced	¼ cup cilantro, chopped
1 cup diced red onion	2 15-oz. cans stewed tomatoes
1 19-oz. can enchilada sauce	1 cup chicken broth
2 15-oz. cans red kidney beans, drained	

Directions:
Into inner pot, add pork, chili powder, salt, black pepper, oregano, garlic, cilantro, onion, tomatoes, enchilada sauce, chicken broth, and kidney beans. Seal the lid, select Manual/Pressure Cook on High, and set time to 15 minutes.
Perform natural pressure release for 10 minutes, then a quick pressure release until remaining steam is out and unlock the lid. Stir, adjust taste with salt and pepper, and dish the chili. Serve warm with tortillas and cheddar cheese.

Nutrition:
Calories: 556, Carbs: 32 g, Fat: 32 g, Protein: 39 g

167. Sriracha Lemon Pork Chops

Preparation time: 5 minutes | **Cooking time:** 50 minutes + marinating time | **Servings:** 2

Ingredients:

4 boneless pork chops	2 tbsp hot sauce
2 tbsp sesame oil	1 lemon, juiced
1 tbsp soy sauce	1 ½ tsp sriracha sauce
2 tbsp olive oil	1 cup chicken broth
Salt to taste	

Directions:
Place pork chops in a plastic zipper bag.
In a small bowl, mix hot sauce, sesame oil, lemon juice, soy sauce, and sriracha sauce. Pour mixture over pork, close bag, and massage marinade into the meat. Marinate in refrigerator for 30 minutes to 1 hour.
Set your Instant Pot to Sauté mode and adjust to medium heat. Heat olive oil in inner pot, take pork out of the fridge and marinade, and sear in oil on both sides until brown, 6 minutes. Pour in chicken broth and season with salt.
Seal the lid, select Manual/Pressure Cook mode on High, and set cooking time to 20 minutes. After cooking, perform a natural pressure release for 10 minutes, then a quick pressure release to let out remaining steam. Unlock the lid. Remove pork onto serving plates, baste with a little sauce, and serve warm.

Nutrition:
Calories: 379, Carbs: 3 g, Fat: 21 g, Protein: 43 g

168. Rosemary Lemon Pork Chops

Preparation time: 5 minutes | **Cooking time:** 55 minutes | **Servings:** 2

Ingredients:

- 1 tbsp olive oil
- Salt and black pepper to taste
- ½ cup chicken broth
- 4 rosemary sprigs
- 4 bone-in pork chops
- 2 tsp garlic powder
- 1 lemon, zested and juiced
- ½ tsp Dijon mustard

Directions:
Set your Instant Pot to Sauté mode and adjust to medium heat. Heat olive oil in inner pot, season pork with salt, black pepper, garlic powder, and sear in oil on both sides until golden brown, 6 minutes. Pour in chicken broth, lemon zest, lemon juice, rosemary sprigs, and mix in Dijon mustard.
Seal the lid, select Manual/Pressure Cook mode on High, and set cooking time to 25 minutes. After cooking, perform a natural pressure release for 10 minutes, then a quick pressure release to let out remaining steam. Unlock the lid. Remove pork onto serving plates, allow sitting for 2 minutes, and serve warm.

Nutrition:
Calories: 373, Carbs: 4 g, Fat: 21 g, Protein: 41 g

169. Instant BBQ Baby Back Ribs

Preparation time: 5 minutes | **Cooking time:** 55 minutes | **Servings:** 2

Ingredients:

- 2 tbsp brown sugar
- ½ tsp garlic powder
- ½ tsp smoked paprika
- 1 cup chicken broth
- 2 tsp hickory liquid smoke
- ¼ tsp onion powder
- Salt and black pepper to taste
- 1 rack baby back ribs
- ½ cup BBQ sauce + more for serving

Directions:
In a small bowl, combine brown sugar, onion powder, garlic powder, salt, black pepper, and paprika. Cut ribs into four pieces each and rub generously with spice mixture. Place in inner pot. Top with chicken broth, BBQ sauce, and liquid smoke. Seal the lid, select Manual/Pressure Cook mode on High, and set cooking time to 35 minutes.
Once done cooking, perform natural pressure release for 10 minutes, then a quick pressure release until remaining steam is out. Unlock the lid. Using tongs, remove ribs into serving plates, brush with BBQ sauce, and serve warm.

Nutrition:
Calories: 895, Carbs: 8 g, Fat: 62 g, Protein: 78 g

170. Beef Stroganoff

Preparation time: 10 minutes | **Cooking time:** 24 minutes | **Servings:** 2

Ingredients:

- 2 lbs. stew meat
- 8 oz mushrooms, sliced
- ½ tsp dried thyme
- 1 tsp onion powder
- ½ cup onion, chopped
- ½ tsp garlic powder
- ⅓ cup flour
- 2 tsp salt
- ½ cup sour cream
- 1 ½ tbsp Worcestershire sauce
- 1 tsp parsley flakes
- 1 ¼ cup beef broth
- 2 tbsp olive oil
- ½ tsp paprika
- 1 tsp pepper

Directions:
Add flour, garlic powder, and paprika into the large zip-lock bag.
Add meat to the bag. Seal bag and shake until well coated.
Add oil into the instant pot and set the pot on sauté mode.
Add onion and meat to the pot and sauté until browned.
Add remaining ingredients except for sour cream and stir well.
Seal pot with lid and cook on manual high pressure for 20 minutes.
Once done then release pressure using the quick-release method than open the lid.
Stir in sour cream and serve.

Nutrition:
Calories: 513, Fat: 29 g, Carbs: 10.1 g, Sugar: 2.2 g, Protein: 50.8 g, Cholesterol: 169 mg

171. Duck and Veggies Recipe

Preparation time: 10 minutes | **Cooking time:** 30 minutes | **Servings:** 2

Ingredients:
- 1 duck, chopped in medium pieces
- 1 small ginger piece, grated
- 3 tbsp. white wine
- Salt and black pepper to the taste
- 1 cup chicken stock
- 3 cucumbers, chopped.
- 2 carrots, chopped

Directions:
In a pan that fits your air fryer, mix duck pieces with cucumbers, wine, carrots, ginger, stock, salt and pepper, toss, introduce in your air fryer and cook at 370°F, for 20 minutes. Divide everything on plates and serve.

Nutrition:
Calories: 200, Fat: 10 g, Fiber: 8 g, Carbs: 20 g, Protein: 22 g

172. Pork Stew

Preparation time: 10 minutes | **Cooking time:** 30 minutes | **Servings:** 2

Ingredients:
- Salt and ground black pepper, to taste
- 1 ½ lbs. pork shoulder, cubed
- 3 tablespoons extra virgin olive oil
- 1 red bell pepper, seeded and chopped
- 4 carrots, peeled and cut into big chunks
- ½ cup chicken stock
- 8 baby potatoes
- 1 yellow onion, peeled and chopped
- 1 rutabaga, cubed
- 2 garlic cloves, peeled and chopped
- 14 oz. canned diced tomatoes

Directions:
Put the Instant Pot in the sauté mode, add 2 tablespoons of oil and heat. Add the pork, salt and pepper, brown on all sides and transfer to a bowl.
Add the onion, garlic, pepper and the rest of the oil to the Instant Pot, stir and cook for 3 minutes. Put the pork back in the pan, add the carrots, potatoes, rutabaga, salt, pepper, tomato and broth, mix, cover and cook the meat / stew for 20 minutes.
Relieve the pressure, uncover the Instant Pot, mix the stew, divide it into bowls and serve.

Nutrition:
Calories: 272, Fat: 6 g, Fiber: 3 g, Carbs: 27 g, Proteins: 24 g

173. Chicken Stew

Preparation time: 10 minutes | **Cooking time:** 1 hour and 15 minutes | **Servings:** 2

Ingredients:
- 6 chicken thighs
- 1 yellow onion, peeled and chopped
- 1 teaspoon vegetable oil
- ½ cup white wine
- 2 cups chicken stock
- 1 ½ lbs. new potatoes
- Salt and ground black pepper, to taste
- 1 celery stalk, chopped
- ½ teaspoon dried thyme
- 2 tablespoons tomato paste
- ¾ lb. baby carrots
- 15 oz. canned diced tomatoes

Directions:
Put the Instant Pot in the sauté mode, add the oil and heat. Add the chicken, salt and pepper, brown for 4 minutes on each side and transfer to a plate.
Add celery, onion, tomato paste, carrot, thyme, salt and pepper, mix and cook for 5 minutes. Add wine, stir, bring to a boil and cook for 3 minutes.
Add the stock, chicken, tomato and potatoes to the Instant Pot steam basket.
Cover the instant pot and cook for 30 minutes in manual mode. Relieve the pressure, uncover the Instant Pot, remove the potatoes from the Instant Pot and place them in a bowl.
Transfer the chicken pieces to a cutting board, let it cool for a few minutes, discard the bones, brandish the meat and put it back in the stew. Add more salt and pepper, if necessary, mix, divide into bowls and serve hot.

Nutrition:
Calories: 271, Fat: 2 g, Fiber: 4 g, Carbs: 18 g, Proteins: 15 g

174. Lamb and Raisins

Preparation time: 10 minutes | **Cooking time:** 30 minutes | **Servings:** 2

Ingredients:

1 cup raisins	1 and ½ lbs. lamb, cubed
1 tablespoon olive oil	1 garlic clove, minced
1 yellow onion, grated	1 tablespoon ginger, grated
2 tablespoons orange juice	A pinch of salt and black pepper
1 cup veggie stock	

Directions:
Heat up a pan with the oil over medium-high heat, add the garlic and the onion and sauté for 5 minutes.
Add the lamb and brown for 5 minutes more.
Add the rest of the ingredients, bring to a simmer and cook over medium heat for 20 minutes.
Divide the mix between plates and serve.

Nutrition:
Calories: 292, Fat: 13.2 g, Fiber: 9.7 g, Carbs: 17.7 g, Protein: 16.3 g

175. Sour Cream Lamb Mix

Preparation time: 10 minutes | **Cooking time:** 2 hours and 15 minutes | **Servings:** 2

Ingredients:

2 lbs. leg of lamb, boneless	2 tablespoons mustard
½ cup avocado oil	2 tablespoons basil, chopped
2 tablespoons tomato paste	2 garlic cloves, minced
Salt and black pepper to the taste	1 cup white wine
½ cup sour cream	

Directions:
Heat up a pan with the avocado oil over medium-high heat, add the meat and brown it for 6 minutes on each side.
Add the rest of the ingredients, introduce the pan in the oven and cook at 370°F for 2 hours.
Divide the mix between plates and serve.

Nutrition:
Calories: 312, Fat: 12.1 g, Fiber: 16.4 g, Carbs: 21.7 g, Protein: 14.2 g

176. Garlic Lamb and Peppers

Preparation time: 10 minutes | **Cooking time:** 1 hour and 30 minutes | **Servings:** 2

Ingredients:

1 red bell pepper, sliced	1 green bell pepper, sliced
1 yellow bell pepper, sliced	2 tablespoons olive oil
⅓ cup mint, chopped	4 garlic cloves, minced
½ cup veggie stock	1 ½ tablespoon lemon juice
4 lamb chops	Salt and black pepper to the taste

Directions:
Heat up a pan with the oil over medium-high heat, add the lamb chops and brown for 4 minutes on each side.
Add the rest of the ingredients, introduce the pan in the oven and bake at 370°F for 1 hour and 20 minutes.
Divide the mix between plates and serve.

Nutrition:
Calories: 300, Fat: 14.1 g, Fiber: 9.4 g, Carbs: 15.7 g, Protein: 24.2 g

177. Lamb and Cauliflower Mix

Preparation time: 10 minutes | **Cooking time:** 1 hour | **Servings:** 2

Ingredients:

2 lbs. lamb meat, roughly cubed	2 tablespoons olive oil
1 teaspoon garlic, minced	1 yellow onion, chopped

1 teaspoon rosemary, chopped
2 cups cauliflower florets
Salt and pepper to the taste
1 cup veggie stock
2 tablespoons sweet paprika

Directions:
Heat up a pot with the oil over medium-high heat, add the onion and the garlic and sauté for 5 minutes.
Add the meat and brown for 5-6 minutes more.
Add the rest of the ingredients, bring to a simmer and cook over medium heat for 50 minutes.
Divide the mix between plates and serve away.

Nutrition:
Calories: 336, Fat: 14.4 g, Fiber: 10.8 g, Carbs: 21.7 g, Protein: 23.2 g

178. Allspice Pork Mix

Preparation time: 10 minutes | **Cooking time:** 8 hours | **Servings:** 2

Ingredients:
2 lbs. pork loin, sliced
Salt and white pepper to the taste
2 teaspoons whole allspice, ground
1 tablespoon tomato paste
1 tablespoon olive oil
2 shallots, chopped
1 cup veggie stock
2 bay leaves

Directions:
In your slow cooker, combine the pork with the oil, salt, pepper and the rest of the ingredients, put the lid on and cook on Low for 8 hours.
Divide the mix between plates and serve right away.

Nutrition:
Calories: 329, Fat: 14.2 g, Fiber: 11.7 g, Carbs: 18.3 g, Protein: 23.4 g

179. Cauliflower Cream

Preparation time: 10 minutes | **Cooking time:** 1 hour and 10 minutes | **Servings:** 2

Ingredients:
1 cauliflower head, florets separated
1 teaspoon garlic powder
2 tablespoons olive oil
Salt and black pepper to the taste
2 tablespoons garlic, minced
1 yellow onion, chopped
5 cups chicken stock
2 ½ cups cheddar cheese, shredded

Directions:
Spread the cauliflower on a baking sheet lined with parchment paper, add garlic powder, half of the oil, salt and pepper and roast at 425 °F for 30 minutes.
Heat up a pot with the rest of the oil over medium heat, add the onion and sauté for 5 minutes.
Add the roasted cauliflower and the rest of the ingredients except the cheddar, stir and simmer the soup for 30 minutes.
Blend the soup using an immersion blender, add the cheese, stir, divide the soup into bowls and serve.

Nutrition:
Calories: 243, Fat: 17 g, Fiber: 2.3 g, Carbs: 41.1 g, Protein: 13.7 g

180. Easy Cilantro Rice

Preparation time: 2 minutes | **Cooking time:** 10 minutes | **Servings:** 2

Ingredients:
1 ⅓ cup white rice
½ yellow onion, diced
2 cups water
½ cup peas
2 oz. can green chilies
¾ tsp. fresh lime juice
½ tbsp. butter
1 garlic clove, minced
½ tbsp. chicken bouillon
½ tsp. cumin
¼ bunch cilantro, chopped.
Salt, to taste

Directions:
Add oil, onion and garlic to Instant Pot and **Sauté** for 4 minutes,
Add all the remaining ingredients to the cooker. Cover and secure the lid. Turn its pressure release handle to the sealing position.
Cook on the Manual function with high pressure for 7 minutes,
When it beeps, do a Natural release and remove the lid. Garnish with fresh cilantro and serve.

Nutrition:
Calories: 167, Carbs: 34.8 g, Protein: 3.1 g, Fat: 1.3 g, Sugar: 0.9 g, Sodium: 83 mg

181. Special Chorizo Pinto Beans

Preparation time: 5 minutes | **Cooking time:** 10 minutes | **Servings:** 2

Ingredients:
- 1 cup dry pinto beans
- 2 oz. dry Spanish chorizo
- 1 ½ garlic cloves
- ½ tsp. freshly cracked pepper
- 7 ½ oz. can diced tomatoes
- ½ tbsp. cooking oil
- ½ yellow onion
- 1 bay leaf
- 1 ½ cups chicken broth

Directions:
Add oil, chorizo, garlic and onion to Instant Pot. Sauté for 5 minutes,
Stir in beans, pepper and bay leaf. Cook for 1 minute then add the broth.
Cover and secure the lid. Turn its pressure release handle to the sealing position.
Cook on the Manual function with high pressure for 35 minutes,
When it beeps, do a Natural release for 20 minutes,
Stir in diced tomatoes and cook for 7 minutes on the Sauté setting. Serve hot with boiled white rice or tortilla chips.

Nutrition:
Calories: 337, Carbs: 50.5 g, Protein: 21.3 g, Fat: 5.7 g, Sugar: 5.4 g, Sodium: 0.67 g

182. Yummy Coconut Rice

Preparation time: 13 minutes | **Cooking time:** 10 minutes | **Servings:** 2

Ingredients:
- 1 can coconut milk
- ½ cup water
- ¼ tsp. salt
- 1 ½ cups jasmine rice
- 1 tsp. sugar

Directions:
Add all the Ingredients to Instant Pot.
Cover and secure the lid. Turn its pressure release handle to the sealing position.
Cook on the Manual function with high pressure for 3 minutes,
When it beeps, do a Natural release for 7 minutes, Serve warm.

Nutrition:
Calories: 255, Carbs: 38.9 g, Protein: 3.9 g, Fat: 9.5 g, Sugar: 2 g, Sodium: 0.10 g

183. Easy Bean Mustard Curry

Preparation time: 4 minutes | **Cooking time:** 10 minutes | **Servings:** 2

Ingredients:
- 2 tsp. mustard powder
- ½ medium onion, chopped
- 1 ½ cans navy beans, rinsed and drained
- ¼ tsp. ground black pepper
- 1 tsp. apple cider vinegar
- ½ cup ketchup
- ½ small green bell pepper, chopped
- 2 tbsp. molasses
- 1 ½ slices bacon, chopped.

Directions:
Select the **Sauté** function on your Instant Pot and add the oil with onion, bacon and bell pepper. Cook for 6 minutes,
Add all the remaining ingredients and secure the lid.
Cook on the **Manual** function for 8 minutes on high pressure,
When it beeps, do a Natural release for 10 minutes, then release the remaining steam with a Quick release,
Garnish with chopped cilantro on top. Serve.

Nutrition:
Calories: 373, Carbs: 64.5 g, Protein: 21.2 g, Fat: 4.7 g, Sugar: 16.1 g, Sodium: 0.50 g

184. Mexican Rice

Preparation time: 5 minutes | **Cooking time:** 10 minutes | **Servings:** 2

Ingredients:
- 1 cup long-grain white rice
- ¼ cup onion, chopped
- 1 tbsp. avocado oil
- 2 garlic cloves, finely chopped.

½ tsp. salt
2 tbsp. cilantro, chopped.
2 cups chicken stock
¼ tsp. garlic powder
2 tbsp. crushed tomatoes
2 tbsp. sun-dried tomatoes
¼ tsp. cumin
¼ tsp. smoked paprika

Directions:
Add oil, onion and garlic to Instant Pot. Sauté for 3 minutes,
Stir in rice and mix well with the onion.
Add all the remaining ingredients to the cooker. Cover and secure the lid. Turn its pressure release handle to the sealing position.
Cook on the Manual function with high pressure for 8 minutes,
When it beeps, do a Natural release, Stir and serve warm.

Nutrition:
Calories: 252, Carbs: 53.1 g, Protein: 5.6 g, Fat: 1.5 g, Sugar: 1.9 g, Sodium: 0.92 g

185. Lentil Risotto

Preparation time: 3 minutes | **Cooking time:** 10 minutes | **Servings:** 2

Ingredients:
½ cup dry lentils, soaked overnight
2 cups vegetable stock
½ medium onion, chopped
1 sprig parsley, chopped
1 garlic clove, lightly mashed
½ tbsp. olive oil
½ celery stalk, chopped.
½ cup Arborio short-grain Italian rice

Directions:
Add oil and onions to Instant Pot and Sauté for 5 minutes,
Add all the remaining ingredient to Instant Pot. Cover and secure the lid. Turn its pressure release handle to the sealing position.
Cook on the Manual function with high pressure for 15 minutes,
When it beeps, do a Natural release for 20 minutes, Stir and serve hot with boiled white rice.

Nutrition:
Calories: 260, Carbs: 47.2 g, Protein: 10.7 g, Fat: 3.5 g, Sugar: 2.2 g, Sodium: 0.24 g

186. Instant Fennel Risotto

Preparation time: 9 minutes | **Cooking time:** 10 minutes | **Servings:** 2

Ingredients:
¼ medium fennel, diced
1 tbsp. olive oil
¼ tsp. salt
1 cup Arborio risotto rice
1 cup chicken stock
3 tbsp. white wine
¼ cup grated Parmesan cheese
½ medium brown onion, finely diced
¼ bunch of asparagus, diced
1 garlic clove, chopped
1 cup vegetable stock
1 tbsp. butter
Zest of ¼ lemon

Directions:
Add oil, onion, fennel and asparagus to Instant Pot and **Sauté** for 4 minutes,
Add all the remaining ingredients except the cheese to the cooker.
Cover and secure the lid. Turn its pressure release handle to the sealing position.
Cook on the Manual function with high pressure for 10 minutes,
When it beeps, do a Natural release and remove the lid. Stir in cheese and serve.

Nutrition:
Calories: 238, Carbs: 24.1 g, Protein: 6.9 g, Fat: 17.5 g, Sugar: 1.8 g, Sodium: 0.52 g

187. Flavorful Onion Rice

Preparation time: 10 minutes | **Cooking time:** 3 minutes | **Servings:** 2

Ingredients:
2 cups white rice, uncooked and rinsed
2 garlic cloves, minced
½ onion, sliced
¼ cup water
¼ cup ghee, melted
1 tbsp fresh parsley, chopped
4 oz mushrooms, sliced
1 ¼ cups chicken broth

10 oz can onion soup   ¼ tsp pepper
¼ tsp kosher salt

Directions:
Add all ingredients into the instant pot and stir well.
Seal pot with lid and cook on manual high pressure for 3 minutes.
Once done then allow to release pressure naturally for 5 minutes then release using the quick-release method. Open the lid.
Fluff rice using a fork and serve.

Nutrition:
Calories: 335, Fat: 9.8 g, Carbs: 53.7 g, Sugar: 2.5 g, Protein: 7 g, Cholesterol: 24 mg

188. Black Bean Rice

Preparation time: 10 minutes | **Cooking time:** 5 minutes | **Servings:** 2

Ingredients:
- 1 ½ cups dry black beans, soaked in water for 2-3 hours and drained
- 3 cups of water
- 2 cups vegetable broth
- 14 oz can tomato, diced
- 1 ½ cups brown rice, rinsed
- 1 tsp olive oil
- ¼ tsp cayenne
- ½ tsp oregano
- 1 tsp chili powder
- 1 tsp cumin
- 2 garlic cloves, minced
- 1 onion, diced
- ½ tsp salt

Directions:
Add oil into the instant pot and set the pot on sauté mode.
Add garlic and onion and sauté for 2-3 minutes.
Add rice, beans, tomatoes, seasonings, broth, and water and stir to combine.
Seal pot with lid and cook on manual high pressure for 30 minutes.
Once done then allow to release pressure naturally for 10 minutes then release using the quick-release method. Open the lid.
Stir well and serve.

Nutrition:
Calories: 383, Fat: 3.4 g, Carbs: 72.7 g, Sugar: 4.4 g, Protein: 16.7 g

189. Easy Baked Beans

Preparation time: 10 minutes | **Cooking time:** 40 minutes | **Servings:** 2

Ingredients:
- 1 lb. navy beans, soak in water for overnight
- ¾ cup maple syrup
- 1 cup of water
- 1 onion, chopped
- 1 lb. bacon, cut into small pieces
- 8 tbsp brown sugar
- ¾ tsp mustard
- 2 tbsp apple cider vinegar
- 1 cup ketchup

Directions:
Add all ingredients into the instant pot and stir well.
Seal pot with lid and cook on manual high pressure for 40 minutes.
Once done then allow to release pressure naturally then open the lid.
Stir well and serve.

Nutrition:
Calories: 258, Fat: 9.9 g, Carbs: 29.1 g, Sugar: 14.4 g, Protein: 13.8 g, Cholesterol: 25 mg

190. Braised Soybeans with Sesame Seeds

Preparation time: 10 minutes | **Cooking time:** 50 minutes | **Servings:** 2

Ingredients:
- 1 cup dried soybeans, soaked overnight and drained
- 4 cups water
- ½ cup soy sauce
- ¼ cup brown sugar
- 1 tsp sesame oil
- 1 tbsp rice vinegar
- 2 garlic cloves, minced
- 2 tsp sesame seeds, for garnishing

Directions:
Pour soybeans and water in inner pot. Seal the lid, select Manual/Pressure Cook on High, and set cooking time to 20 minutes. After cooking, perform a natural pressure release for 10 minutes, then a quick pressure release to let out remaining steam. Unlock the lid.

Meanwhile, in a bowl, combine soy sauce, brown sugar, sesame oil, rice vinegar, and garlic. Set aside.

On the Instant Pot, press Sauté and adjust to medium heat. Add soy sauce mixture, stir and cook for 15 minutes. Spoon beans onto a serving platter and garnish with sesame seeds. Serve warm.

Nutrition:
Calories: 240, Carbs: 24 g, Fat: 12 g, Protein: 11 g

191. Pork & Pinto Bean Casserole

Preparation time: 10 minutes | **Cooking time:** 35 minutes | **Servings:** 2

Ingredients:

2 tbsp olive oil	1 lb. pork roast, cubed
Salt and black pepper to taste	1 cup dried pinto beans, soaked overnight and rinsed
2 cups chicken broth	1 small red onion, chopped
1 cup tomato sauce	2 green chilies, chopped
1 tsp garlic powder	1 tsp chili powder
¼ cup chopped parsley	

Directions:
Set your Instant Pot to Sauté and adjust to medium heat. Heat olive oil in inner pot, season pork with salt and black pepper, and fry in oil until brown, 4 minutes. Add beans, chicken broth, red onion, tomato sauce, green chilies, garlic powder, and chili powder.

Seal the lid, select Manual/Pressure Cook on High, and set cooking time to 10 minutes. After cooking, perform natural pressure release for 10 minutes, then a quick pressure release to let out the remaining steam. Unlock the lid, stir in parsley and adjust taste with salt and black pepper. Serve stew.

Nutrition:
Calories: 579, Carbs: 56 g, Fat: 20 g, Protein: 45 g

192. Rosemary Navy Beans with Mushrooms & Spinach

Preparation time: 10 minutes | **Cooking time:** 35 minutes | **Servings:** 2

Ingredients:

1 tbsp olive oil	1 medium white onion, diced
1 lb. white button mushrooms, quartered	1 medium butternut squash, peeled and chopped
Salt and black pepper to taste	¼ tsp dried rosemary
1 cup chopped tomatoes	2 cups chicken broth
2 cups baby spinach	1 15 oz. can navy beans, drained and rinsed
1 lemon, juiced	

Directions:
Set your Instant Pot to Sauté and heat olive oil. Sauté onion, mushroom, and squash until softened, 6 minutes. Season with salt, black pepper, rosemary, and cook further for 1 minute. Stir in tomato and chicken broth.

Seal the lid, select Manual/Pressure Cook on High, and set cooking time to 3 minutes. After cooking, perform natural pressure release for 10 minutes, and then quick pressure to release steam, and unlock the lid. Press Sauté, add spinach, navy beans, and allow spinach to wilt, 3 minutes. Top with lemon juice, adjust taste with salt and black pepper and serve.

Nutrition:
Calories: 239, Carbs: 37 g, Fat: 9 g, Protein: 10 g

193. Italian Bean Chowder with Crispy Prosciutto

Preparation time: 10 minutes | **Cooking time:** 45 minutes | **Servings:** 2

Ingredients:

6 prosciutto slices, chopped	1 celery stalk, chopped
1 medium carrot, chopped	1 cup chopped white onion
1 small Yukon gold potato, cubed	1 tsp mixed dried herbs

1 cup dried navy beans, soaked overnight and drained	3 cups chicken broth
Salt and black pepper to taste	4 tbsp heavy cream

Directions:
Set your Instant Pot to Sauté and adjust to medium heat. Add prosciutto to inner pot and cook until brown and crispy, 5 minutes. Transfer to a paper towel-lined plate and set aside.
Sauté celery, carrots, onion, and potatoes in prosciutto grease until slightly tender, 5 minutes. Stir in mixed herbs, navy beans, chicken broth, salt, and black pepper.
Seal the lid, select Manual/Pressure Cook on High, and set cooking time to 25 minutes. Perform a quick pressure release to let out all the steam and unlock the lid. Turn Instant Pot off and stir in heavy cream. Serve chowder and top with prosciutto pieces.

Nutrition:
Calories: 369, Carbs: 57 g, Fat: 9 g, Protein: 18 g

194. Moroccan Chickpea Curry

Preparation time: 10 minutes | **Cooking time:** 30 minutes | **Servings:** 2

Ingredients:

2 ½ cups canned chickpeas, drained	2 medium carrots, chopped
1 celery stalk, chopped	4 garlic cloves, minced
1 large yellow onion, finely chopped	1 green bell pepper, deseeded and chopped
1 red bell pepper, deseeded and chopped	½ cup chopped tomatoes
2 cups vegetable broth	2 tbsp ras el hanout
½ tsp turmeric powder	Salt and black pepper to taste
2 tsp dried thyme	2 red chilies, minced
2 tbsp chopped parsley	2 tbsp chopped scallions, for garnishing

Directions:
In inner pot, combine chickpeas, carrots, celery, garlic, onion, bell peppers, tomatoes, vegetable broth, ras el hanout, turmeric, salt, black pepper, thyme, and red chilies. Seal the lid, select Manual/Pressure Cook on High, and set cooking time to 10 minutes.
After cooking, perform natural pressure release for 10 minutes, then a quick pressure release to let out the remaining steam. Unlock the lid and stir half of parsley into curry. Adjust taste with salt and black pepper. Spoon curry into serving bowls and garnish with scallions. Serve chickpea curry with cooked white rice.

Nutrition:
Calories: 554, Carbs: 88 g, Fat: 12 g, Protein: 28 g

195. Bean & Fennel Tempeh Chops

Preparation time: 10 minutes | **Cooking time:** 30 minutes | **Servings:** 2

Ingredients:

2 tbsp olive oil	2 lb. tempeh, chopped
1 large yellow onion, chopped	1 small fennel bulb, chopped
3 carrots, cubed	3 large garlic cloves, roughly chopped
1 cinnamon stick	1 bay leaf
1 ½ tsp ground allspice	1 tsp ras el hanout
½ tsp ginger paste	6 large tomatoes, chopped
2 ½ cups vegetable broth	1 15-oz. can white beans

Directions:
Add the oil to your Instant Pot and select Sauté. Pour in the tempeh and fry until golden brown on all sides. Remove to a plate. Put onion, fennel, carrots, and garlic into the pot and sauté for 6 minutes. Drop in cinnamon stick, followed by bay leaf, allspice, ras el hanout, and ginger paste. Stir-fry for 2 minutes. Pour in tomatoes and broth and stir.
Seal the lid, select Manual/Pressure Cook on High, and set time to 2 minutes. Once the pot beeps, naturally release the pressure until all the steam escapes, for 15 minutes, and open the lid. Select Sauté. Stir in the tempeh and white beans,

cook to warm both through, 3 minutes. Serve with pita bread.

Nutrition:
Calories: 648, Carbs: 50 g, Fat: 34.9 g, Protein: 46.9 g

196. Spicy Kidney Bean Dip

Preparation time: 10 minutes | **Cooking time:** 45 minutes | **Servings:** 2

Ingredients:

1 tbsp coconut oil	1 red onion, finely chopped
4 garlic cloves, minced	Salt and black pepper to taste
2 tbsp tomato paste	1 tbsp curry paste
1 cup dried kidney beans, soaked overnight and rinsed	4 cups vegetable stock
1 tbsp Sriracha sauce	1 lemon, juiced
1 tsp honey	

Directions:
Set your Instant Pot to Sauté and adjust to medium heat. Heat coconut oil and stir-fry onion and garlic until softened, 3 minutes. Season with salt and black pepper. Add tomato paste and curry paste, cook for 2 minutes, stirring frequently. Mix in kidney beans, vegetable stock, and Sriracha sauce.
Seal the lid, select Manual/Pressure Cook on High, and set cooking time to 30 minutes. After cooking, perform a quick pressure release. Unlock the lid. Mix in lemon juice, honey, and using an immersion blender, puree ingredients until very smooth. Spoon bean dip into small ramekins and serve with julienned vegetables.

Nutrition:
Calories: 266, Carbs: 34 g, Fat: 6 g, Protein: 12 g

197. Cheesy Bean Spread

Preparation time: 10 minutes | **Cooking time:** 50 minutes | **Servings:** 2

Ingredients:

1 cup kidney beans, soaked overnight and drained	4 cups chicken broth
Salt and black pepper to taste	¼ cup grated mozzarella cheese
¼ cup grated Gouda cheese	¼ cup grated Parmesan cheese + extra for topping

Directions:
Pour beans and chicken broth in inner pot. Seal the lid, select Manual/Pressure Cook on High, and set cooking time to 30 minutes. After cooking, perform a natural pressure release for 10 minutes. Unlock the lid.
Stir in cheeses until melted, 2 minutes. Turn Instant Pot off. Spoon cheesy beans over toasts and top with Parmesan cheese.

Nutrition:
Calories: 279, Carbs: 28 g, Fat: 6 g, Protein: 17 g

198. White Beans and Orange Soup

Preparation time: 10 minutes | **Cooking time:** 37 minutes | **Servings:** 2

Ingredients:

1 yellow onion, chopped	5 celery sticks, chopped
4 carrots, chopped	1 cup olive oil
½ teaspoon oregano, dried	1 bay leaf
3 orange slices, peeled	30 oz. canned white beans, drained
2 tablespoons tomato paste	2 cups water
6 cups chicken stock	

Directions:
Heat up a pot with the oil over medium heat, add the onion, celery, carrots, the bay leaf and the oregano, stir and sauté for 5 minutes.
Add the orange slices and cook for 2 minutes more.
Add the rest of the ingredients, stir, bring to a simmer and cook over medium heat for 30 minutes.
Ladle the soup into bowls and serve.

Nutrition:
Calories: 273, Fat: 16.3 g, Fiber: 8.4 g, Carbs: 15.6 g, Protein: 7.4 g

199. Basil Zucchini Soup

Preparation time: 10 minutes | **Cooking time:** 20 minutes | **Servings:** 2

Ingredients:
- 2 tablespoons olive oil
- 1 yellow onion, chopped
- 4 cups chicken stock
- ½ cup basil, chopped
- 3 garlic cloves, minced
- 4 zucchinis, cubed
- Zest of 1 lemon, grated
- Salt and black pepper to the taste

Directions:
Heat up a pot with the oil over medium heat, add the onion and the garlic and sauté for 5 minutes.
Add the zucchinis and the rest of the ingredients except the basil, bring to a simmer and cook over medium heat for 15 minutes.
Add the basil, stir, divide the soup into bowls and serve.

Nutrition:
Calories: 274, Fat: 11.1 g, Fiber: 4.5 g, Carbs: 16.5 g, Protein: 4.5 g

200. Chicken and Leeks Soup

Preparation time: 10 minutes | **Cooking time:** 50 minutes | **Servings:** 2

Ingredients:
- 2 lbs. chicken breast, skinless, boneless and cubed
- 2 leeks, sliced
- 1 small green cabbage head, shredded
- 4 cups veggie stock
- A pinch of nutmeg, ground
- ½ cup olive oil
- 4 spring onions, chopped
- 4 celery sticks, chopped
- ½ teaspoon sweet paprika
- Salt and black pepper to the taste

Directions:
Heat up a pot with the oil over medium-high heat, add the chicken and brown for 2 minutes on each side.
Add the leeks, onions and celery and sauté for 1 minute more.
Add the rest of the ingredients, bring to a simmer and cook over medium heat for 45 minutes.
Ladle the soup into bowls and serve.

Nutrition:
Calories: 310, Fat: 15.3 g, Fiber: 8.7 g, Carbs: 24.6 g, Protein: 18.4 g

201. Lemony Lamb Soup

Preparation time: 10 minutes | **Cooking time:** 1 hour and 5 minutes | **Servings:** 2

Ingredients:
- ½ cup olive oil
- 5 cups water
- 2 tablespoons dill, chopped
- Salt and black pepper to the taste
- 1 cup baby spinach
- 2 lbs. lamb meat, cubed
- 5 spring onions, chopped
- Juice of 2 lemons
- 3 eggs, whisked

Directions:
Heat up a pot with the oil over medium heat, add the lamb and brown for 10 minutes stirring from time to time.
Add the onions and sauté for 3 minutes more.
Add the water, salt and pepper, stir and simmer over medium heat for 30 minutes.
Add the spinach, eggs whisked with the lemon juice and some of the soup, whisk the soup well and cook for 20 minutes more.
Add the dill, stir, ladle the soup into bowls and serve.

Nutrition:
Calories: 275, Fat: 28.5 g, Fiber: 1 g, Carbs: 2.8 g, Protein: 5 g

202. Sausage and Beans Soup

Preparation time: 10 minutes | **Cooking time:** 20 minutes | **Servings:** 2

Ingredients:
- 1-lb. Italian pork sausage, sliced
- 1 carrot, chopped
- ¼ cup olive oil
- 1 yellow onion, chopped

1 celery stalk, chopped
½ lb. kale, chopped
28 oz. canned cannellini beans, drained and rinsed
1 teaspoon rosemary, dried
½ cup parmesan, grated
2 garlic cloves, minced
4 cups chicken stock
1 bay leaf
Salt and black pepper to the taste

Directions:
Heat up a pot with the oil over medium heat, add the sausage and brown for 5 minutes.
Add the onion, carrots, garlic and celery and sauté for 3 minutes more.
Add the rest of the ingredients except the parmesan, bring to a simmer and cook over medium heat for 30 minutes.
Discard the bay leaf, ladle the soup into bowls, sprinkle the parmesan on top and serve.

Nutrition:
Calories: 564, Fat: 26.5 g, Fiber: 15.4 g, Carbs: 37.4 g, Protein: 26.6 g

203. Fish Soup

Preparation time: 10 minutes | **Cooking time:** 20 minutes | **Servings:** 2

Ingredients:
2 tablespoons olive oil
½ cup tomatoes, crushed
1-quart veggie stock
¼ teaspoon rosemary, dried
1 tablespoon garlic, minced
1 yellow onion, chopped
1-lb. cod, skinless, boneless and cubed
A pinch of salt and black pepper

Directions:
Heat up a pot with the oil over medium heat, add the onion and the garlic and sauté for 5 minutes.
Add the rest of the ingredients, toss, simmer over medium heat for 15 minutes more, divide into bowls and serve for lunch.

Nutrition:
Calories: 198, Fat: 8.1 g, Fiber: 1 g, Carbs: 4.2 g, Protein: 26.4 g

204. Chickpeas Soup

Preparation time: 10 minutes | **Cooking time:** 1 hour | **Servings:** 2

Ingredients:
3 tomatoes, cubed
2 tablespoons olive oil
½ cup parsley, chopped
16 oz. canned chickpeas, drained and rinsed
1 teaspoon cumin, ground
1 teaspoon turmeric powder
½ teaspoon ginger, grated
2 yellow onions, chopped
4 celery stalks, chopped
2 garlic cloves, minced
6 cups water
Juice of ½ lemon
½ teaspoon cinnamon powder
Salt and black pepper to the taste

Directions:
Heat up a pot with the oil over medium heat, add the onion and the garlic and sauté for 5 minutes.
Add the tomatoes, celery, cumin, turmeric, cinnamon and the ginger, stir and sauté for 5 minutes more.
Add the remaining ingredients, bring the soup to a boil over medium heat and simmer for 50 minutes.
Ladle the soup into bowls and serve.

Nutrition:
Calories: 300, Fat: 15.4 g, Fiber: 4.5 g, Carbs: 29.5 g, Protein: 15.4 g

205. Tomato Soup

Preparation time: 10 minutes | **Cooking time:** 55 minutes | **Servings:** 2

Ingredients:
4 lbs. tomatoes, halved
6 garlic cloves, minced
Salt and black pepper to the taste
½ teaspoon red pepper flakes
½ cup parmesan, grated
2 tablespoons olive oil
1 yellow onion, chopped
4 cups chicken stock
½ cup basil, chopped

Directions:
Arrange the tomatoes in a roasting pan, add half of the oil, salt and pepper, toss, and bake at 400°F for 20 minutes.
Heat up a pot with the rest of the oil over medium heat, add the onion and sauté for 5 minutes.
Add the tomatoes and the rest of the ingredients except the basil and the parmesan, bring to a simmer and cook for 30 minutes.
Blend the soup using an immersion blender, add the basil and the parmesan, stir, divide into bowls and serve.

Nutrition:
Calories: 237, Fat: 10 g, Fiber: 3.4 g, Carbs: 15.3 g, Protein: 7.4 g

206. Oyster Stew

Preparation time: 10 minutes | **Cooking time:** 1 hour and 10 minutes | **Servings:** 2

Ingredients:
- 2 garlic cloves, minced
- 2 teaspoons oregano, chopped
- 1 tablespoon red wine vinegar
- 1 teaspoon red pepper flakes
- 1 ½ cups chicken stock
- 1 ½ cups canned black eyed peas, drained
- ¼ cup jarred roasted red peppers
- 1 lb. lamb meat, ground
- Salt and black pepper to the taste
- 2 tablespoons olive oil
- 36 oysters, shucked

Directions:
Heat up a pot with the oil over medium heat, add the meat and the garlic and brown for 5 minutes.
Add the peppers and the rest of the ingredients, bring to a simmer and cook for 15 minutes.
Divide the stew into bowls and serve.

Nutrition:
Calories: 264, Fat: 9.3 g, Fiber: 1.2 g, Carbs: 2.3 g, Protein: 1.2 g

207. Potatoes and Lentils Stew

Preparation time: 10 minutes | **Cooking time:** 35 minutes | **Servings:** 2

Ingredients:
- 4 cups water
- 1 yellow onion, chopped
- 1 cup celery, chopped
- 2 lbs. gold potatoes, cubed
- ½ teaspoon smoked paprika
- Salt and black pepper to the taste
- ½ cup cilantro, chopped
- 1 cup carrots, sliced
- 1 tablespoon olive oil
- 2 garlic cloves, minced
- 1 and ½ cup lentils, dried
- ½ teaspoon oregano, dried
- 14 oz. canned tomatoes, chopped

Directions:
Heat up a pot with the oil over medium-high heat, add the onion, garlic, celery and carrots, stir and cook for 5 minutes.
Add the rest of the ingredients except the cilantro, stir, bring to a simmer and cook over medium heat for 25 minutes.
Add the cilantro, divide the stew into bowls and serve.

Nutrition:
Calories: 325, Fat: 17.3 g, Fiber: 6.8 g, Carbs: 26.4 g, Protein: 16.4 g

208. Lamb and Potatoes Stew

Preparation time: 10 minutes | **Cooking time:** 1 hour and 20 minutes | **Servings:** 2

Ingredients:
- 2 lbs. lamb shoulder, boneless and cubed
- 1 yellow onion, chopped
- 3 tomatoes, grated
- 2 and ½ lbs. gold potatoes, cubed
- 1 tablespoon cilantro, chopped
- Salt and black pepper to the taste
- 3 tablespoons olive oil
- 2 cups chicken stock
- ¾ cup green olives, pitted and sliced

Directions:
Heat up a pot with the oil over medium-high heat, add the lamb, and brown for 5 minutes on each side.
Add the onion and sauté for 5 minutes more.
Add the rest of the ingredients, bring to a simmer and cook over medium heat and cook for 1 hour and 10 minutes.
Divide the stew into bowls and serve.

Nutrition:
Calories: 411, Fat: 17.4 g, Fiber: 8.4 g, Carbs: 25.5 g, Protein: 34.3 g

209. Ground Pork and Tomatoes Soup

Preparation time: 10 minutes | **Cooking time:** 40 minutes | **Servings:** 2

Ingredients:

1 lb. pork meat, ground	Salt and black pepper to the taste
2 garlic cloves, minced	2 teaspoons thyme, dried
2 tablespoons olive oil	4 cups beef stock
A pinch of saffron powder	15 oz. canned tomatoes, crushed
1 tablespoons parsley, chopped	

Directions:
Heat up a pot with the oil over medium heat, add the meat and the garlic and brown for 5 minutes.
Add the rest of the ingredients except the parsley, bring to a simmer and cook for 25 minutes.
Divide the soup into bowls, sprinkle the parsley on top and serve.

Nutrition:
Calories: 372, Fat: 17.3 g, Fiber: 5.5 g, Carbs: 28.4 g, Protein: 17.4 g

210. Peas Soup

Preparation time: 10 minutes | **Cooking time:** 10 minutes | **Servings:** 2

Ingredients:

1 white onion, chopped	1 tablespoon olive oil
1 quart veggie stock	2 eggs
3 tablespoons lemon juice	2 cups peas
2 tablespoons parmesan, grated	Salt and black pepper to the taste

Directions:
Heat up a pot with the oil over medium-high heat, add the onion and sauté for 4 minutes.
Add the rest of the ingredients except the eggs, bring to a simmer and cook for 4 minutes.
Add whisked eggs, stir the soup, cook for 2 minutes more, divide into bowls and serve.

Nutrition:
Calories: 293, Fat: 11.2 g, Fiber: 3.4 g, Carbs: 27 g, Protein: 4.45 g

211. Minty Lamb Stew

Preparation time: 10 minutes | **Cooking time:** 1 hour and 45 minutes | **Servings:** 2

Ingredients:

3 cups orange juice	½ cup mint, chopped
Salt and black pepper to the taste	2 lbs. lamb shoulder, boneless and cubed
3 tablespoons olive oil	1 carrot, chopped
1 yellow onion, chopped	1 celery rib, chopped
1 tablespoon ginger, grated	28 oz. canned tomatoes, crushed
1 tablespoon garlic, minced	1 cup apricots, dried and halved
½ cup mint, chopped	15 oz. canned chickpeas, drained
6 tablespoons Greek yogurt	

Directions:
Heat up a pot with 2 tablespoons oil over medium-high heat, add the meat and brown for 5 minutes.
Add the carrot, onion, celery, garlic and the ginger, stir and sauté for 5 minutes more.
Add the rest of the ingredients except the yogurt, bring to a simmer and cook over medium heat for 1 hour and 30 minutes.
Divide the stew into bowls, top each serving with the yogurt and serve.

Nutrition:
Calories: 355, Fat: 14.3 g, Fiber: 6.7 g, Carbs: 22.6 g, Protein: 15.4 g

212. Peas and Orzo Soup

Preparation time: 10 minutes | **Cooking time:** 10 minutes | **Servings:** 2

Ingredients:
- ½ cup orzo
- 1 ½ cups cheddar, shredded
- 2 teaspoons oregano, dried
- 3 cups baby spinach
- ½ cup peas
- 6 cups chicken soup
- Salt and black pepper to the taste
- ¼ cup yellow onion, chopped
- 2 tablespoons lime juice

Directions:
Heat up a pot with the soup over medium heat, add the orzo and the rest of the ingredients except the cheese, bring to a simmer and cook for 10 minutes.
Add the cheese, stir, divide into bowls and serve.

Nutrition:
Calories: 360, Fat: 10.2 g, Fiber: 4.7 g, Carbs: 43.3 g, Protein: 22.3 g

213. Turmeric Chard Soup

Preparation time: 10 minutes | **Cooking time:** 40 minutes | **Servings:** 2

Ingredients:
- 2 tablespoons olive oil
- 1 teaspoon coriander seeds, ground
- 2 teaspoons garlic, minced
- ¼ teaspoon cardamom, ground
- 1 yellow onion, chopped
- Salt and black pepper to the taste
- 3 tablespoons cilantro, chopped
- 1 lb. chard, chopped
- 2 teaspoons mustard seeds
- 1 tablespoon ginger, grated
- ¼ teaspoon turmeric powder
- ¾ cup rhubarb, sliced
- 5 cups water
- 6 tablespoons yogurt

Directions:
Heat up a pan with the oil over medium heat, add the coriander, mustard seeds, garlic, ginger, cardamom, turmeric and the onion, stir and sauté for 5 minutes.
Add the rest of the ingredients except the cilantro and the yogurt, bring to a simmer and cook for 20 minutes.
Divide the soup into bowls, top each serving with cilantro and yogurt and serve.

Nutrition:
Calories: 189, Fat: 8.3 g, Fiber: 3.4 g, Carbs: 11.7 g, Protein: 4.5 g

214. Turmeric Shrimp Mix

Preparation time: 5 minutes | **Cooking time:** 20 minutes | **Servings:** 2

Ingredients:
- 1 lb. shrimp, peeled and deveined
- 1 tablespoon avocado oil
- 1 tablespoon lime juice
- ¼ cup chives, chopped
- 2 spring onions, chopped
- ½ teaspoon turmeric powder
- A pinch of salt and black pepper

Directions:
In a sous vide bag, mix the shrimp with the spring onions and the other ingredients, seal the bag and cook in the water oven at 160°F for 20 minutes.
Divide everything into bowls and serve.

Nutrition:
Calories: 281, Fat: 7 g, Fiber: 7 g, Carbs: 8 g, Protein: 5 g

215. Whiskey Infused Apples

Preparation time: 10 minutes | **Cooking time:** 1 hour | **Servings:** 2

Ingredients:
- 4 Gala apples
- 2 tablespoons maple whiskey
- 2 tablespoons brown sugar

Directions:
Preheat your Sous Vide cooker to 175°F

Peel, core, and slice apples.
Place the apple slices, sugar, and whiskey into Sous Vide bag.
Vacuum seal and submerge in water.
Cook 1 hour.
Remove the bag from the water.
Serve apples with ice cream while hot.

Nutrition:
Calories: 99, Fat: 5 g, Carbs: 24 g, Fiber: 2 g, Protein: 2 g

216. Blueberry Lime Compote

Preparation time: 10 minutes | **Cooking time:** 1 hour | **Servings:** 2

Ingredients:

1lb. fresh blueberries	1 tablespoon lime zest
½ cup caster sugar	1 tablespoon lime juice
1 tablespoon tapioca starch	

Directions:
Preheat the Sous Vide cooker to 180°F.
In a large bowl, whisk the lime zest, sugar, lime juice, and tapioca starch.
Toss in the blueberries and stir gently to coat.
Transfer the blueberries to Sous Vide bag.
Seal the bag by using the water immersion sealing technique.
Cook the blueberries 1 hour.
Remove the bag with blueberries from the water.
Open the bag and serve blueberries while hot.

Nutrition:
Calories: 171, Fat: 4 g, Carbs: 47 g, Fiber: 3 g, Protein: 9 g

217. Apricot Dates Compote

Preparation time: 10 minutes | **Cooking time:** 30 minutes | **Servings:** 2

Ingredients:

10oz. fresh apricots	6oz. pitted dates
1-star anise	1 tablespoon Pernod
4 tablespoons brown sugar	1 tablespoon unsalted butter
2 tablespoons maple syrup	

Directions:
Set the Sous Vide cooker to 180°F.
In a large Sous Vide bag, combine all ingredients. Shake gently.
Vacuum seal the bag and submerge in water.
Cook the figs and dates 30 minutes.
Remove the bag from the Sous Vide cooker.
Open the bag and transfer the content to the bowl.
Allow cooling before serving.

Nutrition:
Calories: 239, Fat: 5 g, Carbs: 52 g, Fiber: 8 g, Protein: 2 g

218. Tropical Pineapple

Preparation time: 10 minutes | **Cooking time:** 2 hours | **Servings:** 2

Ingredients:

14oz. pineapple slices	¾ cup rum
1 cup brown sugar	1 vanilla pod, split, seeds scraped

Directions:
Set the Sous vide cooker to 135°F.
Combine the pineapple slices, rum, brown sugar, and vanilla seeds (from the pod in a Sous Vide cooking bag.
Seal the bag using water immersion technique.
Submerge the pineapple in water and cook 2 hours.
Remove the bag with pineapple from the cooker.
Strain the pineapple liquid in saucepan. Place the pineapple aside.
Simmer the cooking juices until thickened.
Serve the pineapple in a bowl and drizzle with thickened sauce.

Nutrition:
Calories: 283, Fat: 1 g, Carbs: 46 g, Fiber: 4 g, Protein: 6 g

219. Stuffed Apples

Preparation time: 20 minutes | **Cooking time:** 90 minutes | **Servings:** 2

Ingredients:
4 golden apples

¼ cup palm sugar + 1 ½ tablespoons	1 tablespoon chopped dates

Ingredients:

- 3 tablespoons raisins
- ¼ teaspoon cinnamon
- 1 ½ tablespoons whipping cream
- 2 tablespoons butter
- ⅓ cup organic apple juice

To garnish:
- A handful of chopped walnuts

Directions:
Preheat your Sous Vide cooker to 185 °F.
Core the apples, leaving the bottom intact.
In a bowl, combine sugar, raisins, dates, butter, and cinnamon.
Fill the apples with prepared mixture.
Place each apple in Sous Vide bag and vacuum seal.
Cook the apples 90 minutes.
Combine the remaining sugar with apple juice in a saucepan.
Simmer until sauce is thick, for 10 minutes. Stir in the whipping cream.

Finishing steps:
Remove the apples from bags and serve on a plate.
Drizzle with sauce and sprinkle with walnuts.

Nutrition:
Calories: 147, Fat: 6 g, Carbs: 27 g, Fiber: 2 g, Protein: 5 g

220. Infused Pineapple with Sorbet

Preparation time: 20 minutes | **Cooking time:** 1 hour | **Servings:** 2

Ingredients:

For the Pineapple:
- 1 pineapple, peeled, cored, and cut into 6 rectangles
- 2 cups sugar
- 10 pink peppercorns
- 1-star anise

For the Sorbet:
- 2 cups passion fruit puree
- 2 large bananas
- 1 ½ cups water
- 1 cup sugar
- 2 tablespoons orange juice

Directions:
Preheat your Sous vide cooker to 149 °F.
Add sugar in a saucepan with a hint of water. Heat until the sugar is dissolved and turns brown.
Pour the caramel over the pineapple.
Once the pineapple is cooled, transfer it to sous vide bag. Add the peppercorns and anise.
Vacuum seal the bag and submerge in water.
Cook the pineapple 60 minutes.

Finishing steps:
While the pineapple is cooking, make the sorbet.
Blend all ingredients in a food blender.
Strain and churn into ice cream making a machine or freeze 4 hours.
Remove the pineapple from the bag and serve with passionfruit sorbet.

Nutrition:
Calories: 405, Fat: 8 g, Carbs: 138 g, Fiber: 18 g, Protein: 6 g

221. Vanilla Poached Peaches

Preparation time: 15 minutes | **Cooking time:** 1 hour | **Servings:** 2

Ingredients:
- 4 peaches, halved, stone removed
- ½ cup white rum
- ¾ cup brown sugar
- 2 tablespoons lemon juice
- ½ vanilla bean, seeds scraped
- ¼ cup Greek yogurt
- 2 tablespoons honey
- ¼ cup chopped pistachios

Directions:
Heat Sous Vide cooker to 165 °F.
In a Sous Vide bag, combine peaches, rum, ¼ cup brown sugar, lemon juice, and vanilla.
Vacuum seal the bag and cook the peaches in the cooker for 1 hour.

Finishing steps:
In a small bowl, combine Greek yogurt and honey.
Open the bag and pour the poaching liquid into a saucepan. Add brown sugar and simmer 6-7 minutes or until thickened.
Serve peaches on a plate. Fill the cavities with Greek yogurt and drizzle all with the syrup.
Serve.

Nutrition:
Calories: 290, Fat: 5 g, Carbs: 51 g, Fiber: 7 g, Protein: 5 g

222. Plums in Red Wine

Preparation time: 5 minutes | **Cooking time:** 30 minutes | **Servings:** 2

Ingredients:
- 4 large plums
- ½ cup granulated sugar
- ½ vanilla seed pod
- 1 cup quality red wine
- 1 teaspoon lime zest

Directions:
Preheat Sous Vide cooker to 170°F.
Cut the plums in half and remove the stone.
Place the plums, wine, sugar, lime zest, and vanilla into Sous Vide bag.
Vacuum seal the bag and cook 30 minutes.
Open the bag and pour the cooking liquid into a plastic container.
Freeze the cooking liquid.
Serve the plums on a plate.
Scrub the poaching liquid with a fork and serve with plums.

Nutrition:
Calories: 323, Fat: 4g, Carbs: 65g, Fiber: 9g, Protein: 1g

223. Orange Compote

Preparation time: 10 minutes | **Cooking time:** 3 hours | **Servings:** 2

Ingredients:
- 4 blood oranges, quartered and thinly sliced
- 1 lemon, juice and zest
- 1 teaspoon beef gelatin powder or agar agar
- 2 cups granulated sugar
- ½ vanilla seed pod

Directions:
Set the Sous Vide cooker to 190°F.
Combine all ingredients in a Sous Vide bag.
Seal using water immersion technique.
Cook the oranges 3 hours.
Remove the bag from the cooker and place into an ice-cold water bath.
Once cooled transfer into a food processor.
Add the gelatin and process until smooth.
Allow cooling completely before serving.

Nutrition:
Calories: 466, Fat: 3 g, Carbs: 121 g, Fiber: 9 g, Protein: 9 g

224. Lime Artichokes

Preparation time: 5 minutes | **Cooking time:** 35 minutes | **Servings:** 2

Ingredients:
- 4 artichokes, trimmed and halved
- 2 tablespoons balsamic vinegar
- A pinch of salt and black pepper
- 1 tablespoon lime juice
- ½ teaspoon coriander, ground

Directions:
In a large sous vide bag, mix the artichokes with the lime juice and the other ingredients, seal the bag, submerge in the water bath, cook at 160°F for 35 minutes, divide between plates and serve.

Nutrition:
Calories: 56, Fat: 8 g, Fiber: 4 g, Carbs: 5 g, Protein: 6 g

225. Basil Green Beans

Preparation time: 10 minutes | **Cooking time:** 35 minutes | **Servings:** 2

Ingredients:
- 1 lb. green beans, trimmed
- 1 tablespoon butter, melted
- 2 tablespoons basil, chopped
- A pinch of red pepper flakes
- 1 tablespoon soy sauce
- Juice of ½ lime
- A pinch of salt and black pepper
- A pinch of salt and black pepper

Directions:
In a sous vide bag, mix the green beans with the soy sauce, butter and the other ingredients, seal the bag, submerge in the water bath, cook at 174°F for 35 minutes, divide the between plates and serve.

Nutrition:
Calories: 10, Fat: 1 g, Fiber: 8 g, Carbs: 6 g, Protein: 6 g

226. Buttery Leeks

Preparation time: 5 minutes | **Cooking time:** 25 minutes | **Servings:** 2

Ingredients:
- 2 leeks, sliced
- 2 tablespoons butter, melted
- ½ teaspoon coriander, ground
- 2 tablespoons lime juice
- 1 tablespoon dill, chopped
- A pinch of salt and black pepper

Directions:
In a sous vide bag, mix the leeks with the melted butter and the other ingredients, seal the bag, submerge in the water oven, cook at 170 °F for 25 minutes, divide the mix between plates and serve.

Nutrition:
Calories: 148, Fat: 8 g, Fiber: 9 g, Carbs: 4 g, Protein: 5 g

227. Green Beans and Capers

Preparation time: 5 minutes | **Cooking time:** 30 minutes | **Servings:** 2

Ingredients:
- 1 lb. green beans, trimmed and halved
- ½ teaspoon chili powder
- 1 tablespoon capers, drained
- 1 tablespoon basil, chopped
- 1 tablespoon balsamic vinegar
- Juice of ½ lemon
- 1 tablespoon sweet paprika
- 2 garlic cloves, chopped

Directions:
In a sous vide bag, mix the green beans with the capers, vinegar and the other ingredients, seal the bag, submerge in the water bath, cook at 164°F for 30 minutes, divide the mix between plates, and serve.

Nutrition:
Calories: 106, Fat: 9 g, Fiber: 2 g, Carbs: 5 g

228. Balsamic Tomatoes

Preparation time: 5 minutes | **Cooking time:** 30 minutes | **Servings:** 2

Ingredients:
- 1 lb. cherry tomatoes, halved
- 2 tablespoons avocado oil
- ½ teaspoon chili powder
- A pinch of salt and black pepper
- 2 tablespoons balsamic vinegar
- 1 tablespoon basil, chopped
- ½ teaspoon sweet paprika
- 1 tablespoon chives, chopped

Directions:
In a sous vide bag, mix the tomatoes with the vinegar, oil and the other ingredients, seal the bag, submerge in the water bath, cook at 167°F for 30 minutes, divide mix between plates and serve.

Nutrition:
Calories: 42, Fat: 2 g, Fiber: 7 g, Carbs: 1 g

229. Mustard Asparagus

Preparation time: 5 minutes | **Cooking time:** 30 minutes | **Servings:** 2

Ingredients:
- 1 lb. asparagus, trimmed
- 2 tablespoons mustard
- A pinch of salt and black pepper
- 1 tablespoon basil, chopped
- 2 tablespoons avocado oil
- 2 tablespoons lime juice
- 1 teaspoon garlic powder

Directions:
In a sous vide bag, mix the asparagus with the oil, mustard and the other ingredients, seal the bag, submerge in the water bath, cook at 170°F for 30 minutes, divide between plates and serve.

Nutrition:
Calories: 102, Fat: 5 g, Fiber: 3 g, Carbs: 1 g, Protein: 4 g

230. Green Beans and Corn

Preparation time: 5 minutes | **Cooking time:** 30 minutes | **Servings:** 2

Ingredients:
- 1 lb. green beans, trimmed and halved
- 1 tablespoon balsamic vinegar
- 2 tablespoons oregano, chopped
- ½ cup chicken stock
- 1 cup corn
- Juice of ½ lime
- A pinch of salt and black pepper

Directions:
In a sous vide bag, mix the green beans with the corn, vinegar and the other ingredients, seal the bag, cook in the water bath at 165°F for 30 minutes, divide everything between plates and serve.

Nutrition:
Calories: 121, Fat: 15 g, Fiber: 8 g, Carbs: 1 g, Protein: 9 g

231. Balsamic Radishes

Preparation time: 5 minutes | **Cooking time:** 30 minutes | **Servings:** 2

Ingredients:
- 1 lb. radishes, halved
- ½ teaspoon garam masala
- 1 tablespoon chives, chopped
- 2 tablespoons balsamic vinegar
- ½ cup chicken stock
- 1 teaspoon chili powder

Directions:
In a sous vide bag, mix the radishes with the vinegar, masala and the other ingredients, seal the bag, submerge in the water bath, cook at 165°F for 30 minutes, divide the mix between plates and serve.

Nutrition:
Calories: 45, Fat: 6 g, Fiber: 1 g, Carbs: 4 g, Protein: 2 g

232. Parsley Artichokes

Preparation time: 5 minutes | **Cooking time:** 30 minutes | **Servings:** 2

Ingredients:
- 4 artichokes, trimmed and halved
- 2 teaspoons lemon zest, grated
- 1 tablespoon lemon juice
- 1 teaspoon chili powder
- A pinch of salt and black pepper
- 1 tablespoon parsley, chopped

Directions:
In a sous vide bag, mix the artichokes with the lemon juice and the other ingredients, seal the bag, submerge in the water bath, cook at 170°F for 30 minutes, divide the mix between plates, and serve.

Nutrition:
Calories: 82, Fat: 5 g, Fiber: 9 g, Carbs: 1 g, Protein: 6 g

233. Balsamic Zucchini Mix

Preparation time: 10 minutes | **Cooking time:** 30 minutes | **Servings:** 2

Ingredients:
- 1 lb. zucchinis, roughly cubed
- 1 tablespoon capers, drained
- 2 garlic cloves, minced
- ½ teaspoon chili powder
- 2 tablespoons balsamic vinegar
- A pinch of salt and black pepper
- 1 tablespoon dill, chopped

Directions:
In a sous vide bag, mix the zucchinis with the vinegar and the other ingredients, seal the bag, cook in the water bath at 165°F for 30 minutes, divide everything between plates and serve.

Nutrition:
Calories: 46, Fat: 7 g, Fiber: 1 g, Carbs: 6 g, Protein: 7 g

234. Garlic Brussels Sprouts

Preparation time: 10 minutes | **Cooking time:** 35 minutes | **Servings:** 2

Ingredients:
- 1 lb. Brussels sprouts, trimmed and halved
- 3 garlic cloves, minced
- Juice of 1 lemon
- ½ teaspoon coriander, ground

½ teaspoon sweet paprika
1 tablespoon rosemary, chopped
A pinch of salt and black pepper

Directions:
In a sous vide bag, mix the sprouts with the lemon juice, garlic and the other ingredients, seal the bag, cook in the water bath at 167°F for 35 minutes, divide the mix between plates and serve.

Nutrition:
Calories: 71, Fat: 1 g, Fiber: 1 g, Carbs: 3 g, Protein: 4 g

235. Creamy Bell Peppers

Preparation time: 10 minutes | **Cooking time:** 30 minutes | **Servings:** 2

Ingredients:
1 lb. red bell peppers, cut into wedges
1 teaspoon turmeric powder
1 tablespoon lime juice
1 cup heavy cream
½ teaspoon coriander, ground
1 tablespoon chives, chopped

Directions:
In a sous vide bag, mix the peppers with the cream, turmeric and the other ingredients, seal the bag, submerge in the water bath, cook at 180°F for 30 minutes, divide the mix between plates and serve.

Nutrition:
Calories: 70, Fat: 8 g, Fiber: 1 g, Carbs: 4 g, Protein: 6 g

236. Cayenne Broccoli

Preparation time: 5 minutes | **Cooking time:** 25 minutes | **Servings:** 2

Ingredients:
1 lb. broccoli florets
Juice of 1 lime
A pinch of salt and black pepper
½ cup chicken stock
A pinch of cayenne pepper
1 tablespoon chives, chopped

Directions:
In a sous vide bag, mix the broccoli with the lime juice, cayenne and the other ingredients, seal the bag, submerge in the water bath, cook at 165°F for 25 minutes, divide the mix between plates and serve.

Nutrition:
Calories: 63, Fat: 7 g, Fiber: 4 g, Carbs: 8 g, Protein: 7 g

237. Nutmeg Brussels Sprouts

Preparation time: 5 minutes | **Cooking time:** 35 minutes | **Servings:** 2

Ingredients:
1 lb. Brussels sprouts, halved
2 tablespoons olive oil
1 tablespoon chives, chopped
2 tablespoons balsamic vinegar
1 teaspoon nutmeg, ground

Directions:
In a sous vide bag, mix the sprouts with the oil and the other ingredients, seal the bag, cook in the water oven at 165°F for 35 minutes, divide the mix between plates and serve.

Nutrition:
Calories: 68, Fat: 2 g, Fiber: 3 g, Carbs: 4 g, Protein: 4 g

238. Garlic Kale

Preparation time: 5 minutes | **Cooking time:** 20 minutes | **Servings:** 2

Ingredients:
1 lb. baby kale
2 tablespoons olive oil
1 teaspoon sweet paprika
3 garlic cloves, minced
A pinch of salt and black pepper
1 teaspoon chives, chopped

Directions:
In a sous vide bag, mix the kale with the garlic, oil and the other ingredients, seal the bag, submerge in the water oven, cook at 160°F for 20 minutes, divide the mix between plates and serve.

Nutrition:
Calories: 32, Fat: 4 g, Fiber: 3 g, Carbs: 9 g, Protein: 3 g

239. Chives Radish SV

Preparation time: 10 minutes | **Cooking time:** 25 minutes | **Servings:** 2

Ingredients:
- 1 lb. radishes, sliced
- 1 tablespoon lime juice
- A pinch of salt and black pepper
- 1 tablespoon olive oil
- 1 teaspoon chili powder
- 1 tablespoon chives, minced

Directions:
In a sous vide bag, mix the radishes with the oil, lime juice and the other ingredients, seal the bag, cook in the water oven at 165°F for 25 minutes, divide mix between plates and serve.

Nutrition:
Calories: 38, Fat: 5 g, Fiber: 2 g, Carbs: 4 g, Protein: 5 g

240. Dill Tomatoes SV

Preparation time: 10 minutes | **Cooking time:** 20 minutes | **Servings:** 2

Ingredients:
- 2 lbs. tomatoes, cut into wedges
- A pinch of salt and black pepper
- 1 teaspoon rosemary, dried
- 1 tablespoon lemon zest, grated
- 1 tablespoon dill, chopped
- 1 teaspoon chili powder

Directions:
In a sous vide bag, mix the tomatoes with the lemon zest and the other ingredients, seal the bag, submerge in the water oven, cook at 170°F for 20 minutes, divide the mix between plates and serve.

Nutrition:
Calories: 161, Fat: 11 g, Fiber: 1 g, Carbs: 5 g, Protein: 6 g

241. Green Beans Sauté SV

Preparation time: 10 minutes | **Cooking time:** 25 minutes | **Servings:** 2

Ingredients:
- 1 lb. green beans, trimmed
- 2 tablespoons olive oil
- ½ teaspoon coriander, ground
- 2 tablespoons garlic, minced
- 1 tablespoon soy sauce
- 2 spring onions, chopped
- A pinch of salt and black pepper
- 1 tablespoon dill, chopped

Directions:
In a sous vide bag, mix the green beans with the soy sauce, oil and the other ingredients, seal the bag, cook in the water oven at 165°F for 25 minutes, divide the mix between plates and serve.

Nutrition:
Calories: 165, Fat: 15 g, Fiber: 8 g, Carbs: 4 g, Protein: 7 g

242. Garlic Spinach

Preparation time: 10 minutes | **Cooking time:** 15 minutes | **Servings:** 2

Ingredients:
- 1 lb. baby spinach
- 1 tablespoon olive oil
- A pinch of salt and black pepper
- Juice of 1 lime
- 4 garlic cloves, minced
- 1 teaspoon chili powder

Directions:
In a sous vide bag, mix the spinach with the lime juice and the other ingredients, seal the bag, cook in the water bath at 160°F for 15 minutes, divide the mix between plates and serve.

Nutrition:
Calories: 95, Fat: 7 g, Fiber: 9 g, Carbs: 4 g, Protein: 8 g

243. Creamy Zucchini SV

Preparation time: 10 minutes | **Cooking time:** 25 minutes | **Servings:** 2

Ingredients:
- 2 tablespoons rosemary, chopped
- 2 tablespoons lime juice
- 1 lb. zucchinis, cut into wedges
- 1 tablespoon olive oil

A pinch of salt and black pepper
½ teaspoon rosemary, dried
1 cup heavy cream
1 tablespoon dill, chopped

Directions:
In a sous vide bag, mix the zucchinis with the rosemary and the other ingredients, seal the bag, submerge in the water bath, cook at 160°F for 25 minutes, divide the mix between plates and serve.

Nutrition:
Calories: 181, Fat: 18 g, Fiber: 2 g, Carbs: 9 g, Protein: 6 g

244. Chicken and Coconut Casserole

Preparation time: 10 minutes | **Cooking time:** 35 minutes | **Servings:** 2

Ingredients:
1 lb. chicken breast, skinless, boneless and cut into thin strips
1 cup veggie stock
1-inch piece, grated
4 Thai chilies, chopped.
6 oz. coconut milk
¼ cup cilantro, chopped
4 lime leaves, torn
1 lemongrass stalk, chopped
8 oz. mushrooms, chopped.
4 tbsp. fish sauce
¼ cup lime juice
Salt and black pepper to the taste

Directions:
Put stock into a pan that fits your air fryer, bring to a simmer over medium heat, add lemongrass, ginger and lime leaves, stir and cook for 10 minutes.
Strain soup, return to pan, add chicken, mushrooms, milk, chilies, fish sauce, lime juice, cilantro, salt and pepper, stir, introduce in your air fryer and cook at 360°F, for 15 minutes. Divide into bowls and serve.

Nutrition:
Calories: 150, Fat: 4 g, Fiber: 4 g, Carbs: 6 g, Protein: 7 g

245. Italian Style Eggplant Sandwich

Preparation time: 10 minutes | **Cooking time:** 26 minutes | **Servings:** 2

Ingredients:
1 eggplant, sliced
½ cup breadcrumbs
½ tsp. garlic powder
2 tbsp. milk
Cooking spray
¾ cup tomato sauce
Salt and black pepper to the taste
2 tsp. parsley, dried
½ tsp. Italian seasoning
½ tsp. onion powder
4 bread slices
½ cup mayonnaise
2 cups mozzarella cheese, grated

Directions:
Season eggplant slices with salt and pepper, leave aside for 10 minutes and then pat dry them well.
In a bowl, mix parsley with breadcrumbs, Italian seasoning, onion and garlic powder, salt and black pepper and stir.
In another bowl, mix milk with mayo and whisk well.
Brush eggplant slices with mayo mix, dip them in breadcrumbs, place them in your air fryer's basket, spray with cooking oil and cook them at 400 °F, for 15 minutes, flipping them after 8 minutes.
Brush each bread slice with olive oil and arrange 2 on a working surface.
Add mozzarella and parmesan on each, add baked eggplant slices, spread tomato sauce and basil and top with the other bread slices, greased side down. Divide sandwiches on plates, cut them in halves and serve for lunch.

Nutrition:
Calories: 324, Fat: 16 g, Fiber: 4 g, Carbs: 39 g, Protein: 12 g

246. Beef Stew

Preparation time: 10 minutes | **Cooking time:** 30 minutes | **Servings:** 2

Ingredients:
2 lbs. beef meat, cut into medium chunks
4 potatoes, chopped
2 carrots, chopped
1-quart veggie stock

½ tsp. smoked paprika
Salt and black pepper to the taste
A handful thyme, chopped

Directions:
In a dish that fits your air fryer, mix beef with carrots, potatoes, stock, salt, pepper, paprika and thyme, stir, place in air fryer's basket and cook at 375 °F, for 20 minutes. Divide into bowls and serve right away for lunch.

Nutrition:
Calories: 260, Fat: 5 g, Fiber: 8 g, Carbs: 20 g, Protein: 22 g

247. Stuffed Meatballs

Preparation time: 10 minutes | **Cooking time:** 20 minutes | **Servings:** 2

Ingredients:
- ⅓ cup breadcrumbs
- 3 tbsp. milk
- 1 egg
- 20 cheddar cheese cubes
- Salt and black pepper to the taste
- ½ tsp. marjoram, dried
- 1 tbsp. ketchup
- 1 lb. lean beef, ground
- 1 tbsp. olive oil

Directions:
In a bowl, mix breadcrumbs with ketchup, milk, marjoram, salt, pepper and egg and whisk well. Add beef, stir and shape 20 meatballs out of this mix.
Shape each meatball around a cheese cube, drizzle the oil over them and rub.
Place all meatballs in your preheated air fryer and cook at 390 °F, for 10 minutes. Serve them for lunch with a side salad.

Nutrition:
Calories: 200, Fat: 5 g, Fiber: 8 g, Carbs: 12 g, Protein: 5 g

248. Air Fryer Bacon Pudding

Preparation time: 10 minutes | **Cooking time:** 40 minutes | **Servings:** 2

Ingredients:
- 4 bacon strips, cooked and chopped.
- 2 cups corn
- 3 cups bread, cubed
- 1 yellow onion, chopped.
- ½ cup red bell pepper, chopped.
- 2 tsp. garlic, minced
- 1 ½ cups milk
- Salt and black pepper to the taste
- 1 tbsp. butter, soft
- 3 eggs, whisked
- 4 tbsp. parmesan, grated
- ¼ cup celery, chopped.
- 1 tsp. thyme, chopped.
- ½ cup heavy cream
- Cooking spray

Directions:
Grease your air fryer's pan with cooking spray. In a bowl, mix bacon with butter, corn, onion, bell pepper, celery, thyme, garlic, salt, pepper, milk, heavy cream, eggs and bread cubes, toss, pour into greased pan and sprinkle cheese all over
Add this to your preheated air fryer at 320°F and cook for 30 minutes. Divide among plates and serve warm for a quick lunch.

Nutrition:
Calories: 276, Fat: 10 g, Fiber: 2 g, Carbs: 20 g, Protein: 10 g

249. Chicken Zucchini Lunch

Preparation time: 10 minutes | **Cooking time:** 30 minutes | **Servings:** 2

Ingredients:
- 1 lb. chicken breasts, skinless, boneless and cubed
- 2 garlic cloves, minced
- 2 cups cherry tomatoes, halved
- Salt and black pepper to the taste
- 2 cups basil
- ½ cup olive oil
- 1 tbsp. lemon juice
- A pinch of salt
- 4 zucchinis, cut with a spiralizer
- 1 tsp. olive oil
- ½ cup almonds, chopped
- For the pesto:
- ¾ cup pine nuts
- 2 cups kale, chopped
- 1 garlic clove

Directions:
In your food processor, mix basil with kale, lemon juice, garlic, pine nuts, oil and a pinch of salt, pulse well and leave aside.
Heat up a pan that fits your air fryer with the oil over medium heat, add garlic, stir and cook for 1 minute.
Add chicken, salt, pepper, stir, almonds, zucchini noodles, garlic, cherry tomatoes and the pesto you've made at the beginning, stir gently, introduce in preheated air fryer and cook at 360°F, for 17 minutes. Divide among plates and serve for lunch.

Nutrition:
Calories: 344, Fat: 8 g, Fiber: 7 g, Carbs: 12 g, Protein: 16 g

250. Special Pancake Mix

Preparation time: 10 minutes | **Cooking time:** 20 minutes | **Servings:** 2

Ingredients:
- 1 cup small shrimp, peeled and de veined
- 3 Eggs, whisked
- ½ cup milk
- 1 tbsp. butter
- ½ cup flour
- 1 cup salsa

Directions:
Preheat your air fryer at a temperature of 400°F.
Add fryer's pan containing 1 tbsp. of butter and melt it.
Mix eggs with flour and milk in a bowl.
Whisk well and pour into air fryer's pan.
Then spread neatly and cook at a temperature of 350°F for 12 minutes.
Move to a plate after cooking.
Mix shrimp with salsa, stir gently
Serve your pancake with this on the side.

Nutrition:
Calories: 200, Fat: 6 g, Fiber: 8 g, Carbs: 12 g, Protein: 4 g

251. Turkish Style Koftas Mix

Preparation time: 10 minutes | **Cooking time:** 25 minutes | **Servings:** 2

Ingredients:
- 2 tbsp feta cheese, crumbled
- 1 Leek, chopped
- 1 tbsp. Parsley, chopped
- ½ lb. lean beef, minced
- 1 tbsp. Mint, chopped
- 1 tsp. Garlic, minced
- 1 tbsp. Cumin, ground
- Salt and black pepper to taste

Directions:
Mix beef with leek, cheese, cumin, mint, parsley, garlic in a bowl.
Sprinkle salt and pepper to taste.
Stir well and shape your kofta s and place them on different sticks.
Add kofta s to your preheated air fryer at a temperature of 360°F and cook them for 15 minutes.
Serve them with a side salad for lunch.

Nutrition:
Calories: 281, Fat: 7 g, Fiber: 8 g, Carbs: 17 g, Protein: 6 g

252. Chicken Wings Recipe

Preparation time: 10 minutes | **Cooking time:** 55 minutes | **Servings:** 2

Ingredients:
- 3 lbs. Chicken wings
- 1 tsp. Lemon juice
- 1 tbsp. old bay seasoning
- ¾ cup potato starch
- ½ cup butter
- Lemon wedges for serving

Directions:
Mix starch with old bay seasoning and chicken wings in a bowl and toss well.
Place the chicken wings in your air fryer's basket and cook them at a temperature of 360°F, for 35 minutes.
Shake the fryer from time to time.
Increase the heat to a temperature of 400°F.
Cook the wings for another 10 minutes and cut them into different plates.
Add heat to a pan using medium heat, then add butter and melt it. Add lemon juice, stir gently and remove the heat.
Drizzle the lemon juice over chicken wings.
Serve lemon wedges on the side for lunch.

Nutrition:
Calories: 271, Fat: 6 g, Fiber: 8 g, Carbs: 18 g, Protein: 18 g

253. Summer Squash Fritters Mix AF

Preparation time: 10 minutes | **Cooking time:** 17 minutes | **Servings:** 2

Ingredients:
- 3 oz. cream cheese
- ½ tsp. Oregano, dried
- ⅔ cup breadcrumbs
- 1 yellow summer squash, grated
- 1 Egg, whisked
- ⅓ cup Carrot, grated
- A pinch of salt and black pepper
- 2 tbsp. Olive oil

Directions:
Mix cream cheese with salt, pepper, oregano, egg, breadcrumbs, carrot and squash in a bowl and stir well.
Shape the medium patties out of this mix and brush them with the oil.
Move the squash patties to your air fryer
Cook them at a temperature of 400°F for about 7 minutes.
Serve them for lunch.

Nutrition:
Calories: 200, Fat: 4 g, Fiber: 7 g, Carbs: 8 g, Protein: 6 g

254. Fresh Style Chicken Recipe AF

Preparation time: 10 minutes | **Cooking time:** 32 minutes | **Servings:** 2

Ingredients:
- 2 chicken breasts, skinless, boneless, and cubed
- 10 oz. alfredo sauce
- 1 red bell pepper, chopped
- 6 bread slices
- ½ tsp. Thyme, dried
- 8 button mushrooms, sliced
- 1 tbsp. olive oil
- 2 tbsp. Butter, soft

Directions:
Mix chicken with mushrooms, bell pepper and oil in the air fryer.
Toss to coat well and cook at a temperature of 350°F, for 15 minutes.
Move the chicken mix to a clean bowl and add thyme and alfredo sauce.
Toss to coat well and return to the air fryer.
Cook again at 350°F, for another 4 minutes.
Spread butter on the bread slices, add it to the fryer.
Butter the side up and cook for another 4 minutes.
Place the toasted bread slices on a platter.
Top each one with some chicken mix and serve for lunch.

Nutrition:
Calories: 172, Fat: 4 g, Fiber: 9 g, Carbs: 12 g, Protein: 4 g

255. Asian Chicken Recipe AF

Preparation time: 10 minutes | **Cooking time:** 40 minutes | **Servings:** 2

Ingredients:
- 2 chicken breasts, skinless, boneless and sliced
- 1 yellow onion, sliced
- 14 oz. pizza dough
- ½ cup jarred cheese sauce
- 1 tsp. olive oil
- 1 tbsp. Worcestershire sauce
- 1 ½ cups cheddar cheese, grated
- Salt and black pepper to the taste

Directions:
Preheat your air fryer at 400°F before adding half of the oil and onions
Fry them for about 8 minutes, stir only once.
Add the chicken pieces, Worcestershire sauce, as well as salt and pepper to taste.
Toss well to coat, then air fry for another 8 minutes, stir once and move everything to a bowl.
Roll the pizza dough on a working surface, then get a rectangle shape out of it.
Spread half of the cheese all over the rectangle dough before adding chicken and onion mix.
Top with cheese sauce.
Roll your dough again and shape into a U.
Place your roll in your air fryer's basket.
Brush with the remaining oil and cook at a temperature of 370°F for 12 minutes.
Flip the roll halfway. Slice your roll neatly while it's still warm
Now you can serve for lunch.

Nutrition:
Calories: 300, Fat: 8 g, Fiber: 17 g, Carbs: 20 g, Protein: 6 g

256. Lamb Ragout *IP*

Preparation time: 15 minutes | **Cooking time:** 1 hour | **Servings:** 2

Ingredients:

- 1½ lbs. mutton, bone-in
- 2 carrots, peeled and sliced
- 6 garlic cloves, peeled and minced
- 4 tomatoes, cored and chopped
- 1 teaspoon dried oregano
- ½ cup parsley, diced
- ½ lbs. mushrooms, sliced
- 1 yellow onion, peeled and chopped
- 2 tablespoons tomato paste
- Salt and ground black pepper, to taste
- 1 teaspoon vegetable oil

Directions:
Put the instant pot in the sauté mode, add the oil and heat. Include the meat and brown on all sides. Add the tomato paste, tomatoes, onions, garlic, mushrooms, oregano, carrots and water to cover everything.
Add salt and pepper, stir, cover the instant pot and cook in the Meat / Stew setting for 1 hour. Relieve the pressure, remove the meat from the Instant Pot, discard the bones and Shred it.
Put the meat into pan again and add the parsley and stir. Add more pepper and salt, if necessary, and serve.

Nutrition:
Calories: 360, Fat: 14 g, Fiber: 3 g, Carbs: 15.1 g, Proteins: 30 g

257. Lamb and Barley Dish *IP*

Preparation time: 15 minutes | **Cooking time:** 45 minutes | **Servings:** 2

Ingredients:

- 5 oz. peas
- 5 carrots, peeled and chopped
- 1 lamb leg, already cooked, boneless and chopped
- Salt and ground black pepper, to taste
- 6 oz. barley
- 6 oz. beef stock
- 3 yellow onions, peeled and chopped
- 12 oz. water

Directions:
In the Instant Pot, mix the broth with water and barley, cover and cook for 10-20 minutes with the Meat / Stew setting minutes.
Release the pressure, uncover the Instant Pot, add the onions, peas and carrots, stir, cover and cook in the Manual setting for 10 minutes.
Relieve the pressure, add the meat, salt and pepper, mix, divide into bowls and serve.

Nutrition:
Calories: 324, Fat: 9 g, Fiber: 4 g, Carbs: 21 g, Proteins: 15 g

258. Lamb and White Beans *IP*

Preparation time: 10 minutes | **Cooking time:** 40 minutes | **Servings:** 2

Ingredients:

- 1½ cups white beans, soaked overnight and drained
- 4 lamb chops
- 2 cups canned diced tomatoes
- 1 teaspoon herbs de Provence
- Salt and ground black pepper, to taste
- 1 cup onion, peeled and chopped
- 1 cup leeks, chopped
- 2 tablespoons garlic, minced
- 2 teaspoons Worcestershire sauce
- 3 cups water

Directions:
Place the lamb chops in the instant pot. Add beans, onions, tomatoes, leeks, garlic, salt, pepper, Provence herbs, Worcestershire sauce and water. Stir, cover and cook for 40 minutes. Relieve the pressure, uncover the Instant Pot, distribute the dishes and serve.

Nutrition:
Calories: 520, Fat: 17 g, Fiber: 7 g, Carbs: 35 g, Proteins: 56 g

259. Mexican-Style Lamb *IP*

Preparation time: 10 minutes
Cooking time: 50 minutes
Servings: 2

Ingredients:

- 3 garlic cloves, peeled and minced
- 1 yellow onion, peeled and chopped

2 tablespoons extra virgin olive oil Salt, to taste
19 oz. enchilada sauce

3 lbs. lamb shoulder, cubed
½ bunch fresh cilantro, diced warm corn tortillas, for serving

lime wedges, for serving refried beans, for serving

Directions:
Put the enchilada sauce in a bowl, add the lamb and the marinade for 24 hours. Put the instant pot in the sauté mode, add the oil and heat. Add onion and garlic, mix and cook for 5 minutes.
Add the lamb, salt and marinade, stir, bring to a boil, cover the Instant Pot and cook for 45 minutes in the Meat / Stew setting.
Release the pressure, take the meat, place it on a cutting board and let it cool for a few minutes. Shred the meat and place it in a bowl. Add the cooking sauce and stir.
Divide the meat over the tortillas, sprinkle with coriander in each one, add the beans, sprinkle with lemon juice, wrap and serve.

Nutrition:
Calories: 484, Fat: 19 g, Fiber: 9 g, Carbs: 28 g, Proteins: 44 g

260. Cacciatore Chicken   IP

Preparation time: 10 minutes | **Cooking time:** 15 minutes | **Servings:** 2

Ingredients:
8 chicken drumsticks

1 teaspoon garlic powder
1 yellow onion, peeled chopped
28 oz. canned crushed tomatoes

1 cup chicken stock Salt, to taste
1 bay leaf

½ cup black olives, pitted and sliced
1 teaspoon dried oregano

Directions:
Put the instant pot in the Sauté mode, add the stock, bay leaf and salt and mix. Add the chicken, garlic powder, onion, oregano and chopped tomatoes, mix, cover the Instant Pot and cook the chicken for 15 minutes.
Release the pressure naturally, uncover the Instant Pot, throw away the bay leaf, divide the cacciatore chicken between the dishes, add a little cooking liquid, sprinkle with olives and serve.

Nutrition:
Calories: 210, Fat: 2.9 g, Fiber: 2.4 g, Carbs: 9.5 g, Proteins: 25.9 g

261. Honey Barbecue Chicken Wings   IP

Preparation time: 10 minutes | **Cooking time:** 25 minutes | **Servings:** 2

Ingredients:
2 lbs. chicken wings

Salt and ground black pepper, to taste
2 teaspoons paprika

½ teaspoon dried basil
½ cup brown sugar

¾ cup honey barbecue sauce Cayenne pepper
½ cup apple juice

1 teaspoon red pepper flakes
½ cup water

Directions:
Place the chicken wings in the Instant Pot, add the barbecue sauce, apple juice, salt, pepper, pepper, sweet pepper, basil, sugar and water. Stir, cover and cook for 10 minutes in the poultry dough.
Relieve the pressure, find the Instant Pot, transfer the chicken to a pan, add the sauce everywhere, put it in a grid pre-heated, cook for 7 minutes, turn the chicken wings, cook for 7 minutes, divide between the dishes and serve.

Nutrition:
Calories: 147.5, Fats: 2.2 g, Fiber: 1 g, Carbs: 8 g, Proteins: 21.8 g

262. Sweet and Tangy Chicken   IP

Preparation time: 10 minutes | **Cooking time:** 10 minutes | **Servings:** 2

Ingredients:
½ cup fish sauce
2 lbs. chicken thighs, boneless and skinless

1 cup lime juice
2 tablespoons coconut nectar

2 teaspoons cilantro, diced
1 teaspoon ginger, grated
¼ cup extra virgin olive oil
1 teaspoon fresh mint, chopped

Directions:
Place the chicken legs in the Instant Pot In a bowl, mix the lemon juice with the fish sauce, olive oil, coconut nectar, ginger, mint and cilantro and beat well.
Pour over the chicken, cover the Instant Pot and cook for 10 minutes in the poultry environment. Relieve the pressure, divide the chicken between the plates and serve.

Nutrition:
Calories: 300, Fat: 5 g, Fiber: 4 g, Carbs: 23 g, Proteins: 32 g

263. Turkey Chili *IP*

Preparation time: 10 minutes | **Cooking time:** 10 minutes | **Servings:** 2

Ingredients:
- 1 lb. turkey meat, ground
- 1 yellow onion, peeled and chopped
- 5 oz. water
- 1½ teaspoons cumin
- 1 yellow bell pepper, seeded and chopped
- 12 oz. vegetable stock
- 15 oz. chickpeas, already cooked
- Salt and ground black pepper, to taste
- 2½ tablespoons chili powder
- Cayenne pepper
- 3 garlic cloves, peeled and chopped

Directions:
Place the turkey meat in the Instant Pot, add the water, mix, cover and cook in the Poultry setting for 5 minutes.
Relieve the pressure, uncover the instant pot and add the chickpeas, pepper, onion, garlic, pepper, cumin, salt, pepper, cayenne and broth. Stir, cover the Instant Pot and cook in the Bean / Chili setting for 5 minutes. You release the pressure naturally for about 10 minutes, then uncover the Instant Pot again, mix the pepper, divide it between the plates and serve.

Nutrition:
Calories: 224, Fat: 7.7 g, Fiber: 6.1 g, Carbs: 18 g, Proteins: 19.7 g

264. Chicken Romano *IP*

Preparation time: 10 minutes | **Cooking time:** 15 minutes | **Servings:** 2

Ingredients:
- 6 chicken thighs, boneless and skinless and cut into medium chunks
- Salt and ground black pepper, to taste
- 10 oz. tomato sauce
- 1 teaspoon white wine vinegar
- 1 tablespoon dried oregano
- 1 teaspoon dried basil
- 1 yellow onion, peeled and chopped
- ½ cup white flour
- 2 tablespoons vegetable oil
- 1 tablespoon sugar
- 4 oz. mushrooms, sliced
- 1 teaspoon garlic, minced
- 1 teaspoon chicken bouillon granules
- 1 cup Romano cheese, grated

Directions:
Put the Instant Pot in the sauté mode, add the oil and heat. Add the chicken pieces, stir and brown 2 minutes
Add onion and garlic, mix and cook for 3 minutes. Add salt, pepper, flour and mix well.
Add the tomato sauce, vinegar, mushrooms, sugar, oregano, basil and broth, mix, cover and cook for 10 minutes in the poultry mixture. Release the pressure naturally for about 10 minutes, uncover the Instant Pot, add the cheese, mix, divide between the dishes and serve.

Nutrition:
Calories: 450, Fat: 11 g, Fiber: 1 g, Carbs: 24.2 g, Proteins: 61.2 g

265. Filipino Chicken *IP*

Preparation time: 10 minutes | **Cooking time:** 15 minutes | **Servings:** 2

Ingredients:
- 5 lbs. chicken thighs
- Salt and ground black pepper, to taste
- 4 garlic cloves, minced
- 3 bay leaves
- ½ cup white vinegar
- 1 teaspoon black peppercorns, crushed
- ½ cup soy sauce

Directions:
Set the instant pot to Poultry mode, add chicken, vinegar, soy sauce, salt, pepper, garlic, pepper and bay leaves, stir, cover and cook for 15 minutes.
Release the pressure naturally for about 10 minutes, then uncover the Instant Pot, throw away the bay leaves, stir, divide the chicken between the plates and serve.

Nutrition:
Calories: 430, Fat: 19.2 g, Fiber: 1 g, Carbs: 2.4 g, Proteins: 76 g

266. Chicken in Tomatillo Sauce IP

Preparation time: 10 minutes | **Cooking time:** 15 minutes | **Servings:** 2

Ingredients:

4 oz. canned chopped green chilies	1 lb. chicken thighs, skinless and boneless
2 tablespoons extra virgin olive oil	1 yellow onion, peeled and sliced thinly
1 garlic clove, peeled and crushed	½ cup cilantro, diced
5 oz. tomatoes, cored and chopped	15 oz. cheddar cheese, grated
Salt and ground black pepper, to taste	15 oz. canned tomatillos, chopped
5 oz. canned garbanzo beans, drained	15 oz. rice, already cooked
4 oz. black olives, pitted and chopped	

Directions:
Put the Instant Pot in the sauté mode, add the oil and heat. Add the onion, mix and cook for 5 minutes. Add the garlic, mix and cook for 15 seconds.
Add the chicken, peppers, salt, pepper, coriander and tomatillos, stir, cover the Instant Pot and cook in Poultry mode for 8 minutes. Release the pressure, uncover the Instant Pot, remove the chicken and Shred it.
Put the chicken back in the pan, add the rice, the beans, put the Instant Pot in the Saute mode and cook for 1 minute.
Add the cheese, tomatoes and olives, mix, cook for 2 minutes, divide between the dishes and serve.

Nutrition:
Calories: 245, Fat: 11.4 g, Fiber: 1.3 g, Carbs: 14.2 g, Proteins: 20 g

267. Beer Coated Duck Breast AF

Preparation time: 15 minutes | **Cooking time:** 20 minutes | **Servings:** 2

Ingredients:

1 tablespoon fresh thyme, chopped	1 cup beer
1: 10½-oz. duck breast	6 cherry tomatoes
1 tablespoon olive oil	1 teaspoon mustard
Salt and ground black pepper, as required	1 tablespoon balsamic vinegar

Directions:
Preheat the Air fryer to 390°F and grease an Air fryer basket.
Mix the olive oil, mustard, thyme, beer, salt, and black pepper in a bowl.
Coat the duck breasts generously with marinade and refrigerate, covered for about 4 hours.
Cover the duck breasts and arrange into the Air fryer basket.
Cook for about 15 minutes and remove the foil from breast.
Set the Air fryer to 355°F and place the duck breast and tomatoes into the Air Fryer basket.
Cook for about 5 minutes and dish out the duck breasts and cherry tomatoes.
Drizzle with vinegar and serve immediately.

Nutrition:
Calories: 332, Fat: 13.7 g, Carbs: 9.2 g, Sugar: 2.5 g, Protein: 34.6 g, Sodium: 88 mg

268. Duck Breast with Figs AF

Preparation time: 20 minutes | **Cooking time:** 45 minutes | **Servings:** 2

Ingredients:

1 lb. boneless duck breast	6 fresh figs, halved

1 tablespoon fresh thyme, chopped
2 tablespoons lemon juice
1 teaspoon olive oil
2 cups fresh pomegranate juice
3 tablespoons brown sugar
Salt and black pepper, as required

Directions:
Preheat the Air fryer to 400°F and grease an Air fryer basket.
Put the pomegranate juice, lemon juice, and brown sugar in a medium saucepan over medium heat.
Bring to a boil and simmer on low heat for about 25 minutes.
Season the duck breasts generously with salt and black pepper.
Arrange the duck breasts into the Air fryer basket, skin side up and cook for about 14 minutes, flipping once in between.
Dish out the duck breasts onto a cutting board for about 10 minutes.
Meanwhile, put the figs, olive oil, salt, and black pepper in a bowl until well mixed.
Set the Air fryer to 400°F and arrange the figs into the Air fryer basket.
Cook for about 5 more minutes and dish out in a platter.
Put the duck breast with the roasted figs and drizzle with warm pomegranate juice mixture.
Garnish with fresh thyme and serve warm.

Nutrition:
Calories: 699, Fat: 12.1 g, Carbs: 90 g, Sugar: 74 g, Protein: 519 g, Sodium: 110 mg

269. Herbed Duck Legs   AF

Preparation time: 10 minutes | **Cooking time:** 30 minutes | **Servings:** 2

Ingredients:
½ tablespoon fresh thyme, chopped
2 duck legs
1 teaspoon five spice powder
½ tablespoon fresh parsley, chopped
1 garlic clove, minced
Salt and black pepper, as required

Directions:
Preheat the Air fryer to 340°F and grease an Air fryer basket.
Mix the garlic, herbs, five spice powder, salt, and black pepper in a bowl.
Rub the duck legs with garlic mixture generously and arrange into the Air fryer basket.
Cook for about 25 minutes and set the Air fryer to 390°F.
Cook for 5 more minutes and dish out to serve hot.

Nutrition:
Calories: 138, Fat: 4.5 g, Carbs: 1 g, Protein: 25 g, Sodium: 82 mg

270. Chicken Wings with Prawn Paste   AF

Preparation time: 20 minutes | **Cooking time:** 8 minutes | **Servings:** 2

Ingredients:
Corn flour, as required
2 tablespoons prawn paste
1½ teaspoons sugar
1 teaspoon Shaoxing wine
2 lbs. mid-joint chicken wings
4 tablespoons olive oil
2 teaspoons sesame oil
2 teaspoons fresh ginger juice

Directions:
Preheat the Air fryer to 360°F and grease an Air fryer basket.
Mix all the ingredients in a bowl except wings and corn flour.
Rub the chicken wings generously with marinade and refrigerate overnight.
Coat the chicken wings evenly with corn flour and keep aside.
Set the Air fryer to 390°F and arrange the chicken wings in the Air fryer basket.
Cook for about 8 minutes and dish out to serve hot.

Nutrition:
Calories: 416, Fat: 31.5 g, Carbs: 11.2 g, Sugar: 1.6 g, Protein: 24.4 g, Sodium: 661 mg

271. Spicy Green Crusted Chicken

Preparation time: 10 minutes | **Cooking time:** 40 minutes | **Servings:** 2

Ingredients:
- 6 eggs, beaten
- 4 teaspoons thyme
- 6 teaspoons oregano
- 4 teaspoons paprika
- 6 teaspoons parsley
- 1 lb. chicken pieces
- Salt and freshly ground black pepper, to taste

Directions:
Preheat the Air fryer to 360°F and grease an Air fryer basket.
Whisk eggs in a bowl and mix all the ingredients in another bowl except chicken pieces.
Dip the chicken in eggs and then coat generously with the dry mixture.
Arrange half of the chicken pieces in the Air fryer basket and cook for about 20 minutes.
Repeat with the remaining mixture and dish out to serve hot.

Nutrition:
Calories: 218, Fat: 10.4 g, Carbs: 2.6 g, Sugar: 0.6 g, Protein: 27.9 g, Sodium: 128 mg

272. Creamy Chicken Tenders AF

Preparation time: 15 minutes | **Cooking time:** 20 minutes | **Servings:** 2

Ingredients:
- 2 lbs. chicken tenders
- 4 tablespoons olive oil
- Salt and black pepper, to taste
- 1 cup feta cheese
- 1 cup cream

Directions:
Preheat the Air fryer to 340°F and grease an Air fryer basket.
Season the chicken tenders with salt and black pepper.
Arrange the chicken tenderloins in the Air fryer basket and drizzle with olive oil.\
Cook for about 15 minutes and set the Air fryer to 390°F.
Cook for about 5 more minutes and dish out to serve warm.
Repeat with the remaining mixture and dish out to serve hot.

Nutrition:
Calories: 344, Fat: 21.1 g, Carbs: 1.7 g, Sugar: 1.4 g, Protein: 35.7 g, Sodium: 317 mg

273. Chicken Breasts with Chimichurri

Preparation time: 15 minutes | **Cooking time:** 35 minutes | **Servings:** 2

Ingredients:
- 1 chicken breast, bone-in, skin-on
- ½ bunch fresh cilantro
- ½ shallot, peeled, cut in quarters
- ½ tablespoon chili powder
- ½ teaspoon black pepper, ground
- 1 teaspoon salt
- ½ teaspoon cumin ground
- Chimichurri
- 4 garlic cloves, peeled
- 1 teaspoon kosher salt
- Chimichurri
- ¼ bunch fresh parsley
- ½ tablespoon paprika ground
- ½ tablespoon fennel ground
- ½ teaspoon onion powder
- ½ teaspoon garlic powder
- ½ tablespoon canola oil
- 2 tablespoons olive oil
- Zest and juice of 1 lemon

Directions:
Preheat the Air fryer to 300°F and grease an Air fryer basket.
Combine all the spices in a suitable bowl and season the chicken with it.
Sprinkle with canola oil and arrange the chicken in the Air fryer basket.
Cook for about 35 minutes and dish out in a platter.
Put all the ingredients in the blender and blend until smooth.
Serve the chicken with chimichurri sauce.

Nutrition:
Calories: 140, Fats: 7.9 g, Carbs: 1.8 g, Sugar: 7.1 g, Proteins: 7.2 g, Sodium: 581 mg

274. Fried Chicken Thighs

Preparation time: 10 minutes | **Cooking time:** 25 minutes | **Servings:** 2

Ingredients:
- ½ cup almond flour
- 1 egg beaten

Ingredients:
- 4 small chicken thighs
- 1 teaspoon seasoning salt
- 1½ tablespoons Old Bay Cajun Seasoning

Directions:
Preheat the Air fryer to 400°F for 3 minutes and grease an Air fryer basket.
Whisk the egg in a shallow bowl and place the old bay, flour and salt in another bowl.
Dip the chicken in the egg and coat with the flour mixture.
Arrange the chicken thighs in the Air fryer basket and cook for about 25 minutes.
Dish out in a platter and serve warm.

Nutrition:
Calories: 180, Fat: 20 g, Carbs: 3 g, Sugar: 1.2 g, Protein: 21 g, Sodium: 686 mg

275. Sweet Sriracha Turkey Legs AF

Preparation time: 10 minutes | **Cooking time:** 35 minutes | **Servings:** 2

Ingredients:
- 1-lb. turkey legs
- 1 tablespoon cilantro
- 1 tablespoon scallions
- 1½ tablespoons soy sauce
- 1 tablespoon butter
- 1 tablespoon chives
- 4 tablespoons sriracha sauce
- ½ lime, juiced

Directions:
Preheat the Air fryer on Roasting mode to 360°F for 3 minutes and grease an Air fryer basket.
Arrange the turkey legs in the Air fryer basket and cook for about 30 minutes, flipping several times in between.
Mix butter, scallions, sriracha sauce, soy sauce and lime juice in the saucepan and cook for about for 3 minutes until the sauce thickens.
Drizzle this sauce over the turkey legs and garnish with cilantro and chives to serve.

Nutrition:
Calories: 361, Fat: 16.3 g, Carbs: 9.3 g, Sugar: 18.2 g, Protein: 33.3 g, Sodium: 515 mg

276. Gyro Seasoned Chicken AF

Preparation time: 10 minutes | **Cooking time:** 30 minutes | **Servings:** 2

Ingredients:
- 2 lbs. chicken thighs
- 2 tablespoons primal palate super gyro seasoning
- 1 tablespoon Himalayan pink salt
- 1 tablespoon avocado oil
- 2 tablespoons primal palate new bae seasoning

Directions:
Preheat the Air fryer to 350°F and grease an Air fryer basket.
Rub the chicken with avocado oil and half of the spices.
Arrange the chicken thighs in the Air fryer basket and cook for about 25 minutes, flipping once in between.
Sprinkle the remaining seasoning and cook for 5 more minutes.
Dish out and serve warm.

Nutrition:
Calories: 545, Fat: 36.4 g, Carbs: 0.7 g, Protein: 42.5 g, Sodium: 272 mg

277. Chicken Curry

Preparation time: 10-20 minutes | **Cooking time:** 15-30 minutes | **Servings:** 2

Ingredients:
- 600g chicken breast
- 2 carrots
- 200 ml of fresh cream
- Salt to taste
- Flour
- 1 onion
- 150 ml
- 100 ml of milk
- 2 spoons of curry

Directions:
Chop the onion in a food processor and cut the carrots into cubes or slices.
Spray the basket and distribute the onion and carrots evenly in the basket.
Brown for 5 minutes at 150°C.
Add the floured chicken, cut into small pieces, the broth, salt, and simmer for another 5 min.
Finally pour the fresh cream, the milk and finish cooking for another 15 min. Ideal accompanied with basmati rice.

Nutrition:
Calories: 243, Fat: 11 g, Carbs: 7.5 g, Sugars: 2 g, Protein: 28 g, Cholesterol: 74 mg

278. Chicken with Yogurt and Mustard

Preparation time: 10 - 20 minutes | **Cooking time:** 15 – 30 minutes | **Servings:** 2

Ingredients:
- 500 g chicken breast
- 40 g mustard
- Salt to taste
- 100 g of white yogurt
- 1 shallot
- Pepper to taste

Directions:
Place the chopped shallot inside the basket previously greased.
Brown for 3 minutes at 150°C.
Add the chicken pieces, salt, pepper and cook for another 15 minutes at 180°C.
Then pour the mustard and yogurt and cook for another 5 minutes.

Nutrition:
Calories: 287.1, Fat: 8.9 g, Carbs: 4.3 g, Sugars: 1.7 g, Protein: 43.6 g, Cholesterol: 99.9 mg

279. Almond Chicken

Preparation time: 10 – 20 minutes | **Cooking time:** 15 – 30 minutes | **Servings:** 2

Ingredients:
- 500 g chicken breast
- ½ onion
- 60 g of soy sauce
- 130g crushed almonds
- 1 tbsp grated fresh ginger
- Water

Directions:
Pour the almonds into the basket.
Roast the almonds for 5 minutes at 150°C.
Remove the almonds and pour the chopped onion and ginger, the oil into the tank and brown for about 2 minutes.
Add lightly floured chicken, salt, pepper and cook for additional 13 minutes.
Pour the soy sauce, a ladle of hot water, the roasted almonds and simmer for additional 5 minutes.

Nutrition:
Calories: 458, Fat: 34 g, Carbs: 22 g, Sugars: 7.3 g, Protein: 20 g, Cholesterol: 24 mg

280. Mushroom Chicken

Preparation time: 10-20 minutes | **Cooking time:** 15-30 minutes | **Servings:** 2

Ingredients:
- 500 g chicken breast
- 100 g of fresh cream
- 300g Mushroom
- 1 shallot

Directions:
Cut the chicken into pieces and sliced mushrooms. Spray the basket and chopped shallot into the basket. Set the temperature to 150°C and lightly brown for 5 minutes.
Add the mushrooms and cook for additional 6 minutes.
Finally pour the chicken, salt, pepper, and simmer for another 10 minutes.
Then add the fresh cream and cook for 5 min. until the sauce has thickened.

Nutrition:
Calories: 220, Fat: 14 g, Carbs: 11 g, Sugar: 4 g, Protein: 12 g, Cholesterol: 50 mg

281. Braised Duck and Potatoes

Preparation time: 10 minutes | **Cooking time:** 20 minutes | **Servings:** 2

Ingredients:
- 1 potato, cut into cubes
- Ground black pepper, to taste
- 4 garlic cloves, peeled and minced
- 4 tablespoons sugar
- 4 tablespoons sherry wine
- Salt, to taste
- 2 duck breasts, boneless, skinless, and cut into small chunks
- 1-inch ginger root, peeled and sliced
- 4 tablespoons soy sauce
- 2 green onions, roughly chopped
- ¼ cup water

Directions:
Put Instant Pot in Stir-Fry mode, add the duck, stir and brown for a few minutes. Add garlic, ginger, green onion, soy sauce, sugar, wine, water and a pinch of salt and pepper, mix, cover, place the Instant Pot in poultry mode and cook for 18 minutes.

Release the pressure, uncover the instant pot, add the potatoes, stir, cover and cook for 5 minutes.

Relieve the pressure, divide the braised duck between the plates and serve.

Nutrition:
Calories: 238, Fat: 18 g, Carbs: 1 g, Proteins: 19 g

282. Goat with Roasted Tomatoes

Preparation time: 10 minutes | **Cooking time:** 60 minutes | **Servings:** 2

Ingredients:

4 oz. tomato paste	17 oz. goat meat, cubed
1 carrot, peeled and chopped	1 celery rib, chopped
1 yellow onion, peeled and chopped	3 garlic cloves, peeled and crushed
½ cup water	Sherry
Salt and ground black pepper, to taste	1 cup chicken stock
Dried rosemary	2 tablespoons extra virgin olive oil
1 tablespoon cumin	2 roasted tomatoes, cored chopped

Directions:
Put the instant pot in the sauté mode, add 1 tablespoon of oil and heat. Add the goat cheese, salt, pepper and brown for a few minutes on each side. Add cumin and rosemary, mix, cook 2 minutes and transfer to a bowl.

Add the remaining oil to the instant flask and heat. Add onion, garlic, salt and pepper, stir and cook for 1 minute. Add the carrot and celery, mix and cook for 2 minutes.

Add sherry, stock, water, goat cheese, tomato paste, more salt and pepper, mix, cover and cook over meat / stew for 40 minutes.

Release the pressure naturally, uncover the Instant Pot, add the tomatoes, mix, divide between the plates and serve.

Nutrition:
Calories: 340, Fat: 3.8 g, Fiber: 4.1 g, Carbs: 30 g, Proteins: 12.6 g

283. Goat and Potatoes

Preparation time: 10 minutes | **Cooking time:** 50 minutes | **Servings:** 2

Ingredients:

5 tablespoons vegetable oil	3 teaspoons turmeric
2½ lbs. goat meat, cut into small cubes	Salt and ground black pepper, to taste
4 cloves	3 cardamom pods
3 potatoes, cut into halves	1 teaspoon sugar
3 onions, peeled and chopped	2-inch cinnamon stick
4 garlic cloves, peeled and minced	2 green chilies, chopped
1-inch piece of ginger, grated	2 tomatoes, cored and chopped
1 teaspoon fresh cilantro, chopped	¾ teaspoon chili powder
2½ cups water	

Directions:
Place the goat in a bowl, add salt, pepper and turmeric, turn to cover and set aside for 10 minutes. Place the instant pot in the sauté mode, add the oil and half the sugar, mix and heat.

Add the potatoes, fry them a little and transfer them to a bowl. Add cloves, cinnamon stick and cardamom in the instant pot and mix. Add ginger, onion, pepper and garlic, mix and cook for 3 minutes. Add the tomato and pepper powder, mix and cook for 5 minutes.

Add the meat, mix and cook for 10 minutes. Add 2 cups of water, stir, cover and cook for 15 minutes in the Meat / Stew setting.

Release the pressure, uncover the Instant Pot, add more salt and pepper, the rest of the sugar, potatoes and ½ cup of water, cover and cook for 5 minutes in the Manual setting.

Release the pressure, uncover the Instant Pot, share the dishes, sprinkle with cilantro and serve.

Nutrition:
Calories: 300, Fat: 17 g, Fiber: 1 g, Carbs: 5 g, Proteins: 30 g

284. Apple Cider Pork

Preparation time: 10 minutes | **Cooking time:** 25 minutes | **Servings:** 2

Ingredients:
2 tablespoons extra virgin olive oil
Salt and ground black pepper, to taste
1 yellow onion, peeled and chopped
2 apples, cored and chopped
2 lbs. pork loin
2 cups apple cider
1 tablespoon dried onion flakes

Directions:
Put the instant pot in the sauté mode, add the oil and heat. Add the pork loin, salt, pepper and dried onion, mix and brown the meat on all sides and transfer to a plate.
Add the onion to the instant pot, stir and cook for 2 minutes. Put the meat back in the Instant Pot, add the cider, apples, more salt and pepper, stir, cover and cook in manual mode for 20 minutes.
Release the pressure, uncover the Instant Pot, transfer the pork to a cutting board, cut it and divide it between the plates. Add the sauce and mix the Instant Pot on the side and serve.

Nutrition:
Calories: 450, Fat: 22 g, Fiber: 2.2 g, Carbs: 29 g, Proteins: 37.2 g

285. Pork Chops and Onion

Preparation time: 10 minutes | **Cooking time:** 15 minutes | **Servings:** 2

Ingredients:
2 tablespoons fresh parsley, chopped
4 pork chops
½ cup milk
2 tablespoons butter
1 lb. onions, peeled and sliced
2 tablespoons cornstarch mixed with
1 tablespoon white flour
1 garlic clove, peeled and minced
2 tablespoons lime juice
Salt and ground black pepper, to taste
2 tablespoons extra virgin olive oil
½ cup white wine
3 tablespoons water

Directions:
Place the instant pot in the sauté mode, add the oil and butter and heat. Add the pork chops, salt and pepper, brown them on all sides and transfer them to a bowl.
Include the onion and garlic in the pan, stir and cook for 2 minutes. Add the wine, lemon juice, milk, parsley and return the pork chops to the pan. Stir, cover and cook in manual setting for 15 minutes.
Relieve the pressure, uncover the Instant Pot, add the dough and cornstarch flour, mix well and cook, in Manual mode for 3 minutes. Divide the pork chops and onions between the dishes, season the sauce everywhere and serve.

Nutrition:
Calories: 222, Fat: 7 g, Fiber: 3 g, Carbs: 9 g, Proteins: 22.2 g

286. Creamy pork chops

Preparation time: 10 minutes | **Cooking time:** 20 minutes | **Servings:** 2

Ingredients:
2 tablespoons extra virgin olive oil
10 oz. canned cream of mushroom soup
1 cup water
½ small bunch fresh parsley, chopped
2 teaspoons chicken bouillon
4 pork chops, boneless
1 cup sour cream
Salt and ground black pepper, to taste

Directions:
Put the instant pot in the sauté mode, add the oil and heat. Add the pork chops, salt and pepper, brown them on all sides, transfer them to a plate and set aside. Add water and broth to the instant flask and mix well.
Return the pork chops, mix, cover and cook manually for 9 minutes. Release the pressure naturally, transfer the pork chops to a plate and set aside. Place the instant cooker in manual mode and heat the cooking liquid.
Add the mushroom soup, mix, and cook for 2 minutes and remove from heat. Add the parsley and sour cream, mix and pour over the pork chops.

Nutrition:
Calories: 284, Fat: 16 g, Fiber: 1 g, Carbs: 10.5 g, Proteins: 23.2 g

287. Beef and Barley Soup

Preparation time: 10 minutes | **Cooking time:** 25 minutes | **Servings:** 2

Ingredients:

- Salt and ground black pepper, to taste
- 1 cup celery, diced
- 2 tablespoons vegetable oil
- 6 cups beef stock
- 1 cup onion, diced
- ½ teaspoon dried thyme
- 1 cup water
- 10 cremini mushrooms, cut into quarters
- 1 ½ lbs. beef stew meat, chopped
- 8 garlic cloves, peeled and minced
- 1 cup carrots, diced
- 2 bay leaves
- 1 potato, chopped
- ⅔ cup barley

Directions:

Put the Instant Pot in the sauté mode, add the oil and heat. Add the meat, salt and pepper, mix, cook 3 minutes and transfer to a plate.

Add the mushrooms, mix and brown for 2 minutes and transfer to a plate.

Add the onion, celery and carrots to the Instant Pot, stir and cook for 4 minutes. Return the meat and mushrooms to the Instant Pot and stir.

Add the bay leaves, thyme, water, stock, salt and pepper, mix, cover and cook for 16 minutes in the Manual setting.

Release the pressure, uncover the Instant Pot, and add the potatoes and barley, mix, cover and cook in the manual for 1 hour.

Relieve the pressure, mix the soup, divide it into bowls and serve.

Nutrition:

Calories: 120, Fat: 3 g, Fiber: 2 g, Carbs: 11 g, Proteins: 5 g

288. Beef stew

Preparation time: 10 minutes | **Cooking time:** 30 minutes | **Servings:** 2

Ingredients:

- 1 yellow onion, peeled and chopped
- 1 tablespoon vegetable oil
- 8 potatoes, cubed
- 5 carrots, peeled and chopped
- 2 lbs. beef stew, cubed
- 2 teaspoons cornstarch
- 2 beef bouillon cubes
- 2 cups water
- Salt and ground black pepper, to taste

Directions:

Put the Instant Pot in the sauté mode, add the oil and heat. Add the meat and onion, stir and cook until golden on all sides. Add the carrot, water and broth, mix, cover and cook in soup mode for 20 minutes.

Put the water in a pan, add a little salt, bring to a boil over medium-high heat, add the potatoes, cook for 10 minutes and drain.

Release the pressure, uncover the Instant Pot and set it to manual mode.

Add the cornstarch mixed with a little water, salt, pepper and potatoes, mix, bring to a boil, remove the heat and divide the stew between the dishes.

Nutrition:

Calories: 300, Fat: 12 g, Fiber: 5 g, Carbs: 1 g, Proteins: 25 g

289. Glazed Chicken and Apples

Preparation time: 30 minutes | **Cooking time:** 30 minutes | **Servings:** 2

Ingredients:

- 3 Apples, sliced and core
- 1 tbsp. Chopped rosemary
- Black pepper
- ⅔ cup Apple cider
- 2 tbsp. Honey
- 2 tbsp. Olive oil
- Salt
- 6 skin-on Chicken thighs
- 1 tbsp. Mustard

Directions:

Heat greased pan over medium heat, add cider, honey, and mustard then whisk it. Let it simmer. Toss in chicken, apples, salt, pepper, and rosemary, cook in the air fryer for 17 minutes at 390°F. Then serve hot

Nutrition:

Calories: 281, Fat: 11 g, Fiber: 12 g, Carbs: 28 g, Protein: 19 g

290. Lemon Chicken and Asparagus

Preparation time: 20 minutes | **Cooking time:** 30 minutes | **Servings:** 2

Ingredients:
- 2 tbsp. Olive oil
- 1 tbsp. Dried oregano
- 1 lb. Chicken thigh
- Black pepper
- 1 Zucchini, roughly cubed
- Juice from 1 lemon
- 3 Minced garlic cloves
- Salt
- ½ lb. Asparagus, trimmed and halved
- 1 Lemon, sliced

Directions:
Mix all the ingredients in a pan, cook for 15 minutes in the air fryer at 380°F. Serve hot.

Nutrition:
Calories: 280, Fat: 8 g, Fiber: 12 g, Carbs: 20 g, Protein: 15 g

291. Turkey with Fig Sauce

Preparation time: 40 minutes | **Cooking time:** 30 minutes | **Servings:** 2

Ingredients:
- 2 Turkey breasts, halved
- ½ tbsp. Garlic powder
- Salt
- 1 cup Chicken stock
- 1 shallot, chopped
- 4 tbsp. Chopped figs
- 1 tbsp. Olive oil
- ¼ tbsp. Sweet paprika:
- Black pepper
- 3 tbsp. Melted butter
- ½ cup Red wine
- 1 tbsp. White flour

Directions:
Heat a greased pan over medium heat. Add shallots and cook for 2 minutes. Add garlic powder, paprika, stock, salt, pepper, wine, and the figs then stir and cook for 8 minutes
Add flour and stir. Cook for 2 minutes. Turn off the heat. This is the seasoning sauce
Use salt and pepper to season the turkey. Drizzle oil over it, cook for 8 minutes each side in the air fryer at 380°F
Top it with the sauce and serve hot.

Nutrition:
Calories 246, Fat: 12 g, Fiber: 4 g, Carbs: 22 g, Protein: 16 g

292. Simple Garlic and Lemon Chicken

Preparation time: 25 minutes | **Cooking time:** 30 minutes | **Servings:** 2

Ingredients:
- 4 Chicken breasts, boneless and skinless
- 2 tbsp. Lemon juice
- Black pepper
- 1 ½ tbsp. Avocado oil
- 4 Garlic heads, peeled with cloves separated and cut into quarters
- Salt
- ½ tbsp. Lemon pepper

Directions:
Mix all the ingredients in a bowl, cook for 15 minutes in the air fryer at 360°F. Serve hot.

Nutrition:
Calories: 240, Fat: 7 g, Fiber: 1 g, Carbs: 17 g, Protein: 18 g

293. Tarragon Chicken Breasts

Preparation time: 25 minutes | **Cooking time:** 30 minutes | **Servings:** 2

Ingredients:
- 2 Chicken breast, skinless and boneless
- ¼ cup Soy sauce
- 8 Chopped tarragon sprigs
- Black pepper
- 1 cup White wine
- 2 Minced garlic cloves
- Salt
- 1 tbsp. Melted butter

Directions:
Mix chicken, wine, soy sauce, garlic, tarragon, salt, pepper, and the butter in a bowl and let it sit aside for 10 minutes
Transfer to a greased pan and cook in the air fryer for 8 minutes each side at 370°F. Serve hot

Nutrition:
Calories: 271, Fat: 12 g, Fiber: 3 g, Carbs: 17 g, Protein: 15 g

294. Chicken and Pear Sauce

Preparation time: 30 minutes | **Cooking time:** 30 minutes | **Servings:** 2

Ingredients:
- 3 cups Ketchup
- ¼ cup Honey
- 1 tbsp. Chili powder
- Salt
- 1 tbsp. Garlic powder
- 1 cup Pear jelly
- ½ tbsp. Smoked paprika
- 1 tbsp. Mustard powder
- Black pepper
- 6 Chicken breasts, skinless and boneless

Directions:
Using salt and pepper, season the chicken, cook for in the air fryer for 10 minutes at 350°F
Heat a greased pan over medium heat. Add pear jelly, honey, smoked paprika, chili powder, mustard powder, garlic powder, Salt, and pepper and whisk then let it cook for 6 minutes
Toss the chicken in it and cook for 4 minutes. Serve hot

Nutrition:
Calories: 283, Fat: 13 g, Fiber: 7 g, Carbs: 19 g, Protein: 17 g

295. Honey Chicken and Dates

Preparation time: 35 minutes | **Cooking time:** 30 minutes | **Servings:** 2

Ingredients:
- 1 Whole chicken, cut into medium pieces
- ⅓ cup Honey
- Black pepper
- 4 Chopped dates
- ¾ cup Water
- Salt
- ¼ cup Olive oil

Directions:
Simmer the water in a pot over medium heat. Add honey and whisk then take off the heat
Use oil to rub the chicken then season it using salt and pepper
Place it in the air fryer basket. Cook it in the air fryer for 10 minutes at 350°F
Brush the chicken with honey and cook for 6 minutes each side. Serve it hot

Nutrition:
Calories: 270, Fat: 14 g, Fiber: 3 g, Carbs: 15 g, Protein: 20 g

296. Chicken and Leeks

Preparation time: 40 minutes | **Cooking time:** 30 minutes | **Servings:** 2

Ingredients:
- 4 Chicken thighs, bone-in
- Black pepper
- 1 cup Chicken stock
- 2 tbsp. Chopped chives
- Salt
- 1 tbsp. Olive oil
- 3 sliced Leeks

Directions:
Heat a greased pan over medium heat. Add stock, leeks and carrots and cover it. Let it cook for 20 minutes
Using salt and pepper, season the chicken. Rub it with olive oil. Cook it in the air fryer for 4 minutes at 350°F.
Place the chicken in the leeks mix. Serve it hot.

Nutrition:
Calories: 237, Fat: 10 g, Fiber: 4 g, Carbs: 19 g, Protein: 16 g

297. Chicken and Yogurt Mix

Preparation time: 1 hour and 15 minutes | **Cooking time:** 30 minutes | **Servings:** 2

Ingredients:
- 17 oz. Chicken meat, boneless and cubed
- 1 Green bell pepper, deseeded and cubed
- 14 oz. Yogurt
- Black pepper
- 1 tbsp. Grated ginger
- 2 tbsp. Coriander powder
- 1 tbsp. Turmeric powder
- 3 Mint leaves, torn
- 1 Red bell pepper, deseeded and cubed
- 1 Yellow bell pepper, deseeded and cubed
- Salt
- 3 ½ oz. Cherry tomato, halved
- 2 tbsp. Red chili powder
- 2 tbsp. Olive oil
- 2 tbsp. Cumin powder

Directions:
Toss and mix all the ingredients in a bowl. Keep it in the fridge for 1 hour
Place them in a pan. Cook them in the air fryer for 8 minutes each side at 400°F. Serve hot

Nutrition:
Calories: 245, Fat: 4 g, Fiber: 5 g, Carbs: 17 g, Protein: 16 g

298. Air Fried Chicken Wings

Preparation time: 55 minutes | **Cooking time:** 30 minutes | **Servings:** 2

Ingredients:
- 16 Chicken wings
- Black pepper
- ¼ cup Clover honey
- Salt
- ¼ cup Melted butter
- 4 tbsp. Minced garlic

Directions:
Season chicken wings using the salt and pepper then place it in the air fryer basket. Cook for 25 minutes in the air fryer at 380°F then for 5 minutes at 400°F heat a greased pan over medium heat

Add garlic and sauté for 5 minutes. Add salt, pepper, the air fried chicken and the honey then stir and let it simmer for 10 minutes

Place the chicken in the pan and let it sit or a few minutes. Serve it hot.

Nutrition:
Calories: 274, Fat: 11 g, Fiber: 3 g, Carbs: 19 g, Protein: 15 g

299. Tomato Duck Breast

Preparation time: 25 minutes | **Cooking time:** 30 minutes | **Servings:** 2

Ingredients:
- 1 Smoked duck breast
- 1 tbsp. Tomato paste
- 1 tbsp. Honey
- ½ tbsp. Apple vinegar

Directions:
Toss and mix all the ingredients in a bowl, cook for 10 minutes each side in the air fryer at 370°F. Cut it into halves and serve hot.

Nutrition:
Calories: 274, Fat: 11 g, Fiber: 3 g, Carbs: 22 g, Protein: 13 g

300. Turkey, Mushrooms and Peas Casserole

Preparation time: 25 minutes | **Cooking time:** 30 minutes | **Servings:** 2

Ingredients:
- 2 lbs. turkey breasts, skinless, boneless
- 1 celery stalk, chopped.
- 1 cup chicken stock
- 1 cup bread cubes
- 1 yellow onion, chopped
- ½ cup peas
- 1 cup cream of mushrooms soup
- Salt and black pepper to the taste

Directions:
In a pan that fits your air fryer, mix turkey with salt, pepper, onion, celery, peas and stock, introduce in your air fryer and cook at 360°F, for 15 minutes.

Add bread cubes and cream of mushroom soup, stir toss and cook at 360°F, for 5 minutes more. Divide among plates and serve hot.

Nutrition:
Calories: 271, Fat: 9 g, Fiber: 9 g, Carbs: 16 g, Protein: 7 g

301. Duck Breast with Fig Sauce Recipe

Preparation time: 25 minutes | **Cooking time:** 30 minutes | **Servings:** 2

Ingredients:
- 2 duck breasts, skin on, halved
- 1 tbsp. olive oil
- ½ cup port wine
- ¼ tsp. sweet paprika
- 3 tbsp. butter, melted
- 4 tbsp. fig preserves
- 1 tbsp. white flour
- ½ tsp. thyme, chopped
- ½ tsp. garlic powder
- 1 cup beef stock
- 1 shallot, chopped
- Salt and black pepper to the taste

Directions:
Season duck breasts with salt and pepper, drizzle half of the melted butter, rub well, put in your air fryer's basket and cook at 350°F, for 5 minutes on each side.

Meanwhile, heat up a pan with the olive oil and the rest of the butter over medium high heat, add shallot, stir and cook for 2 minutes.

Add thyme, garlic powder, paprika, stock, salt, pepper, wine and figs, stir and cook for 7-8 minutes.

Add flour, stir well, cook until sauce thickens a bit and take off heat.

Divide duck breasts on plates, drizzle figs sauce all over and serve.

Nutrition:
Calories: 246, Fat: 12 g, Fiber: 4 g, Carbs: 22 g, Protein: 3 g

302. Chicken Thighs and Baby Potatoes

Preparation time: 25 minutes | **Cooking time:** 40 minutes | **Servings:** 2

Ingredients:

8 chicken thighs	2 tbsp. olive oil
1 lb. baby potatoes, halved	2 tsp. oregano, dried
2 tsp. rosemary, dried	2 garlic cloves, minced
1 red onion, chopped	2 tsp. thyme, chopped.
½ tsp. sweet paprika	Salt and black pepper to the taste

Directions:
In a bowl, mix chicken thighs with potatoes, salt, pepper, thyme, paprika, onion, rosemary, garlic, oregano and oil.

Toss to coat, spread everything in a heat proof dish that fits your air fryer and cook at 400°F, for 30 minutes, shaking halfway. Divide among plates and serve.

Nutrition:
Calories: 364, Fat: 14 g, Fiber: 13 g, Carbs: 21 g, Protein: 34 g

303. Cream-Poached Pork Loin

Preparation time: 30 minutes | **Cooking time:** 4 hours | **Servings:** 2

Ingredients:

1 – 3 lbs. boneless pork loin roast	Kosher salt and pepper as needed
2 thinly sliced onion	¼ cup cognac
1 cup whole milk	1 cup heavy cream

Directions:
Prepare the Sous Vide water bath using your immersion circulator and raise the temperature to 145°F

Season the pork with pepper and salt, take a large iron skillet and place it over medium heat for 5 minutes.

Add the pork and sear for 15 minutes until all sides are browned.

Transfer to a platter, add the onion to the rendered fat (in the skillet) and cook for 5 minutes.

Add the cognac and bring to a simmer. Allow it to cool for 10 minutes.

Add the pork, onion, milk, and cream to a resealable zipper bag and seal using the immersion method. Submerge underwater and cook for 4 hours.

Once cooked, remove the bag from the water and take the pork out, transfer the pork to cutting board and cover it to keep it warm.

Pour the bag contents to a skillet and bring the mixture to a simmer over medium heat, keep cooking for 10 minutes and season with salt and pepper.

Slice the pork and serve with the cream sauce.

Nutrition:
Calories: 1809, Carbs: 23 g, Protein: 109 g, Fat: 140 g, Sugar: 19 g, Sodium: 621 mg

304. Hoisin Glazed Pork Tenderloin

Preparation time: 20 minutes | **Cooking time:** 3 hours | **Servings:** 2

Ingredients:

1-piece pork tenderloin, trimmed	1 teaspoon kosher salt
½ teaspoon freshly ground black pepper	3 tablespoons hoisin sauce

Directions:
Prepare the Sous Vide water bath using your immersion circulator and raise the temperature to 145°F.

Take the tenderloins and season it with pepper and salt and transfer to a resealable zip bag.

Seal using the immersion method and cook for 3 hours.
Remove the bag and then the pork, brush with hoisin sauce.
Heat up your grill to high grill and add the tenderloin, sear for 5 minutes until all sides are caramelized.
Allow it to rest and slice the tenderloin into medallions, serve!

Nutrition:
Calories: 287, Carbs: 13 g, Protein: 33 g, Fat: 11 g, Sugar: 7 g, Sodium: 417 mg

305. Beef and Tomato Mix

Preparation time: 10 minutes | **Cooking time:** 1 hour | **Servings:** 2

Ingredients:
- 1 lb. beef stew meat, ground
- ¼ tablespoon balsamic vinegar
- 1 tablespoon olive oil
- ½ teaspoon garam masala
- A pinch of salt and black pepper
- 1 cup cherry tomatoes, halved
- 1 red onion, chopped
- 1 teaspoon cumin, ground
- ½ teaspoon oregano, dried
- ¼ cup chives, chopped

Directions:
In a sous vide bag, mix the beef with the tomatoes, vinegar and the other ingredients, toss, seal the bag, submerge in the water oven and cook at 160°F for 1 hours.
Divide everything into bowls and serve.

Nutrition:
Calories: 354, Fat: 2 g, Fiber: 5 g, Carbs: 7 g, Protein: 2 g

306. Lentils and Quinoa Stew

Preparation time: 10 minutes | **Cooking time:** 30 minutes | **Servings:** 2

Ingredients:
- 1 cup canned lentils, drained and rinsed
- 1 zucchini, cubed
- 1 cup quinoa, cooked
- 1 yellow onion, chopped
- ½ cup tomato passata
- ½ teaspoon sweet paprika
- 1 tablespoon cilantro, chopped
- 1 tablespoon olive oil
- ½ teaspoon red pepper flakes, crushed
- Salt and black pepper to the taste

Directions:
In a sous vide bag, mix the lentils with the quinoa, zucchini and the other ingredients, toss, seal the bag and cook in the water oven at 160°F for 30 minutes.
Divide into bowls and serve for lunch.

Nutrition:
Calories: 263, Fat: 5 g, Fiber: 5 g, Carbs: 8 g, Protein: 5 g

307. Chickpeas Stew

Preparation time: 10 minutes | **Cooking time:** 30 minutes | **Servings:** 2

Ingredients:
- 2 cups canned chickpeas, drained
- 1 yellow onion, chopped
- Juice of 1 lime
- Salt and black pepper to the taste
- ½ teaspoon rosemary, dried
- ½ cup tomato passata
- 1 carrot, peeled and sliced
- ¼ cup dill, chopped
- ½ teaspoon sweet paprika

Directions:
In a sous vide bag, mix the chickpeas with the passata, onion and the other ingredients, toss, seal the bag and cook in the water oven at 160°F for 30 minutes.
Divide into bowls and serve.

Nutrition:
Calories: 264, Fat: 5 g, Fiber: 8 g, Carbs: 7 g, Protein: 3 g

308. Chickpeas Bowls

Preparation time: 10 minutes | **Cooking time:** 30 minutes | **Servings:** 2

Ingredients:
- 15 oz. canned chickpeas, drained
- 1 red onion, chopped

- 1 teaspoon curry powder
- 1 tablespoon olive oil
- ½ cup baby spinach
- 2 teaspoons ground turmeric
- A pinch of salt and black pepper
- 1 avocado, pitted, peeled and sliced

Directions:
Spread the chickpeas, onion and the other ingredients except the spinach on a lined baking sheet and bake at 350°F for 30 minutes.
Divide the spinach into bowls, add the chickpeas mix, toss and serve.

Nutrition:
Calories: 230, Fat: 5.4 g, Fiber: 7 g, Carbs: 7.6 g, Protein: 7 g

309. Broccoli Salad

Preparation time: 10 minutes | **Cooking time:** 15 minutes | **Servings:** 2

Ingredients:
- 1 lb. broccoli head, florets separated
- 1 cup baby spinach
- 3 tablespoons avocado oil
- A pinch of salt and black pepper
- 1 tablespoon lime juice
- 2 carrots, shredded
- 1 cup cherry tomatoes, halved
- 2 garlic cloves, minced
- Juice of ½ lemon

Directions:
Spread the broccoli on a lined baking sheet, add the rest of the ingredients, toss and cook at 360°F for 15 minutes.
Divide into bowls and serve for lunch.

Nutrition:
Calories: 182, Fat: 5.4 g, Fiber: 6 g, Carbs: 5.4 g, Protein: 6.6 g

310. Herbed Mushrooms

Preparation time: 10 minutes | **Cooking time:** 40 minutes | **Servings:** 2

Ingredients:
- 1 lb. white mushroom caps
- 2 sweet potatoes, cut into wedges
- 2 tablespoons avocado oil
- 1 teaspoon curry powder
- 1 cup chopped parsley
- 1 teaspoon hot paprika
- 1 tablespoon lemon juice
- 2 tablespoons Italian seasoning

Directions:
Spread the mushroom caps on a lined baking sheet, add the rest of the ingredients, toss and bake at 365°F for 40 minutes.
Divide between plates and serve for lunch.

Nutrition:
Calories: 241, Fat: 5.4 g, Fiber: 4.3 g, Carbs: 5.6 g, Protein: 5.4 g

311. Balsamic Sprouts

Preparation time: 10 minutes | **Cooking time:** 30 minutes | **Servings:** 2

Ingredients:
- 2 lb. Brussels sprouts, trimmed and halved
- 2 tablespoons olive oil
- 3 tablespoons balsamic vinegar
- 1 garlic clove, minced
- 1 teaspoon coriander, ground
- A pinch of salt and black pepper
- 1 small red onion, cubed
- 1 cup cherry tomatoes, halved
- 1 tablespoon mustard
- 1 teaspoon sweet paprika
- 1 teaspoon basil, dried

Directions:
Spread the sprouts on a lined baking sheet, add the onion and the other ingredients, toss and bake at 370°F for 30 minutes.
Divide into bowls and serve for lunch.

Nutrition:
Calories: 206, Fat: 6.1 g, Fiber: 6 g, Carbs: 7.4 g, Protein: 6.5 g

312. Mushroom Cream

Preparation time: 10 minutes | **Cooking time:** 30 minutes | **Servings:** 2

Ingredients:
- 1 yellow onion, chopped
- 1 tablespoon olive oil

6 garlic cloves, minced
1 teaspoon turmeric powder
1 teaspoon cumin, ground
5 cups veggie stock
1 lb. white mushrooms, sliced
1 teaspoon coriander, ground
A pinch of salt and black pepper
2 carrots, sliced

Directions:
Heat up a pot with the oil over medium heat, add the onion and garlic and cook for 5 minutes.
Add the mushrooms and cook for another 5 minutes.
Add the rest of the ingredients, stir, bring to a simmer and cook for 20 minutes more.
Blend using an immersion blender, divide into bowls and serve.

Nutrition:
Calories: 192, Fat: 7.4 g, Fiber: 8 g, Carbs: 16 g, Protein: 11.4 g

313. Lentils Cakes

Preparation time: 10 minutes | **Cooking time:** 10 minutes | **Servings:** 2

Ingredients:
2 garlic cloves, peeled
2 cups canned lentils, drained and rinsed
2 tablespoons almond flour
A pinch of salt and black pepper
3 tablespoons olive oil
1 yellow onion, peeled and chopped
2 tablespoons chives, chopped
1 teaspoon chili powder
A pinch of cayenne pepper

Directions:
In a blender, combine the garlic with lentils and the other ingredients except the oil and pulse well.
Shape the cakes and arrange them on a platter.
Heat up a pan with the oil over medium-high heat, add the cakes, cook for 4 minutes on each side and serve with a side salad.

Nutrition:
Calories: 261, Fat: 4 g, Fiber: 7 g, Carbs: 15 g, Protein: 7 g

314. Coconut and Lime Sweet Potatoes

Preparation time: 10 minutes | **Cooking time:** 45 minutes | **Servings:** 2

Ingredients:
1 lb. sweet potatoes, peeled and cubed
A pinch of salt and black pepper
1 teaspoon turmeric powder
Juice of 1 lime
2 tablespoons avocado oil
1 teaspoon cumin, ground
1 cup coconut cream
2 tablespoons chives, chopped

Directions:
Heat up a pan with the oil over medium heat, add sweet potatoes and cook for 5 minutes.
Add the rest of the ingredients except the chives, stir and simmer over medium heat for 40 minutes more.
Divide into bowls and serve with the chives sprinkled on top.

Nutrition:
Calories: 222, Fat: 6.2 g, Fiber: 7 g, Carbs: 6.5 g, Protein: 5.4 g

315. Lemony Cauliflower Soup

Preparation time: 10 minutes | **Cooking time:** 1 hour | **Servings:** 2

Ingredients:
1 lb. cauliflower florets
1 yellow onion, chopped
3 garlic cloves, minced
A pinch of salt and black pepper
32 oz. veggie stock
1 tablespoon chives, chopped
1 tablespoon olive oil
1 celery stalk, chopped
1 carrot, shredded
1 teaspoon turmeric powder
Juice of 3 small lemons

Directions:
Heat up a pot with the oil over medium heat, add the onion, garlic and celery and cook for 5 minutes.

Add the cauliflower, stir and cook for another 5 minutes.
Add the rest of the ingredients, cook for 40 minutes more, ladle into bowls and serve.

Nutrition:
Calories: 283, Fat: 4.5 g, Fiber: 6.1 g, Carbs: 7.6 g, Protein: 8 g

316. Spinach Bowls

Preparation time: 10 minutes | **Cooking time:** 0 minutes | **Servings:** 2

Ingredients:

- 3 cups spinach leaves, torn
- 1 tablespoon kalamata olives, pitted and chopped
- 1 cup cherry tomatoes, halved
- 1 teaspoon olive oil
- 3 tablespoons chives, chopped
- 1 tablespoon chopped parsley
- 1 tablespoon black olives, pitted and chopped
- 1 tablespoon capers, drained
- 1 tablespoon chopped red bell pepper
- salt and black pepper to the taste
- 2 tablespoons coconut cream

Directions:
In a bowl, mix the spinach with the olives and the other ingredients, toss and serve for lunch.

Nutrition:
Calories: 187, Fat: 5.8 g, Fiber: 2 g, Carbs: 5.6 g, Protein: 6.5 g

317. Black Bean Patties

Preparation time: 10 minutes | **Cooking time:** 10 minutes | **Servings:** 2

Ingredients:

- 3 tablespoons chives, chopped
- 15 oz. canned black beans, no-salt-added, drained and rinsed
- 2 tablespoons flax meal mixed with 3 tablespoons water
- 2 garlic cloves, minced
- 1 teaspoon sweet paprika
- Cooking spray
- 1 tablespoon lime juice

Directions:
In a blender, mix the beans with the garlic and the other ingredients except the cooking spray and blend.
Shape medium patties out of this mix
Heat up a pan over medium-high heat, grease with cooking spray, add beans patties, cook them for 5 minutes on each side and transfer to plates.
Serve with a side salad.

Nutrition:
Calories: 200, Fat: 4.2 g, Fiber: 6.5 g, Carbs: 12 g, Protein: 8 g

318. Rice and Avocado Bowls

Preparation time: 10 minutes | **Cooking time:** 0 minutes | **Servings:** 2

Ingredients:

- 1 teaspoon olive oil
- 1 avocado, peeled, pitted and cubed
- 1 cup brown rice, cooked
- 2 tablespoons chives, chopped
- 1 cup red bell peppers, cut into strips
- 1 cup cherry tomatoes, halved
- 3 tablespoons salsa
- A pinch of salt and black pepper

Directions:
In a bowl mix the peppers with the tomatoes and the other ingredients, toss and serve for lunch.

Nutrition:
Calories: 219, Fat: 4.4 g, Fiber: 4 g, Carbs: 12.1 g, Protein: 5.4 g

319. Pesto Mushroom Bowls

Preparation time: 10 minutes | **Cooking time:** 15 minutes | **Servings:** 2

Ingredients:

- ½ lb. mushrooms, roughly sliced
- 1 tablespoon olive oil
- 2 tablespoons pesto
- 1 tablespoon chives, chopped
- 1 cup coconut cream
- 1 red onion, sliced
- 2 tomato, chopped
- 1 teaspoon turmeric powder

Directions:
Heat up a pan with the oil over medium heat, add the onion and cook for 5 minutes.
Add the mushrooms and turmeric and cook for another 5 minutes.
Add the rest of the ingredients, toss, simmer for 5 minutes, divide into bowls and serve for lunch.

Nutrition:
Calories: 198, Fat: 3.4 g, Fiber: 4 g, Carbs: 14 g, Protein: 5.4 g

320. Veggie and Pasta Soup

Preparation time: 10 minutes | **Cooking time:** 16 minutes | **Servings:** 2

Ingredients:
- 2 teaspoons olive oil
- 1 celery stalk, chopped
- 1 cup zucchinis, cubed
- 1 ½ cups whole wheat pasta
- 1 ½ cups carrot, shredded
- 1 cup yellow onion, chopped
- 5 cups low-sodium veggie stock
- 2 tablespoons parsley, chopped

Directions:
Heat up a pot with the oil over medium-high heat, add the onion and celery and cook for 5 minutes.
Add the rest of the ingredients except the parsley, bring to a boil and cook for 11 minutes more.
Divide into bowls, top each with parsley and serve.

Nutrition:
Calories: 212, Fat: 5.4 g, Fiber: 5.3 g, Carbs: 13 g, Protein: 8 g

321. Avocado Salad

Preparation time: 10 minutes | **Cooking time:** 0 minutes | **Servings:** 2

Ingredients:
- 2 tablespoon balsamic vinegar
- 1 tablespoon chives, chopped
- 1 avocado, peeled, pitted and sliced
- 2 tablespoons mint, chopped
- A pinch of black pepper
- 4 cups baby spinach
- ½ cup cherry tomatoes, halved
- 1 and ½ cups strawberries, sliced

Directions:
In a salad bowl, combine the spinach with avocado and the other ingredients, toss and serve.

Nutrition:
Calories: 209, Fat: 4.3 g, Fiber: 4 g, Carbs: 6.2 g, Protein: 8 g

322. Peppers Stew

Preparation time: 10 minutes | **Cooking time:** 25 minutes | **Servings:** 2

Ingredients:
- ½ lb. red bell peppers, cut into strips
- 1 red onion, chopped
- 2 garlic cloves, minced
- 2 tablespoons tomato paste
- ½ cup cherry tomatoes, halved
- 1 tablespoon olive oil
- A pinch of salt and black pepper
- ¼ cup parsley, chopped

Directions:
In a sous vide bag, mix the peppers with the tomatoes and the other ingredients, seal the bag, and cook in the water oven at 165°F for 25 minutes.
Divide the stew into bowls and serve.

Nutrition:
Calories: 273, Fat: 2 g, Fiber: 4 g, Carbs: 7 g, Protein: 6 g

323. Potato Stew

Preparation time: 10 minutes | **Cooking time:** 30 minutes | **Servings:** 2

Ingredients:
- 1 red onion, chopped
- 1 lb. gold potatoes, peeled and cut into wedges
- 1 carrot, sliced
- 2 tablespoons ginger, grated
- 1 tablespoon chives, chopped
- 1 tablespoon olive oil
- ½ cup tomato passata
- ½ cup cilantro, chopped
- 1 teaspoon turmeric powder
- A pinch of salt and black pepper

Directions:
In a sous vide bag, mix the potatoes with the onion, the oil and the other ingredients, seal the bag, submerge in the water oven and cook at 170°F for 30 minutes.
Divide into bowls and serve.

Nutrition:
Calories: 238, Fat: 3 g, Fiber: 3 g, Carbs: 32 g, Protein: 14 g

324. Green Beans Salad

Preparation time: 10 minutes | **Cooking time:** 25 minutes | **Servings:** 2

Ingredients:
- 1 red onion, chopped
- 1 tablespoon lime juice
- 1 cup kalamata olives, pitted and halved
- 1 lb. green beans, trimmed and halved
- ½ teaspoon chili powder
- 1 tablespoon olive oil
- 1 cup cherry tomatoes, halved
- 2 tablespoons balsamic vinegar
- ½ teaspoon turmeric powder
- A pinch of salt and black pepper

Directions:
In a sous vide bag, mix the green beans with the onion, oil and the other ingredients, seal the bag and cook in the water oven at 165°F for 25 minutes.
Divide into bowls and serve for lunch.

Nutrition:
Calories: 264, Fat: 5 g, Fiber: 5 g, Carbs: 7 g, Protein: 5 g

325. The Simplest No-Sear Sous Vide Chicken Breast

Preparation time: 5 minutes | **Cooking time:** 1 hour
Serving: 2

Ingredients:
- Boneless chicken breast
- Pepper as needed
- Salt as needed
- Garlic powder as needed

Directions:
Prepare your sous vide water bath to a temperature of 150°F
Drain your chicken breast gently by patting them dry
Season the breast all over with pepper, salt and garlic powder
Place them in your sous vide zip bag or a good quality resealable bag and lock the bag up using the immersion method
Drop them into your water bath and cook for about 1 hour (for 1-inch thickness) or 2 hours (for 2-inch thickness)
Once done, take them out and serve!

Nutrition:
Calories: 232, Fat: 17 g, Protein: 18 g, Fiber: 2 g

326. Delicious Rosemary Salmon Meal

Preparation time: 5 minutes | **Cooking time:** 30 minutes
Serving: 2

Ingredients:
- 1 lb. of wild salmon
- 1 tablespoonful of chopped rosemary
- Juice of one lemon
- ¼ teaspoonful of black pepper
- 2 tablespoonfuls of olive oil
- Zest of one lemon
- ¼ teaspoonful of garlic powder
- ⅛ teaspoonful of sea salt

Directions:
Prepare your Sous Vide water bath and increase the temperature to 115°F.
Take a small bowl and add oil, lemon juice, rosemary, zest, pepper, salt and garlic powder.
Mix them well until emulsified.
Place them in your resealable bag/sous vide zip bag alongside the salmon.
Use the water immersion method to release air and lock up the bag.
Place the bag in your bath and cook for 30 minutes.
While it is cooking, slice up two garlic cloves very thinly.
Once done, remove them from your bath and pour the contents in your plate (make sure to keep the juices). Heat up about 1 tablespoonful

of olive oil in your frying pan over medium high heat.
Add garlic slices and Sauté them until golden.
Remove them and let them rest.
In the very same oil, add salmon and cook them for 3 minutes.
Remove the salmon and garnish with some garlic slices.
Serve!

Nutrition:
Calories: 438, Fat: 30 g, Protein: 37 g, Fiber: 2 g

327. Slightly Spicy Garam Masala Encrusted Lamb Rack

Preparation time: 10 minutes | **Cooking time:** 1 hour 30 minutes
Serving: 2

Ingredients:

- 1 – 5 lb. of frenched baby lamb racks
- ½ a teaspoonful of salt
- 2 teaspoonfuls of Garam Masala spice blend
- ½ a teaspoonful of pepper

Directions:
Prepare your sous vide water bath to a temperature of 135°F.
Generously season your lamb rack with pepper and salt on all sides.
Once done, rub them with the Garam masala.
Place them in your sous vide zip bag or a good quality resealable bag and lock the bag up using the immersion method, making sure to put the meat first and bone upward.
Drop them into your water bath and cook for about 1 hour and 30 minutes.
Remove the meat once cooked and path them dry.
Sear them a bit over the pan or with a blow torch.
Slice it between the bones to get nice lamb lollipops and serve!
Drizzle some honey to elevate its flavor to a heavenly level.

Nutrition:
Calories: 190, Fat: 10 g, Protein: 23 g

328. Honey Drizzled Dijon Lamb Rack

Preparation time: 5 minutes | **Cooking time:** 60 minutes
Serving: 2

Ingredients:

- 1 trimmed lamb on rack
- 2 tablespoonfuls of Dijon mustard
- ¼ teaspoonful of salt
- 3 tablespoonfuls of runny honey
- 1 teaspoonful of sherry wine vinegar
- 2 tablespoonfuls of avocado

Toasted mustard seeds and chopped up green onion for garnish

Directions:
Prepare your Sous Vide water bath and increase the temperature to 135°F.
Take a small sized bowl and add everything except the lamb.
Mix everything well to combine them.
Place your trimmed-up lamb in your zip bag/sous vide bag and pour over the prepared sauce.
Use the water immersion method to seal the bag.
Place the bag in your bath and cook for 1 hour.
Remove the bag from the water and take out the lamb and place it on your serving plate.
Heat up about 2 tablespoonfuls of oil in your frying pan by placing it over medium-high heat.
Once it shimmers, add the lamb with the meaty side down and sear it for 2 minutes.
Turn it over and repeat the process for the other side.
Slice them up into chops and drizzle with the sauce in the bag.
Garnish with some green onion and toasted mustard seeds.
Enjoy!

Nutrition:
Calories: 301, Fat: 27 g, Protein: 12 g, Fiber: 4 g

329. Interesting Salmon with Hollandaise

Preparation time: 5 minutes | **Cooking time:** 60 minutes
Serving: 2

Ingredients:

2 salmon fillets	Salt as needed
Hollandaise Sauce	4 tablespoonfuls of butter
1 egg yolk	1 teaspoonful of lemon juice
1 teaspoonful of water	½ of a diced shallot
Just a pinch of cayenne	Salt as needed

Directions:
Gently dry bring your salmon and rubbing it with salt on both sides and chilling it in your fridge for 30 minutes.
Preheat your Sous Vide water by 148°F.
Take a large sized Sous Vide bag or resealable bag and add all the ingredients of your Hollandaise sauce.
Submerge it using the water displacement method and cook it for about 45 minutes.
Once the sauce it done, lower the temperature of your bath to the temperature required for your salmon.
Add the salmon to another resealable bag and add the salmon, seal it well using the immersion method.
Cook it for 30 minutes under water.
Remove the sauce from your water bath and pour it in a blender.
Blend it well until a light-yellow texture appears.
Remove the Salmon from your bath and pat them dry.
Sear if needed and serve with the hollandaise sauce.

Nutrition:
Calories: 418, Fat: 28 g, Protein: 33 g, Fiber: 2 g

330. Blackberry Hibiscus Delight

Preparation time: 10 minutes | **Cooking time:** 1 hour 30 minutes | **Servings:** 2

Ingredients:

1lb. fresh blackberries	½ cup red wine vinegar
½ cup caster sugar	2 teaspoons crushed hibiscus flowers
3 bay leaves	

Directions:
Preheat your Sous Vide cooker to 140°F.
In a saucepot, combine red wine vinegar, caster sugar, hibiscus, and bay leaves.
Heat until the sugar is dissolved. Allow cooling.
Place the blackberries and cooled syrup in a Sous vide bag.
Vacuum seal and submerge in water.
Cook 1 hour 30 minutes. Remove the bag from the cooker and place in ice-cold water 10 minutes.
Open carefully and transfer the content to a bowl.
Serve.

Nutrition:
Calories: 149, Fat: 6 g, Carbs: 32 g, Fiber: 6 g, Protein: 6 g

331. Smoked Sausage & Cabbage Potatoes

Preparation time: 25 minutes | **Cooking time:** 2 hours | **Servings:** 2

Ingredients:

½ head green cabbage, cored and thinly sliced	1 Granny smith apple, peeled and cored, cut up into small dices
24 oz. red potatoes cut up into quarters and into ¼ inch thick wedges	1 small onion thinly sliced
¼ teaspoon celery salt	2 tablespoons cider vinegar
2 tablespoons packed brown sugar	Salt and black pepper, as needed
1-lb. precooked smoked pork sausage sliced up into 4 portions with each portion sliced into half lengthwise	½ cup chicken broth
2 tablespoons unsalted butter	

Directions:
Prepare the Sous Vide water bath using your immersion circulator and raise the temperature to 185-°F
Take a large bowl and add the cabbage, potatoes, onion, apple, cider vinegar, brown sugar, and celery salt. Season with salt and pepper Divide

the mixture and sausage among 2 resealable zip bags and add ¼ cup of chicken broth to each bag. Seal using the immersion method and cook for 2 hours.
Take a skillet and place it over medium-high heat and add 1 tablespoon of butter, heat it up and add the bag contents to the skillet.
Bring it to a boil and reduce the heat, cook until the liquid evaporates. It should take about 5-6 minutes for the onion, potatoes, cabbage to be browned.
Transfer to a serving platter and repeat the process with the remaining cabbage-sausage mix.
Serve!

Nutrition:
Calories: 510, Carbs: 39 g, Protein: 18 g, Fat: 32 g, Sugar: 10 g, Sodium: 496 mg

332. Boneless Pork Ribs

Preparation time: 30 minutes | **Cooking time:** 8 hours | **Servings:** 2

Ingredients:

⅓ cup unsweetened coconut milk	2 tablespoons peanut butter
2 tablespoons soy sauce	2 tablespoons light brown sugar
2 tablespoons dry white wine	2-inch fresh lemongrass
1 tablespoon Sriracha sauce	1 inch peeled fresh ginger
2 garlic cloves	2 teaspoons sesame oil
12 oz. boneless country style pork ribs	Chopped up fresh cilantro and steamed basmati rice for serving

Directions:
Prepare the Sous Vide water bath using your immersion circulator and increase the temperature to 134-°F.
Add the coconut milk, peanut butter, soy sauce, brown sugar, wine, lemongrass, ginger, Sriracha sauce, sesame oil and garlic to a blender, blend until smooth.
Add the ribs to a resealable zip bag alongside the sauce and seal using the immersion method. Cook for 8 hours.

Once done, remove the bag and take the ribs out from the bag, transfer to plate.
Pour the bag contents to a large skillet and place it over medium-high heat, bring to a boil and lower heat to medium-low. Simmer for 10-15 minutes.
Then, add the ribs to the sauce and turn well to coat it.
Simmer for 5 minutes.
Garnish with fresh cilantro and serve with the rice!

Nutrition:
Calories: 840, Carbs: 24 g, Protein: 53 g, Fat: 59 g, Sugar: 12 g, Sodium: 534 mg

333. Coffee-Chili Pork Porterhouse

Preparation time: 20 minutes | **Cooking time:** 2 hours 30 minutes | **Servings:** 2

Ingredients:

2 pieces bone-in pork porterhouse	1 tablespoon ancho chilis powder
1 tablespoon ground coffee	1 tablespoon light brown sugar
1 tablespoon garlic salt	1 tablespoon extra-virgin olive oil

Directions:
Prepare your Sous Vide water bath using your immersion circulator and increase the temperature to 145°F.
Add the pork to a resealable bag and seal using the immersion method. Cook for 2 ½ hours.
Make your seasoning mixture by adding the chili powder, coffee, brown sugar, and garlic salt to a small bowl.
Remove the bag. Then take the pork out from the bag, pat it dry using kitchen towel.
Rub the chop with seasoning.
Take a cast iron skillet and put it over high heat and add the olive oil and sear the pork for 1-2 minutes per side.
Once done, transfer the pork to a cutting board and allow it to rest for 5 minutes, slice and serve!

Nutrition:
Calories: 813, Carbs: 4 g, Protein: 56 g, Fat: 63 g, Sodium: 475 mg

334. Balsamic Glazed Pork Rib Chop

Preparation time: 20 minutes | **Cooking time:** 180 minutes | **Servings:** 2

Ingredients:
- 1-piece bone-in pork chop
- 1 tablespoon extra-virgin olive oil
- Kosher salt and black pepper, as needed
- 4 tablespoons aged balsamic vinegar

Directions:
Prepare your Sous Vide water bath using your immersion circulator and increase the temperature to 145°F.

Take the pork and carefully season it with pepper and salt, transfer to a resealable zipper bag and seal using the immersion method.

Cook for 3 hours and remove the bag from the water bath and then the pork and pat it dry.

Take a sauté pan and place it over high heat for 5 minutes, add the olive oil and the pork chops. Sear until browned on both sides.

Add 3 tablespoons of balsamic vinegar to the skillet and bring to a rapid simmer, keep simmer while spooning the vinegar over the chop. Keep repeating for 1 minute.

Once done, transfer the dish to your serving plate and serve it with the rest of the balsamic.

Nutrition:
Calories: 529, Carbs: 45 g, Protein: 23 g, Fat: 29 g, Sugar: 13 g, Sodium: 155 mg

335. Siu-Style Chinese Baby Back Ribs

Preparation time: 30 minutes | **Cooking time:** 4 hours | **Servings:** 2

Ingredients:
- ⅓ cup hoisin sauce
- ⅓ cup granulated sugar
- 3 tablespoons sherry vinegar
- 2 teaspoons sesame oil
- 1-inch piece fresh grated ginger
- ⅓ cup dark soy sauce
- 3 tablespoons honey
- 1 tablespoon fermented bean paste
- 2 crushed garlic cloves
- 1 ½ teaspoon five spice powder
- ½ teaspoon salt
- ½ teaspoon fresh ground black pepper
- Cilantro leaves for garnishing
- ½ teaspoon white pepper
- 3 lbs. baby back ribs with the membrane removed

Directions:
Prepare the Sous Vide water bath using your immersion circulator and raise the temperature to 167°F.

Take a large bowl and add the hoisin sauce, dark soy sauce, sugar, sherry vinegar, honey, bean paste, sesame oil, garlic, five spice powder, salt, ginger, white pepper, and black pepper.

Take a small-sized bowl and add ⅓ cup of the marinade, chill for later use.

Add the ribs to the remaining marinade and mix well to coat the ribs.

Divide the mixture among 3 large resealable bags and seal using the immersion method. Cook for 4 hours.

Heat up the grill to 400-°F and transfer the ribs to the grill, brush with the reserved marinade and cook for 3 minutes.

Flip them up and brush with more marinade, cook for another 3 minutes.

Transfer the dish to the cutting board and allow it to rest for 5 minutes, slice the rack into ribs and garnish with cilantro leaves. Serve!

Nutrition:
Calories: 1041, Carbs: 33 g, Protein: 52 g, Fat: 77 g, Sugar: 26 g, Sodium: 567 mg

336. Lamb and Cucumber Mix

Preparation time: 10 minutes | **Cooking time:** 1 hour and 30 minutes | **Servings:** 2

Ingredients:
- 2 lbs. lamb stew meat, roughly cubed
- 1 cup cucumbers, cubed
- ¼ cup beef stock
- A pinch of salt and black pepper
- 2 tablespoons olive oil
- 1 teaspoon cumin, ground
- 4 garlic cloves, minced
- 1 tablespoon cilantro, chopped

Directions:
In a large sous vide bag mix the lamb with the oil, cucumber and the other ingredients, seal the bag, cook in the water oven at 180°F for 1 hour and 30 minutes, divide the mix between plates and serve.

Nutrition:
Calories: 244, Fat: 12 g, Fiber: 2 g, Carbs: 5 g, Protein: 16 g

337. Ground Lamb and Carrots Mix

Preparation time: 10 minutes | **Cooking time:** 1 hour | **Servings:** 2

Ingredients:

- 2 lbs. lamb stew meat, ground
- 1 red onion, sliced
- 3 carrots, peeled and grated
- ¼ cup red wine
- A pinch of salt and black pepper
- 1 tablespoon balsamic vinegar
- 2 tablespoons olive oil
- 1 parsnip, peeled and sliced
- 1 tablespoon chives, chopped

Directions:
In a large sous vide bag, mix the lamb with the vinegar, onion and the other ingredients, seal the bag, submerge in the water oven, cook at 175°F for 1 hour, divide the mix into bowls and serve.

Nutrition:
Calories: 254, Fat: 14 g, Fiber: 3 g, Carbs: 6 g, Protein: 17 g

338. Pork with Tomatoes and Potatoes

Preparation time: 10 minutes | **Cooking time:** 1 hour and 40 minutes | **Servings:** 2

Ingredients:

- 2 lbs. pork stew meat, roughly cubed
- ½ lb. gold potatoes, peeled and cut into wedges
- Juice of 1 lime
- 1 cup cherry tomatoes, halved
- 1 teaspoon sweet paprika
- 1 red onion, chopped
- 2 tablespoons avocado oil
- 1 tablespoon chives, chopped
- 3 garlic cloves, minced

Directions:
In a large sous vide bag, mix the pork with the tomatoes, potatoes and the other ingredients, seal the bag, submerge in the water bath, cook at 180°F for 1 hour and 40 minutes, divide the mix between plates and serve.

Nutrition:
Calories: 253, Fat: 14 g, Fiber: 2 g, Carbs: 6 g, Protein: 18 g

339. Lamb and Savoy Cabbage Mix

Preparation time: 10 minutes | **Cooking time:** 1 hour and 20 minutes | **Servings:** 2

Ingredients:

- 2 lbs. lamb shoulder, cubed
- 1 cup Savoy cabbage, shredded
- 2 spring onions, chopped
- A pinch of salt and black pepper
- 1 tablespoon chives, chopped
- 2 tablespoons olive oil
- 1 tablespoon balsamic vinegar
- 1 tablespoon balsamic vinegar
- Juice of 1 lime

Directions:
In a large sous vide bag, mix the lamb with the cabbage, oil and the other ingredients, seal the bag, submerge in the water bath, cook at 180°F for 1 hour and 20 minutes, divide everything between plates and serve.

Nutrition:
Calories: 264, Fat: 14 g, Fiber: 3 g, Carbs: 6 g, Protein: 17 g

340. Beef with Carrots and Cabbage

Preparation time: 10 minutes | **Cooking time:** 1 hour and 30 minutes | **Servings:** 2

Ingredients:

- 2 tablespoons olive oil
- 2 carrots, peeled and sliced

Ingredients:
- 1 cup red cabbage, shredded
- 2 tablespoons balsamic vinegar
- 1 red onion, chopped
- ½ teaspoon cumin, ground
- Juice of 1 lime
- 2 lbs. beef stew meat, roughly cubed
- A pinch of salt and black pepper
- 1 tablespoon chives, chopped

Directions:
In a sous vide bag, mix the beef with the oil, carrots and the other ingredients, seal the bag, submerge in the water oven and cook at 186°F for 1 hour and 30 minutes.
Divide the mix into bowls and serve.

Nutrition:
Calories: 273, Fat: 13 g, Fiber: 2 g, Carbs: 6 g, Protein: 15 g

341. Orange Lamb

Preparation time: 10 minutes | **Cooking time:** 1 hour | **Servings:** 2

Ingredients:
- 2 lbs. lamb chops
- Juice of 2 oranges
- ½ teaspoon turmeric powder
- 1 tablespoon chives, chopped
- 2 tablespoons olive oil
- 2 tablespoons orange zest, grated
- A pinch of salt and black pepper

Directions:
In a large sous vide bag, mix the lamb chops with the oil, orange juice and the other ingredients, seal the bag, submerge in the water bath, cook at 180°F for 1 hour, divide between plates and serve.

Nutrition:
Calories: 274, Fat: 14, Fiber: 2, Carbs: 6, Protein: 16

342. Ginger Pork

Preparation time: 10 minutes | **Cooking time:** 1 hour and 10 minutes | **Servings:** 2

Ingredients:
- 2 lbs. pork shoulder, boneless and cubed
- 2 spring onions, chopped
- 1 tablespoon ginger, grated
- ½ teaspoon coriander, ground
- ¼ cup beef stock
- ½ teaspoon chili powder
- A pinch of salt and black pepper
- 1 tablespoon cilantro, chopped

Directions:
In a sous vide bag, mix the pork with the ginger, spring onions and the other ingredients, seal the bag, submerge in the water bath, cook at 175°F for 1 hour and 10 minutes, divide the mix between plates and serve with a side salad.

Nutrition:
Calories: 264, Fat: 14 g, Fiber: 2 g, Carbs: 8 g, Protein: 12 g

343. Beef and Swiss Chard

Preparation time: 10 minutes | **Cooking time:** 1 hour and 10 minutes | **Servings:** 2

Ingredients:
- 2 lbs. beef stew meat, roughly cubed
- 1 cup red chard, torn
- 1 tablespoon olive oil
- ½ teaspoon turmeric powder
- A pinch of salt and black pepper
- 2 scallions, chopped
- Juice of 1 lime
- 1 teaspoon hot paprika
- 1 tablespoon chives, chopped

Directions:
In a large sous vide bag, mix the beef with the scallions, chard and the other ingredients, seal the bag, submerge in the water bath, cook at 176°F for 1 hour and 10 minutes, divide the mix between plates and serve with a side salad.

Nutrition:
Calories: 200, Fat: 9 g, Fiber: 2 g, Carbs: 6 g, Protein: 12 g

344. Nutmeg Pork Roast

Preparation time: 10 minutes | **Cooking time:** 1 hour and 40 minutes | **Servings:** 2

Ingredients:
- 2 lbs. pork roast, sliced
- 1 teaspoon nutmeg, ground

Juice of ½ lemon
2 tablespoons olive oil
½ cup red wine
½ tablespoon lemon zest, grated
A pinch of salt and black pepper
1 tablespoon chives, chopped

Directions:
In a large sous vide bag, mix the pork roast with the nutmeg, lemon juice and the other ingredients, seal the bag, submerge in the water bath, cook at 180°F for 1 hour and 40 minutes, divide roast between plates and serve with a side salad.

Nutrition:
Calories: 234, Fat: 11 g, Fiber: 3 g, Carbs: 7 g, Protein: 15 g

345. Lamb with Ginger Artichokes

Preparation time: 10 minutes | **Cooking time:** 1 hour and 10 minutes | **Servings:** 2

Ingredients:
2 lbs. lamb meat, cubed
1 tablespoon ginger, grated
Juice of ½ lime
½ teaspoon turmeric powder
2 tablespoons olive oil
1 cup canned artichoke hearts, drained and quartered
1 red onion, sliced
½ teaspoon chili powder
1 cup beef stock
1 tablespoon parsley, chopped

Directions:
In a large sous vide bag, mix the lamb with the artichokes, ginger, and the other ingredients, seal the bag, submerge in the water bath, cook at 180°F for 1 hour and 10 minutes, divide the mix between plates and serve.

Nutrition:
Calories: 273, Fat: 14 g, Fiber: 2 g, Carbs: 6 g, Protein: 15 g

346. Chicken and Apricot Sauce Recipe

Preparation time: 10 minutes | **Cooking time:** 30 minutes | **Servings:** 2

Ingredients:
1 whole chicken, cut into medium pieces
1 tbsp. olive oil
¼ cup white wine
¼ cup apricot preserves
½ tsp. marjoram, dried
Salt and black pepper to the taste
2 tbsp. honey
½ tsp. smoked paprika
2 tbsp. white vinegar
1 ½ tsp. ginger, grated
¼ cup chicken stock

Directions:
Season chicken with salt, pepper, marjoram and paprika, toss to coat, add oil, rub well, place in your air fryer and cook at 360°F, for 10 minutes. Transfer chicken to a pan that fits your air fryer, add stock, wine, vinegar, ginger, apricot preserves and honey, toss, put in your air fryer and cook at 360 °F, for 10 minutes more. Divide chicken and apricot sauce on plates and serve.

Nutrition:
Calories: 200, Fat: 7 g, Fiber: 19 g, Carbs: 20 g, Protein: 14 g

347. Creamy Chicken Casserole Recipe

Preparation time: 10 minutes | **Cooking time:** 22 minutes | **Servings:** 2

Ingredients:
10 oz. spinach, chopped
½ cup heavy cream
3 tbsp. flour
2 cup chicken breasts, skinless, boneless and cubed
Salt and black pepper to the taste
½ cup parmesan, grated
4 tbsp. butter
1 ½ cups milk
1 cup breadcrumbs

Directions:
Heat up a pan with the butter over medium heat, add flour and stir well.

Add milk, heavy cream and parmesan, stir well, cook for 1-2 minutes more and take off heat.
In a pan that fits your air fryer, spread chicken and spinach.
Add salt and pepper and toss.
Add cream mix and spread, sprinkle breadcrumbs on top, introduce in your air fryer and cook at 350 for 12 minutes. Divide chicken and spinach mix on plates and serve.

Nutrition:
Calories: 321, Fat: 9 g, Fiber: 12 g, Carbs: 22 g, Protein: 17 g

348. Chicken and Garlic Sauce Recipe

Preparation time: 10 minutes | **Cooking time:** 30 minutes | **Servings:** 2

Ingredients:

4 chicken breasts, skin on and bone-in	1 tbsp. butter, melted
1 tbsp. olive oil	Salt and black pepper to the taste
40 garlic cloves, peeled and chopped.	2 thyme springs
¼ cup chicken stock	2 tbsp. parsley, chopped
¼ cup dry white wine	

Directions:
Season chicken breasts with salt and pepper, rub with the oil, place in your air fryer, cook at 360°F, for 4 minutes on each side and transfer to a heat proof dish that fits your air fryer.
Add melted butter, garlic, thyme, stock, wine and parsley, toss, introduce in your air fryer and cook at 350°F, for 15 minutes more. Divide everything on plates and serve.

Nutrition:
Calories: 227, Fat: 9 g, Fiber: 13 g, Carbs: 22 g, Protein: 12 g

349. Pork in Creamy Sauce

Preparation time: 5 minutes | **Cooking time:** 60 minutes | **Servings:** 2

Ingredients:

1 tbsp olive oil	1 tbsp butter
1 pork shoulder, cut into 2-inch cubes	1 tsp dried thyme
Salt and black pepper to taste	½ tsp dried mustard powder
1 small yellow onion, diced	3 garlic cloves, minced
1 ½ cups chicken broth	¾ cup heavy cream
1 tbsp cornstarch	1 tsp dried parsley
1 tsp dried basil	

Directions:
Set your Instant Pot to Sauté mode and adjust to medium heat. Heat olive oil and butter in inner pot, season pork with thyme, salt, black pepper, and mustard powder. Sear in oil until golden on the outside, 7 minutes. Transfer to a plate. Sauté onion until softened, 3 minutes. Stir in garlic and cook until fragrant, 30 seconds. Pour in chicken broth and return meat to inner pot.
Seal the lid, select Manual/Pressure Cook mode on High, and set cooking time to 20 minutes. After cooking, perform a natural pressure release for 10 minutes, then a quick pressure release to let out remaining steam. Unlock the lid. Transfer pork to a plate and select Sauté mode.
Into sauce, whisk heavy cream, cornstarch, basil, and parsley. Cook for 2 minutes and return pork to sauce. Allow heating through for 3 minutes. Spoon pork with sauce onto plates and serve warm.

Nutrition:
Calories: 484, Carbs: 12 g, Fat: 34 g, Protein: 28 g

350. Salsa Verde Pork with Velveeta Cheese

Preparation time: 5 minutes | **Cooking time:** 30 minutes | **Servings:** 2

Ingredients:

2 tbsp olive oil	1 lb. ground pork
Salt and black pepper to taste	1 cup milk
2 tbsp white Velveeta cheese	1 16 ozjar salsa verde
16 oz sour cream	2 jalapeño peppers, sliced

Directions:
Set your Instant Pot to Sauté mode and heat olive oil. Cook pork until brown, 5 minutes. Season with a little salt and black pepper. Add in milk and seal the lid. Select Manual/Pressure Cook and set time to 15 minutes. When ready, do a quick pressure release.
Press Sauté, mix in Velveeta cheese, salsa verde, sour cream, and jalapeño peppers. Cook with frequent stirring until cheese melts. Dish into serving bowls and serve warm.

Nutrition:
Calories: 739, Carbs: 30 g, Fat: 27 g, Protein: 51 g

351. Pork Chops with Caramelized Apples

Preparation time: 5 minutes | **Cooking time:** 55 minutes | **Servings:** 2

Ingredients:

2 tbsp olive oil	4 bone-in pork chops
Salt and black pepper to taste	2 garlic cloves, minced
2 tbsp chopped sage	1 lb. apples, peeled and sliced
3 tbsp butter	4 tbsp honey
½ cup apple cider vinegar	½ cup chicken broth
½ cup heavy cream	2 tbsp chopped parsley

Directions:
Set your Instant Pot to Sauté mode. Heat olive oil, season pork with salt and pepper, and sear in oil until golden brown on the outside, 6 minutes. Set aside. Add garlic and sage to oil and stir-fry until fragrant, 30 seconds. Pour in apples, butter, and honey, cook until apples caramelize, 5 minutes. Top with apple cider vinegar, broth, and pork.
Seal the lid, select Manual/Pressure Cook mode on High, and set cooking time to 20 minutes. After cooking, perform a natural pressure release for 10 minutes. Unlock the lid and stir in heavy cream. Simmer in Sauté mode for 2 to 3 minutes. Spoon food into serving plates with a generous topping of sauce. Garnish with parsley and serve warm.

Nutrition:
Calories: 766, Carbs: 59 g, Fat: 41 g, Protein: 43 g

352. Broccoli & Cabbage Pork Ramen

Preparation time: 5 minutes | **Cooking time:** 50 minutes | **Servings:** 2

Ingredients:

2 3 oz packs ramen noodles	¼ cup soy sauce
2 tbsp Worcestershire sauce	2 tbsp ketchup
2 tsp granulated sugar	¼ tsp red chili flakes
3 tsp olive oil, divided	1 lb boneless pork chops, cut in ½ inch strips
1 cup broccoli florets	1 cup shredded red cabbage
1 cup shredded green cabbage	4 garlic cloves, minced
1 ½ cups chicken broth	

Directions:
In inner pot, add ramen noodles discard seasoning, 2 ½ cups of water, and salt. Seal the lid, select Manual/Pressure Cook mode on High, and set cooking time to 1 minute. After cooking, perform a quick pressure release to let out steam and unlock the lid. Drain noodles through a colander, set aside, and clean inner pot.
Select Sauté mode and adjust to medium heat. In a small bowl, mix soy sauce, Worcestershire sauce, ketchup, sugar, red chili flakes, and 2 teaspoons of olive oil. Pour mixture into inner pot, allow heating for 1 minute, and add pork, cook until no longer pink. Using a slotted spoon, strain pork and transfer to a plate.
In the pot, add broccoli, cabbages, garlic, and chicken broth. Cook for 2 minutes and return pork to inner pot. Seal the lid, select Manual/Pressure Cook on High, and set time to 15 minutes. After cooking, perform a natural pressure release for 10 minutes. Stir in ramen. Press Sauté and heat noodles for 2 minutes. Spoon into serving plates and serve.

Nutrition:
Calories: 425, Carbs: 44 g, Fat: 12 g, Protein: 34 g

353. Tuscan Pork Chops

Preparation time: 5 minutes | **Cooking time:** 45 minutes | **Servings:** 2

Ingredients:
- 1 tbsp olive oil
- Salt and black pepper to taste
- 5 garlic cloves, minced
- 2 tsp dried oregano
- 1 tsp dried sage
- 4 pork chops, fat trimmed
- 1 large red onion, chopped
- 1 ½ chopped tomatoes
- 1 tsp dried basil
- ½ cup chicken broth

Directions:
Set your Instant Pot to Sauté mode. Heat olive oil, season pork with salt, pepper, and sear in oil until golden brown on both sides, 6 to 8 minutes. Stir in onion and garlic until softened and fragrant, 2 minutes. Add tomatoes, oregano, basil, sage, and cook for 2 minutes, turn meat halfway. Pour in chicken broth and season with salt and pepper.
Seal the lid, select Manual/Pressure Cook mode on High, and set cooking time to 15 minutes. After cooking, perform a natural pressure release for 10 minutes, then a quick pressure release to let out remaining steam. Unlock the lid, stir, and plate. Serve warm.

Nutrition:
Calories: 517, Carbs: 18 g, Fat: 35 g, Protein: 33 g

354. Balsamic Beef Roast

Preparation time: 5 minutes | **Cooking time:** 65 minutes | **Servings:** 2

Ingredients:
- 1 cup Homemade Beef Broth
- 4 tbsp Balsamic Vinegar
- 1 tbsp Coconut Oil, melted
- ½ tsp Garlic Powder
- Pinch of Pepper
- 1 tbsp Olive Oil
- 3 lbs. Beef Roast
- ½ tsp Thyme
- ¼ tsp Onion Powder

Directions:
Heat the olive oil in your Instant Pot on SAUTE. Add the beef and sear on all sides until it becomes browned.
Whisk together the remaining ingredients and pour the mixture over the beef.
Close the lid and set the IP to MANUAL.
Cook on HIGH for 40 minutes.
Do a natural pressure release.
Serve and enjoy!

Nutrition:
Calories: 530, Fats: 23 g, Carbs: 0.5 g, Protein: 75 g

355. Lamb with Tomatoes and Zucchini

Preparation time: 5 minutes | **Cooking time:** 3 hours and 40 minutes | **Servings:** 2

Ingredients:
- 1-lb. Lamb, cut into cubes
- 2 Large Tomatoes, diced
- ½ Yellow Onion, diced
- ½ cup Coconut Milk
- ½ tsp ground Ginger
- 1 tbsp Ghee
- 1 Zucchini, diced
- 2 Carrots, sliced
- 1 tsp minced Garlic

Directions:
In a bowl, combine the coconut milk, lamb, ginger, and garlic.
Cover and let sit in the fridge for 3 hours.
Dump the lamb along with the coconut milk into the IP.
Add the tomatoes, carrots, onion, and ghee, and close the lid.
Set the IP to MANUAL and cook on HIGH for 20 minutes.
Open the lid with a quick pressure release and stir in the zucchini.
Set the IP to SAUTE and cook for 5 minutes.
Serve and enjoy!

Nutrition:
Calories: 340, Fats: 22 g, Carbs: 12.5 g, Protein: 24 g, Fiber: 3 g

356. Mushroom Beef Ribs

Preparation time: 5-8 minutes | **Cooking time:** 15 minutes | **Servings:** 2

Ingredients:

- 1 lb. beef ribs, cut into pieces
- 2 teaspoon olive oil
- 2 garlic cloves, minced
- 1 teaspoon sea salt
- 4 cremini mushrooms, chopped
- 2 scallions, minced
- 2 teaspoons coconut aminos
- Black pepper to taste

Directions:

Take your instant pot, open the lid.
Add the ingredients to the pot and stir.
Seal the lid and put the valve in sealing position, press "MANUAL" setting. Cook for 15 minutes on "HIGH" pressure mode.
Press "CANCEL." Use the NPR function for natural pressure release.
Open the lid, transfer the recipe in serving plates. Serve warm.

Nutrition:

Calories: 329, Fat: 12 g, Carbs: 6 g, Fiber: 1 g, Sodium: 523 mg, Protein: 46 g

357. Steak Salad with Feta Cheese

Preparation time: 40 minutes | **Cooking time:** 20 minutes | **Servings:** 2

Ingredients:

- ½ cup feta cheese, crumbled
- 1 cup water
- 2 tablespoons wine vinegar
- 2 sweet peppers, cut into strips
- Sea salt and ground black pepper, to taste
- 1 butterhead lettuce, separate into leaves
- ½ cup black olives, pitted and sliced
- ¼ cup extra-virgin olive oil
- 1 red onion, thinly sliced
- ½ cup red wine
- ½ teaspoon red pepper flakes
- 1 ½ lbs. steak

Directions:

Add the steak, red wine, salt, black pepper, red pepper, and water to the inner pot.
Secure the lid. Choose the "Manual" mode and cook for 25 minutes at High pressure. Once cooking is complete, use a natural pressure release for 10 minutes, carefully remove the lid. Thinly slice the steak against the grain and transfer to a salad bowl. Toss with the olive oil and vinegar.
Add the red onion, peppers, and lettuce, toss to combine well. Top with cheese and olives and serve.

Nutrition:

Calories: 474, Fat: 28.8 g, Carbs: 3.6 g, Protein: 50.6 g, Sugars: 1.7 g

358. Rustic Beef Brisket with Vegetables

Preparation time: 1 hour 25 minutes | **Cooking time:** 20 minutes | **Servings:** 2

Ingredients:

- 2 sprigs thyme
- ½ lb. rutabaga, peeled and cut into 1-inch chunks
- 2 tablespoons olive oil
- 1 medium leek, sliced
- 2 cloves peeled garlic
- 2 ½ lbs. corned beef brisket
- 1 sprig rosemary
- ½ lb. turnips, peeled and cut into 1-inch chunks
- 1 cup chicken broth
- 2 parsnips, cut into 1-inch chunks
- 2 bell peppers, halved
- ¼ cup tomato puree

Directions:

Place the beef brisket, garlic, thyme, rosemary, olive oil, chicken broth, and tomato puree in the inner pot.
Secure the lid. Choose the "Manual" mode and cook for 80 minutes at High pressure. Once cooking is complete, use a quick pressure release, carefully remove the lid.
Add the other ingredients. Gently stir to combine.

Secure the lid. Choose the "Manual" mode and cook for 4 minutes at High pressure. Once cooking is complete, use a quick pressure release, carefully remove the lid.

Nutrition:

Calories: 563, Fat: 35.8 g, Carbs: 19.5 g, Protein: 39.3 g, Sugars: 6.5 g

359. Pork Bean Dip

Preparation time: 5 minutes | **Cooking time:** 27 minutes | **Servings:** 2

Ingredients:

- 1 tbsp olive oil
- ½ lb. ground pork

Salt and black pepper to taste	2 cups black beans, soaked overnight, rinsed
4 tbsp chicken broth	1 tbsp coriander powder
1 tbsp cumin powder	¼ cup grated cheddar cheese

Directions:
Set your Instant Pot to Sauté and heat olive oil. Season pork with salt and black pepper, and sear until brown, 10 minutes. Plate and set aside. Pour black beans, chicken broth, coriander powder, and cumin powder into inner pot. Seal the lid, select Manual/Pressure Cook mode on High, and set cooking time to 15 minutes. After cooking, perform a quick pressure release until steam is out and unlock the lid. Using an immersion blender, puree ingredients and stir in pork. Adjust taste with salt and black pepper. Dish, top with cheddar cheese and serve.

Nutrition:
Calories: 225, Carbs: 6 g, Fat: 12 g, Protein: 25 g

360. Beef with Wontons and Cream Cheese

Preparation time: 30 minutes | **Cooking time:** 20 minutes | **Servings:** 2

Ingredients:

1 ½ lbs. beef brisket, cut into 2-inch cubes	6 oz. wonton noodles
¾ cup cream cheese	2 tablespoons toasted sesame seeds
2 sprigs dried rosemary, leaves picked	1 teaspoon red pepper flakes, crushed
2 garlic cloves, minced	2 sprigs dried thyme, leaves picked
1 ½ tablespoons flaxseed meal	½ cup chicken stock
1 shallot, diced	1 tablespoon lard, at room temperature
1 teaspoon caraway seeds	Sea salt and freshly ground pepper, to taste

Directions:
Press the "Sauté" button to preheat your Instant Pot. Now, melt the lard, once hot, sweat the shallot for 2 to 3 minutes.

Toss the beef brisket with salt, ground pepper, and red pepper flakes. Add the beef to the Instant pot, continue cooking for 3 minutes more or until it is no longer pink.
After that, stir in the garlic, rosemary, thyme, and caraway seeds, cook an additional minute, stirring continuously.
Add the flaxseed meal, chicken stock, and wonton noodles. Stir to combine well and seal the lid. Choose the "Meat/Stew" setting and cook at High pressure for 20 minutes.
Once cooking is complete, use a quick release, remove the lid. Divide the beef mixture among 6 serving bowls.
To serve, stir in the cream cheese and garnish with toasted sesame seeds.

Nutrition:
Calories: 485, Fat: 30.9 g, Carbs: 12.8 g, Protein: 37.1 g, Sugars: 2.4 g

361. Minty Balsamic Lamb

Preparation time: 10 minutes | **Cooking time:** 11 minutes | **Servings:** 2

Ingredients:

2 red chilies, chopped	2 tablespoons balsamic vinegar
1 cup mint leaves, chopped	Salt and black pepper to the taste
2 tablespoons olive oil	4 lamb fillets
1 tablespoon sweet paprika	

Directions:
Heat up a pan with half of the oil over medium-high heat, add the chilies, the vinegar and the rest of the ingredients except the lamb, whisk and cook over medium heat for 5 minutes.
Brush the lamb with the rest of the oil, season with salt and black pepper, place on preheated grill and cook over medium heat for 3 minutes on each side.
Divide the lamb between plates, drizzle the minty vinaigrette all over and serve.

Nutrition:
Calories: 312, Fat: 12.1 g, Fiber: 9.1 g, Carbs: 17.7 g, Protein: 17.2 g

362. Tasty Lamb Ribs

Preparation time: 10 minutes | **Cooking time:** 2 hours | **Servings:** 2

Ingredients:

- 2 garlic cloves, minced
- 2 tablespoons fish sauce
- 2 tablespoons olive oil
- 1 tablespoon coriander seeds, ground
- Salt and black pepper to the taste
- ¼ cup shallot, chopped
- ½ cup veggie stock
- 1 and ½ tablespoons lemon juice
- 1 tablespoon ginger, grated
- 2 lbs. lamb ribs

Directions:

In a roasting pan, combine the lamb with the garlic, shallots and the rest of the ingredients, toss, introduce in the oven at 300°F and cook for 2 hours.

Divide the lamb between plates and serve with a side salad.

Nutrition:

Calories: 293, Fat: 9.1 g, Fiber: 9.6 g, Carbs: 16.7 g, Protein: 24.2 g

363. Cinnamon and Coriander Lamb

Preparation time: 10 minutes | **Cooking time:** 6 hours | **Servings:** 2

Ingredients:

- 2 ½ lbs. lamb shoulder, cubed
- 1 garlic clove, minced
- Salt and black pepper to the taste
- 1 bunch coriander, chopped
- 2 tomatoes, chopped
- 1 tablespoon cinnamon powder
- ½ cup veggie stock

Directions:

In your slow cooker, combine the lamb with the tomatoes and the rest of the ingredients, put the lid on and cook on Low for 6 hours.

Divide everything between plates and serve.

Nutrition:

Calories: 352, Fat: 15.2 g, Fiber: 10.7 g, Carbs: 18.7 g, Protein: 15.3 g

364. Lamb and Plums Mix

Preparation time: 5 minutes | **Cooking time:** 6 hours and 10 minutes | **Servings:** 2

Ingredients:

- 4 lamb shanks
- 2 tablespoons olive oil
- 1 tablespoon sweet paprika
- Salt and pepper to the taste
- 1 red onion, chopped
- 1 cup plums, pitted and halved
- 2 cups chicken stock

Directions:

Heat up a pan with the oil over medium-high heat, add the lamb, brown for 5 minutes on each side and transfer to your slow cooker.

Add the rest of the ingredients, put the lid on and cook on High for 6 hours.

Divide the mix between plates and serve right away.

Nutrition:

Calories: 293, Fat: 13.2 g, Fiber: 9.7 g, Carbs: 15.7 g, Protein: 14.3 g

365. Rosemary Lamb

Preparation time: 10 minutes | **Cooking time:** 6 hours | **Servings:** 2

Ingredients:

- 2 lbs. lamb shoulder, cubed
- 3 garlic cloves, minced
- 4 bay leaves
- 1 tablespoon rosemary, chopped
- ½ cup lamb stock
- Salt and black pepper to the taste

Directions:

In your slow cooker, combine the lamb with the rosemary and the rest of the ingredients, put the lid on and cook on High for 6 hours.

Divide the mix between palates and serve.

Nutrition:

Calories: 292, Fat: 13.2 g, Fiber: 11.6 g, Carbs: 18.3 g, Protein: 14.2 g

366. Lemony Lamb and Potatoes

Preparation time: 10 minutes | **Cooking time:** 2 hours and 10 minutes | **Servings:** 2

Ingredients:

- 2-lb. lamb meat, cubed
- 2 springs rosemary, chopped
- 1 tablespoon lemon rind, grated
- 2 tablespoons lemon juice
- 1 cup veggie stock
- 2 tablespoons olive oil
- 2 tablespoons parsley, chopped
- 3 garlic cloves, minced
- 2 lbs. baby potatoes, scrubbed and halved

Directions:

In a roasting pan, combine the meat with the oil and the rest of the ingredients, introduce in the oven and bake at 400°F for 2 hours and 10 minutes.
Divide the mix between plates and serve.

Nutrition:
Calories: 302, Fat: 15.2 g, Fiber: 10.6 g, Carbs: 23.3 g, Protein: 15.2 g

367. Lamb and Feta Artichokes

Preparation time: 10 minutes | **Cooking time:** 8 hours and 5 minutes | **Servings:** 2

Ingredients:

- 2 lbs. lamb shoulder, boneless and roughly cubed
- 1 tablespoon olive oil
- 1 tablespoon lemon juice
- 1 ½ cups veggie stock
- ½ cup feta cheese, crumbled
- 2 spring onions, chopped
- 3 garlic cloves, minced
- Salt and black pepper to the taste
- 6 oz. canned artichoke hearts, drained and quartered
- 2 tablespoons parsley, chopped

Directions:

Heat up a pan with the oil over medium-high heat, add the lamb, brown 5 minutes and transfer to your slow cooker.
Add the rest of the ingredients except the parsley and the cheese, put the lid on and cook on Low for 8 hours.
Add the cheese and the parsley, divide the mix between plates and serve.

Nutrition:
Calories: 330, Fat: 14.5 g, Fiber: 14.1 g, Carbs: 21.7 g, Protein: 17.5 g

368. Lamb and Mango Sauce

Preparation time: 10 minutes | **Cooking time:** 1 hour | **Servings:** 2

Ingredients:

- 2 cups Greek yogurt
- 1 yellow onion, chopped
- 1 lb. lamb, cubed
- Salt and black pepper to the taste
- ¼ teaspoon cinnamon powder
- 1 cup mango, peeled and cubed
- ⅓ cup parsley, chopped
- ½ teaspoon red pepper flakes
- 2 tablespoons olive oil

Directions:

Heat up a pan with the oil over medium-high heat, add the meat and brown for 5 minutes.
Add the onion and sauté for 5 minutes more.
Add the rest of the ingredients, toss, bring to a simmer and cook over medium heat for 45 minutes.
Divide everything between plates and serve.

Nutrition:
Calories: 300, Fat: 15.5 g, Fiber: 9.1 g, Carbs: 15.7 g, Protein: 15.5 g

369. Pork Chops with Sweet Peppers and Cabbage

Preparation time: 10 minutes | **Cooking time:** 23 minutes | **Servings:** 2

Ingredients:

- 4 pork chops
- 2 teaspoons olive oil
- 2 spring onions, chopped
- 1 teaspoon rosemary, dried
- 3 tablespoons wine vinegar
- ½ green cabbage head, shredded

| 4 sweet peppers, chopped | Salt and black pepper to the taste |

Directions:
Heat up a pan with half of the oil over medium-high heat, add spring onions and sauté for 3 minutes.
Add the rest of the ingredients except the pork chops and rosemary, stir, simmer for 10 minutes and take off the heat.
Rub the pork chops with the rest of the oil, season with salt, pepper and the rosemary, place on preheated grill and cook over medium-high heat for 5 minutes on each side.
Divide the chops between plates, add the cabbage and peppers mix on the side and serve.

Nutrition:
Calories: 219, Fat: 18 g, Fiber: 9.3 g, Carbs: 16.5 g, Protein: 12.4 g

370. Greek Lamb and Eggplant

Preparation time: 10 minutes | **Cooking time:** 1 hour | **Servings:** 2

Ingredients:

4 eggplants, cubed	3 tablespoons olive oil
2 yellow onions, chopped	1 and ½ lbs. lamb meat, roughly cubed
2 tablespoons tomato paste	½ cup parsley, chopped
4 garlic cloves, minced	½ cup Greek yogurt

Directions:
Heat up a pan with the olive oil over medium-high heat, add the onions and garlic and sauté for 4 minutes.
Add the meat and brown for 6 minutes.
Add the eggplants and the other ingredients except the parsley, bring to a simmer and cook over medium heat for 50 minutes more stirring from time to time.
Divide everything between plates and serve.

Nutrition:
Calories: 299, Fat: 18 g, Fiber: 14.3 g, Carbs: 21.5 g, Protein: 14.4 g

371. Roasted Baby Potatoes

Preparation time: 10 minutes | **Cooking time:** 13 minutes | **Servings:** 2

Ingredients:

1 lb. baby potatoes	½ tbsp garlic, minced
1 tbsp olive oil	¼ tsp pepper
½ tsp salt	

Directions:
Add oil into the instant pot and set the pot on sauté mode.
Add garlic and potatoes and sauté for 4-5 minutes.
Remove potatoes from pot and place in baking dish. Season with pepper and salt.
Pour 1 cup of water into the instant pot then place the trivet in the pot.
Place baking dish on top of the trivet and cook on manual high pressure for 8 minutes.
Once done then allow to release pressure naturally for 5 minutes then release using the quick-release method. Open the lid.
Serve and enjoy.

Nutrition:
Calories: 98, Fat: 3.6 g, Carbs: 14.5 g, Protein: 3 g

372. Indian Peppers with Coconut Flour Naan

Preparation time: 20 minutes | **Cooking time:** 10 Minutes | **Servings:** 2

Ingredients:

3 teaspoons canola oil	⅓ teaspoon cumin seeds
2 red bell pepper, seeded and sliced	1 green bell pepper, seeded and sliced
1 garlic clove, minced	1 teaspoon dhania
1 teaspoon chili powder	½ teaspoon haldi
Sea salt and ground black pepper, to taste	1 tablespoon fresh lemon juice

For the Coconut Flour Naan:

| ½ cup coconut flour | ½ teaspoon baking powder |
| 1 ½ tablespoons ground psyllium husk powder | ½ teaspoon salt |

¼ cup coconut oil, melted
1 tablespoon coconut oil, for frying
1 ½ cups boiling water

Directions:
Press the "Sauté" button to heat up your Instant Pot. Heat the canola oil until sizzling. Once hot, sauté cumin seeds for 40 seconds.
Now, add peppers, garlic, and spices.
Secure the lid. Choose "Manual" mode and Low pressure, cook for 4 minutes.
Once cooking is complete, use a quick pressure release, carefully remove the lid. Add lemon juice.
To make naan, in a mixing bowl, combine coconut flour with baking powder, psyllium and salt, mix to combine well.
Add ¼ cup of coconut oil, add the hot water to form a dough, let it rest for 10 minutes at room temperature.
Now, divide the dough into 6 balls, flatten the balls on a working surface.
Heat up a pan with 1 tablespoon of coconut oil over a medium-high flame. Fry naan breads until they are golden.
Serve these naans with Indian peppers and enjoy!

Nutrition:
Calories: 348, Fat: 38.7 g, Carbs: 3.2 g, Protein: 0.6 g, Sugars: 1.7 g

373. Tofu with Zhoug Sauce

Preparation time: 10 minutes | **Cooking time:** 10 Minutes | **Servings:** 2

Ingredients:
1 tablespoon grapeseed oil
½ cup vegetable stock
For the Herby Sauce:
1 Hungarian wax pepper, stemmed and chopped
½ cup fresh cilantro leaves
1 12-oz. block extra-firm tofu, pressed and cubed
1 teaspoon dried rosemary
2 cloves garlic, chopped
Kosher salt and ground black pepper, to taste
½ teaspoon ground cumin
1 teaspoon sherry vinegar
⅓ cup extra-virgin olive oil

Directions:
Press the "Sauté" button to heat up your Instant Pot. Heat the oil until sizzling. Once hot, cook tofu until it has begun to brown.
Add vegetable stock and rosemary.
Secure the lid. Choose "Manual" mode and High pressure, cook for 3 minutes. Once cooking is complete, use a quick pressure release, carefully remove the lid.
Then, mix all ingredients for the sauce in your food processor. Store in your refrigerator until ready to use.
Serve tofu with Zhoug sauce on the side. Enjoy!

Nutrition:
Calories: 308, Fat: 28.3 g, Carbs: 4.5 g, Protein: 12.3 g, Sugars: 1.4 g

374. Classic Vegan Cauliflower Soup

Preparation time: 15 minutes | **Cooking time:** 10 minutes | **Servings:** 2

Ingredients:
3 teaspoons sesame oil
2 cloves garlic, minced
¾ lb. cauliflower, broken into florets
4 vegan bouillon cubes
½ teaspoon ground cumin
Himalayan salt and freshly ground black pepper, to taste
2 tablespoons fresh parsley, chopped
1 shallot, chopped
1 celery stalk, chopped
4 cups water
1 teaspoon fresh coriander, chopped
1 teaspoon paprika
½ cup almond milk, unsweetened

Directions:
Press the "Sauté" button to heat up your Instant Pot. Heat the oil and sauté the shallot until tender or about 2 minutes.
Add garlic and continue to cook for 30 seconds more, stirring frequently.

Add celery, cauliflower, water, bouillon cubes, fresh coriander, cumin, paprika, salt, and black pepper.

Secure the lid. Choose "Manual" mode and Low pressure, cook for 3 minutes. Once cooking is complete, use a quick pressure release, carefully remove the lid.

Then, add almond milk, press the "Sauté" button again and let it simmer an additional 4 minutes or until everything is heated through.

Afterwards, purée the soup with an immersion blender until smooth and uniform, then, return the soup to the Instant Pot.

Ladle into soup bowls, garnish with fresh parsley, and serve warm. Enjoy!

Nutrition:
Calories: 144, Fat: 11.4 g, Carbs: 9.2 g, Protein: 3.3 g, Sugars: 3.5 g

375. Thai Cream of Celery Soup

Preparation time: 10 minutes | **Cooking time:** 10 minutes | **Servings:** 2

Ingredients:

2 tablespoons olive oil	½ cup leeks, chopped
3 cups celery with leaves, chopped	2 cloves garlic, smashed
1 2-inch piece young galangal, peeled and chopped	1 teaspoon shallot powder
2 fresh bird chilies, seeded and finely chopped	4 cups water
2 tablespoons vegetable bouillon granules	½ teaspoon Thai white peppercorns, ground
Sea salt, to taste	1 bay leaf
¼ cup coconut cream, unsweetened	2 sprigs cilantro, coarsely chopped

Directions:

Press the "Sauté" button to heat up your Instant Pot. Heat the oil and sauté the leeks until tender or about 2 minutes.

Add celery, garlic, and galangal, continue to cook an additional 2 minutes.

Next, add shallot powder, bird chilies, water, vegetable bouillon granules, Thai white peppercorns, salt, and bay leaf.

Secure the lid. Choose "Manual" mode and High pressure, cook for 2 minutes. Once cooking is complete, use a quick pressure release, carefully remove the lid.

Afterwards, purée the soup with an immersion blender until smooth and uniform, then, return the soup to the Instant Pot.

Add the coconut cream and press the "Sauté" button again. Let it simmer until everything is heated through.

Ladle into soup bowls, garnish with cilantro, and serve hot. Enjoy!

Nutrition:
Calories: 141, Fat: 11.1 g, Carbs: 9.1 g, Protein: 2.2 g, Sugars: 4.2 g

376. Cauliflower Tikka Masala

Preparation time: 3 minutes | **Cooking time:** 7 minutes | **Servings:** 2

Ingredients:

1 large cauliflower head, chopped into florets	½ cup unsweetened coconut cream or unsweetened non-dairy yogurt
1 medium beet, peeled, peeled, diced	½ cup pumpkin puree
½ cup organic low-sodium bone broth	2 Tablespoons ghee or non-dairy butter
1 medium red onion, finely chopped	4 garlic cloves, minced
1 1-inch fresh ginger, peeled, grated	1 Tablespoon dried fenugreek leaves
1 Tablespoon fresh parsley, finely chopped	1 Tablespoon garam masala
1 teaspoon smoked or regular paprika	1 teaspoon organic ground turmeric
1 teaspoon organic chili powder	Garnish: roasted cashews, finely chopped cilantro

Directions:

Press "Sauté" function on Instant Pot. Add the ghee.

Once melted, add onion. Cook 3 minutes. Add garlic, grated ginger. Cook 2 minutes more. Add fenugreek, paprika, chili powder, turmeric, garam masala, and parsley. Cook 1 minute, stirring frequently.

In a blender, combine the beet, pumpkin puree, and bone broth. Blend until slightly chunky. Add to ingredients in the Instant Pot. Stir in the cauliflower.

Lock and seal the lid. Press "Manual" button. Cook on HIGH 2 minutes.

When done, allow to sit for 1 minute before quick releasing pressure. Remove lid.

Stir in cream until well combined. Ladle in bowls. Garnish with roasted cashews, cilantro. Serve.

Nutrition:
Calories: 243, Fat: 8.3 g, Carbs: 33.23 g, Fiber: 11.96 g, Protein: 13.4 g

377. Barbecue Jackfruit

Preparation time: 5 minutes | **Cooking time:** 10 minutes | **Servings:** 2

Ingredients:

2 x 8-oz. cans jackfruit, drained, chopped	½ cup homemade low-sodium vegetable broth
½ cup ghee or non-dairy butter, melted	½ cup vinegar
Juice from 1 fresh lemon	½ Tablespoon Worcestershire sauce
½ teaspoons paprika	¼ teaspoon onion powder
¼ teaspoon garlic powder	½ teaspoons salt
¼ teaspoon pepper	Lettuce leaves for serving

Directions:
Add jackfruit and vegetable broth to Instant Pot. Lock and seal the lid. Press "Manual" button. Cook on HIGH 5 minutes.

When done, naturally release pressure. Remove the lid.

Using a colander, drain liquid from jackfruit. Return fruit to Instant Pot. Using a potato masher, smash the fruit slightly.

In a bowl, combine melted ghee, vinegar, lemon juice, Worcestershire sauce, paprika, garlic powder, onion powder, salt, and black pepper. Stir well. Pour mixture over the jackfruit.

Press "Sauté" function. Warm for 5 minutes. Ladle over lettuce leaves. Serve.

Nutrition:
Calories: 488, Fat: 34.8 g, Carbs: 45.7 g, Dietary Fiber: 3 g, Protein: 3.7 g

378. Green Beans with Scallions and Mushrooms

Preparation time: 10 minutes | **Cooking time:** 10 minutes | **Servings:** 2

Ingredients:

2 tablespoons olive oil	½ cup scallions, chopped
2 cloves garlic, minced	1 cup white mushrooms, chopped
¾ lb. green beans	1 cup vegetable broth
Sea salt and ground black pepper, to taste	1 teaspoon red pepper flakes, crushed

Directions:
Press the "Sauté" button to heat up your Instant Pot. Heat the oil and sauté scallions until softened or about 2 minutes.

Then, add garlic and mushrooms, continue to cook an additional minute or so.

Add the other ingredients, gently stir to combine.

Secure the lid. Choose "Manual" mode and Low pressure, cook for 3 minutes. Once cooking is complete, use a quick pressure release, carefully remove the lid.

Serve warm and enjoy!

Nutrition:
Calories: 106, Fat: 7.7 g, Carbs: 7 g, Protein: 3.5 g, Sugars: 1.7 g

379. Ranch Broccoli Dip

Preparation time: 10 minutes | **Cooking time:** 10 minutes | **Servings:** 2

Ingredients:

2 cups broccoli, cut into florets	2 ripe tomatoes, diced
1 yellow onion, chopped	2 garlic cloves, sliced
1 teaspoon fresh coriander, chopped	Seasoned salt, to taste
½ teaspoon ground black pepper	½ teaspoon cayenne pepper

½ teaspoon dried dill weed
½ cup vegan mayonnaise
1 teaspoon Ranch seasoning mix

Directions:
Prepare your Instant Pot by adding 1 cup of water and a steamer basket to its bottom.
Place broccoli florets in the steamer basket.
Secure the lid. Choose "Manual" mode and Low pressure, cook for 5 minutes. Once cooking is complete, use a quick pressure release, carefully remove the lid.
Add the broccoli florets along with the remaining ingredients to your food processor. Process until everything is well incorporated.
Serve well chilled with vegetable sticks. Enjoy!

Nutrition:
Calories: 74, Fat: 6.1 g, Carbs: 3.5 g, Protein: 1.7 g, Sugars: 1.5 g

380. Pork Bowls

Preparation time: 10 minutes | **Cooking time:** 30 minutes | **Servings:** 2

Ingredients:
- 1 lb. pork stew meat, cubed
- 1 tablespoon olive oil
- ½ teaspoon chili powder
- 2 garlic cloves, minced
- ⅓ cup parsley, chopped
- 2 sweet potatoes, peeled and cubed
- 1 yellow onion, chopped
- A pinch of salt and black pepper
- ½ cup tomato passata

Directions:
In s sous vide bag, mix the pork with the sweet potatoes and the other ingredients, toss, seal the bag, submerge in the water oven and cook at 170°F for 30 minutes.
Divide into bowls and serve for lunch.

Nutrition:
Calories: 435, Fat: 5 g, Fiber: 6 g, Carbs: 8 g, Protein: 6 g

381. Shrimp and Sweet Potato Bowls

Preparation time: 10 minutes | **Cooking time:** 20 minutes | **Servings:** 2

Ingredients:
- 1 cup sweet potatoes, peeled and cubed
- ½ lb. shrimp, peeled and deveined
- 1 tablespoon chives, chopped
- ½ teaspoon chili powder
- Juice of ½ lemon
- 1 tablespoon balsamic vinegar
- 2 spring onions, chopped
- ½ teaspoon sweet paprika
- A pinch of salt and black pepper

Directions:
In a sous vide bag, mix the shrimp with the vinegar, potatoes and the other ingredients, toss, seal the bag, submerge in the water oven and cook at 140°F for 20 minutes.
Divide everything into bowls and serve.

Nutrition:
Calories: 253, Fat: 5 g, Fiber: 4 g, Carbs: 5 g, Protein: 2 g

382. Chicken and Eggplants

Preparation time: 10 minutes | **Cooking time:** 30 minutes | **Servings:** 2

Ingredients:
- 1 lb. chicken breast, skinless, boneless and cubed
- Juice of 1 lime
- 2 eggplants, cubed
- ½ teaspoon hot paprika
- ¼ cup parsley, chopped
- 2 spring onions, chopped
- ½ cup tomato passata
- ½ teaspoon chili powder
- 2 tablespoons balsamic vinegar

Directions:
In a sous vide bag, mix the chicken with the eggplants and the other ingredients, toss, seal the bag, submerge in the water oven and cook at 170°F for 30 minutes.
Divide everything between plates and serve for lunch.

Nutrition:
Calories: 266, Fat: 2 g, Fiber: 5 g, Carbs: 7 g, Protein: 7 g

383. Turkey Hash

Preparation time: 10 minutes | **Cooking time:** 30 minutes | **Servings:** 2

Ingredients:

- 1 red onion, chopped
- 1 lb. turkey breast, skinless, boneless and cubed
- ¼ cup chicken stock
- ¼ teaspoon garlic powder
- ¼ cup parsley, chopped
- 1 cup hash browns
- 1 tablespoon olive oil
- ¼ teaspoon red pepper flakes, crushed
- 2 tablespoons lemon juice

Directions:
In a sous vide bag, mix the turkey with the onion, hash browns and the other ingredients, seal the bag and cook in the water oven at 170°F for 30 minutes.
Divide between plates and serve for lunch.

Nutrition:
Calories: 364, Fat: 8 g, Fiber: 5 g, Carbs: 8 g, Protein: 4 g

384. Eggplant Stew

Preparation time: 10 minutes | **Cooking time:** 25 minutes | **Servings:** 2

Ingredients:

- 1 lb. eggplant, cubed
- 1 red onion, chopped
- ½ teaspoon cumin, ground
- A pinch of salt and black pepper
- 1 tablespoon parsley, chopped
- 2 tablespoons olive oil
- 2 garlic cloves, minced
- Zest and juice of 1 lemon
- 1 cup tomato passata

Directions:
In a sous vide bag, mix the eggplants with the onion and the other ingredients, seal the bag and cook in the water oven at 170°F for 25 minutes. Divide the stew into bowls and serve.

Nutrition:
Calories: 512, Fat: 4 g, Fiber: 5 g, Carbs: 78 g, Protein: 2 g

385. Chicken and Rice Soup

Preparation time: 10 minutes | **Cooking time:** 35 minutes | **Servings:** 2

Ingredients:

- 6 cups chicken stock
- 1 bay leaf
- 2 tablespoons olive oil
- 1 egg, whisked
- 1 cup asparagus, trimmed and halved
- ½ cup dill, chopped
- 1 ½ cups chicken meat, cooked and shredded
- 1 yellow onion, chopped
- ⅓ cup white rice
- Juice of ½ lemon
- 1 cup carrots, chopped
- Salt and black pepper to the taste

Directions:
Heat up a pot with the oil over medium heat, add the onions and sauté for 5 minutes.
Add the stock, dill, the rice and the bay leaf, stir, bring to a boil over medium heat and cook for 10 minutes.
Add the rest of the ingredients except the egg and the lemon juice, stir and cook for 15 minutes more.
Add the egg whisked with the lemon juice gradually, whisk the soup, cook for 2 minutes more, divide into bowls and serve.

Nutrition:
Calories: 263, Fat: 18.5 g, Fiber: 4.5 g, Carbs: 19.8 g, Protein: 14.5 g

386. Chicken and Carrots Soup

Preparation time: 10 minutes | **Cooking time:** 1 hour and 20 minutes | **Servings:** 2

Ingredients:
- 1 whole chicken, cut into medium pieces
- 4 eggs, whisked
- ¼ cup dill, chopped
- 8 cups water
- 3 carrots, sliced
- Juice of 2 lemons
- Salt and black pepper to the taste

Directions:
Put the chicken pieces in a pot, add the water, bring to a boil over medium heat, cover the pot and simmer for 1 hour.
Transfer the chicken to a plate, cool it down, discard bones, return the meat to the pot and heat it up again over medium heat.
Add the rest of the ingredients except the eggs, stir and simmer the soup for 10 minutes more.
Add the eggs mixed with 2 cups of stock, stir the soup, cook for 2-3 minutes more, divide into bowls and serve.

Nutrition:
Calories: 264, Fat: 17.5 g, Fiber: 4.8 g, Carbs: 28.7 g, Protein: 16.3 g

387. Roasted Peppers Soup

Preparation time: 10 minutes | **Cooking time:** 55 minutes | **Servings:** 2

Ingredients:
- 2 tomatoes, halved
- 1 yellow onion, quartered
- 2 tablespoons olive oil
- A pinch of salt and black pepper
- ¼ cup parsley, chopped
- ¼ teaspoon sweet paprika
- 3 red bell peppers, halved and deseeded
- 2 garlic cloves, peeled and halved
- 2 cups veggie stock
- 2 tablespoons tomato paste
- ¼ teaspoon Italian seasoning

Directions:
Spread the bell peppers, tomatoes, onion and garlic on a baking sheet lined with parchment paper, add oil, salt and pepper and bake at 375°F for 45 minutes.
Heat up a pot with the stock over medium heat, add the roasted vegetables and the rest of the ingredients, stir, bring to a simmer and cook for 10 minutes.
Blend the mix using an immersion blender, divide the soup into bowls and serve.

Nutrition:
Calories: 273, Fat: 11.2 g, Fiber: 3.4 g, Carbs: 15.7 g, Protein: 5.6 g

388. Lentils Soup

Preparation time: 10 minutes | **Cooking time:** 45 minutes | **Servings:** 2

Ingredients:
- 1 yellow onion, chopped
- 2 celery stalks, chopped
- ⅓ cup parsley, chopped
- 2 and ½ tablespoons garlic, minced
- 1 teaspoon turmeric powder
- 1 teaspoon cinnamon powder
- 15 oz. canned chickpeas, drained and rinsed
- 8 cups chicken stock
- 2 tablespoons olive oil
- 1 carrot, sliced
- ½ cup cilantro, chopped
- 2 tablespoons ginger, grated
- 2 teaspoons sweet paprika
- 1 and ¼ cups red lentils
- 28 oz. canned tomatoes and juice, crushed
- A pinch of salt and black pepper

Directions:
Heat up a pot with the oil over medium heat, add the onion, ginger, garlic, celery and carrots and sauté for 5 minutes.
Add the rest of the ingredients, stir, bring to a simmer over medium heat and cook for 35 minutes.
Ladle the soup into bowls and serve right away.

Nutrition:
Calories: 238, Fat: 7.3 g, Fiber: 6.3 g, Carbs: 32 g, Protein: 14 g

389. White Bean Soup

Preparation time: 10 minutes | **Cooking time:** 8 hours | **Servings:** 2

Ingredients:
- 1 cup celery, chopped
- 1 cup carrots, chopped

1 yellow onion, chopped
4 garlic cloves, minced
½ teaspoon basil, dried
1 teaspoon thyme, dried
6 cups veggie stock
2 cup navy beans, dried
½ teaspoon sage, dried
A pinch of salt and black pepper

Directions:
In your slow cooker, combine the beans with the stock and the rest of the ingredients, put the lid on and cook on Low for 8 hours.
Divide the soup into bowls and serve right away.

Nutrition:
Calories: 264, Fat: 17.5 g, Fiber: 4.5 g, Carbs: 23.7 g, Protein: 11.5 g

390. Veggie Soup

Preparation time: 10 minutes | **Cooking time:** 45 minutes | **Servings:** 2

Ingredients:
1 yellow onion, chopped
½ cup carrots, chopped
1 yellow squash, peeled and cubed
3 tablespoons olive oil
30 oz. canned cannellini beans, drained and rinsed
4 cups veggie stock
¼ teaspoon thyme, dried
A pinch of salt and black pepper
¼ cup parmesan, grated
4 garlic cloves, minced
1 zucchini, chopped
2 tablespoons parsley, chopped
¼ cup celery, chopped
30 oz. canned red kidney beans, drained and rinsed
2 cups water
½ teaspoon basil, dried
4 cups baby spinach

Directions:
Heat up a pot with the oil over medium heat, add the onion, garlic, carrots, squash, zucchini, parsley and the celery, stir and sauté for 5 minutes.
Add the rest of the ingredients except the spinach and the parmesan, stir, bring to a simmer over medium heat and cook for 30 minutes.
Add the spinach, cook the soup for 10 minutes more, divide into bowls, sprinkle the cheese on top and serve.

Nutrition:
Calories: 300, Fat: 11.3 g, Fiber: 3.4 g, Carbs: 17.5 g, Protein: 10 g

391. Seafood Gumbo

Preparation time: 10 minutes | **Cooking time:** 30 minutes | **Servings:** 2

Ingredients:
¼ cup tapioca flour
1 cup celery, chopped
1 red bell pepper, chopped
1 red chili, chopped
2 garlic cloves, minced
1 teaspoon thyme, dried
1 bay leaf
1 lb. shrimp, peeled and deveined
Salt and black pepper to the taste
¼ cup olive oil
1 white onion, chopped
1 green bell pepper, chopped
2 cups okra, chopped
1 cup canned tomatoes, crushed
2 cups fish stock
16 oz. canned crab meat, drained
¼ cup parsley, chopped

Directions:
Heat up a pot with the oil over medium heat, add the flour, whisk to obtain a paste and cook for about 5 minutes.
Add the bell peppers, the onions, celery and the okra and sauté for 5 minutes.
Add the rest of the ingredients except the crab, shrimp, and parsley, stir, bring to a simmer and cook for 15 minutes.
Add the remaining ingredients, simmer the soup for 10 minutes more, divide into bowls and serve.

Nutrition:
Calories: 363, Fat: 2 g, Fiber: 5 g, Carbs: 18 g, Protein: 40 g

392. Chicken and Orzo Soup

Preparation time: 10 minutes | **Cooking time:** 11 minutes | **Servings:** 2

Ingredients:

- ½ cup carrot, chopped
- 12 cups chicken stock
- 3 cups chicken meat, cooked and shredded
- ¼ cup lemon juice
- 1 yellow onion, chopped
- 2 cups kale, chopped
- 1 cup orzo
- 1 tablespoon olive oil

Directions:
Heat up a pot with the oil over medium heat, add the onion and sauté for 3 minutes.
Add the carrots and the rest of the ingredients, stir, bring to a simmer and cook for 8 minutes more.
Ladle into bowls and serve hot.

Nutrition:
Calories: 300, Fat: 12.2 g, Fiber: 5.4 g, Carbs: 16.5 g, Protein: 12.2 g

393. Lentils Soup

Preparation time: 10 minutes | **Cooking time:** 8 hours | **Servings:** 2

Ingredients:

- 2 cups red lentils, dried
- 2 celery stalks, chopped
- 3 garlic cloves, minced
- 2 chipotle chili peppers, chopped
- 1 ½ teaspoons cumin, ground
- 2 teaspoons adobo sauce
- 2 tablespoons lime juice
- 1 yellow onion, chopped
- 2 carrots, sliced
- 15 oz. canned tomatoes, chopped
- 7 cups veggie stock
- Salt and black pepper to the taste
- ¼ cup cilantro, chopped

Directions:
In your slow cooker, combine the lentils with the tomatoes, chili peppers and the rest of the ingredients except the cilantro and the lime juice, put the lid on and cook on Low for 8 hours.
Add the cilantro and the lime juice, stir, ladle the soup into bowls and serve.

Nutrition:
Calories: 276, Fat: 1 g, Fiber: 21 g, Carbs: 48 g, Protein: 17 g

394. Zucchini Soup

Preparation time: 10 minutes | **Cooking time:** 20 minutes | **Servings:** 2

Ingredients:

- 2 ½ lbs. zucchinis, roughly chopped
- 1 yellow onion, chopped
- 4 cups chicken stock
- Salt and black pepper to the taste
- 2 tablespoons olive oil
- 4 garlic cloves, minced
- ½ cup basil, chopped

Directions:
Heat up a pot with the oil over medium heat, add the zucchinis and the onion and sauté for 5 minutes.
Add the garlic and the rest of the ingredients except the basil, stir, bring to a simmer and cook for 15 minutes over medium heat.
Add the basil, blend the soup using an immersion blender, ladle into bowls and serve.

Nutrition:
Calories: 182, Fat: 7.6 g, Fiber: 1.5 g, Carbs: 12.6 g, Protein: 2.3 g

395. Spanish-Style Carrot Dip

Preparation time: 10 minutes | **Cooking time:** 10 minutes | **Servings:** 2

Ingredients:

- 1 lb. carrots, trimmed, peeled, and chopped
- ½ teaspoon ground cumin
- ¼ teaspoon dried dill weed
- 1 teaspoon smoked Spanish paprika
- 1 tablespoon apple cider vinegar
- ¼ cup sesame oil
- 2 garlic cloves, crushed
- ½ teaspoon dried basil
- Salt and ground white pepper, to your liking

Directions:
Add all ingredients to your Instant Pot.
Secure the lid. Choose "Manual" mode and High pressure, cook for 1 minute. Once cooking is complete, use a quick pressure release, carefully remove the lid.

Transfer to a serving bowl and serve. Enjoy!

Nutrition:
Calories: 89, Fat: 7.1 g, Carbs: 6.4 g, Protein: 0.7 g, Sugars: 3.1 g

396. Cauliflower Risotto

Preparation time: 10 minutes | **Cooking time:** 27 minutes | **Servings:** 2

Ingredients:

- 12 asparagus, remove woodsy stem, diced
- 1 cup organic baby carrots
- 2 garlic cloves, minced
- ½ bunch chives, thinly sliced
- 1 ½ cups cauliflower rice
- 2 Tablespoons olive oil
- ½ teaspoon garlic powder
- 1 teaspoon fresh lemon zest
- ¼ cup ghee or non-dairy butter
- 1 cup organic fresh broccoli florets
- 1 cup fresh leeks, finely chopped
- 1 cup fresh baby spinach
- 1 medium yellow onion, finely chopped
- 4 cups homemade low-sodium vegetable broth
- 1 teaspoon fresh thyme
- ¼ teaspoon red pepper flakes
- 2 Tablespoons fresh lemon juice
- Pinch of salt, pepper

Directions:
Line a baking sheet with parchment paper. Place asparagus, broccoli, and carrots in a single layer on the tray. Drizzle olive oil. Season with salt and pepper.
Place baking sheet in 400°F oven 15 minutes, until broccoli is tender. Remove, set aside. Once cooled, dice in small pieces.
Press "Sauté" function on Instant Pot. Add 1 tablespoon of olive oil.
Once hot, add onion. Cook 4 minutes. Add garlic, leeks. Cook 2 minutes. Add cauliflower rice. Sauté 1 minute.
Stir in vegetable broth, ghee or non-dairy butter, and fresh thyme.
Lock and seal the lid. Press "Manual" button. Cook on HIGH 7 minutes.
When done, quick release pressure. Remove the lid.
Press "Sauté" function. Stir in asparagus, broccoli, carrots, leeks, spinach, garlic powder, red pepper flakes, lemon zest, and lemon juice. Sauté 1 minute, until spinach wilts. Ladle in bowls. Garnish with chives. Serve.

Nutrition:
Calories: 278, Fat: 21.5 g, Carbs: 15.3 g, Fiber: 4.3 g, Protein: 8.4 g

397. Spicy Chickpea Curry

Preparation time: 10 minutes | **Cooking time:** 18 minutes | **Servings:** 2

Ingredients:

- 2 cans chickpeas, rinsed and drained
- 3 tomatoes, diced
- 1 tsp turmeric
- 2 tsp garam masala
- 1 tbsp olive oil
- 1 onion, chopped
- 14 oz coconut milk
- 1 tsp chili powder
- 1 ½ tsp cumin
- 1 ½ tsp coriander
- 2 garlic cloves, chopped
- 1 tsp salt

Directions:
Add oil into the instant pot and set the pot on sauté mode.
Add onion and garlic and sauté until onion is softened.
Add remaining ingredients and stir everything well.
Seal pot with lid and cook on manual high pressure for 15 minutes.
Once done then allow to release pressure naturally for 10 minutes then release using the quick-release method. Open the lid.
Stir well and serve over rice.

Nutrition:
Calories: 659, Fat: 33.8 g, Carbs: 73.9 g, Sugar: 17.7 g, Protein: 23.1 g

398. Tasty Mushroom Stroganoff

Preparation time: 10 minutes | **Cooking time:** 12 minutes | **Servings:** 2

Ingredients:

- 8 oz pasta, uncooked
- 1 tbsp flour

2 tbsp mustard	2 cups vegetable broth
¼ cup white wine	15 oz mushrooms, sliced
2 garlic cloves, chopped	½ onion, diced
3 tbsp olive oil	½ tsp pepper
¾ tsp salt	

Directions:
Add oil into the instant pot and set the pot on sauté mode.
Add mushrooms, garlic, onion, pepper, and salt and cook for 5-8 minutes.
Add flour, mustard, broth, wine, and pasta and stir well.
Seal pot with lid and cook on high pressure for 4 minutes.
Once done then release pressure using the quick-release method than open the lid.
Stir well and serve.

Nutrition:
Calories: 349, Fat: 14.4 g, Carbs: 40.8 g, Sugar: 3.3 g, Protein: 14.1 g, Cholesterol: 41 mg

399. Chinese-Style Bok Choy

Preparation time: 15 minutes | **Cooking time:** 10 minutes | **Servings:** 2

Ingredients:

1 ½ lbs. Bok choy	2 cloves garlic, pressed
2 tablespoons rice wine vinegar	2 teaspoons sesame oil
4 tablespoons soy sauce	1 cup water

Directions:
Press the "Sauté" button and heat the oil. Now, cook the garlic for 1 minute or until it is fragrant but not browned.
Add the Bok choy and water to the inner pot.
Secure the lid. Choose the "Manual" mode and cook for 5 minutes at High pressure. Once cooking is complete, use a quick pressure release, carefully remove the lid.
Meanwhile, in a mixing bowl, whisk the rice vinegar and soy sauce. Drizzle this sauce over the Bok choy and serve immediately.

Nutrition:
Calories: 92, Fat: 5.4 g, Carbs: 8.1 g, Protein: 3.8 g, Sugars: 5.1 g

400. Spanish Salmorejo with Pepitas

Preparation time: 15 minutes | **Cooking time:** 10 minutes | **Servings:** 2

Ingredients:

1 lb. ripe tomatoes, puréed	2 tablespoons pepitas
½ teaspoon dried marjoram	1 teaspoon sweet paprika
2 carrots, roughly chopped	1 red chili pepper, seeded and chopped
1 zucchini, chopped	1 teaspoon dried rosemary
2 cloves garlic, crushed	½ teaspoon dried basil
1 cup vegetable stock	2 tablespoons fresh chives, chopped
2 tablespoons olive oil	½ cup green onions, chopped
Sea salt and ground black pepper, to taste	

Directions:
Press the "Sauté" button to preheat your Instant Pot. Then, heat the oil until sizzling.
Now, cook the green onions and garlic until tender and fragrant. Add the carrots, chili pepper, tomatoes, zucchini, seasonings, and stock.
Secure the lid. Choose the "Manual" mode and cook for 6 minutes under High pressure. Once cooking is complete, use a quick release, carefully remove the lid.
Then, purée the mixture with an immersion blender until the desired thickness is reached.
Ladle into soup bowls, serve garnished with fresh chives and pepitas. Enjoy!

Nutrition:
Calories: 125, Fat: 9.4 g, Carbs: 8.1 g, Protein: 4.2 g, Sugars: 1.8 g

401. Pork Kebabs

Preparation time: 10 minutes | **Cooking time:** 14 minutes | **Servings:** 2

Ingredients:

- 1 yellow onion, chopped
- 3 tablespoons cilantro, chopped
- 1 garlic clove, minced
- Salt and black pepper to the taste
- 1 lb. pork meat, ground
- 1 tablespoon lime juice
- 2 teaspoon oregano, dried
- A drizzle of olive oil

Directions:

In a bowl, mix the pork with the other ingredients except the oil, stir well and shape medium kebabs out of this mix.

Divide the kebabs on skewers and brush them with a drizzle of oil.

Place the kebabs on your preheated grill and cook over medium heat for 7 minutes on each side.

Divide the kebabs between plates and serve with a side salad.

Nutrition:
Calories: 229, Fat: 14 g, Fiber: 8.3 g, Carbs: 15.5 g, Protein: 12.4 g

402. Cilantro Pork and Olives

Preparation time: 10 minutes | **Cooking time:** 20 minutes | **Servings:** 2

Ingredients:

- 2 lbs. pork loin, sliced
- 2 tablespoons olive oil
- Salt and black pepper to the taste
- Salt and black pepper to the taste
- Juice of 1 lime
- 1 cup black olives, pitted and halved
- ½ cup tomato puree
- ½ cup mixed cilantro, chopped
- 4 garlic cloves, minced

Directions:

Heat up a pan with the oil over medium-high heat, add the garlic and the meat and brown for 5 minutes.

Add the rest of the ingredients, bring to a simmer and cook over medium heat for 15 minutes more.

Divide the mix between plates and serve.

Nutrition:
Calories: 249, Fat: 12 g, Fiber: 8.3 g, Carbs: 21.5 g, Protein: 12.6 g

403. Pork and Parsley Sauce

Preparation time: 10 minutes | **Cooking time:** 20 minutes | **Servings:** 2

Ingredients:

- 1 lb. pork stew meat, cubed
- 1 cup parsley, chopped
- Salt and black pepper to the taste
- ½ cup olive oil
- 1 tablespoon walnuts, chopped
- 2 garlic cloves, minced
- 2 cups Greek yogurt

Directions:

In a blender, combine the parsley with garlic, walnuts, yogurt, salt, pepper and half of the oil and pulse well.

Heat up a pan with the rest of the oil over medium-high heat, add the meat and cook for 5 minutes.

Add the parsley sauce, toss, bring to a simmer and cook over medium heat for 15 minutes more.

Divide the mix into bowls and serve.

Nutrition:
Calories: 264, Fat: 11 g, Fiber: 5.4 g, Carbs: 20.1 g, Protein: 18.5 g

404. Pork Tenderloin and Dill Sauce

Preparation time: 10 minutes | **Cooking time:** 20 minutes | **Servings:** 2

Ingredients:

- 1 lb. pork tenderloin, sliced
- 3 tablespoons coriander seeds, ground
- ⅓ cup heavy cream
- Salt and black pepper to the taste
- 2 tablespoons olive oil
- ½ cup dill, chopped

Directions:

Heat up a pan with the oil over medium-high heat, add the meat and brown for 4 minutes on each side.

Add the rest of the ingredients, bring to a simmer and cook over medium heat for 12 minutes more.
Divide the mix between plates and serve.

Nutrition:
Calories: 320, Fat: 14.5 g, Fiber: 9.1 g, Carbs: 13.7 g, Protein: 17.5 g

405. Lamb and Couscous

Preparation time: 10 minutes | **Cooking time:** 30 minutes | **Servings:** 2

Ingredients:
- 1 and ½ cups couscous
- 2 cups chicken stock
- Salt and black pepper to the taste
- ¼ cup parsley, chopped
- ¼ cup spring onions, chopped
- 2 tablespoons avocado oil
- 1 tablespoon cilantro, chopped
- 1 and ½ lb. lamb meat, cubed
- 4 oz. feta cheese, crumbled

Directions:
Heat up a pan with the oil over medium-high heat, add the lamb and brown for 6 minutes.
Add the couscous and brown for 4 minutes more.
Add the rest of the ingredients except the cheese, bring to a simmer and cook over medium heat for 20 minutes more.
Add the cheese, toss, divide the mix between plates and serve.

Nutrition:
Calories: 370, Fat: 24.5 g, Fiber: 11 g, Carbs: 16.7 g, Protein: 27.5 g

406. Pork Meatloaf

Preparation time: 10 minutes | **Cooking time:** 1 hour and 20 minutes | **Servings:** 2

Ingredients:
- 1 red onion, chopped
- 2 garlic cloves, minced
- 1 cup almond milk
- Cooking spray
- 2 lbs. pork stew, ground
- ¼ cup feta cheese, crumbled
- 2 eggs, whisked
- 4 tablespoons oregano, chopped
- ⅓ cup kalamata olives, pitted and chopped
- Salt and black pepper to the taste

Directions:
In a bowl, mix the meat with the onion, garlic and the other ingredients except the cooking spray, stir well, shape your meatloaf and put it in a loaf pan greased with cooking spray.
Bake the meatloaf at 370°F for 1 hour and 20 minutes.
Serve the meatloaf warm.

Nutrition:
Calories: 350, Fat: 23 g, Fiber: 1 g, Carbs: 17 g, Protein: 24 g

407. Marjoram Pork

Preparation time: 10 minutes | **Cooking time:** 1 hour | **Servings:** 2

Ingredients:
- 1 cup marjoram, chopped
- 1 tablespoons capers, drained
- 1 and ½ lbs. pork loin, cubed
- Salt and black pepper to the taste
- 1 garlic clove, minced
- 2 tablespoons olive oil
- 1 cup veggie stock
- ½ cup feta cheese, crumbled

Directions:
Heat up a pan with the oil over medium-high heat, add the meat and brown for 5 minutes.
Add the rest of the ingredients except the cheese, toss, bring to a simmer and cook over medium heat for 30 minutes.
Add the cheese, toss gently, divide between plates and serve.

Nutrition:
Calories: 304, Fat: 14.1 g, Fiber: 8.2 g, Carbs: 15.9 g, Protein: 33.2 g

408. Simple Fish Chowder

Preparation time: 10 minutes | **Cooking time:** 10 minutes | **Servings:** 2

Ingredients:
- ¾ cup bacon, chopped
- 2 celery ribs, chopped
- 3 cups potatoes, cubed
- 4 cups chicken stock
- 1 lb. haddock fillets
- 2 cups heavy cream
- 1 tablespoon potato starch
- 1 yellow onion, peeled and chopped
- 2 garlic cloves, peeled and chopped
- 1 carrot, peeled and chopped
- 1 cup frozen corn
- 2 tablespoons butter
- Salt and ground white pepper, to taste

Directions:
Put the Instant Pot in the sauté mode, add the butter and melt. Add the bacon, mix and cook until crispy.
Add the garlic, celery and onion, mix and cook for 3 minutes. Add salt, pepper, fish, potato, corn and broth, mix, cover and cook for 5 minutes in the Manual setting.
Release the pressure naturally, uncover the Instant Pot, add the cream mixed with potato starch, mix well, put the Instant Pot in Soup mode and cook for 3 minutes. Divide into bowls and serve.

Nutrition:
Calories: 195, Fat: 4.4 g, Fiber: 2 g, Carbs: 21 g, Proteins: 17 g

409. Pulled Pork

Preparation time: 10 minutes | **Cooking time:** 1 hour and 20 minutes | **Servings:** 2

Ingredients:
- 8 oz. water
- 11 oz. beer
- 3 oz. white sugar
- Salt, to taste
- For the sauce:
- 12 oz. apple cider vinegar
- 4 oz. hot water
- Salt and ground black pepper, to taste
- 3 lbs. pork shoulder, boneless and cut into large chinks
- 2 teaspoons dry mustard
- 2 teaspoons smoked paprika
- 2 tablespoons brown sugar
- Cayenne pepper
- 2 teaspoons dry mustard

Directions:
In a bowl, mix white sugar with smoked pepper, 2 teaspoons of dried mustard and salt. Rub the pork with this mixture and place the pieces in the instant pot. Add the beer and 3 oz. of water, stir, cover the instant pot and cook in the Meat / Stew setting for 75 minutes.
Release the pressure, uncover the Instant Pot, transfer the pork to a cutting board, Shred with 2 forks and reserve the dish.
Discard half of the cooking liquid from the Instant Pot. In a bowl, mix brown sugar with 4 oz. of hot water, vinegar, cayenne pepper, salt, pepper and 2 teaspoons of dry mustard and mix well. Pour this sauce from the instant pot, stir, cover and cook for 3 minutes in the Manual setting.
Relieve the pressure, divide the pork between the dishes, season the sauce everywhere and serve.

Nutrition:
Calories: 440, Fat: 12 g, Fiber: 4 g, Carbs: 40 g, Proteins: 32 g

410. Pork Roast with Fennel

Preparation time: 10 minutes
Cooking time: 1 hour and 20 minutes
Servings: 2

Ingredients:
- 2 tablespoons extra virgin olive oil
- 2 garlic cloves, peeled and minced
- 5 oz. chicken stock
- 5 oz. white wine
- Salt and ground black pepper, to taste
- 2 lbs. pork meat, boneless
- 1 yellow onion, peeled and chopped
- 1-lb. fennel bulbs, sliced

Directions:
Put the instant pot in the sauté mode, add the oil and heat. Add the pork, salt and pepper, mix, brown on all sides and transfer to a plate. Add the garlic, wine and broth to the Instant Pot, stir and cook for 2 minutes.
Return the pork to the pan, cover and cook for 40 minutes in the Manual setting. Release the pressure, uncover the Instant Pot, add the onion and fennel, stir, cover and cook for 15 minutes in the Manual setting.

Relieve the pressure, mix the mixture, transfer the pork to a cutting board, cut and divide between the plates. Serve with onion and fennel on the side, with all the sauce.

Nutrition:
Calories: 428, Fat: 16 g, Fiber: 1.1 g, Carbs: 29 g, Proteins: 38 g

411. Chinese Barbecue Pork

Preparation time: 10 minutes | **Cooking time:** 50 minutes | **Servings:** 2

Ingredients:

- 4 tablespoons soy sauce
- 1-quart chicken stock
- 2 tablespoons honey
- 8 tablespoons char siu sauce
- 2 tablespoons dry sherry
- 2 lbs. pork belly
- 1 teaspoon peanut oil
- 2 teaspoons sesame oil

Directions:
Put the instant pot in manual mode, add sherry, stock, soy sauce and half of the siu sauce, mix and cook for 8 minutes. Add the pork, mix, cover and cook for 30 minutes in the Meat / Stew setting.

Release the pressure naturally, transfer the pork to a cutting board, let it cool and cut into small pieces.

Heat a pan with peanut oil over medium-high heat, add the pork, stir and cook for a few minutes. In a bowl, mix the sesame oil with the rest of the char siu sauce and the honey. Brush the pork with the sauce, mix and cook for 10 minutes.

Heat another pan over medium-high heat, add the cooking liquid to the Instant Pot and bring to a boil. Cook for 3 minutes and remove from heat.

Divide the pork between the dishes, add the sauce and serve.

Nutrition:
Calories: 400, Fat: 23 g, Fiber: 1 g, Carbs: 15 g, Sugar: 14 g, Proteins: 41 g

Chapter 3: Dinner

412. Shrimp and Dill Sauce

Preparation time: 10 minutes | **Cooking time:** 10 minutes | **Servings:** 2

Ingredients:
- 1 tablespoon yellow onion, chopped
- 2 tablespoons shortening
- 1 teaspoon fresh dill, chopped
- ¾ cup milk
- 1 cup white wine
- 2 tablespoons cornstarch
- 1 lb. shrimp, peeled and deveined

Directions:
Put the Instant Pot in Sauté mode, add the fat and heat. Add the onion, mix and cook for 2 minutes.
Add the shrimp and wine, stir, cover and cook for 2 minutes in the Manual setting. Release the pressure, uncover the Instant Pot and set it to Manual mode.
In a bowl, mix the cornstarch with the milk and stir.
Add this to the shrimp and stir until it thickens. Add the dill, stir, cook for 5 minutes, divide between the bowls and serve.

Nutrition:
Calories: 300, Fat: 10 g, Carbs: 7 g, Proteins: 10 g

413. Lemon Rainbow Trout

Preparation time: 10 minutes | **Cooking time:** 15 minutes | **Servings:** 2

Ingredients:
- 2 rainbow trout
- 3 tablespoons olive oil
- A pinch of salt and black pepper
- Juice of 1 lemon
- 4 garlic cloves, minced

Directions:
Line a baking sheet with parchment paper, add the fish and the rest of the ingredients and rub. Bake at 400°F for 15 minutes, divide between plates and serve with a side salad.

Nutrition:
Calories: 521, Fat: 29 g, Fiber: 5 g, Carbs: 14 g, Protein: 52 g

414. Trout and Peppers Mix

Preparation time: 10 minutes | **Cooking time:** 20 minutes | **Servings:** 2

Ingredients:
- 4 trout fillets, boneless
- 1 tablespoon capers, drained
- A pinch of salt and black pepper
- 1 yellow bell pepper, chopped
- 1 green bell pepper, chopped
- 2 tablespoons kalamata olives, pitted and chopped
- 2 tablespoons olive oil
- 1 and ½ teaspoons chili powder
- 1 red bell pepper, chopped

Directions:
Heat up a pan with the oil over medium-high heat, add the trout, salt and pepper and cook for 10 minutes.
Flip the fish, add the peppers and the rest of the ingredients, cook for 10 minutes more, divide the whole mix between plates and serve.

Nutrition:
Calories: 572, Fat: 17.4 g, Fiber: 6 g, Carbs: 71 g, Protein: 33.7 g

415. Cod and Cabbage

Preparation time: 10 minutes | **Cooking time:** 15 minutes | **Servings:** 2

Ingredients:
- 3 cups green cabbage, shredded
- A pinch of salt and black pepper
- 4 teaspoons olive oil
- ¼ cup green olives, pitted and chopped
- 1 sweet onion, sliced
- ½ cup feta cheese, crumbled
- 4 cod fillets, boneless

Directions:
Grease a roasting pan with the oil, add the fish, the cabbage and the rest of the ingredients, introduce in the pan and cook at 450°F for 15 minutes.
Divide the mix between plates and serve.

Nutrition:
Calories: 270, Fat: 10 g, Fiber: 3 g, Carbs: 12 g, Protein: 31 g

416. Mediterranean Mussels

Preparation time: 10 minutes | **Cooking time:** 10 minutes | **Servings:** 2

Ingredients:
- 1 white onion, sliced
- 2 teaspoons fennel seeds
- 1 teaspoon red pepper, crushed
- 1 cup chicken stock
- 2 and ½ lbs. mussels, scrubbed
- ½ cup tomatoes, cubed
- 3 tablespoons olive oil
- 4 garlic cloves, minced
- A pinch of salt and black pepper
- 1 tablespoon lemon juice
- ½ cup parsley, chopped

Directions:
Heat up a pan with the oil over medium-high heat, add the onion and the garlic and sauté for 2 minutes.
Add the rest of the ingredients except the mussels, stir and cook for 3 minutes more.
Add the mussels, cook everything for 6 minutes more, divide everything into bowls and serve.

Nutrition:
Calories: 276, Fat: 9.8 g, Fiber: 4.8 g, Carbs: 6.5 g, Protein: 20.5 g

417. Mussels Bowls

Preparation time: 10 minutes | **Cooking time:** 10 minutes | **Servings:** 2

Ingredients:
- 2 lbs. mussels, scrubbed
- 1 tablespoon basil, chopped
- 6 tomatoes, cubed
- 2 tablespoons olive oil
- 1 tablespoon garlic, minced
- 1 yellow onion, chopped
- 1 cup heavy cream
- 1 tablespoon parsley, chopped

Directions:
Heat up a pan with the oil over medium-high heat, add the garlic and the onion and sauté for 2 minutes.
Add the mussels and the rest of the ingredients, toss, cook for 7 minutes more, divide into bowls and serve.

Nutrition:
Calories: 266, Fat: 11.8 g, Fiber: 5.8 g, Carbs: 16.5 g, Protein: 10.5 g

418. Calamari and Dill Sauce

Preparation time: 10 minutes | **Cooking time:** 15 minutes | **Servings:** 2

Ingredients:

- 1 ½ lb. calamari, sliced into rings
- 2 tablespoons olive oil
- 2 tablespoons balsamic vinegar
- A pinch of salt and black pepper
- 10 garlic cloves, minced
- Juice of 1 ½ lime
- 3 tablespoons dill, chopped

Directions:
Heat up a pan with the oil over medium-high heat, add the garlic, lime juice and the other ingredients except the calamari and cook for 5 minutes.
Add the calamari rings, cook everything for 10 minutes more, divide between plates and serve.

Nutrition:
Calories: 282, Fat: 18.6 g, Fiber: 4 g, Carbs: 9.2 g, Protein: 18.5 g

419. Chili Calamari and Veggie Mix

Preparation time: 10 minutes | **Cooking time:** 40 minutes | **Servings:** 2

Ingredients:

- 1 lb. calamari rings
- 2 tablespoons olive oil
- 14 oz. canned tomatoes, chopped
- 1 tablespoon thyme, chopped
- 2 tablespoons capers, drained
- 2 red chili peppers, chopped
- 3 garlic cloves, minced
- 2 tablespoons tomato paste
- Salt and black pepper to the taste
- 12 black olives, pitted and halved

Directions:
Heat up a pan with the oil over medium-high heat, add the garlic and the chili peppers and sauté for 2 minutes.
Add the rest of the ingredients except the olives and capers, stir, bring to a simmer and cook for 22 minutes.
Add the olives and capers, cook everything for 15 minutes more, divide everything into bowls and serve.

Nutrition:
Calories: 274, Fat: 11.6 g, Fiber: 2.8 g, Carbs: 13.5 g, Protein: 15.4 g

420. Cheesy Crab and Lime Spread

Preparation time: 10 minutes | **Cooking time:** 25 minutes | **Servings:** 2

Ingredients:

- 1 lb. crab meat, flaked
- 1 tablespoon chives, chopped
- 1 teaspoon lime zest, grated
- 4 oz. cream cheese, soft
- 1 teaspoon lime juice

Directions:
In a baking dish greased with cooking spray, combine the crab with the rest of the ingredients and toss.
Introduce in the oven at 350°F, bake for 25 minutes, divide into bowls and serve.

Nutrition:
Calories: 284, Fat: 14.6 g, Fiber: 5.8 g, Carbs: 16.5 g, Protein: 15.4 g

421. Horseradish Cheesy Salmon Mix

Preparation time: 1 hour | **Cooking time:** 0 minutes | **Servings:** 2

Ingredients:

- 2 oz. feta cheese, crumbled
- 3 tablespoons already prepared horseradish
- 2 teaspoons lime zest, grated
- 3 tablespoons chives, chopped
- 4 oz. cream cheese, soft
- 1 lb. smoked salmon, skinless, boneless and flaked
- 1 red onion, chopped

Directions:

In your food processor, mix cream cheese with horseradish, goat cheese and lime zest and blend very well.

In a bowl, combine the salmon with the rest of the ingredients, toss and serve cold.

Nutrition:

Calories: 281, Fat: 17.9 g, Fiber: 1 g, Carbs: 4.2 g, Protein: 25.3 g

422. Greek Trout Spread

Preparation time: 5 minutes | **Cooking time:** 0 minutes | **Servings:** 2

Ingredients:

- 4 oz. smoked trout, skinless, boneless and flaked
- 1 cup Greek yogurt
- Salt and black pepper to the taste
- 1 tablespoon lemon juice
- tablespoon dill, chopped
- A drizzle of olive oil

Directions:

In a bowl, combine the trout with the lemon juice and the rest of the ingredients and whisk well.

Divide the spread into bowls and serve.

Nutrition:

Calories: 258, Fat: 4.5 g, Fiber: 2 g, Carbs: 5.5 g, Protein: 7.6 g

423. Scallions and Salmon Tartar

Preparation time: 5 minutes | **Cooking time:** 0 minutes | **Servings:** 2

Ingredients:

- 4 tablespoons scallions, chopped
- 1 tablespoon chives, minced
- 1 lb. salmon, skinless, boneless and minced
- 1 tablespoon parsley, chopped
- 2 teaspoons lemon juice
- 1 tablespoon olive oil
- Salt and black pepper to the taste

Directions:

In a bowl, combine the scallions with the salmon and the rest of the ingredients, stir well, divide into small molds between plates and serve.

Nutrition:

Calories: 224, Fat: 14.5 g, Fiber: 5.2 g, Carbs: 12.7 g, Protein: 5.3 g

424. Salmon and Green Beans

Preparation time: 10 minutes | **Cooking time:** 15 minutes | **Servings:** 2

Ingredients:

- 3 tablespoons balsamic vinegar
- 1 garlic clove, minced
- ½ teaspoon lime zest, grated
- Salt and black pepper to the taste
- 4 salmon fillets, boneless
- 2 tablespoons olive oil
- ½ teaspoons red pepper flakes, crushed
- 1 ½ lbs. green beans, chopped
- 1 red onion, sliced

Directions:

Heat up a pan with half of the oil, add the vinegar, onion, garlic and the other ingredients except the salmon, toss, cook for 6 minutes and divide between plates.

Heat up the same pan with the rest of the oil over medium-high heat, add the salmon, salt and pepper, cook for 4 minutes on each side, add next to the green beans and serve.

Nutrition:

Calories: 224, Fat: 15.5 g, Fiber: 8.2 g, Carbs: 22.7 g, Protein: 16.3 g

425. Cayenne Cod and Tomatoes

Preparation time: 10 minutes | **Cooking time:** 25 minutes | **Servings:** 2

Ingredients:

- 1 teaspoon lime juice
- 1 teaspoon sweet paprika
- 2 tablespoons olive oil
- Salt and black pepper to the taste
- 1 teaspoon cayenne pepper
- 1 yellow onion, chopped

2 garlic cloves, minced

A pinch of cloves, ground

½ lb. cherry tomatoes, cubed

4 cod fillets, boneless

½ cup chicken stock

Directions:

Heat up a pan with the oil over medium-high heat add the cod, salt, pepper and the cayenne, cook for 4 minutes on each side and divide between plates.

Heat up the same pan over medium-high heat, add the onion and garlic and sauté for 5 minutes. Add the rest of the ingredients, stir, bring to a simmer and cook for 10 minutes more.

Divide the mix next to the fish and serve.

Nutrition:

Calories: 232, Fat: 16.5 g, Fiber: 11.1 g, Carbs: 24.8 g, Protein: 16.5 g

426. Salmon and Watermelon Gazpacho

Preparation time: 4 hours | **Cooking time:** 0 minutes | **Servings:** 2

Ingredients:

¼ cup basil, chopped

1 lb. watermelon, cubed

⅓ cup avocado oil

1 cup smoked salmon, skinless, boneless and cubed

1 lb. tomatoes, cubed

¼ cup red wine vinegar

2 garlic cloves, minced

A pinch of salt and black pepper

Directions:

In your blender, combine the basil with the watermelon and the rest of the ingredients except the salmon, pulse well and divide into bowls.

Top each serving with the salmon and serve cold.

Nutrition:

Calories: 252, Fat: 16.5 g, Fiber: 9.1 g, Carbs: 24.8 g, Protein: 15.5 g

427. Shrimp and Dill Mix

Preparation time: 10 minutes | **Cooking time:** 10 minutes | **Servings:** 2

Ingredients:

1 lb. shrimp, cooked, peeled and deveined

1 cup spring onion, chopped

2 tablespoons capers, chopped

Salt and black pepper to the taste

½ cup raisins

2 tablespoons olive oil

2 tablespoons dill, chopped

Directions:

Heat up a pan with the oil over medium-high heat, add the onions and raisins and sauté for 2-3 minutes.

Add the shrimp and the rest of the ingredients, toss, cook for 6 minutes more, divide between plates and serve with a side salad.

Nutrition:

Calories: 218, Fat: 12.8 g, Fiber: 6.2 g, Carbs: 22.2 g, Protein: 4.8 g

428. Minty Sardines Salad

Preparation time: 10 minutes | **Cooking time:** 0 minutes | **Servings:** 2

Ingredients:

4 oz. canned sardines in olive oil, skinless, boneless and flaked

2 tablespoons mint, chopped

1 avocado, peeled, pitted and cubed

2 tomatoes, cubed

2 teaspoons avocado oil

A pinch of salt and black pepper

1 cucumber, cubed

2 spring onions, chopped

Directions:

In a bowl, combine the sardines with the oil and the rest of the ingredients, toss, divide into small cups and keep in the fridge for 10 minutes before serving.

Nutrition:

Calories: 261, Fat: 7.6 g, Fiber: 2.2 g, Carbs: 22.8 g, Protein: 12.5 g

429. Salmon and Zucchini Rolls

Preparation time: 10 minutes | **Cooking time:** 0 minutes | **Servings:** 2

Ingredients:

- 8 slices smoked salmon, boneless
- 1 cup ricotta cheese, soft
- 1 tablespoon dill, chopped
- Salt and pepper to the taste
- 2 zucchinis, sliced lengthwise in 8 pieces
- 2 teaspoons lemon zest, grated
- 1 small red onion, sliced

Directions:

In a bowl, mix the ricotta cheese with the rest of the ingredients except the salmon and the zucchini and whisk well.

Arrange the zucchini slices on a working surface and divide the salmon on top.

Spread the cheese mix all over, roll and secure with toothpicks and serve right away.

Nutrition:

Calories: 297, Fat: 24.3 g, Fiber: 11.6 g, Carbs: 15.4 g, Protein: 11.6 g

430. Wrapped Scallops

Preparation time: 10 minutes | **Cooking time:** 6 minutes | **Servings:** 2

Ingredients:

- 12 medium scallops
- 2 teaspoons lemon juice
- A pinch of chili powder
- Salt and black pepper to the taste
- 12 thin bacon slices
- 2 teaspoons olive oil
- A pinch of cloves, ground

Directions:

Wrap each scallop in a bacon slice and secure with toothpicks.

Heat up a pan with the oil over medium-high heat, add the scallops and the rest of the ingredients, cook for 3 minutes on each side, divide between plates and serve.

Nutrition:

Calories: 297, Fat: 24.3 g, Fiber: 9.6 g, Carbs: 22.4 g, Protein: 17.6 g

431. Chorizo Shrimp and Salmon Mix

Preparation time: 10 minutes | **Cooking time:** 20 minutes | **Servings:** 2

Ingredients:

- 3 tablespoons olive oil
- 1 lb. salmon, skinless, boneless and cubed
- Salt and black pepper to the taste
- 1 red onion, chopped
- ¼ teaspoon red pepper flakes, crushed
- 1 tablespoon cilantro, chopped
- 1 lb. shrimp, peeled and deveined
- 4 oz. chorizo, chopped
- 3 cups canned tomatoes, crushed
- 2 garlic cloves, minced
- 1 cup chicken stock

Directions:

Heat up a pan with the olive oil over medium-high heat, add the chorizo and cook for 2 minutes.

Add salt, pepper, tomatoes, and the rest of the ingredients except the shrimp, salmon and the cilantro, stir, bring to a simmer and cook for 10 minutes.

Add the remaining ingredients, cook everything for 8 minutes more, divide into bowls and serve.

Nutrition:

Calories: 232, Fat: 15.5 g, Fiber: 10.5 g, Carbs: 20.9 g, Protein: 16.8 g

432. Garlic Scallops and Peas Mix

Preparation time: 10 minutes | **Cooking time:** 20 minutes | **Servings:** 2

Ingredients:

- 12 oz. scallops
- 4 garlic cloves, minced
- ½ cup chicken stock
- ½ tablespoon balsamic vinegar
- 1 tablespoon basil, chopped
- 2 tablespoons olive oil
- A pinch of salt and black pepper
- 1 cup snow peas, sliced
- 1 cup scallions, sliced

Directions:
Heat up a pan with half of the oil over medium-high heat, add the scallops, cook for 5 minutes on each side and transfer to a bowl.
Heat up the pan again with the rest of the oil over medium heat, add the scallions and the garlic and sauté for 2 minutes.
Add the rest of the ingredients, stir, bring to a simmer and cook for 5 minutes more.
Add the scallops to the pan, cook everything for 3 minutes, divide into bowls and serve.

Nutrition:
Calories: 296, Fat: 11.8 g, Fiber: 9.8 g, Carbs: 26.5 g, Protein: 20.5 g

433. Kale, Beets, and Cod Mix

Preparation time: 10 minutes | **Cooking time:** 20 minutes | **Servings:** 2

Ingredients:

2 tablespoons apple cider vinegar	½ cup chicken stock
1 red onion, sliced	4 golden beets, trimmed, peeled and cubed
2 tablespoons olive oil	Salt and black pepper to the taste
4 cups kale, torn	2 tablespoons walnuts, chopped
1 lb. cod fillets, boneless, skinless and cubed	

Directions:
Heat up a pan with the oil over medium-high heat, add the onion and the beets and cook for 3-4 minutes.
Add the rest of the ingredients except the fish and the walnuts, stir, bring to a simmer and cook for 5 minutes more.
Add the fish, cook for 10 minutes, divide between plates and serve.

Nutrition:
Calories: 285 g, Fat: 7.6 g, Fiber: 6.5 g, Carbs: 16.7 g, Protein: 12.5 g

434. Salmon, Calamari, and Mango Mix

Preparation time: 10 minutes | **Cooking time:** 10 minutes | **Servings:** 2

Ingredients:

½ lb. smoked salmon, skinless, boneless and cubed	½ lb. calamari rings
1 tablespoon garlic chili sauce	2 tablespoons olive oil
¼ cup lime juice	½ teaspoon smoked paprika
½ teaspoon cumin, ground	2 garlic cloves, minced
A pinch of salt and black pepper	1 cup mango, peeled and cubed

Directions:
Heat up a pan with the oil over medium-high heat, add the garlic sauce, lime juice and the rest of the ingredients except the salmon and the calamari, stir and simmer for 3 minutes.
Add the remaining ingredients, cook everything for 7 minutes, divide into bowls and serve.

Nutrition:
Calories: 274, Fat: 11.6 g, Fiber: 2.8 g, Carbs: 11.5 g, Protein: 15.4 g

435. Squid and Cucumber Mix

Preparation time: 10 minutes | **Cooking time:** 15 minutes | **Servings:** 2

Ingredients:

10 oz. squid, cut in medium pieces	2 cucumbers, chopped
2 tablespoons cilantro, chopped	1 hot jalapeno pepper, chopped
3 tablespoons balsamic vinegar	2 tablespoons olive oil
A pinch of salt and black pepper	1 tablespoon dill, chopped

Directions:
Heat up a pan with the oil over medium-high heat, add the squid and cook for 5 minutes.
Add the cucumbers and the rest of the ingredients, stir, cook for 10 minutes more, divide everything between plates and serve.

Nutrition:
Calories: 224, Fat: 14.5 g, Fiber: 11.2 g, Carbs: 22.7 g, Protein: 11.3 g

436. Octopus and Radish Salad

Preparation time: 2 hours | **Cooking time:** 1 hour and 30 minutes | **Servings:** 2

Ingredients:

1 big octopus, cleaned and tentacles separated	2 oz. calamari rings
3 garlic cloves, minced	1 white onion, chopped
¾ cup chicken stock	2 cups radicchio, sliced
2 cups radish, sliced	1 cup parsley, chopped
1 tablespoons olive oil	Salt and black pepper to the taste

Directions:
Put the octopus tentacles in a pot, add the stock, add the calamari rings, salt and pepper, bring to a simmer and cook over medium heat for 1 hour and 30 minutes.
Drain everything, cut the tentacles into pieces and transfer them with the calamari rings to a bowl.
Add the rest of the ingredients, toss and keep the salad in the fridge for 2 hours before serving.

Nutrition:
Calories: 287, Fat: 9.9 g, Fiber: 5.6 g, Carbs: 22 g, Protein: 8.4 g

437. Shrimp and Mushrooms Mix

Preparation time: 10 minutes | **Cooking time:** 12 minutes | **Servings:** 2

Ingredients:

1 lb. shrimp, peeled and deveined	2 green onions, sliced
½ lb. white mushrooms, sliced	2 tablespoons balsamic vinegar
2 tablespoons sesame seeds, toasted	2 teaspoons ginger, minced
2 teaspoons garlic, minced	3 tablespoons olive oil
2 tablespoons dill, chopped	

Directions:
Heat up a pan with the oil over medium-high heat, add the green onions and the garlic and sauté for 2 minutes.
Add the rest of the ingredients except the shrimp and cook for 6 minutes more.
Add the shrimp, cook for 4 minutes, divide everything between plates and serve.

Nutrition:
Calories: 245, Fat: 8.5 g, Fiber: 45.8 g, Carbs: 11.8 g, Protein: 17.7 g

438. Scallops and Carrots Mix

Preparation time: 10 minutes | **Cooking time:** 15 minutes | **Servings:** 2

Ingredients:

1 lb. sea scallops, halved	2 celery stalks, sliced
2 tablespoons olive oil	3 garlic cloves, minced
Salt and black pepper to the taste	Juice of 1 lime
4 oz. baby carrots, trimmed	1 tablespoon capers, chopped
1 tablespoon mayonnaise	1 tablespoon rosemary, chopped
1 cup chicken stock	

Directions:
Heat up a pan with the oil over medium-high heat, add the celery and the garlic and sauté for 2 minutes.
Add the carrots and the rest of the ingredients except the scallops and the mayonnaise, stir, bring to a simmer and cook over medium heat for 8 minutes.
Add the scallops and the mayo, toss, cook for 5 minutes, divide everything into bowls and serve.

Nutrition:
Calories: 305, Fat: 14.5 g, Fiber: 5.8 g, Carbs: 31.8 g, Protein: 7.7 g

439. Shrimp and Potato

Preparation time: 10 minutes | **Cooking time:** 15 minutes | **Servings:** 2

Ingredients:

- 4 tablespoons extra virgin olive oil
- 2 lbs. shrimp, peeled and deveined
- 8 potatoes, cut into quarters
- 1 tablespoon watercress, chopped
- 1 teaspoon curry powder Juice of
- 4 onions, peeled and chopped
- 1 lb. tomatoes, cored, peeled, and chopped
- 1 teaspoon coriander
- Salt, to taste
- 1 lemon

Directions:

Place the potatoes in the basket for the Instant Pot, add a little water, cover and cook for 10 minutes.

Relieve the pressure, transfer the potatoes to a bowl and dry the pan immediately. Put the Instant Pot in the sauté mode, add the oil and heat. Add the onion, mix and cook for 5 minutes. Add salt, coriander and curry powder, mix and cook for 5 minutes.

Add tomato, shrimp, lemon juice and potatoes. Stir, cover and cook for 3 minutes in Manual setting. Relieve the pressure, divide between the bowls and serve with watercress on top.

Nutrition:

Calories: 140, Fat: 2 g, Carbs: 5 g, Proteins: 19 g

440. Parsley Cod

Preparation time: 5 minutes | **Cooking time:** 30 minutes | **Servings:** 2

Ingredients:

- 1 lb. cod fillets, boneless
- 1 tablespoon parsley, chopped
- ½ teaspoon turmeric powder
- 1 tablespoon olive oil
- A pinch of salt and black pepper
- 1 tablespoon capers, drained
- 1 cup heavy cream
- Juice of 1 lime
- ½ teaspoon garam masala

Directions:

In a sous vide bag, mix the cod with the capers, parsley and the other ingredients, toss gently, seal the bag, and cook in the water bath at 180°F for 30 minutes.

Divide between plates and serve.

Nutrition:

Calories: 200, Fat: 12 g, Fiber: 2 g, Carbs: 6 g, Protein: 9 g

441. Cod, Olives, and Zucchinis

Preparation time: 10 minutes | **Cooking time:** 30 minutes | **Servings:** 2

Ingredients:

- 1 lb. cod fillets, boneless and roughly cubed
- 2 zucchinis, cubed
- 3 spring onions, chopped
- 1 tablespoon lime juice
- A pinch of salt and black pepper
- 1 cup black olives, pitted and halved
- 2 tablespoons olive oil
- ¼ cup chicken stock
- ½ teaspoon sweet paprika
- 2 tablespoons chives, chopped

Directions:

Divide the cod, olives, zucchinis and the other ingredients between 2 sous vide bags, seal them and cook in the water bath at 180°F for 30 minutes.

Divide between plates and serve.

Nutrition:

Calories: 200, Fat: 12 g, Fiber: 2 g, Carbs: 5 g, Protein: 6 g

442. Creamy Salmon Mix

Preparation time: 5 minutes | **Cooking time:** 30 minutes | **Servings:** 2

Ingredients:

- 1 lb. salmon fillets, boneless and roughly cubed
- 1 tablespoon lime juice
- 1 yellow onion, chopped
- ½ teaspoon chili powder
- 1 tablespoon chives, chopped
- 1 cup heavy cream
- 1 tablespoon lime zest, grated
- ½ teaspoon turmeric powder
- A pinch of salt and black pepper

Directions:
In a big sous vide bag, mix the salmon with the cream, lime juice and the other ingredients, seal the bag and cook in the water bath at 175°F for 30 minutes Divide the mix into bowls and serve.

Nutrition:
Calories: 210, Fat: 9 g, Fiber: 2 g, Carbs: 6 g, Protein: 7 g

443. Trout and Capers Mix

Preparation time: 10 minutes | **Cooking time:** 30 minutes | **Servings:** 2

Ingredients:
- 1 lb. trout fillets, boneless
- 1 red onion, sliced
- ½ cup white wine
- 2 tablespoons chives, chopped
- A pinch of salt and black pepper
- 2 tablespoons capers, drained
- 1 tablespoon olive oil
- Juice of 1 lime
- ½ teaspoon chili powder

Directions:
In a large sous vide bag, mix the trout fillets with the capers, onion and the other ingredients, seal the bag and cook in the water bath at 175°F for 30 minutes.
Divide the mix between plates and serve.

Nutrition:
Calories: 200, Fat: 10 g, Fiber: 2 g, Carbs: 5 g, Protein: 9 g

444. Balsamic Sea Bass

Preparation time: 5 minutes | **Cooking time:** 30 minutes | **Servings:** 2

Ingredients:
- 1 lb. sea bass fillets, boneless
- 1 cup kalamata olives, pitted and halved
- 2 tablespoons garlic, minced
- 2 tablespoons balsamic vinegar
- 2 tablespoons olive oil
- A pinch of salt and black pepper

Directions:
In a sous vide bag, mix the sea bass with the vinegar, olives and the other ingredients, seal the bag, submerge in the water bath and cook at 180°F for 30 minutes.
Divide everything between plates and serve.

Nutrition:
Calories: 200, Fat: 13 g, Fiber: 3 g, Carbs: 6 g, Protein: 11 g

445. Creole Calamari

Preparation time: 5 minutes | **Cooking time:** 35 minutes | **Servings:** 2

Ingredients:
- 1 lb. calamari rings
- 2 tablespoons avocado oil
- 1 tablespoon Creole seasoning
- 1 tablespoon chives, chopped
- ½ cup white wine
- 1 tablespoon lime juice
- ½ teaspoon chili powder

Directions:
In a sous vide bag, mix the calamari rings with the wine, oil and the other ingredients, seal the bag, submerge in the water bath and cook at 190°F for 35 minutes.
Divide the mix into bowls and serve.

Nutrition:
Calories: 211, Fat: 12 g, Fiber: 3 g, Carbs: 6 g, Protein: 7 g

446. Clams and Wine Sauce

Preparation time: 10 minutes | **Cooking time:** 25 minutes | **Servings:** 2

Ingredients:
- 1 lb. clams, scrubbed
- Juice of ½ lemon
- A pinch of salt and black pepper
- ½ cup white wine
- Zest of 1 lemon, grated
- 1 tablespoon chives, chopped

Directions:
In a sous vide bag, mix the clams with the wine, lemon juice and the other ingredients, seal the bag and cook in the water bath at 175°F for 25 minutes.
Divide the mix into bowls and serve.

Nutrition:
Calories: 198, Fat: 7 g, Fiber: 2 g, Carbs: 6 g, Protein: 7 g

447. Tarragon Trout

Preparation time: 10 minutes | **Cooking time:** 30 minutes | **Servings:** 2

Ingredients:

- 1 tablespoon avocado oil
- ½ teaspoon chili powder
- ½ cup chicken stock
- Juice of ½ lemon
- 1 lb. trout fillets, boneless
- 1 tablespoon tarragon, chopped
- A pinch of salt and black pepper

Directions:
In a large sous vide bag, mix the trout with the oil, chili powder and the other ingredients, seal the bag and cook in the water bath at 180°F for 30 minutes.
Divide the mix between plates and serve.

Nutrition:
Calories: 221, Fat: 8 g, Fiber: 3 g, Carbs: 6 g, Protein: 7 g

448. Shrimp, Corn, and Tomato Bowls

Preparation time: 5 minutes | **Cooking time:** 20 minutes | **Servings:** 2

Ingredients:

- 1 lbs. shrimp, peeled and deveined
- 1 cup cherry tomatoes, halved
- 1 tablespoon olive oil
- 3 garlic cloves, crushed
- ½ cup chicken stock
- 1 cup corn
- Juice of 1 lime
- ½ teaspoon rosemary, dried
- 2 tablespoons chives, chopped
- A pinch of salt and black pepper

Directions:
In a large sous vide bag, mix the shrimp with the corn, tomatoes and the other ingredients, seal the bag and cook in the water bath at 175°F for 20 minutes.
Divide into bowls and serve.

Nutrition:
Calories: 235, Fat: 8 g, Fiber: 4 g, Carbs: 7 g, Protein: 9 g

449. Shrimp, Crab, and Avocado Bowls

Preparation time: 10 minutes | **Cooking time:** 20 minutes | **Servings:** 2

Ingredients:

- 1 tablespoon olive oil
- 1 lb. shrimp, peeled and deveined
- Juice of 1 lime
- ½ teaspoon chili powder
- 1 teaspoon sweet paprika
- 1 cup crab meat
- 1 cup avocado, peeled, pitted and cubed
- 1 tablespoon lime zest, grated
- 1 cup chicken stock
- A pinch of salt and black pepper

Directions:
In a sous vide bag, mix the crab with the shrimp and the other ingredients, seal the bag and cook in the water bath at 180°F for 20 minutes.
Divide everything into bowls and serve.

Nutrition:
Calories: 211, Fat: 8 g, Fiber: 4 g, Carbs: 8 g, Protein: 8 g

450. Salmon and Kale

Preparation time: 10 minutes | **Cooking time:** 30 minutes | **Servings:** 2

Ingredients:

- 1 lb. salmon fillets, boneless and cubed
- Juice of 1 lime
- 1 tablespoon smoked paprika
- 2 garlic cloves, minced
- 1 cup baby kale
- 2 tablespoons avocado oil
- A pinch of salt and black pepper
- 1 tablespoon cilantro, chopped

Directions:
In a sous vide bag, mix the salmon with the kale and the other ingredients, seal the bag and cook in the water bath at 180°F for 30 minutes.
Transfer the mix to bowls and serve.

Nutrition:
Calories: 193, Fat: 7 g, Fiber: 3 g, Carbs: 6 g, Protein: 6 g

451. Fried Chicken

Preparation time: 15 minutes | **Cooking time:** 2 hours | **Servings:** 2

Ingredients:
- 3 lb. chicken drums
- 1 tablespoon fine salt

For the coating:
- 3 cups all-purpose flour
- 1 tablespoon onion powder
- 1 teaspoon garlic powder
- ½ tablespoon dried basil
- 1 tablespoon salt
- 2 cup buttermilk

Directions:
Preheat Sous Vide cooker to 155°F.
Season chicken with salt.
Place the chicken drums in Sous Vide bags. Vacuum seal.
Submerge in water and cook 2 hours.

Finishing steps:
Heat 3-inches oil in a pot.
Remove the chicken from bags and pat dry.
Combine all dry breading ingredients in a large bowl. Place buttermilk in a separate bowl.
Dredge chicken drums through flour, buttermilk, and flour again.
Fry chicken in batches, until golden and crispy.
Serve warm with fresh salad and favorite sauce.

Nutrition:
Calories: 357, Fat: 10 g, Carb: 6 g, Fiber: 4 g, Protein: 4 g

452. Sticky Duck Wings

Preparation time: 20 minutes | **Cooking time:** 2 hours | **Servings:** 2

Ingredients:
- 3 lb. duck wings
- 1 tablespoon mustard
- ½ cup honey
- 1 tablespoon soy sauce
- ¼ cup ketchup
- 1 tablespoon hot sauce
- 2 tablespoons Cajun spice blend
- ¼ cup butter
- Salt and pepper, to taste

Directions:
Preheat Sous Vide cooker to 150°F.
Cut the wings into portions and rub with Cajun blend. Season with some salt and pepper.
Transfer the wings into cooking bags and add butter.
Vacuum seal the wings and submerge in water. Cook the wings 2 hours.

Finishing steps:
Preheat your broiler.
Combine remaining ingredients in a bowl.
Remove the wings from the cooker and toss with prepared sauce.
Arrange the wings on baking sheet and broil 10 minutes, basting with any remaining sauce during that time.
Serve warm.

Nutrition:
Calories: 305, Fat: 1 g, Carb: 27 g, Fiber: 7 g, Protein: 8 g

453. Cauliflower soup

Preparation time: 10 minutes | **Cooking time:** 10 minutes | **Servings:** 2

Ingredients:
- 1 cauliflower head, separated into florets and chopped
- 2 tablespoons butter
- 1 small onion, peeled and chopped
- 3 cups chicken stock
- 4 oz. cream cheese, cubed
- 1 cup cheddar cheese, grated
- Salt and ground black pepper, to taste
- 1 teaspoon garlic powder
- ½ cup half and half

Directions:
Put the Instant Pot in the sauté mode, add the butter and melt. Add the onion, mix and cook for 3 minutes. Add the cauliflower, broth, salt, pepper and garlic powder, mix, cover and cook for 5 minutes in the soup.
Release the pressure, uncover the Instant Pot, mix everything using an immersion blender, add more salt and pepper, if necessary, cream cheese, grated cheese and a half and a half.

Stir, place the Instant Pot in manual mode, heat for 2 minutes, divide into bowls and serve.

Nutrition:
Calories: 78, Fat: 1.2 g, Fiber: 1 g, Carbs: 10 g, Proteins: 3 g

454. Turkey and Cranberry Sauce

Preparation time: 10 minutes | **Cooking time:** 50 minutes | **Servings:** 2

Ingredients:

- 1 cup chicken stock
- ½ cup cranberry sauce
- 1 yellow onion, roughly chopped
- 2 tablespoons avocado oil
- 1 big turkey breast, skinless, boneless and sliced
- Salt and black pepper to the taste

Directions:
Heat up a pan with the avocado oil over medium-high heat, add the onion and sauté for 5 minutes.
Add the turkey and brown for 5 minutes more.
Add the rest of the ingredients, toss, introduce in the oven at 350°F and cook for 40 minutes

Nutrition:
Calories: 382, Fat: 12.6 g, Fiber: 9.6 g, Carbs: 26.6 g, Protein: 17.6 g

455. Sage Turkey Mix

Preparation time: 10 minutes | **Cooking time:** 40 minutes | **Servings:** 2

Ingredients:

- 1 big turkey breast, skinless, boneless and roughly cubed
- 2 tablespoons avocado oil
- 2 tablespoons sage, chopped
- 1 cup chicken stock
- Juice of 1 lemon
- 1 red onion, chopped
- 1 garlic clove, minced

Directions:
Heat up a pan with the avocado oil over medium-high heat, add the turkey and brown for 3 minutes on each side.

Add the rest of the ingredients, bring to a simmer and cook over medium heat for 35 minutes.
Divide the mix between plates and serve with a side dish.

Nutrition:
Calories: 382, Fat: 12.6 g, Fiber: 9.6 g, Carbs: 16.6 g, Protein: 33.2 g

456. Turkey and Asparagus Mix

Preparation time: 10 minutes | **Cooking time:** 30 minutes | **Servings:** 2

Ingredients:

- 1 bunch asparagus, trimmed and halved
- 1 teaspoon basil, dried
- A pinch of salt and black pepper
- 1 tablespoon chives, chopped
- 1 big turkey breast, skinless, boneless and cut into strips
- 2 tablespoons olive oil
- ½ cup tomato sauce

Directions:
Heat up a pan with the oil over medium-high heat, add the turkey and brown for 4 minutes.
Add the asparagus and the rest of the ingredients except the chives, bring to a simmer and cook over medium heat for 25 minutes.
Add the chives, divide the mix between plates and serve.

Nutrition:
Calories: 337, Fat: 21.2 g, Fiber: 10.2 g, Carbs: 21.4 g, Protein: 17.6 g

457. Herbed Almond Turkey

Preparation time: 10 minutes | **Cooking time:** 40 minutes | **Servings:** 2

Ingredients:

- 1 big turkey breast, skinless, boneless and cubed
- ½ cup chicken stock
- 1 tablespoon rosemary, chopped
- 1 tablespoon olive oil
- 1 tablespoon basil, chopped
- 1 tablespoon oregano, chopped

1 tablespoon parsley, chopped
½ cup almonds, toasted and chopped
3 garlic cloves, minced
3 cups tomatoes, chopped

Directions:
Heat up a pan with the oil over medium-high heat, add the turkey and the garlic and brown for 5 minutes.
Add the stock and the rest of the ingredients, bring to a simmer over medium heat and cook for 35 minutes.
Divide the mix between plates and serve.

Nutrition:
Calories: 297, Fat: 11.2 g, Fiber: 9.2 g, Carbs: 19.4 g, Protein: 23.6 g

458. Thyme Chicken and Potatoes

Preparation time: 10 minutes | **Cooking time:** 50 minutes | **Servings:** 2

Ingredients:
1 tablespoon olive oil
A pinch of salt and black pepper
12 small red potatoes, halved
1 cup red onion, sliced
2 tablespoons basil, chopped
4 garlic cloves, minced
2 teaspoons thyme, dried
2 lbs. chicken breast, skinless, boneless and cubed
¾ cup chicken stock

Directions:
In a baking dish greased with the oil, add the potatoes, chicken and the rest of the ingredients, toss a bit, introduce in the oven and bake at 400°F for 50 minutes.
Divide between plates and serve.

Nutrition:
Calories: 281, Fat: 9.2 g, Fiber: 10.9 g, Carbs: 21.6 g, Protein: 13.6 g

459. Lemony Turkey and Pine Nuts

Preparation time: 10 minutes | **Cooking time:** 30 minutes | **Servings:** 2

Ingredients:
2 turkey breasts, boneless, skinless and halved
2 tablespoons avocado oil
1 tablespoon rosemary, chopped
¼ cup pine nuts, chopped
A pinch of salt and black pepper
Juice of 2 lemons
3 garlic cloves, minced
1 cup chicken stock

Directions:
Heat up a pan with the oil over medium-high heat, add the garlic and the turkey and brown for 4 minutes on each side.
Add the rest of the ingredients, bring to a simmer and cook over medium heat for 20 minutes.
Divide the mix between plates and serve with a side salad.

Nutrition:
Calories: 293, Fat: 12.4 g, Fiber: 9.3 g, Carbs: 17.8 g, Protein: 24.5 g

460. Yogurt Chicken and Red Onion Mix

Preparation time: 10 minutes | **Cooking time:** 30 minutes | **Servings:** 2

Ingredients:
2 lbs. chicken breast, skinless, boneless and sliced
¼ cup Greek yogurt
½ teaspoon onion powder
4 red onions, sliced
3 tablespoons olive oil
2 garlic cloves, minced
A pinch of salt and black pepper

Directions:
In a roasting pan, combine the chicken with the oil, the yogurt and the other ingredients, introduce in the oven at 375°F and bake for 30 minutes.
Divide chicken mix between plates and serve hot.

Nutrition:
Calories: 278, Fat: 15 g, Fiber: 9.2 g, Carbs: 15.1 g, Protein: 23.3 g

461. Chicken and Mint Sauce

Preparation time: 10 minutes | **Cooking time:** 30 minutes | **Servings:** 2

Ingredients:
- 2 and ½ tablespoons olive oil
- 3 tablespoons garlic, minced
- 1 tablespoon red wine vinegar
- 2 tablespoons mint, chopped
- 2 lbs. chicken breasts, skinless, boneless and halved
- 2 tablespoons lemon juice
- ⅓ cup Greek yogurt
- A pinch of salt and black pepper

Directions:
In a blender, combine the garlic with the lemon juice and the other ingredients except the oil and the chicken and pulse well.
Heat up a pan with the oil over medium-high heat, add the chicken and brown for 3 minutes on each side.
Add the mint sauce, introduce in the oven and bake everything at 370°F for 25 minutes.
Divide the mix between plates and serve.

Nutrition:
Calories: 278, Fat: 12 g, Fiber: 11.2 g, Carbs: 18.1 g, Protein: 13.3 g

462. Turkey and sweet potato soup

Preparation time: 10 minutes | **Cooking time:** 12 minutes | **Servings:** 2

Ingredients:
- 1 lb. Italian turkey sausage, chopped
- 2 carrots, peeled and chopped
- 2 celery stalks, chopped
- 1 teaspoon dried oregano
- 1 teaspoon red pepper flakes
- 5 oz. spinach, chopped
- Salt and ground black pepper, to taste
- 1 yellow onion, peeled and chopped
- 1 big sweet potato, cubed
- 5 cups turkey stock
- 2 garlic cloves, peeled and minced
- 1 teaspoon dried basil
- 2 bay leaves
- 1 teaspoon dried thyme

Directions:
Put the Instant Pot in Sauté mode, add the sausage, brown and transfer to a plate. Add onion, celery and carrot, mix and cook for 2 minutes.
Add the potato, stir and cook for 2 minutes. Add stock, garlic, pepper flakes, salt, pepper, basil, oregano, thyme, spinach and bay leaves. Stir, cover and cook for 4 minutes in the Soup setting. Relieve the pressure, uncover the instant pot, throw away the bay leaves, divide the soup into bowls and serve.

Nutrition:
Calories: 190, Fat: 12 g, Fiber: 1 g, Carbs: 2 g, Proteins: 5 g

463. Chicken meatball soup

Preparation time: 10 minutes | **Cooking time:** 20 minutes | **Servings:** 2

Ingredients:
- 2 tablespoons arrowroot powder
- Salt and ground black pepper, to taste
- 1 teaspoon garlic powder
- ½ tablespoon dried basil
- ½ tablespoon dried oregano
- 1½ lbs. chicken breast, ground
- ½ teaspoon crushed red pepper
- 1 teaspoon onion powder
- 2 tablespoons nutritional yeast

For the soup:
- 2 yellow onions, dried chopped
- 4 celery stalks, chopped
- 6 cups chicken stock
- ½ teaspoon red pepper flakes
- 2 garlic cloves, dried minced
- 1 bunch kale, chopped
- 3 carrots, dried chopped
- 2 teaspoons dried thyme
- 2 eggs, whisked
- 2 tablespoons extra virgin olive oil

Directions:
Put the Instant Pot in the sauté mode, add the oil and heat. Add onion, celery and carrot, mix and cook for 3 minutes.
Add garlic, salt, pepper, black cabbage, broth, 2 teaspoons of thyme and half a teaspoon of red pepper, mix and cook for 10 minutes.

In a bowl, mix the chicken with arrowroot, salt, pepper, ½ teaspoon of pepper, garlic powder, onion powder, oregano, basil and yeast and mix well.

Shape the meatballs with your hands and gently toss them in the soup. Cover the Instant Pot and cook in the soup for 15 minutes.

Release the pressure, uncover the Instant Pot and set it in Sauté mode. Add the eggs slowly, mix and cook for 2 minutes. Divide into bowls and serve hot.

Nutrition:
Calories: 190, Fat: 2.8 g, Fiber: 2.3 g, Carbs: 10 g, Proteins: 29 g

464. Shrimp Creole

Preparation time: 10 minutes | **Cooking time:** 5 minutes | **Servings:** 2

Ingredients:
- 2 teaspoons vinegar
- 1 cup shrimp, already cooked
- Salt, to taste
- 1 teaspoons chili powder
- 1 yellow onion, peeled and chopped
- 1 cup tomato juice
- 1½ cups rice, already cooked
- ½ teaspoon sugar
- 2 tablespoons shortening
- 1 cup celery, chopped

Directions:
Put the Instant Pot in Sauté mode, add the fat and heat. Add onion and celery, mix and cook for 2 minutes.

Add salt, chili powder, tomato juice, vinegar, sugar and shrimp and rice. Stir, cover and cook manually for 3 minutes.

Relieve the pressure, uncover the Instant Pot, distribute the dishes and serve.

Nutrition:
Calories: 29, Fat: 9 g, Fiber: 1.5 g, Carbs: 27 g, Proteins: 24 g

465. Teriyaki Shrimp

Preparation time: 10 minutes
Cooking time: 4 minutes
Servings: 2

Ingredients:
½ lb. pea pods
1 lbs. shrimp, peeled and deveined
2 tablespoons soy sauce
3 tablespoons vinegar
3 tablespoons sugar
¾ cup pineapple juice
1 cup chicken stock

Directions:
Place the shrimp and pea pods in the Instant Pot. In a bowl, mix the soy sauce with the vinegar, pineapple juice, broth and sugar and mix well. Pour into the Instant Pot, stir, cover and cook in manual setting for 3 minutes.

Release the pressure, uncover, divide between the plates and serve.

Nutrition:
Calories: 200, Fat: 4.2 g, Fiber: 0.7 g, Carbs: 13 g, Proteins: 38 g

466. Rice Flour Coated Shrimp

Preparation time: 20 minutes | **Cooking time:** 20 minutes | **Servings:** 2

Ingredients:
- 3 tablespoons rice flour
- 2 tablespoons olive oil
- Salt and black pepper, as required
- 1 lb. shrimp, peeled and deveined
- 1 teaspoon powdered sugar

Directions:
Preheat the Air fryer to 325°F and grease an Air fryer basket.

Mix rice flour, olive oil, sugar, salt, and black pepper in a bowl.

Stir in the shrimp and transfer half of the shrimp to the Air fryer basket.

Cook for about 10 minutes, flipping once in between.

Dish out the mixture onto serving plates and repeat with the remaining mixture.

Nutrition:
Calories: 299, Fat: 12 g, Carbs: 11.1 g, Sugar: 0.8 g, Protein: 35 g, Sodium: 419 mg

467. Shrimp Kebabs

Preparation time: 15 minutes | **Cooking time:** 10 minutes | **Servings:** 2

Ingredients:

- ¾ lb. shrimp, peeled and deveined
- Wooden skewers, presoaked
- 1 teaspoon garlic, minced
- ½ teaspoon ground cumin
- 1 tablespoon fresh cilantro, chopped
- 2 tablespoons fresh lemon juice
- ½ teaspoon paprika
- Salt and ground black pepper, as required

Directions:

Preheat the Air fryer to 350°F and grease an Air fryer basket.
Mix lemon juice, garlic, and spices in a bowl.
Stir in the shrimp and mix to coat well.
Thread the shrimp onto presoaked wooden skewers and transfer to the Air fryer basket.
Cook for about 10 minutes, flipping once in between.
Dish out the mixture onto serving plates and serve garnished with fresh cilantro.

Nutrition:
Calories: 212, Fat: 3.2 g, Carbs: 3.9 g, Sugar: 0.4 g, Protein: 39.1 g, Sodium: 497 mg

468. Garlic Parmesan Shrimp

Preparation time: 20 minutes | **Cooking time:** 10 minutes | **Servings:** 2

Ingredients:

- 1 lb. shrimp, deveined and peeled
- ¼ cup cilantro, diced
- 1 teaspoon salt
- 1 tablespoon lemon juice
- ½ cup parmesan cheese, grated
- 1 tablespoon olive oil
- 1 teaspoon fresh cracked pepper
- 6 garlic cloves, diced

Directions:

Preheat the Air fryer to 350°F and grease an Air fryer basket.
Drizzle shrimp with olive oil and lemon juice and season with garlic, salt and cracked pepper.
Cover the bowl with plastic wrap and refrigerate for about 3 hours.
Stir in the parmesan cheese and cilantro to the bowl and transfer to the Air fryer basket.
Cook for about 10 minutes and serve immediately.

Nutrition:
Calories: 602, Fat: 23.9 g, Carbs: 46.5 g, Sugar: 2.9 g, Protein: 11.3 g, Sodium: 886 mg

469. Prawn Burgers

Preparation time: 20 minutes | **Cooking time:** 6 minutes | **Servings:** 2

Ingredients:

- ½ cup prawns, peeled, deveined and finely chopped
- 2-3 tablespoons onion, finely chopped
- ½ teaspoon ginger, minced
- ½ teaspoon red chili powder
- ¼ teaspoon ground turmeric
- ½ cup breadcrumbs
- 3 cups fresh baby greens
- ½ teaspoon garlic, minced
- ½ teaspoon ground cumin
- Salt and ground black pepper, as required

Directions:

Preheat the Air fryer to 390°F and grease an Air fryer basket.
Mix the prawns, breadcrumbs, onion, ginger, garlic, and spices in a bowl.
Make small-sized patties from the mixture and transfer to the Air fryer basket.
Cook for about 6 minutes and dish out in a platter.
Serve immediately warm alongside the baby greens.

Nutrition:
Calories: 240, Fat: 2.7 g, Carbs: 37.4 g, Sugar: 4 g, Protein: 18 g, Sodium: 371 mg

470. Buttered Scallops

Preparation time: 15 minutes | **Cooking time:** 4 minutes | **Servings:** 2

Ingredients:

- ¾ lb. sea scallops, cleaned and patted very dry
- 1 tablespoon butter, melted
- ½ tablespoon fresh thyme, minced
- Salt and black pepper, as required

Directions:
Preheat the Air fryer to 390°F and grease an Air fryer basket.
Mix scallops, butter, thyme, salt, and black pepper in a bowl.
Arrange scallops in the Air fryer basket and cook for about 4 minutes.
Dish out the scallops in a platter and serve hot.

Nutrition:
Calories: 202, Fat: 7.1 g, Carbs: 4.4 g, Protein: 28.7 g, Sodium: 393 mg

471. Scallops with Capers Sauce

Preparation time: 15 minutes | **Cooking time:** 6 minutes | **Servings:** 2

Ingredients:
- 10: 1-oz.ea scallops, cleaned and patted very dry
- 2 teaspoons capers, finely chopped
- ¼ cup extra-virgin olive oil
- ½ teaspoon garlic, finely chopped
- 2 tablespoons fresh parsley, finely chopped
- Salt and ground black pepper, as required
- 1 teaspoon fresh lemon zest, finely grated

Directions:
Preheat the Air fryer to 390°F and grease an Air fryer basket.
Season the scallops evenly with salt and black pepper.
Arrange the scallops in the Air fryer basket and cook for about 6 minutes.
Mix parsley, capers, olive oil, lemon zest and garlic in a bowl.
Dish out the scallops in a platter and top with capers sauce.

Nutrition:
Calories: 344, Fat: 26.3 g, Carbs: 4.2 g, Sugar: 0.1 g, Protein: 24 g, Sodium: 393 mg

472. Bulgur and Avocado Mix

Preparation time: 30 minutes | **Cooking time:** 0 minutes | **Servings:** 2

Ingredients:
- 1 cup bulgur
- A pinch of sea salt and black pepper
- 1 cup cherry tomatoes, halved
- 1 cucumber, chopped
- 2 tablespoons balsamic vinegar
- 2 cups hot water
- Black pepper to taste
- 2 avocados, peeled, pitted and cubed
- 2 tablespoons lemon juice
- 2 tablespoons olive oil

Directions:
In a bowl, mix bulgur with water, cover, leave aside for 25 minutes, fluff with a fork and transfer to a salad bowl.
Add the rest of the ingredients, toss to coat well and serve.

Nutrition:
Calories: 150, Fat: 3.5 g, Fiber: 4.1 g, Carbs: 3.3 g, Protein: 6 g

473. Lettuce and Tomato Mix

Preparation time: 10 minutes | **Cooking time:** 0 minutes | **Servings:** 2

Ingredients:
- 3 tablespoons olive oil
- 1 cucumber, chopped
- 5 medium tomatoes, chopped
- 5 green bell peppers, chopped
- 5 radishes, sliced
- Salt and black pepper to taste
- ¼ teaspoon allspice, ground
- 1 red beet, baked, peeled and cubed
- 1 heart lettuce, chopped
- ½ teaspoon oregano, dried
- 1 cup parsley, chopped
- Juice from 1 ½ limes
- 1 teaspoon sumac

Directions:
In a bowl, mix the beet with the cucumber, lettuce and the other ingredients, toss and serve.

Nutrition:
Calories: 201, Fat: 5.5 g, Fiber: 6.1 g, Carbs: 5 g, Protein: 11 g

474. Avocado and Cucumber Mix

Preparation time: 10 minutes | **Cooking time:** 0 minutes | **Servings:** 2

Ingredients:

- 2 avocados, peeled, pitted and cubed
- 1 long green pepper, chopped
- 1 tablespoon dill weed, chopped
- 2 tablespoons oregano, chopped
- 3 tablespoons olive oil
- 10 big black olives, pitted and sliced
- ¾ lb. cucumbers, chopped
- 2 spring onions, chopped
- ¼ cup parsley, chopped
- Salt and black pepper to taste
- 3 tablespoons lemon juice

Directions:
In a large bowl, mix the avocados with the cucumbers and the other ingredients, toss and serve.

Nutrition:
Calories: 241, Fat: 3 g, Fiber: 2 g, Carbs: 5 g, Protein: 6.2 g

475. Delicious Shrimp Risotto

Preparation time: 10 minutes | **Cooking time:** 17 minutes | **Servings:** 2

Ingredients:

- 1 lb. shrimp, peeled, deveined, and chopped
- ½ tbsp paprika
- 1 red pepper, chopped
- ½ cup parmesan cheese, grated
- 3 cups chicken stock
- 2 tbsp butter
- ½ tsp salt
- 1 ½ cups Arborio rice
- ½ tbsp oregano, minced
- 1 onion, chopped
- 1 cup clam juice
- ¼ cup dry sherry
- ¼ tsp pepper

Directions:
Add butter into the instant pot and set the pot on sauté mode.
Add onion and pepper and sauté until onion is softened.
Add paprika, oregano, pepper, and salt. Stir for minute.
Add rice and stir for a minute.
Add sherry, clam juice, and stock. Stir well.
Seal pot with lid and cook on manual high pressure for 10 minutes.
Once done then release pressure using the quick-release method than open the lid.
Add shrimp and cook on sauté mode for 2 minutes.
Stir in cheese and serve.

Nutrition:
Calories: 530, Fat: 10.4 g, Carbs: 71.6 g, Sugar: 5.3 g, Protein: 34.5 g, Cholesterol: 259 mg

476. Lentils and Beets Salad

Preparation time: 10 minutes | **Cooking time:** 15 minutes | **Servings:** 2

Ingredients:

- 1 cup canned green lentils, drained
- 2 tablespoons olive oil
- 1 carrot, grated
- ½ cup mint, chopped
- Salt and black pepper to taste
- 2 beets, baked, peeled and cubed
- 2 spring onions, chopped
- 1 cup parsley, chopped
- Juice of 1 lemon

Directions:
Heat a pan with the oil over medium high heat, add the spring onions, carrot and beets and cook for 5 minutes.
Add the rest of the ingredients, toss, cook for 10 minutes more, divide between plates and serve.

Nutrition:
Calories: 200, Fat: 5.9 g, Fiber: 3.3 g, Carbs: 5 g, Protein: 7 g

477. Corn and Peas Salad

Preparation time: 10 minutes | **Cooking time:** 20 minutes | **Servings:** 2

Ingredients:

- 2 cups corn
- 1 cup cherry tomatoes, halved
- 1 red onion, chopped
- 1 teaspoon sweet paprika

1 teaspoon coriander, ground
3 tablespoons olive oil
2 carrots, cubed
½ cup sweet peas
¼ cup parsley, chopped
1 tablespoon mint, chopped
Salt to taste

Directions:
Heat up a pan with the oil over medium heat, add the onion, paprika and coriander and cook for 5 minutes.
Add the corn, tomatoes and the other ingredients, toss and cook for 15 minutes more. Divide between plates and serve.

Nutrition:
Calories: 210, Fat: 8.1 g, Fiber: 3.4 g, Carbs: 4 g, Protein: 7 g

478. Cucumber and Carrot Salad

Preparation time: 10 minutes | **Cooking time:** 0 minutes | **Servings:** 2

Ingredients:

2 garlic cloves, minced	2 carrots, peeled and grated
Salt to taste	1 tablespoon balsamic vinegar
1 tablespoon dill weed, chopped	3 medium cucumbers, sliced
1 tablespoon olive oil	1 tablespoon mint, chopped
1 teaspoon coriander, ground	

Directions:
In a bowl, mix the carrots with the cucumbers and the other ingredients, toss and serve.

Nutrition:
Calories: 210, Fat: 6.1 g, Fiber: 2 g, Carbs: 5.4 g, Protein: 4.4 g

479. Carrot Soup

Preparation time: 10 minutes | **Cooking time:** 25 minutes | **Servings:** 2

Ingredients:

1 yellow onion, chopped	2 tablespoons coconut oil, melted
3 small carrots, cubed	1 ½ tablespoon almond flour
1 teaspoon turmeric powder	1 teaspoon cumin, ground
2 ½ cups chicken stock	Salt and black pepper to taste

Directions:
Heat a large saucepan with the oil over medium high heat, add onion and carrots, stir and cook for 3-4 minutes.
Add the flour and cook for 5 more minutes stirring often.
Add the rest of the ingredients, toss and cook for 15-20 minutes. Discard bay leaf, blend using an immersion blender, ladle into bowls and serve.

Nutrition:
Calories: 198, Fat: 3.8 g, Fiber: 3.1 g, Carbs: 6 g, Protein: 8 g

480. Tomato and Spinach Soup

Preparation time: 10 minutes | **Cooking time:** 20 minutes | **Servings:** 2

Ingredients:

4 medium tomatoes, grated	1 green bell pepper, chopped
1 cup baby spinach	1 garlic clove, minced
1 tablespoon olive oil	½ teaspoon turmeric powder
1 teaspoon chili flakes	½ tablespoon peppercorns
Salt and black pepper to taste	3 cups hot water
½ bunch parsley, chopped	

Directions:
Heat a large saucepan with the olive oil over medium heat, add the garlic, pepper, chili, peppercorns and turmeric and cook for 5 minutes.
Add the rest of the ingredients, stir and cook over medium heat for 15 minutes. Ladle into bowls and serve.

Nutrition:
Calories: 200, Fat: 9 g, Fiber: 3 g, Carbs: 5 g, Protein: 7 g

481. Salmon Burger

Preparation time: 10 minutes | **Cooking time:** 30 minutes | **Servings:** 2

Ingredients:
- 2 cups salmon
- 3 eggs
- 1 cup green onions
- 4 English muffins
- 2 ½ cup breadcrumbs
- ¾ cup celery
- 2 tablespoons oil
- Salt, pepper, fries as per need

Directions:
Set the sous vide machine to 19 °F.
Take the salmon in a sous vide bag and apply vacuum to remove the air.
Place this bag in the water bath for 10 minutes.
Take a large bowl and beat the eggs.
Add the cooked salmon, breadcrumbs, celery, green onions, salt, pepper and mix.
Make 4 patties from the above dough and cook in oil for 10 minutes on medium flame. Flip and repeat.
Place the patty on the toasted English muffin and garnish with favorite salads.

Nutrition:
Calories: 138, Fat: 6 g, Carbs: 4 g, Protein: 18 g

482. Crunchy Coconut Shrimps

Preparation time: 5 minutes | **Cooking time:** 15 minutes | **Servings:** 2

Ingredients:
- 24 shrimps
- 3 tablespoon flour
- ¼ cup cornflakes
- ¼ cup skim milk
- ½ cup coconut

Directions:
Set the sous vide machine to 195°F.
Take the shrimps in a Ziplock bag and apply vacuum to remove the air.
Place this bag in the water bath for 5 minutes.
Make a mixture of milk and flour in a mixing bowl. Toss the above shrimps in it.
In another mixing bowl, make a mixture of coconut and cornflakes crumbs.
Add the shrimps to the above mixture and coat it uniformly.
Preheat the oven to 450 °F. Grease the baking tray with cooking spray.
Place the shrimps on this tray and bake for 5 minutes. Flip and repeat.
Serve hot.

Nutrition:
Calories: 260, Fat: 14 g, Carbs: 27 g, Protein: 7 g

483. Salmon Cakes

Preparation time: 25 minutes | **Cooking time:** 20 minutes | **Servings:** 2

Ingredients:
- 1 ½ lbs. boiled potatoes
- 1 teaspoon lemon juice
- 4 tablespoon oil
- 1 tablespoon grated ginger
- 1 teaspoon soy sauce
- Salt, pepper, mayonnaise as per taste
- 1 teaspoon lemon zest
- 1 lb. chopped salmon
- 1 onion
- 1 egg
- 6 lettuce leaves

Directions:
Set the sous vide machine to 195°F.
Take salmon in the Ziplock bag and remove air.
Place this bag in the water bath for 5 minutes.
In a pan heat oil and cook the onions and ginger.
Add boiled potatoes and mash the mixture.
Add salmon, egg, pepper, salt and mix.
Make 12 small cakes from this mixture.
Heat oil in the skillet and cook these salmon cakes for 6 minutes until brown. Flip and repeat.
In a small bowl add lemon juice, soy sauce, ginger, mayonnaise and mix.
Serve the salmon cakes with the above mixture.

Nutrition:
Calories: 280, Fat: 16 g, Carbs: 14 g, Protein: 17 g

484. Crispy Catfish Fingers

Preparation time: 10 minutes | **Cooking time:** 10 minutes | **Servings:** 2

Ingredients:
- 1 ½ lb. catfish fillets
- 1 cup cornmeal
- Salt as per taste
- 3 cups canola oil
- ¼ cup cayenne pepper

Directions:
Take a mixing bowl and toss the catfish with salt and cayenne pepper.
Set the sous vide machine to 195°F.
Take the catfish fillets in a Ziplock bag. Seal it.
Place this bag in the water bath for 5 minutes.
Spread the cornmeal in a place and keep aside.
Coat the fish with cornmeal and fry them in oil at 350 °F until golden.
Transfer it to a baking sheet pat to remove excess oil.
Serve hot.

Nutrition:
Calories: 460, Fat: 28 g, Protein: 45 g

485. Chicken with Asparagus & Jasmine Rice

Preparation time: 10 minutes | **Cooking time:** 40 minutes | **Servings:** 2

Ingredients:

1 tbsp olive oil	4 chicken breasts
1 tsp garlic salt	½ cup onion, finely diced
2 garlic cloves, minced	1 cup jasmine rice
1 lemon, zested and juiced	2 ¼ cups chicken broth
1 cup asparagus, chopped	1 tbsp parsley for garnish
Black pepper to taste	Lemon slices to garnish

Directions:
Set your Instant Pot to Sauté mode and adjust to medium heat. Heat olive oil in inner pot, season chicken with garlic salt and black pepper, and sear chicken on both sides until golden brown, 6 minutes. Place on a plate and set aside.
Add onion and cook until softened, 3 minutes. Stir in garlic, allow to release fragrant for 30 seconds. Stir in rice and cook until translucent, 2 to 3 minutes. Add lemon zest, lemon juice, chicken broth, asparagus, salt, black pepper, and place chicken on top.
Seal the lid, select Manual/Pressure Cook mode on High, and set cooking time to 5 minutes. After cooking, perform natural pressure release for 15 minutes, then quick pressure release to let out the remaining steam. Unlock the lid, fluff rice, and plate. Garnish with parsley and lemon slices, serve warm.

Nutrition:
Calories: 646, Carbs: 22 g, Fat: 25 g, Protein: 88 g

486. Chicken with Rotini, Mushrooms & Spinach

Preparation time: 10 minutes | **Cooking time:** 30 minutes | **Servings:** 2

Ingredients:

2 tbsp butter	4 chicken breasts, cut into cubes
Salt and black pepper to taste	1 small yellow onion, diced
4 cups sliced white mushrooms	1 garlic clove, minced
1 lb. rotini pasta	1 cup chicken broth
1 tsp chopped oregano	4 cups chopped baby spinach
½ cup crumbled goat cheese	

Directions:
Set your Instant Pot to Sauté mode and adjust to medium heat. Melt butter in inner pot, season chicken with salt and black pepper, and sear in oil until golden brown, 4 minutes. Place in a plate and set aside.
Add onion and mushroom and cook until softened, 4 minutes. Stir in garlic, allow to release fragrant for 30 seconds. Return chicken to pot, stir in rotini, chicken broth, and oregano. Seal the lid, select Manual/Pressure Cook on High, and set cooking time to 3 minutes. After cooking, do a natural pressure release for 10 minutes, then a quick pressure release to let out remaining steam.
Select Sauté mode and unlock the lid. Stir in spinach, allow wilting, and mix in goat cheese until properly incorporated. Adjust taste with salt, black pepper, and serve warm.

Nutrition:
Calories: 687, Carbs: 35 g, Fat: 32 g, Protein: 63 g

487. Lemon Butter chicken

Preparation time: 10 minutes | **Cooking time:** 15 minutes | **Servings:** 2

Ingredients:

- 4 chicken thighs, bone-in
- 1 lemon juice
- 1 small onion, diced
- 1 tsp parsley flakes
- 2 tbsp butter, melted
- ½ tsp salt
- ½ tsp oregano
- 2 garlic cloves, diced
- 1 cup chicken broth
- 1 tsp lemon pepper seasoning
- ¼ tsp pepper

Directions:

Add all ingredients into the instant pot and stir well.

Seal pot with lid and cook on manual high pressure for 15 minutes.

Once done then allow to release pressure naturally for 10 minutes then release using quick-release method. Open the lid.

Serve and enjoy.

Nutrition:

Calories: 679, Fat: 33.2 g, Carbs: 6 g, Sugar: 2.2 g, Protein: 84.4 g, Cholesterol: 280 mg

488. Instant Pot Turkey Breast

Preparation time: 10 minutes | **Cooking time:** 30 minutes | **Servings:** 2

Ingredients:

- 6 lbs. turkey breast
- 1 onion, quartered
- 1 ¼ tsp thyme
- Salt
- 1 ½ cups chicken broth
- ½ cup celery, chopped
- Pepper

Directions:

Add broth, onion, celery, and thyme to the instant pot and stir well.

Season turkey breast with pepper and salt.

Place trivet into the pot then place turkey breast on top of the trivet.

Seal pot with lid and cook on manual high pressure for 30 minutes.

Once done then allow to release pressure naturally then open the lid.

Slice and serve.

Nutrition:

Calories: 368, Fat: 5.9 g, Carbs: 16.1 g, Sugar: 12.7 g, Protein: 59.2 g, Cholesterol: 146 mg

489. Thai Chicken Curry Rice

Preparation time: 10 minutes | **Cooking time:** 35 minutes | **Servings:** 2

Ingredients:

- 4 chicken thighs
- 1 tbsp olive oil
- 1 red bell pepper, deseeded and thinly sliced
- 1 garlic clove, minced
- 2 cups basmati rice
- 1 cup coconut milk
- 1 lime, cut into wedges to garnish
- Salt and black pepper to taste
- 2 medium carrots, julienned
- 2 tbsp red curry paste
- 1 tsp ginger paste
- 3 cups chicken broth
- 2 tbsp chopped cilantro to garnish

Directions:

Set your Instant Pot to Sauté and adjust to medium heat. Heat olive oil in inner pot, season chicken with salt and black pepper, and sear in oil until golden brown on both sides, 6 minutes. Place on a plate and set aside.

Add carrots and bell pepper to oil and cook until softened, 4 minutes. Stir in curry paste, garlic, and ginger, sauté for 1 minute. Add rice, broth, coconut milk and give ingredients a good stir. Arrange chicken on top. Seal the lid, select Manual/Pressure Cook mode on High, and set cooking time to 10 minutes.

After cooking, do a natural pressure release for 10 minutes, then quick pressure release to let out remaining steam. Unlock the lid, fluff rice, and adjust taste with salt and black pepper. Garnish with cilantro, lime wedges, and serve.

Nutrition:

Calories: 715, Carbs: 38 g, Fat: 48 g, Protein: 43 g

490. Rich Louisiana Chicken with Quinoa

Preparation time: 10 minutes | **Cooking time:** 20 minutes | **Servings:** 2

Ingredients:

- 2 tbsp olive oil
- 4 chicken breasts, thinly sliced

1 tsp Creole seasoning	2 green bell peppers, deseeded and sliced
1 cup dry rainbow quinoa	2 cups chicken broth
Salt to taste	1 lemon, zested and juiced
2 chives, chopped	2 tbsp chopped parsley

Directions:
Set your Instant Pot to Sauté and adjust to medium heat. Heat olive oil in inner pot, season chicken with Creole seasoning, and fry with bell peppers in oil until chicken is golden brown on both sides, 5 minutes and peppers soften. Stir in quinoa, chicken broth, and salt.
Seal the lid, select Manual/Pressure Cook mode on High, and set cooking time to 1 minute. After cooking, perform quick pressure release, and select Sauté mode. Unlock the lid, fluff quinoa, and stir in lemon zest, lemon juice, chives, and parsley. Dish meal into serving bowls and serve warm with hard-boiled eggs.

Nutrition:
Calories: 523, Carbs: 32 g, Fat: 17 g, Protein: 37 g

491. Creamy Peanut Butter Chicken

Preparation time: 10 minutes | **Cooking time:** 20 minutes | **Servings:** 2

Ingredients:
2 lbs. chicken breasts, skinless, boneless and cut into chunks	1 ½ tsp ginger powder
1 ½ tsp garlic powder	2 tbsp honey
1 tbsp sriracha sauce	1 tbsp vinegar
4 tbsp soy sauce	4 tbsp peanut butter
1 cup chicken broth	1 tbsp sesame oil
1 tbsp olive oil	2 tbsp peanuts, roasted chopped
Pepper	Salt

Directions:
Add oil into the instant pot and set the pot on sauté mode.
Add chicken, ginger powder, garlic powder, honey, sriracha sauce, vinegar, soy sauce, peanut butter, broth, pepper, and salt and stir well.
Seal pot with lid and cook on manual mode for 9 minutes.
Once done then release pressure using the quick-release method than open the lid.
Stir everything well and cook on sauté mode until sauce thickens.
Garnish with peanuts and serve.

Nutrition:
Calories: 668, Fat: 34.4 g, Carbs: 15.3 g, Sugar: 11 g, Protein: 73.3 g, Cholesterol: 202 mg

492. BBQ Pulled Chicken

Preparation time: 10 minutes | **Cooking time:** 24 minutes | **Servings:** 2

Ingredients:
2 ½ lbs. chicken breasts, skinless and boneless	½ tsp allspice
1 tsp chipotle powder	2 tsp garlic powder
2 tsp Dijon mustard	1 ½ tsp molasses
1 tbsp onion powder	1 tbsp liquid smoke
4 tbsp Dietz sweet	2 tbsp soy sauce
¼ cup apple cider vinegar	7 oz tomato paste
¾ cup chicken broth	2 tsp salt

Directions:
Place chicken into the instant pot.
Whisk together remaining ingredients and pour over chicken.
Seal pot with lid and cook on poultry mode for 24 minutes.
Once done then release pressure using the quick-release method than open the lid.
Remove chicken from pot and shred using a fork. Return shredded chicken to the pot and stir well. Serve and enjoy.

Nutrition:
Calories: 614, Fat: 21.7 g, Carbs: 14.9 g, Sugar: 2.5 g, Protein: 86.1 g, Cholesterol: 252 mg

493. Buffalo Chicken Breasts

Preparation time: 5 minutes | **Cooking time:** 20 minutes | **Servings:** 2

Ingredients:
- 1 lb. chicken breasts, skinless and boneless
- ¾ cup water
- ¼ cup buffalo sauce

Directions:
Place chicken into the instant pot then pour water and buffalo sauce over the chicken.
Seal pot with lid and cook on manual high pressure for 20 minutes.
Once done then release pressure using the quick-release method than open the lid.
Remove chicken from pot and shred using the fork.
Return shredded chicken to the pot and stir well.
Serve and enjoy.

Nutrition:
Calories: 219, Fat: 8.4 g, Carbs: 0.5 g, Protein: 32.8 g, Cholesterol: 101 mg

494. Green Chicken

Preparation time: 8 minutes | **Cooking time:** 20 minutes | **Servings:** 2

Ingredients:
- 1 ⅓ lbs. Chicken Breasts, cubed
- ⅓ cup Basil Leaves
- ⅔ cup Homemade Chicken Broth
- 1 tbsp Olive Oil
- 1 cup chopped Spinach
- ⅓ cup Coconut Cream
- 1 tsp minced Garlic

Directions:
Heat the oil in the Instant Pot on SAUTE.
Add the garlic and cook for 1 minute.
Add the chicken and cook until it is no longer pink.
Stir in the rest of the ingredients.
Put the lid on and seal.
Set the IP to MANUAL.
Cook on HIGH for 8 minutes.
Do a quick pressure release.
Serve and enjoy!

Nutrition:
Calories: 320, Fats 14 g, Carbs: 4 g, Protein 35 g, Fiber: 1 g

495. Cheesy Chicken Stuffed Peppers

Preparation time: 20 minutes | **Cooking time:** 18 minutes | **Servings:** 2

Ingredients:
- 1 tablespoon butter, at room temperature
- ½ cup scallions, chopped
- ½ teaspoon sea salt
- ¼ teaspoon shallot powder
- 6 oz. goat cheese, crumbled
- ½ cup sour cream
- 1 lb. chicken, ground
- ½ teaspoon chili powder
- ⅓ teaspoon paprika
- ⅓ teaspoon ground cumin
- 5 bell peppers, tops, membrane and seeds removed

Directions:
Press the "Sauté" button to heat up the Instant Pot. Melt the butter.
Once hot, cook the chicken and scallions for 2 to 3 minutes. Add chili powder, salt, paprika, shallot powder, and cumin, stir to combine. Now, add crumbled goat cheese, stir, and reserve.
Then, clean your Instant Pot and add 1 ½ cups of water and a metal trivet to the bottom of the inner pot.
Fill bell peppers with enough of the meat/scallion mixture, don't pack the peppers too tightly.
Place the peppers on the trivet and secure the lid. Choose "Poultry" mode and High pressure, cook for 15 minutes.
Once cooking is complete, use a natural pressure release, carefully remove the lid. Serve with a dollop of sour cream and enjoy!

Nutrition:
Calories: 335, Fat: 19.6 g, Carbs: 8.9 g, Protein: 30 g, Sugars: 3.9 g

496. Holiday BBQ Chicken

Preparation time: 10 minutes | **Cooking time:** 40 minutes | **Servings:** 2

Ingredients:
- 1 ½ cups chopped sweet pineapple
- ¼ tsp salt
- ¼ cup chicken broth
- ¾ cup BBQ sauce

4 chicken breasts, cut into 1-inch cubes

Directions:
In inner pot, combine pineapples, chicken broth, salt, BBQ sauce, and chicken. Seal the lid, select Manual/Pressure Cook on High, and set cooking time to 12 minutes.

After cooking, perform a natural pressure release for 10 minutes, then a quick pressure release to let out remaining steam, and unlock the lid. Remove chicken onto a plate and select Sauté mode. Cook sauce until boiled down by half, 4 minutes, and stir in chicken. Serve chicken and sauce with rice.

Nutrition:
Calories: 447, Carbs: 12 g, Fat: 27 g, Protein: 32 g

497. Spicy Chicken Manchurian

Preparation time: 10 minutes | **Cooking time:** 35 minutes | **Servings:** 2

Ingredients:

½ cup olive oil	4 tbsp cornstarch, divided
2 eggs, beaten	2 tbsp soy sauce, divided
Salt and black pepper to taste	4 chicken breasts, cubed
2 tbsp sesame oil	1 tbsp fresh garlic paste
1 tbsp fresh ginger paste	1 red chili, sliced
2 tbsp hot sauce	½ tsp honey
½ cup chicken broth	2 scallions, sliced for garnishing

Directions:
Set your Instant Pot to Sauté and adjust to medium heat. Heat olive oil in inner pot. Meanwhile, in a medium bowl, whisk cornstarch, eggs, soy sauce, salt, and black pepper. Pour chicken into mixture and stir to coat well.

Fry coated chicken in oil until cooked through and golden brown on all sides, 6 to 8 minutes. Transfer to a paper towel-lined plate to drain grease. Empty inner pot, wipe clean with a paper towel, and return to base.

Heat in sesame oil and sauté garlic, ginger, and red chili until fragrant and chili softened, 1 minute. Stir in hot sauce, honey, chicken broth, and arrange chicken in sauce.

Seal the lid, select Manual/Pressure Cook mode on High, and set cooking time to 3 minutes. After cooking, perform natural pressure release for 10 minutes, then quick pressure release to let out the remaining steam.

Unlock the lid, stir, and adjust taste with salt and black pepper. Spoon into serving bowls and garnish generously with scallions. Serve warm with rice.

Nutrition:
Calories: 722, Carbs: 14 g, Fat: 46 g, Protein: 61 g

498. Maple Balsamic & Thyme Chicken

Preparation time: 10 minutes | **Cooking time:** 40 minutes | **Servings:** 2

Ingredients:

¼ cup balsamic vinegar	2 tbsp maple syrup
1 tbsp Dijon mustard	½ cup chicken broth
1 medium brown onion, chopped	2 garlic cloves, minced
½ tsp dried thyme	4 chicken breasts

Directions:
In inner pot, mix balsamic vinegar, maple syrup, Dijon mustard, chicken broth, onion, garlic, thyme, and chicken. Seal the lid, select Manual/Pressure Cook on High, and set cooking time to 12 minutes.

After cooking, perform a natural pressure release for 10 minutes, then a quick pressure release to let out remaining steam. Unlock the lid and remove chicken onto a plate and select Sauté mode. Shred chicken with two forks and returns to sauce. Cook until sauce thickens, 5 minutes. Serve immediately.

Nutrition:
Calories: 464, Carbs: 14 g, Fat: 25 g, Protein: 32 g

499. Sweet & Saucy Chicken

Preparation time: 10 minutes | **Cooking time:** 25 minutes | **Servings:** 2

Ingredients:

2 tbsp olive oil	4 chicken thighs, bone-in
Salt and black pepper to taste	3 tbsp Dijon mustard
1 tbsp tamarind sauce	1 tbsp honey
½ cup chicken broth	3 garlic cloves, minced
1 tbsp chopped parsley	

Directions:
Set your Instant Pot to Sauté mode and heat olive oil. Season chicken with salt and black pepper, and sear in oil until golden brown on both sides, 6 minutes.

Meanwhile, in a bowl, combine mustard, tamarind sauce, honey, chicken broth, and pour into pot along with garlic. Seal the lid, select Manual/Pressure Cook mode on High, and set cooking time to 2 minutes.

After cooking, do a natural pressure release for 10 minutes, then quick pressure release to let out remaining steam. Unlock the lid, stir in parsley, and adjust taste with salt and black pepper. Dish chicken with sauce and serve.

Nutrition:
Calories: 521, Carbs: 8 g, Fat: 39 g, Protein: 33 g

500. Sausage & Red Kidney Stew

Preparation time: 5 minutes | **Cooking time:** 35 minutes | **Servings:** 2

Ingredients:

6 bacon slices, chopped	½ lb. kielbasa sausage, chopped
1 cup chopped tomatoes	2 red bell peppers, deseeded and diced
1 red onion, chopped	1 cup dried red kidney beans, soaked overnight
3 cups chicken broth	¼ cup honey
1 cup ketchup	1 tbsp Worcestershire sauce
1 tsp mustard powder	

Directions:
Set your Instant Pot to Sauté and fry bacon until brown and crispy, 5 minutes. Remove to a plate. Add sausages to inner pot and cook until brown on both sides, 5 minutes. Set aside next to bacon. Wipe inner pot clean and combine bell peppers, onion, kidney beans, chicken broth, honey, ketchup, Worcestershire sauce, and mustard powder. Seal the lid, select Manual/Pressure Cook on High, and set time to 10 minutes. After cooking, perform a quick pressure release. Stir in bacon and sausage, and simmer on Sauté mode for 5 minutes. Serve stew with bread or cooked white rice.

Nutrition:
Calories: 498, Carbs: 47 g, Fat: 28 g, Protein: 26 g

501. Classic Beef Stew

Preparation time: 5 minutes | **Cooking time:** 40 minutes | **Servings:** 2

Ingredients:

2 tbsp olive oil	1 lb beef stew meat, cubed
Salt and black pepper to taste	2 shallots, chopped
2 garlic cloves, minced	1 carrot, peeled and chopped
2 red bell peppers, chopped	2 tomatoes, chopped
2 bay leaves	1 tsp dried mixed herbs
1 ½ cups beef broth	1 tsp cornstarch

Directions:
Set your Instant Pot to Sauté mode and adjust to medium heat. Heat olive oil in inner pot, season beef with salt and black pepper, and brown on both sides, 5 minutes. Set aside. To the pot, add shallots, garlic, carrot, bell peppers, and cook for 5 minutes. Stir in tomatoes, mixed herbs, bay leaves, and beef broth, and return the beef.

Seal the lid, select Manual/Pressure Cook mode on High, and set cooking time to 20 minutes. Do a natural pressure release for 10 minutes, then a quick pressure release, and unlock the lid. Discard bay leaves. Stir in cornstarch and thicken sauce on Sauté mode for 1 to 2 minutes. Adjust taste with salt, black pepper, and serve.

Nutrition:
Calories: 355, Carbs: 8 g, Fat: 12 g, Protein: 27 g

502. Moroccan Beef Stew with Couscous

Preparation time: 5 minutes | **Cooking time:** 45 minutes | **Servings:** 2

Ingredients:

1 ¼ lb. beef stew meat, cut into bite-size pieces	1 tbsp ras el hanout
Salt and black pepper to taste	3 carrots, peeled and julienned
1 celery root, cut into 1-inch chunks	¾ cup pitted prunes, chopped
2 cups chicken broth	2 tbsp tomato paste
1 cup couscous	2 tsp harissa paste, plus more for serving
¼ cup chopped cilantro for garnishing	

Directions:
Season beef with ras el hanout, salt, and pepper, and add to inner pot. Pour in carrots, celery, prunes, chicken broth, tomatoes, and stir. Seal the lid, select Manual/Pressure Cook mode on High, and set cooking time to 30 minutes.
Meanwhile, pour couscous into a medium bowl, season with salt, and pour in 1 cup of boiling water. Cover the bowl with a napkin and allow water to absorb.
Once Instant Pot beeps, perform a natural pressure release. Unlock the lid. Stir in harissa paste, adjust taste with salt, black pepper, and dish stew into serving bowls. Garnish with cilantro and serve beef stew with couscous.

Nutrition:
Calories: 288, Carbs: 39 g, Fat: 13 g, Protein: 6 g

503. Tomato Soup

Preparation time: 10 minutes | **Cooking time:** 25 minutes | **Servings:** 2

Ingredients:

3 lbs. fresh tomatoes, chopped	2 teaspoons dried parsley, crushed
2 tablespoons homemade tomato sauce	4 cups low-sodium vegetable broth
Freshly ground black pepper, to taste	¼ cup fresh basil, chopped
1 tablespoon olive oil	1 garlic clove, minced
2 tablespoons sugar	1 medium onion, chopped
2 teaspoons dried basil, crushed	1 tablespoon balsamic vinegar

Directions:
Put the oil, garlic and onion in the Instant Pot and select "Sauté".
Sauté for 4 minutes and add the tomatoes, herbs, tomato sauce, broth and black pepper.
Cook for about 3 minutes and lock the lid.
Set the Instant Pot to "Soup" and cook for 10 minutes at high pressure.
Release the pressure quickly and stir in the vinegar and sugar.
Put the mixture in the immersion blender and puree the soup.
Garnish with basil and serve.

Nutrition:
Calories: 146, Fat: 4.5 g, Carbs: 23.5 g, Sugars: 16.4 g, Protein: 5.4 g

504. Healthy Vegetable Soup

Preparation time: 10 minutes | **Cooking time:** 30 minutes | **Servings:** 2

Ingredients:

12 oz frozen peas	12 oz frozen corn
12 oz frozen green beans	12 oz frozen okra
4 potatoes, peeled and chopped	3 garlic cloves, chopped
½ onion, chopped	4 carrots, chopped
2 celery stalks, chopped	4 cups chicken broth
¼ tsp pepper	1 tsp salt

Directions:
Add all ingredients into the instant pot and stir well.
Seal pot with lid and cook on soup mode for 30 minutes.
Once done then allow to release pressure naturally then open the lid.
Stir well and serve.

Nutrition:
Calories: 248, Fat: 2.5 g, Carbs: 51.4 g, Sugar: 9.4 g, Protein: 10.6 g

505. Curried Lentil Stew

Preparation time: 10 minutes | **Cooking time:** 5 minutes | **Servings:** 2

Ingredients:

- 1 ½ cups dry green lentils
- ½ cup fresh cilantro, chopped
- 2 bell peppers, diced
- 14 oz can coconut milk
- 1 tbsp curry powder
- 1 tbsp ginger root, minced
- 2 onion, diced
- ½ tsp salt
- 2 cups jasmine rice, cooked
- 2 cups spinach, chopped
- 2 ½ cups vegetable broth
- 1 tsp cumin
- 1 tbsp turmeric
- 2 garlic cloves, minced
- 1 tbsp olive oil

Directions:

Add oil, broth, milk, lentils, cumin, curry powder, turmeric, ginger, garlic, onions, and salt and stir well.
Seal pot with lid and cook on manual high pressure for 5 minutes.
Once done then release pressure using the quick-release method than open the lid.
Add bell peppers and stir well and let sit for 5 minutes.
Add spinach and stir until spinach is wilted.
Pour soup to the bowl and top with rice and cilantro.
Serve and enjoy.

Nutrition:
Calories: 592, Fat: 18.1 g, Carbs: 88.4 g, Sugar: 5 g, Protein: 21.3 g

506. Carrot Broccoli Soup

Preparation time: 5 minutes | **Cooking time:** 40 minutes | **Servings:** 2

Ingredients:

- 2 cups broccoli florets, chopped
- 2 tbsp olive oil
- 2 celery stalks, sliced
- 1 ½ cup heavy whipping cream
- ½ tsp salt
- 32 oz chicken broth
- 2 small carrots, diced
- 1 onion, diced
- ½ tsp pepper

Directions:
Add oil into the instant pot and set the pot on sauté mode.
Add onion, carrots, and celery and sauté for 4-5 minutes.
Add remaining ingredients except whipping cream and stir well.
Seal pot with lid and cook on soup mode for 25 minutes.
Allow to release pressure naturally for 10 minutes then release using quick release method.
Add heavy whipping cream and stir well.
Serve and enjoy.

Nutrition:
Calorie: 290, Carbs: 10.6 g, Protein: 7.4 g, Fat: 25 g, Sugar: 4 g, Sodium: 1069 mg

507. Squid Potato Stew

Preparation time: 5 minutes | **Cooking time:** 20 minutes | **Servings:** 2

Ingredients:

- 2 tbsp olive oil
- 4 potatoes, peeled and diced
- ¼ tsp smoked paprika
- 1 ¼ cups frozen squid rings, defrosted
- Salt and black pepper to taste
- 1 medium white onion, chopped
- 2 garlic cloves, minced
- ¼ tsp curry powder
- 1 cup chicken broth
- ¼ cup parsley leaves, chopped

Directions:
Set your Instant Pot to Sauté and heat olive oil. Cook onion, garlic, paprika, curry powder, and potatoes for 3 minutes. Pour in squid rings, chicken broth, salt, and pepper.
Seal the lid, select Manual/Pressure Cook on High, and set time to 10 minutes.
After cooking, do a quick pressure release. Spoon stew into bowls and garnish with parsley.
Serve.

Nutrition:
Calories: 415, Carbs: 63 g, Fat: 9 g, Protein: 15 g

508. Trout Radish Stew

Preparation time: 5 minutes | **Cooking time:** 20 minutes | **Servings:** 2

Ingredients:

4 tbsp olive oil, divided	1 red onion, thinly sliced
4 garlic cloves, minced	½ cup dry white wine
8 oz bottle clam juice	2 ½ cups chicken broth
½ lb. radishes, diced	1 15 oz. can diced tomatoes with juice
Salt and black pepper to taste	¼ tsp red chili flakes
4 trout fillets, cut into 2-inch cubes	1 lemon, juiced

Directions:
Set your Instant Pot to Sauté mode.
Heat olive and sauté onion and garlic until softened, 3 minutes.
Pour in white wine, cook until reduced by one-third, and add clam juice, chicken broth, radishes, tomatoes, salt, pepper, and red chili flakes, stir and add in the fish.
Seal the lid, select Manual/Pressure Cook on High, and set time to 3 minutes.
After cooking, do a quick pressure release to let out steam, and unlock the lid. Stir and adjust taste with salt and black pepper. Mix in lemon juice.
Spoon into serving bowls and serve warm.

Nutrition:
Calories: 488, Carbs: 25 g, Fat: 33 g, Protein: 26 g

509. Lamb & Mushroom Stew

Preparation time: 5 minutes | **Cooking time:** 50 minutes | **Servings:** 2

Ingredients:

1 tbsp olive oil	1 ½ lb. lamb shoulder, cut into 1-inch cubes
Salt and black pepper to taste	1 small onion, chopped
½ lb. baby Bella mushrooms, chopped	1 garlic clove, minced
½ tbsp tomato paste	1 cup cherry tomatoes, halved
1 cup chicken broth	½ cup chopped parsley

Directions:
Set your Instant Pot to Sauté mode.
Heat olive oil, season lamb with salt and pepper, and sear meat in oil until brown on the outside, 6 to 7 minutes. Stir in onion and mushrooms, and cook until softened, 5 minutes. Add garlic and cook until fragrant, 30 seconds. Mix in tomato paste, cherry tomatoes, chicken broth, and season with salt and pepper.
Seal the lid, select Manual/Pressure Cook mode on High, and set cooking time to 15 minutes. After cooking, perform natural pressure release for 10 minutes, then a quick pressure release. Sprinkle with parsley and serve.

Nutrition:
Calories: 345, Carbs: 12 g, Fat: 18 g, Protein: 36 g

510. Tunisian Lamb Stew

Preparation time: 5 minutes | **Cooking time:** 55 minutes | **Servings:** 2

Ingredients:

2 tbsp olive oil	1 lb. lamb shoulder, cube d
1 medium red onion, thinly sliced	8 cloves garlic, thickly sliced
2-3 tsp ras-el-hanout	1 tsp turmeric
1 tsp red chili flakes	1 tbsp rosemary leaves
¼ cup thyme leaves	1 cup chopped parsley + a little extra for garnishing
2 tomatoes, roughly chopped	2 red bell peppers, peeled and cut into thick strips
2 russet potatoes, peeled and cut into 8 wedges each	2 cups vegetable stock
Salt to taste	

Directions:
Set your Instant Pot to Sauté mode. Heat olive oil and cook lamb until brown on the outside, 6 to 7 minutes. Add onion and garlic, cook until onion softens, 3 minutes. Stir in ras el hanout, turmeric, red chili flakes, rosemary, thyme, and

parsley. Cook until fragrant, 3 minutes. Mix in tomatoes, bell peppers, potatoes, vegetable stock, and salt.

Seal the lid, select Manual/Pressure Cook mode on High, and set cooking time to 20 minutes. After cooking, perform natural pressure release for 10 minutes. Spoon into serving bowls, garnish with parsley, and serve.

Nutrition:
Calories: 450, Carbs: 44 g, Fat: 18 g, Protein: 31 g

511. Easy Beef Stew

Preparation time: 5 minutes | **Cooking time:** 50 minutes | **Servings:** 2

Ingredients:

1 ½ lbs. beef stew meat	¼ cup flour
2 tbsp olive oil	6 cups beef broth
1 onion, cut into wedges	2 carrots, chopped
2 tomatoes, chopped	5 cloves garlic, minced
1 tbsp oregano	4 potatoes, cubed
3 celery stalks, chopped	Salt and black pepper to taste
2 tbsp parsley, chopped for garnish	

Directions:
Coat the beef with the flour in a bowl. Set your Instant Pot to Sauté mode and heat olive oil. Cook the meat for 5 minutes, until browned. Add in the onion and cook for 3 minutes. Pour in the broth.
Seal the lid, select Manual/Pressure Cook mode on High, and set time to 30 minutes. When done, perform a quick pressure release, unlock the lid, and put in the carrots, tomatoes, garlic, oregano, potatoes, celery, salt, and pepper.
Seal the lid again, select Manual/Pressure Cook mode on High, and set time to 5 minutes. When done, perform a quick pressure release.
Sprinkle with parsley to serve.

Nutrition:
Calories: 429, Carbs: 49 g, Fat: 22 g, Protein: 11 g

512. Green Bean and Turkey Soup

Preparation time: 5 minutes | **Cooking time:** 35 minutes | **Servings:** 2

Ingredients:

⅔ cup Green Beans	½ lbs. Turkey Breasts, diced
⅓ cup diced Onions	⅓ cup diced Carrots
1 small Tomato, chopped	2 cups Chicken Stock
1 tbsp chopped Parsley	½ Turnip, chopped
¼ tsp Salt	

Directions:
Place everything except the green beans in the Instant Pot.
Close the lid and set the pot to SOUP.
Cook for 20 minutes and then release the pressure quickly.
Stir in the green beans and cook for additional 30 minutes.
Release the pressure quickly. Serve and enjoy!

Nutrition:
Calories: 140, Fats 1.5 g, Carbs: 15 g Protein 7 g, Fiber: 3.2 g

513. Homemade German Soup

Preparation time: 5 minutes | **Cooking time:** 30 minutes | **Servings:** 2

Ingredients:

4 tbsp butter	2 Yukon gold potatoes, cubed
4 shallots, chopped	1 celery stalk, chopped
2 carrots, chopped	¼ cup flour
6 cups chicken broth	1 tbsp Dijon mustard
½ small head cabbage, shredded	1 lb. cooked bratwurst, sliced
2 cups buttermilk	Black pepper to taste
3 cups shredded cheddar cheese	

Directions:
Set your Instant Pot to Sauté mode and melt the butter.
Cook the potatoes, shallots, celery and carrots for 5 minutes, until tender. Stir in the flour and broth. Add in the mustard and stir until there

are no lumps. Put the cabbage and bratwurst. Seal the lid, select Manual/Pressure Cook mode on High, and set time to 5 minutes.

When done, perform a natural pressure release for 10 minutes, then a quick pressure release to let out the remaining steam. Unlock the lid and pour in buttermilk and black pepper. Stir in the cheese until it is completely melted. Serve.

Nutrition:
Calories: 473, Carbs: 28 g, Fat: 32 g, Protein: 19 g

514. Pumpkin-Ginger Soup

Preparation time: 5 minutes | **Cooking time:** 20 minutes | **Servings:** 2

Ingredients:
- 3 tbsp olive oil
- 1 small red onion, finely chopped
- 3 tbsp chopped mint + parsley + sage leaves
- 1 cup almond milk
- Salt and black pepper to taste
- 1 tbsp chopped cilantro
- 1 medium pumpkin, peeled and chopped
- 1 tbsp ginger paste
- 3 cups vegetable stock
- ½ tbsp chili powder
- 1 lime, juiced

Directions:
Set your Instant Pot to Sauté mode and adjust to medium heat. Heat olive oil and sauté pumpkin, onion, and ginger paste until vegetables soften, 5 minutes.

Mix in fresh herbs, allow releasing of fragrance, and pour in vegetable stock, almond milk, chili powder, salt, and black pepper.

Seal the lid, select Manual/Pressure Cook mode on High, and set cooking time to 3 minutes.

After cooking, perform a quick pressure release to let out steam. Unlock the lid, stir in lime juice, and ladle into individual bowls.

Garnish with cilantro and serve.

Nutrition:
Calories: 330, Carbs: 11 g, Fat: 28 g, Protein: 14 g

515. Mango Salad

Preparation time: 10 minutes | **Cooking time:** 0 minutes | **Servings:** 2

Ingredients:
- 1 avocado, pitted, peeled and chopped
- 1 cup cherry tomatoes, halved
- 1 small cucumber, chopped
- 2 tablespoons olive oil
- 2 tablespoons lime juice
- Salt and black pepper to taste
- 1 cup red bell pepper, chopped
- 1 cup baby arugula
- 2 mangos, peeled and cubed
- 1 garlic clove, minced
- 1 tablespoon chives, chopped

Directions:
In a bowl, mix the avocado with bell pepper and the rest of the ingredients, toss to coat and serve.

Nutrition:
Calories: 200, Fat: 4 g, Fiber: 4.1 g, Carbs: 3.2 g, Protein: 6 g

516. Crispy Scallops

Preparation time: 15 minutes | **Cooking time:** 6 minutes | **Servings:** 2

Ingredients:
- 18 sea scallops, cleaned and patted very dry
- 1 tablespoon 2% milk
- ¼ cup cornflakes, crushed
- Salt and black pepper, as required
- ⅛ cup all-purpose flour
- ½ egg
- ½ teaspoon paprika

Directions:
Preheat the Air fryer to 400°F and grease an Air fryer basket.

Mix flour, paprika, salt, and black pepper in a bowl.

Whisk egg with milk in another bowl and place the cornflakes in a third bowl.

Coat each scallop with the flour mixture, dip into the egg mixture and finally, dredge in the cornflakes.

Arrange scallops in the Air fryer basket and cook for about 6 minutes.

Dish out the scallops in a platter and serve hot.

Nutrition:
Calories: 150, Fat: 1.7 g, Carbs: 8 g, Sugar: 0.4 g, Protein: 24 g, Sodium: 278 mg

517. Scallops with Spinach

Preparation time: 20 minutes | **Cooking time:** 10 minutes | **Servings:** 2

Ingredients:

- 1 12-oz. package frozen spinach, thawed and drained
- Olive oil cooking spray
- Salt and ground black pepper, as required
- 1 tablespoon tomato paste
- 8 jumbo sea scallops
- 1 tablespoon fresh basil, chopped
- ¾ cup heavy whipping cream
- 1 teaspoon garlic, minced

Directions:
Preheat the Air fryer to 350°F and grease an Air fryer pan.
Season the scallops evenly with salt and black pepper.
Mix cream, tomato paste, garlic, basil, salt, and black pepper in a bowl.
Place spinach at the bottom of the Air fryer pan, followed by seasoned scallops and top with the cream mixture.
Transfer into the Air fryer and cook for about 10 minutes.
Dish out in a platter and serve hot.

Nutrition:
Calories: 203, Fat: 18.3 g, Carbs: 12.3 g, Sugar: 1.7 g, Protein: 26.4 g, Sodium: 101 mg

518. Bacon Wrapped Scallops

Preparation time: 15 minutes | **Cooking time:** 12 minutes | **Servings:** 2

Ingredients:

- 5 center-cut bacon slices, cut each in 4 pieces
- Olive oil cooking spray
- ½ teaspoon paprika
- 20 sea scallops, cleaned and patted very dry
- 1 teaspoon lemon pepper seasoning
- Salt and ground black pepper, to taste

Directions:
Preheat the Air fryer to 400°F and grease an Air fryer basket.
Wrap each scallop with a piece of bacon and secure each with a toothpick.
Season the scallops evenly with lemon pepper seasoning and paprika.
Arrange half of the scallops into the Air fryer basket and spray with cooking spray.
Season with salt and black pepper and cook for about 6 minutes.
Repeat with the remaining half and serve warm.

Nutrition:
Calories: 330, Fat: 16.3 g, Carbs: 4.5 g, Protein: 38.7 g, Sodium: 1118 mg

519. Glazed Calamari

Preparation time: 20 minutes | **Cooking time:** 13 minutes | **Servings:** 2

Ingredients:

- ½ lb. calamari tubes, cut into ¼ inch rings
- 1 cup flour
- Salt and black pepper, to taste
- 1 cup club soda
- ½ tablespoon red pepper flakes, crushed

For the Sauce:
- ½ cup honey
- ¼ teaspoon red pepper flakes, crushed
- 2 tablespoons Sriracha sauce

Directions:
Preheat the Air fryer to 375°F and grease an Air fryer basket.
Soak the calamari in the club soda in a bowl and keep aside for about 10 minutes.
Mix flour, red pepper flakes, salt, and black pepper in another bowl.
Drain the club soda from calamari and coat the calamari rings evenly with flour mixture.
Arrange calamari rings into the Air fryer basket and cook for about 11 minutes.
Meanwhile, mix the honey, Sriracha sauce and red pepper flakes in a bowl.
Coat the calamari rings with the honey sauce and cook for 2 more minutes.

Dish out the calamari rings onto serving plates and serve hot.

Nutrition:
Calories: 307, Fats: 1.4 g, Carbs: 62.1 g, Sugar: 35 g, Proteins: 12 g, Sodium: 131 mg

520. Buttered Crab Shells

Preparation time: 20 minutes | **Cooking time:** 10 minutes | **Servings:** 2

Ingredients:
- 4 soft crab shells, cleaned
- 3 eggs
- 2 tablespoons butter, melted
- 1½ teaspoons lemon zest, grated
- 1 cup buttermilk
- 2 cups panko breadcrumb
- 2 teaspoons seafood seasoning

Directions:
Preheat the Air fryer to 375°F and grease an Air fryer basket.
Place the buttermilk in a shallow bowl and whisk the eggs in a second bowl.
Mix the breadcrumbs, seafood seasoning, and lemon zest in a third bowl.
Soak the crab shells into the buttermilk for about 10 minutes, then dip in the eggs.
Dredge in the breadcrumb mixture and arrange the crab shells into the Air fryer basket.
Cook for about 10 minutes and dish out in a platter.
Drizzle melted butter over the crab shells and immediately serve.

Nutrition:
Calories: 521, Fat: 16.8 g, Carbs: 11.5 g, Sugar: 3.3 g, Protein: 47.8 g, Sodium: 1100 mg

521. Crab Cakes

Preparation time: 20 minutes | **Cooking time:** 20 minutes | **Servings:** 2

Ingredients:
- 1-lb. lump crab meat
- ¼ cup scallion, finely chopped
- ⅓ cup panko breadcrumbs
- 2 large eggs
- 2 tablespoons mayonnaise
- 1 teaspoon Worcestershire sauce
- Ground black pepper, as required
- 1 teaspoon Dijon mustard
- 1½ teaspoons Old Bay seasoning

Directions:
Preheat the Air fryer to 375°F and grease an Air fryer basket.
Mix all the ingredients in a large bowl and cover to refrigerate for about 1 hour.
Make 8 equal-sized patties from the mixture and transfer 4 patties into the Air fryer.
Cook for about 10 minutes, flipping once in between and repeat with the remaining patties.
Dish out and serve warm.

Nutrition:
Calories: 183, Fat: 14.8 g, Carbs: 5.9 g, Sugar: 1.1 g, Protein: 20.1 g, Sodium: 996 mg

522. Spicy Shrimp and Rice

Preparation time: 20 minutes | **Cooking time:** 10 minutes | **Servings:** 2

Ingredients:
- ½ tablespoon mustard seeds
- ¼ cup vegetable oil
- 2 onions, diced
- 1 teaspoon turmeric
- Rice, already cooked, for serving
- 18 oz. shrimp, peeled and deveined Salt, to taste
- 2 green chilies, cut into halves lengthwise
- 2 teaspoons dry mustard
- 1-inch piece of ginger, peeled and chopped
- 4 oz. curd, beaten

Directions:
Place the mustard seeds in a bowl, add enough water to cover, set aside for 10 minutes, drain and grind very well.
Put the shrimp in a bowl, and include the oil, dry mustard, saffron, mustard paste, salt, onion, pepper, curd and ginger, turn to cover and set aside for 10 minutes.
Transfer everything to the Instant Pot, cover and cook in steam mode for 10 minutes. Relieve

the pressure, divide between the dishes and serve with boiled rice.

Nutrition:
Calories: 200, Fat: 2 g, Fiber: 1 g, Carbs: 7 g, Proteins: 11 g

523. Shrimp Scampi

Preparation time: 10 minutes | **Cooking time:** 4 minutes | **Servings:** 2

Ingredients:
- 1-lb. shrimp, cooked, peeled and deveined
- ¼ teaspoon dried oregano
- 10 oz. canned diced tomatoes
- 1 tablespoon fresh parsley, diced
- ⅓ cup water
- 2 tablespoons extra virgin olive oil
- 1 garlic clove, peeled and minced
- ⅓ cup tomato paste
- 1 cup Parmesan cheese, grated
- Spaghetti noodles, already cooked, for serving

Directions:
Put the Instant Pot in the sauté mode, add the oil and heat. Add the garlic, mix and cook for 2 minutes.
Add the shrimp, tomato paste, tomato, water, oregano and parsley, mix, cover and cook in Manual setting of 3 minutes.
Release the pressure, divide between the plates, add the spaghetti, sprinkle with cheese and serve.

Nutrition:
Calories: 288, Fat: 20 g, Carbs: 0.01 g, Proteins: 23 g

524. Fish and shrimp

Preparation time: 10 minutes | **Cooking time:** 10 minutes | **Servings:** 2

Ingredients:
- ½ lb. shrimp, cooked, peeled and deveined
- 2 lbs. flounder
- 4 lemon wedges
- 2 tablespoons butter
- Salt and ground black pepper, to taste
- ½ cup water

Directions:
Season the fish with pepper and salt, and place it in the Instant Pot steam basket
Add water to the Instant Pot, cover and steam for 10 minutes. Release the pressure, uncover the Instant Pot, transfer the fish to the plates and set aside.
Discard the water, clean the Instant Pot and set to Sauté mode. Add the butter and melt. Add the shrimp, salt and pepper, mix and distribute between the fish dishes and serve with lemon slices on the side.

Nutrition:
Calories: 200, Fat: 0.2 g, Fiber: 0.2 g, Carbs: 1 g, Proteins: 12 g

525. Shrimp with Risotto and Herbs

Preparation time: 10 minutes | **Cooking time:** 20 minutes | **Servings:** 2

Ingredients:
- 2 garlic cloves, peeled and minced
- 1½ cups Arborio rice
- Salt and ground black pepper, to taste
- 2 tablespoons dry white wine
- ¾ cup Parmesan cheese, grated
- ⅛ cup fresh tarragon, chopped
- 1 yellow onion, peeled and chopped
- 4 tablespoons butter
- 1 lb. shrimp, peeled and deveined
- 4½ cups chicken stock
- ⅛ cup fresh parsley, chopped

Directions:
Put the Instant Pot in the sauté mode, add 2 tablespoons of butter and melt them. Add the garlic and onion, mix and cook for 4 minutes.
Add the rice, mix and cook for 1 minute. Add wine, stir and cook for 30 seconds. Add 3 cups of broth, salt and pepper, stir, cover and cook for 9 minutes on rice.
Release the pressure, uncover the Instant Pot, add the shrimp and the rest of the broth, put the Instant Pot in the sauté mode and cook for 5 minutes, stirring occasionally.
Add the cheese, the rest of the butter, tarragon and parsley, mix, divide between the plates and serve.

Nutrition:
Calories: 400, Fat: 8 g, Fiber: 4 g, Carbs: 15 g, Proteins: 29 g

526. Celery soup

Preparation time: 10 minutes | **Cooking time:** 17 minutes | **Servings:** 2

Ingredients:
- 1 teaspoon extra virgin olive oil
- 1 yellow onion, peeled and chopped
- Salt and ground black pepper, to taste
- ½ cup parsley, chopped, for serving
- 1 teaspoon celery seeds
- 3 potatoes, chopped
- 7 celery stalks, chopped
- 4 cups vegetable stock
- 1 tablespoon curry powder

Directions:
Put the Instant Pot in the sauté mode, add the oil and heat. Add the onion, celery seeds and curry, mix and cook for 1 minute.
Add celery and potatoes, mix and cook for 5 minutes. Add the stock, salt, pepper, mix, cover and cook with manual adjustment for 10 minutes.
Relieve the pressure, uncover the Instant Pot, mix well using an immersion blender, add the parsley, stir, divide into bowls and serve.

Nutrition:
Calories: 90, Fat: 4 g, Fiber: 4 g, Carbs: 8.5 g, Proteins: 2 g

527. Chestnut soup

Preparation time: 10 minutes | **Cooking time:** 25 minutes | **Servings:** 2

Ingredients:
- 1 yellow onion, peeled and chopped
- 1 lb. canned chestnuts, drained and rinsed
- 4 tablespoons butter
- 1 bay leaf
- 2 tablespoons rum
- 1 sage leaf, chopped
- 1 celery stalk, chopped
- Salt and ground white pepper, to taste
- 4 cups chicken stock
- 1 potato, chopped
- Nutmeg
- Heavy cream, for serving
- Sage leaves, chopped, for serving

Directions:
Put the Instant Pot in the sauté mode, add the butter and melt. Add onion, sage, celery, salt and pepper, mix and cook for 5 minutes.
Add chestnuts, potatoes, bay leaves and broth, mix, cover and cook in soup mode for 20 minutes.
Release the pressure, uncover the Instant Pot, add the nutmeg and rum, throw away the bay leaf and mix the soup with a blender.
Divide the soup into bowls, add the cream and sage leaves and serve.

Nutrition:
Calories:
Calories: 230, Fat: 13 g, Fiber: 2 g, Carbs: 22 g, Proteins: 2.1 g

528. Fennel soup

Preparation time: 10 minutes | **Cooking time:** 15 minutes | **Servings:** 2

Ingredients:
- 2 cups water
- 1 fennel bulb, chopped
- 1 tablespoon extra-virgin olive oil
- 2 teaspoons Parmesan cheese, grated
- 1 leek, chopped
- 1 bay leaf
- Salt and ground black pepper, to taste
- ½ cube vegetable bouillon

Directions:
In the Instant Pot, mix the fennel with leeks, bay leaves, vegetable stock and water. Stir, cover and cook for 15 minutes in the Soup setting.
Relieve the pressure, uncover the Instant Pot, add the cheese, oil, salt and pepper, mix, divide into bowls and serve.

Nutrition:
Calories: 100, Fats: 2.2 g, Fiber: 4 g, Carbs: 15 g, Proteins: 5 g

529. Curry Sea Bass

Preparation time: 10 minutes | **Cooking time:** 40 minutes | **Servings:** 2

Ingredients:
- 1 lb. sea bass fillets, boneless
- ½ teaspoon rosemary, dried
- ½ teaspoon curry powder
- A pinch of salt and black pepper
- 1 tablespoon olive oil
- Juice of 1 lime
- 1 red onion, chopped
- 2 tablespoons cilantro, chopped

Directions:
In a sous vide bag, mix the sea bass with the oil and the other ingredients, seal the bag, submerge in the water bath and cook at 180°F for 40 minutes.
Divide the mix between plates and serve with a side salad.

Nutrition:
Calories: 200, Fat: 12 g, Fiber: 2 g, Carbs: 6 g, Protein: 11 g

530. Calamari and Mushrooms

Preparation time: 10 minutes | **Cooking time:** 35 minutes | **Servings:** 2

Ingredients:
- 1 lb. calamari rings
- 4 scallions, minced
- 2 tablespoons avocado oil
- 1 tablespoon rosemary, dried
- 1 tablespoon parsley, chopped
- 1 cup brown mushrooms, halved
- ½ cup white wine
- Juice of 1 lime
- Salt and black pepper to the taste

Directions:
In a sous vide bag, mix the calamari with the mushrooms, scallions and the other ingredients, seal the bag, submerge in the water bath and cook at 180°F for 35 minutes.
Divide the mix between plates and serve.

Nutrition:
Calories: 200, Fat: 12 g, Fiber: 2 g, Carbs: 6 g, Protein: 9 g

531. Curry Trout and Green Beans

Preparation time: 10 minutes | **Cooking time:** 35 minutes | **Servings:** 2

Ingredients:
- 4 trout fillets, boneless
- 1 tablespoon green curry paste
- 1 tablespoon avocado oil
- ½ teaspoon curry powder
- ½ lb. green beans, trimmed and halved
- 1 cup coconut cream
- ½ teaspoon basil, dried
- A pinch of salt and black pepper

Directions:
In a sous vide bag, mix the trout with the green beans, curry paste and the other ingredients, seal the bag, submerge in the water bath and cook at 180°F for 35 minutes.
Divide the whole mix between plates and serve.

Nutrition:
Calories: 211, Fat: 13 g, Fiber: 2 g, Carbs: 7 g, Protein: 11 g

532. Coriander Shrimp Mix

Preparation time: 5 minutes | **Cooking time:** 20 minutes | **Servings:** 2

Ingredients:
- 1 lb. shrimp, peeled and deveined
- 1 tablespoon olive oil
- ½ teaspoon turmeric powder
- A pinch of salt and black pepper
- Juice of 1 lime
- ½ cup white wine
- 2 tablespoons coriander, chopped

Directions:
In a sous vide bag, mix the shrimp with the oil, lime juice and the other ingredients, seal the bag, submerge in the water bath and cook at 180°F for 20 minutes.
Divide the mix into bowls and serve.

Nutrition:
Calories: 200, Fat: 12 g, Fiber: 4 g, Carbs: 6 g, Protein: 8 g

533. Shrimp and Mustard Sauce

Preparation time: 5 minutes | **Cooking time:** 20 minutes | **Servings:** 2

Ingredients:

- 1 lb. shrimp, peeled and deveined
- 1 cup heavy cream
- 1 tablespoon lime zest, grated
- A pinch of salt and black pepper
- 1 tablespoon mustard
- ½ teaspoon garam masala
- ½ teaspoon rosemary, dried
- 1 tablespoon cilantro, chopped

Directions:

In a sous vide bag, mix the shrimp with the mustard, heavy cream and the other ingredients, seal the bag and cook in the water bath and cook at 175°F for 25 minutes.
Divide the mix into bowls and serve.

Nutrition:

Calories: 232, Fat: 7 g, Fiber: 3 g, Carbs: 7 g, Protein: 9 g

534. Vegetable Soup

Preparation time: 10 minutes | **Cooking time:** 15 minutes | **Servings:** 2

Ingredients:

- Salt and ground black pepper, to taste
- 1 tablespoon coconut oil
- 6 mushrooms, sliced
- 2 celery sticks, chopped
- 4 garlic cloves, peeled and minced
- 3.5 oz. kale leaves, chopped
- 4 cups vegetable stock
- ½ cup fresh parsley, chopped
- 1 onion, peeled and chopped
- ½ red chili, chopped
- 2 carrots, peeled and chopped
- ½ cup dried porcini mushrooms
- 1 zucchini, chopped
- 1 cup tomatoes, chopped
- 1 bay leaf
- 1 teaspoon lemon zest

Directions:

Put the Instant Pot in the sauté mode, add the oil and heat. Add onion, celery, carrot, salt and pepper, mix and cook for 1 minute.
Add pepper, mushrooms, garlic, mix and cook for 2 minutes. Add the cabbage leaves, zucchini, tomatoes, bay leaves and broth, mix, cover and cook for 10 minutes.
Release the pressure naturally, uncover the Instant Pot, divide the soup into bowls, add the lemon zest and parsley and serve.

Nutrition:

Calories: 80, Fat: 1 g, Fiber: 2 g, Carbs: 14 g, Proteins: 2 g

535. Chicken Chili Soup

Preparation time: 10 minutes | **Cooking time:** 30 minutes | **Servings:** 2

Ingredients:

- 1 white onion, peeled and chopped
- 4 garlic cloves, peeled and minced
- 1 jalapeño pepper, chopped
- 1 lb. chicken breast, skinless and boneless
- ½ teaspoon red pepper flakes
- Fresh cilantro, chopped, for serving
- Cannellini beans, drained
- Lime wedges, for serving
- 2 tablespoons olive oil
- 2 teaspoons dried oregano
- 1 teaspoon cumin
- 30 oz. canned
- 3 cups chicken stock
- Tortilla chips, for serving
- Salt and ground black pepper, to taste

Directions:

Put the Instant Pot in the sauté mode, add the oil and heat. Add the jalapeno pepper and onion, stir and cook for 3 minutes.
Add the garlic, mix and cook for 1 minute. Add oregano, cumin, pepper flakes, stock, chicken, beans, salt and pepper, mix, cover and cook the soup for 30 minutes.
Release the pressure, uncover the Instant Pot, cut the meat into pieces with 2 forks, add more salt and pepper, mix and divide into bowls.
Serve with cilantro on top and tortilla chips and lemon slices on the side.

Nutrition:

Calories: 200, Fat: 8 g, Fiber: 6 g, Carbs: 17 g, Proteins: 19 g

536. Simple Cracker Mix

Preparation time: 20 minutes | **Cooking time:** 30 minutes | **Servings:** 2

Ingredients:
- Diced garlic cloves, 8 pieces
- Olive oil, ⅓ cup
- Rough and slashed green olives, 1½ kitchen spoon
- Salt and black pepper to taste
- Lime peel, 1 kitchen spoon
- Deboned crackers, 4 average sized pieces
- Lime juice, from 2 limes

Directions:
Barring the fish, place all ingredients in a pan.
Toss and mix properly.
Insert the fish and flip lightly.
Set your air fryer to 360°F. Insert the fish and cook for 15 minutes.
Share into dishes and serve.

Nutrition:
Calories: 191, Fat: 2 g, Fiber: 3 g, Carbs: 18 g, Protein: 12 g

537. Simple Char Mix

Preparation time: 23 minutes | **Cooking time:** 30 minutes | **Servings:** 2

Ingredients:
- Deboned char strips, 2
- Diced red pepper, 1 piece
- Olive oil, 1 kitchen spoon
- Salt and black pepper to taste
- Lemon juice, 1 kitchen spoon
- Shredded garlic, 1 kitchen spoon

Directions:
Make a mixture of all ingredients barring the char.
Coat the char with this mixture.
Set your air fryer to 360°F. Insert the char and cook for 13 minutes
Share into dishes and serve.

Nutrition:
Calories: 271, Fat: 4 g, Fiber: 2 g, Carbs: 15 g, Protein: 11 g

538. Coriander Char Strips

Preparation time: 17 minutes | **Cooking time:** 30 minutes | **Servings:** 2

Ingredients:
- 4 Deboned char strips
- 1 cup Rough and diced olives
- 1 kitchen spoon Olive oil
- 4 pieces Diced garlic cloves
- 3 kitchen spoons Chopped coriander

Directions:
Mix all the ingredients in a pan.
Set your air fryer to 360°F. Insert and cook for 6 minutes.
Flip and cook for a further 6 minutes.
Share into dishes and serve.

Nutrition:
Calories: 251, Fat: 7 g, Fiber: 3 g, Carbs: 16 g, Protein: 12 g

539. Kipper and Jasmine Rice

Preparation time: 35 minutes | **Cooking time:** 30 minutes | **Servings:** 2

Ingredients:
- 2 Deboned wild kipper strips
- ½ cup Jasmine rice
- 1 kitchen spoon Thawed margarine
- Salt and black pepper to taste
- 1 cup Chicken broth
- ¼ teaspoon Saffron

Directions:
Barring the fish, place all ingredients in a pan
Flip and mix well
Set your air fryer 360°F
Insert the ingredients and cook for 15 minutes.
Insert the fish, place on the lid
Cook 12 minutes more at the same temperature
Share into dishes and serve immediately

Nutrition:
Calories: 271, Fat: 8 g, Fiber: 9 g, Carbs: 15 g, Protein: 8 g

540. Kipper and Carrots

Preparation time: 25 minutes | **Cooking time:** 30 minutes | **Servings:** 2

Ingredients:

2 Deboned kipper strips	3 Diced garlic cloves
1 kitchen spoon Olive oil	¼ cup Veggie broth
1 cup Baby carrots	Salt and black pepper to taste

Directions:
Mix the ingredients in a pan.
Set your air fryer to 370°F. Insert the mixture and cook for 20 minutes.
Share into dishes and serv

Nutrition:
Calories: 200, Fat: 6 g, Fiber: 6 g, Carbs: 18 g, Protein: 11 g

541. Tasty Cod

Preparation time: 15 minutes | **Cooking time:** 30 minutes | **Servings:** 2

Ingredients:

4 Deboned cod strips	2 kitchen spoons assorted chili peppers
Lemon juice from 1 lemon	1 Chopped up lemon
Salt and black pepper to taste	

Directions:
Mix the chili pepper with the cod, the lemon juice, as well as the salt and pepper in a pan.
Set your air fryer to 360°F.
Place the lemon slices atop the cod mixture.
Insert in the air fryer and cook for 10 minutes.
Share the strips into dishes and serve.

Nutrition:
Calories: 200, Fat: 4 g, Fiber: 8 g, Carbs: 16 g, Protein: 7 g

542. Italian Barramundi Fillets

Preparation time: 15 minutes | **Cooking time:** 18 minutes | **Servings:** 2

Ingredients:

2 barramundi fillets, boneless	1 tbsp. olive oil+ 2 tsp.
2 tsp. Italian seasoning	¼ cup green olives, pitted and chopped
¼ cup cherry tomatoes, chopped	¼ cup black olives, chopped.
2 tbsp. parsley, chopped	1 tbsp. lemon zest
2 tbsp. lemon zest	Salt and black pepper to the taste

Directions:
Rub fish with salt, pepper, Italian seasoning and 2 tsp. olive oil, transfer to your air fryer and cook at 360°F, for 8 minutes, flipping them halfway. In a bowl, mix tomatoes with black olives, green olives, salt, pepper, lemon zest and lemon juice, parsley and 1 tbsp. olive oil and toss well. Divide fish on plates, add tomato salsa on top and serve.

Nutrition:
Calories: 270, Fat: 4 g, Fiber: 2 g, Carbs: 18 g, Protein: 27 g

543. Endive Risotto

Preparation time: 10 minutes | **Cooking time:** 20 minutes | **Servings:** 2

Ingredients:

2 Belgian endives, trimmed, cut into halves lengthwise, and roughly chopped	¾ cup rice
½ yellow onion, peeled and chopped	2 tablespoons extra virgin olive oil
2 cups vegetable stock	½ cup white wine
2 oz. Parmesan cheese, grated	Salt and ground black pepper, to taste
3 tablespoons heavy cream	

Directions:
Put the Instant Pot in the sauté mode, add the oil and heat. Add the onion, stir and fry for 4 minutes.
Add the endives, mix and cook for 4 minutes. Add rice, wine, salt, pepper, stock, mix, cover and cook for 10 minutes.
Quickly release the pressure, uncover the Instant Pot and set it to Sauté mode. Add the cheese and cream, mix, cook for 1 minute, transfer to the dishes and serve.

Nutrition:
Calories: 260, Fat: 5 g, Fiber: 5 g, Carbs: 13 g, Proteins: 16 g

544. Eggplant Ratatouille

Preparation time: 15 minutes | **Cooking time:** 8 minutes | **Servings:** 2

Ingredients:
- Salt and ground black pepper, to taste
- 1 eggplant, peeled and thinly sliced
- 3 tablespoons extra virgin olive oil
- 1 red bell pepper, seeded and chopped
- ½ cup water
- 1 cup fresh basil, chopped
- 1 cup onion, peeled and chopped
- 2 garlic cloves, peeled and minced
- 1 green bell pepper, seeded and chopped
- 1 teaspoon dried thyme
- 14 oz. canned diced tomatoes
- Sugar

Directions:
Put the Instant Pot in the sauté mode, add the oil and heat. Add the peppers, onions and garlic, mix and cook for 3 minutes.
Add the eggplant, water, salt, pepper, thyme, sugar and tomato, cover the Instant Pot and cook for 4 minutes.
Quickly release the pressure, uncover the Instant Pot, add the basil, mix gently, divide between the dishes and serve.

Nutrition:
Calories: 109, Fat: 5 g, Fiber: 3 g, Carbs: 14 g, Proteins: 2 g

545. Eggplant Marinara

Preparation time: 10 minutes | **Cooking time:** 8 minutes | **Servings:** 2

Ingredients:
- 1 tablespoon extra-virgin olive oil
- 1 tablespoon onion powder
- Salt and ground black pepper, to taste
- Spaghetti noodles, already cooked
- 3 garlic cloves, peeled and minced
- 4 cups eggplant, cubed
- 1 cup marinara sauce
- ½ cup water

Directions:
Put the Instant Pot in the sauté mode, add the oil and heat. Add the garlic, mix and cook for 2 minutes.
Add eggplant, salt, pepper, onion powder, marinara sauce and water, mix gently, cover and cook for 8 minutes.
Relieve the pressure, uncover the Instant Pot and serve with spaghetti.

Nutrition:
Calories: 130, Fat: 3 g, Fiber: 2 g, Carbs: 3 g, Proteins: 3 g

546. Babaganoush

Preparation time: 10 minutes | **Cooking time:** 4 minutes | **Servings:** 2

Ingredients:
- ½ cup water
- Salt and ground black pepper, to taste
- 4 garlic cloves, peeled
- 1 tablespoon tahini
- 3 olives, pitted and sliced
- 2 lbs. eggplant, peeled and cut into medium chunks
- ⅓ cup extra virgin olive oil
- 1 bunch thyme, chopped
- ¼ cup lemon juice

Directions:
Place the eggplant pieces in the Instant Pot, add ¼ cup of oil, place the Instant Pot in the sauté mode and heat.
Add the garlic, water, salt and pepper, mix, cover and cook for 3 minutes.
Release the pressure, uncover the Instant Pot, transfer the pieces of eggplant and garlic to the blender, add the lemon juice and tahini and beat well. Add the thyme and mix again.
Transfer eggplant spread in a bowl, cover with slices of olive and a drizzle of oil and serve.

Nutrition:
Calories: 70, Fat: 2 g, Fiber: 2 g, Carbs: 7 g, Proteins: 1 g

547. Eggplant Surprise

Preparation time: 10 minutes | **Cooking time:** 7 minutes | **Servings:** 2

Ingredients:

Salt and ground black pepper, to taste
1 eggplant, roughly chopped
3 tomatoes, cored and sliced
3 tablespoons extra virgin olive oil
1 teaspoon dried thyme
3 zucchinis, roughly chopped
2 tablespoons lemon juice
1 teaspoon dried oregano

Directions:

Place the eggplant pieces in the instant pot. Add the zucchini and the tomato.
In a bowl, mix the lemon juice with salt, pepper, thyme, oregano and oil and mix well. Pour over the vegetables, mix well, cover the Instant Pot and cook for 7 minutes.
Relieve the pressure, uncover the Instant Pot, distribute the dishes and serve.

Nutrition:

Calories: 140, Fat: 3.4 g, Fiber: 7 g, Carbs: 20 g, Proteins: 5 g

548. Braised Fennel

Preparation time: 10 minutes | **Cooking time:** 12 minutes | **Servings:** 2

Ingredients:

Salt and ground black pepper, to taste
2 fennel bulbs, trimmed and cut into quarters
1 dried red pepper
¾ cup vegetable stock Juice of
¼ cup Parmesan cheese, grated
1 garlic clove, peeled and chopped
3 tablespoons extra virgin olive oil
¼ cup white wine
½ lemon

Directions:

Put the Instant Pot in the sauté mode, add the oil and heat. Add garlic and pepper, mix, cook 2 minutes and discard the garlic.
Add the fennel, mix and brown for 8 minutes. Add salt, pepper, broth, wine, cover and cook for 4 minutes at steam temperature.
Release the pressure, uncover the Instant Pot, add the lemon juice, more salt and pepper, if necessary, and the cheese. Mix to cover, divide between plates and serve.

Nutrition:

Calories: 70, Fat: 1 g, Fiber: 2 g, Carbs: 2 g, Proteins: 1 g

549. Fennel Risotto

Preparation time: 10 minutes | **Cooking time:** 10 minutes | **Servings:** 2

Ingredients:

1 fennel bulb, trimmed and chopped
1 yellow onion, peeled and chopped
1 tablespoon extra-virgin olive oil
¼ cup white wine
Salt and ground black pepper, to taste
3 tablespoons tomato paste
2 tablespoons butter
3 cups chicken stock
1½ cups Arborio rice
½ teaspoon thyme, dried
⅓ cup Parmesan cheese, grated

Directions:

Put the Instant Pot in the sauté mode, add the butter and melt. Add the fennel and onion, mix, brown for 4 minutes and transfer to a bowl.
Add the oil to the instant flask and heat. Add the rice, mix and cook for 3 minutes.
Add the tomato paste, stock, fennel, onion, wine, salt, pepper and thyme, stir, cover and cook for 8 minutes in the Manual setting.
Release the pressure, uncover, add the cheese, mix, divide between the dishes and serve.

Nutrition:

Calories: 200, Fat: 10 g, Fiber: 2 g, Carbs: 20 g, Proteins: 12 g

550. Kale with Garlic and Lemon

Preparation time: 10 minutes | **Cooking time:** 5 minutes | **Servings:** 2

Ingredients:

½ cup water
1 tablespoon extra-virgin olive oil
3 garlic cloves, peeled and chopped
Juice of ½ lemon
1 lb. kale, trimmed
Salt and ground black pepper, to taste

Directions:
Put the Instant Pot in the sauté mode, add the oil and heat. Add the garlic, mix and cook for 2 minutes.
Add the cabbage and water, cover and cook for 5 minutes in the steamer.
Release the pressure, uncover the instant pot, add salt, pepper and lemon juice, mix, divide between the dishes and serve.

Nutrition:
Calories: 60, Fat: 3 g, Fiber: 1 g, Carbs: 2.4 g, Proteins: 0.7 g

551. Braised Kale

Preparation time: 10 minutes | **Cooking time:** 10 minutes | **Servings:** 2

Ingredients:
- 1 yellow onion, peeled and sliced thin
- 10 oz. kale, chopped
- 3 carrots, peeled and sliced
- Salt and ground black pepper, to taste
- 1 tablespoon butter
- 1 tablespoon kale
- ¼ teaspoon red pepper flakes
- 5 garlic cloves, peeled and chopped
- ½ cup chicken stock
- Balsamic vinegar

Directions:
Put the Instant Pot in Saute mode, add the butter and melt. Add the carrots and onion, mix and brown for 2 minutes.
Add the garlic, mix and cook for 1 minute. Add the cabbage, stock, salt and pepper, mix, cover and cook for 7 minutes in the Manual setting.
Relieve the pressure, uncover the Instant Pot, add the vinegar and pepper flakes, toss to coat, divide between the plates and serve.

Nutrition:
Calories: 60, Fat: 2 g, Fiber: 2 g, Carbs: 4 g, Proteins: 1 g

552. Kale and Bacon

Preparation time: 10 minutes | **Cooking time:** 10 minutes | **Servings:** 2

Ingredients:
- 1 tablespoon vegetable oil
- 1 onion, peeled and sliced thin
- 6 garlic cloves, peeled and chopped
- 1 teaspoon red chili peppers
- 2 tablespoons apple cider vinegar
- 6 bacon slices, chopped
- 1 tablespoon brown sugar
- 1½ cups chicken stock
- 1 teaspoon liquid smoke
- 10 oz. kale leaves, chopped

Directions:
Put the Instant Pot in the sauté mode, add the oil and heat. Add the bacon, mix and cook for 1 to 2 minutes.
Add the onion, mix and cook for 3 minutes. Add the garlic, mix and cook for 1 minute. Add vinegar, broth, sugar, liquid smoke, red pepper, salt, pepper, black cabbage, stir, cover and cook for 5 minutes in manual setting.
Quickly release the pressure, uncover, divide between the plates and serve.

Nutrition:
Calories: 140, Fat: 7 g, Fiber: 1 g, Carbs: 7 g, Proteins: 2 g

553. Baked Trout and Fennel

Preparation time: 10 minutes | **Cooking time:** 22 minutes | **Servings:** 2

Ingredients:
- 1 fennel bulb, sliced
- 1 yellow onion, sliced
- 4 rainbow trout fillets, boneless
- ½ cup kalamata olives, pitted and halved
- 2 tablespoons olive oil
- 3 teaspoons Italian seasoning
- ¼ cup panko breadcrumbs
- Juice of 1 lemon

Directions:
Spread the fennel the onion and the rest of the ingredients except the trout and the breadcrumbs on a baking sheet lined with parchment paper, toss them and cook at 400°F for 10 minutes.
Add the fish dredged in breadcrumbs and seasoned with salt and pepper and cook it at 400°F for 6 minutes on each side.

Divide the mix between plates and serve.

Nutrition:
Calories: 306, Fat: 8.9 g, Fiber: 11.1 g, Carbs: 23.8 g, Protein: 14.5 g

554. Seafood Noodles

Preparation time: 25 minutes | **Cooking time:** 40 minutes | **Servings:** 2

Ingredients:
- 12 shrimps
- 8 cup chicken broth
- 2 tablespoon grated ginger
- 4 mushrooms
- 12 snow peas
- Salt, pepper, cilantro as per need
- 12 sea scallops
- 1 cup cooked noodles
- 3 tablespoon soy sauce
- 4 cabbage leaves
- 3 scallions

Directions:
Set the sous vide machine to 195 °F.
Take all the ingredients of the seafood in a large Ziplock bag.
In another Ziplock bag take all the required vegetables and seal the bag.
Apply vacuum to remove the air.
Place these bags in the water bath for 30 minutes.
Take a large cooking pan. Add broth, soy sauce and boil for 10 minutes.
Take the serving bowl. Add the noodles, cooked seafood and vegetables, broth.
Sprinkle cilantro, salt, pepper and serve.

Nutrition:
Calories: 287

555. Caramel Shrimp Chili

Preparation time: 15 minutes | **Cooking time:** 30 minutes | **Servings:** 2

Ingredients:
- 1 cup cooked rice noodles
- 1 chopped green onion
- 1 tablespoon water
- 3 garlic cloves
- 1 lb. cooked broccoli
- 3 tablespoon sugar
- 1 tablespoon oil
- ¼ teaspoon crushed red pepper
- 1 tablespoon fish sauce
- ¼ cup cilantro
- 1 lb. shrimp
- Salt, pepper

Directions:
In a bowl, toss broccoli, green onion and salt.
In a saucepan, cook water and sugar until it starts to caramelize. Add ginger, oil, pepper, fish sauce. Add cilantro and pepper.
Set the sous vide machine to 195°F.
Take the shrimps in a sous vide bag and seal it.
Place this bag in the water bath for 20 minutes.
In a serving bowl, add the noodles, shrimps and top with broccoli.
Add the shrimps with sauce and serve.

Nutrition:
Calories: 340

556. Mediterranean Tilapia Stew

Preparation time: 10 minutes | **Cooking time:** 30 minutes | **Servings:** 2

Ingredients:
- 1 lb. tilapia fillets
- 4 red potatoes
- 1 cup marinara sauce
- 2 tablespoon chopped cilantro
- 2 teaspoons olive oil
- 2 garlic cloves
- ¼ cup sliced green olives
- Salt, pepper, water as per need

Directions:
Set the sous vide machine to 195°F.
Take the fish in a Ziplock bag and apply vacuum to remove the air.
Place this bag in the water bath for 20 minutes.
Take a large nonstick skillet and heat oil. Add the potatoes, pepper, garlic and cook for 5 minutes.
Add water cook until potatoes are tender.
Then, add marinara sauce and bring it to boil.
Add cooked fish and simmer for 5 minutes.
Garnish with cilantro, olives and serve.

Nutrition:
Calories: 359

557. Tomatoes Stuffed with Tuna

Preparation time: 15 minutes | **Cooking time:** 15 minutes | **Servings:** 2

Ingredients:
- 4 tomatoes
- 2 cups white tuna

2 celery stalks	2 tablespoons capers
1 tablespoon olive oil	1 tablespoon red wine vinegar
½ cup parsley	Salt, pepper as per need

Directions:
Set the sous vide machine to 195°F.
Take tuna is a sous vide Ziplock bag.
Place this bag in the water bath for 10 minutes.
Cut off the top and bottom thin slices of tomatoes. Remove the seeds and pulp using the spoon. Take this seeds and pulp in a mixing bowl. To this, add tuna, oil vinegar, celery, salt, pepper, capers, parsley and mix.
Cook this mixture for 5 minutes.
Add the tuna mixture into the tomato cavities and serve.

Nutrition:
Calories: 162

558. Walnut Coated Halibut

Preparation time: 15 minutes | **Cooking time:** 25 minutes | **Servings:** 2

Ingredients:
1 egg white	1 cup walnut
4 halibut fillets	2 tablespoons all-purpose flour
3 oranges	½ tablespoon red onion
2 tablespoon cilantros	1 jalapeno pepper
1 teaspoon vinegar	Salt, pepper, mashed potatoes

Directions:
Add flour, salt and pepper in one bowl.
Beat the egg with water in another bowl.
Take crushed walnut in the third bowl.
Coat the fish with flour mixture, dip it in egg mixture and coat it with the crushed walnut.
Set the sous vide machine to 195°F.
Place this fish pieces in a large Ziplock bag in a side-by-side manner.
Apply vacuum to remove the air.
Place this bag in the water bath for 30 minutes.
In a bowl toss onion, oranges, cilantro, vinegar and jalapeno.
Serve the above salad with the cooked fish.

Nutrition:
Calories: 453

559. Poached Halibut

Preparation time: 10 minutes + inactive time | **Cooking time:** 30 minutes | **Servings:** 2

Ingredients:
2 5oz. halibut fillets	⅓ cup sea salt
⅓ cup sugar	¼ cup Vin Jaune

For the Sauce:
½ cup Vin Jaune	¾ cup chicken stock
1 cup unsalted butter	2 tablespoon chopped chives

Salt, to taste

Directions:
Preheat Sous Vide cooker to 132°F.
Sprinkle the fish fillets with salt and sugar. Place aside minutes.
Place the halibut fillets into separate Sous Vide bags. Add Vin Jaune.
Vacuum seal the bags and submerge in water. Cook the fish 30 minutes.
Make the sauce, simmer Vin Jaune and chicken stock in a saucepan until reduced by half.
Add the butter and whisk until sauce-like consistency. Season to taste.
Remove the fish from the bags and arrange on a plate.
Drizzle with sauce and sprinkle with chives. Serve.

Nutrition:
Calories: 575, Fat: 45 g, Carbs: 38 g, Fiber: 1 g, Protein: 32 g

560. Eggplant Cream

Preparation time: 15 minutes | **Cooking time:** 1 hour | **Servings:** 2

Ingredients:
2 big eggplants, sliced	3 tomatoes, halved
2 leeks, chopped	2 tablespoons olive oil
6 garlic cloves	4 cups veggie stock
1 tablespoon rosemary, chopped	1 cup coconut cream
Salt and black pepper to taste	

Directions:
Arrange tomatoes, eggplant, garlic and leeks on a lined baking sheet, brush with oil and bake at 400°F for 45 minutes.
Scoop out pulp from veggies, transfer to a pan, heat over medium heat, add the rest of the ingredients and simmer for 15 minutes more.
Transfer soup to a blender, pulse well, divide into bowls and serve.

Nutrition:
Calories: 200, Fat: 3 g, Fiber: 3 g, Carbs: 5 g, Protein: 8 g

561. Hot Peppers and Garlic Soup

Preparation time: 10 minutes | **Cooking time:** 35 minutes | **Servings:** 2

Ingredients:
- 1 cup roasted red peppers, chopped
- 1 red onion, chopped
- 2 celery stalks, chopped
- 2 garlic cloves, minced
- Salt and black pepper to taste
- 1 tablespoon basil leaves, chopped
- ½ lb. red bell peppers, chopped
- 2 tablespoons olive oil
- 1 jalapeno, chopped
- 4 cups veggie stock
- 1 tablespoon balsamic vinegar

Directions:
Heat a large saucepan with the oil over medium high heat, add the onion, celery, jalapeno and garlic and cook for 5 minutes.
Add the rest of the ingredients except the basil, stir and simmer over medium heat for 20 minutes.
Blend with an immersion blender, stir and cook for 10 minutes more. Ladle into bowls, sprinkle basil on top and serve.

Nutrition:
Calories: 198, Fat: 3.9 g, Fiber: 7.1 g, Carbs: 7 g, Protein: 10 g

562. Broccoli Soup

Preparation time: 30 minutes | **Cooking time:** 0 minutes | **Servings:** 2

Ingredients:
- 1 broccoli head, florets separated and chopped
- 1 tablespoon rosemary, chopped
- 1 tablespoon balsamic vinegar
- 1 tablespoon olive oil
- 1 teaspoon basil, dried
- A pinch of red pepper flakes
- 1 garlic clove, minced
- 1 cup coconut cream
- 2 leeks, chopped
- A pinch of sea salt and black pepper
- 1 avocado, peeled and pitted
- 1 and ½ cups water

Directions:
In a blender, combine the broccoli with the garlic and the other ingredients, blend and keep in the fridge for 30 minutes before serving.

Nutrition:
Calories: 182, Fat: 4.4 g, Fiber: 3 g, Carbs: 5 g, Protein: 4.9 g

563. Onion and Mushroom Soup

Preparation time: 10 minutes | **Cooking time:** 25 minutes | **Servings:** 2

Ingredients:
- 2 tablespoons olive oil
- 1 red onion, chopped
- 3 tablespoons tomato paste
- ½ tablespoon rosemary, dried
- 1 teaspoon fennel seeds
- 1 cup coconut cream
- A pinch of salt and black pepper
- 1 yellow onion, chopped
- 1 lb. brown mushrooms, sliced
- ½ teaspoon garlic powder
- 1 teaspoon basil, dried
- 6 cups veggie stock
- 1 tablespoon chives, chopped

Directions:
Heat a pot with the oil over medium-high heat, add the mushrooms, stir and sauté for 5 minutes.
Add the onions, stir and cook for 5 minutes more. Add the rest of the ingredients except the coconut cream, stir and simmer for 15 more minutes.

Add the cream, stir, blend with an immersion blender, ladle into bowls and serve.

Nutrition:
Calories: 233, Fat: 13 g, Fiber: 6.4 g, Carbs: 9 g, Protein: 11.3 g

564. Corn Soup

Preparation time: 10 minutes | **Cooking time:** 0 minutes | **Servings:** 2

Ingredients:

- 1 leek, chopped
- ½ zucchini, chopped
- ½ cup coconut cream
- A pinch of sea salt and black pepper
- 1 teaspoon dill, dried
- 1 teaspoon saffron
- 1 cup corn
- 2 cups water
- 1 teaspoon turmeric powder
- 1 tablespoon balsamic vinegar
- 1 tablespoon olive oil

Directions:
In a blender, mix the corn with leek and the other ingredients, pulse well, divide into bowls and serve.

Nutrition:
Calories: 200, Fat: 4 g, Fiber: 3 g, Carbs: 5 g, Protein: 3.9 g

565. Green Onions Soup

Preparation time: 10 minutes | **Cooking time:** 0 minutes | **Servings:** 2

Ingredients:

- 5 green onions, chopped
- ⅓ cup dill weed, chopped
- 1 teaspoon lime zest, grated
- ½ cup water
- 1 teaspoon chili powder
- 1 big avocado, peeled, pitted and cubed
- 1 tablespoon lime juice
- A pinch of sea salt and black pepper
- ½ cup coconut cream
- A drizzle of olive oil

Directions:
In a blender, mix the green onions with the dill, avocado and the other ingredients, blend, ladle into bowls and serve.

Nutrition:
Calories: 187, Fat: 3 g, Fiber: 2 g, Carbs: 6 g, Protein: 4 g

566. Spinach Soup

Preparation time: 10 minutes | **Cooking time:** 0 minutes | **Servings:** 2

Ingredients:

- 2 cups water
- ½ cups walnuts, chopped
- 1 cup cucumbers, chopped
- 1 garlic clove, minced
- Juice of ½ lemon
- ½ cup coconut cream
- 1 cup spinach
- 1 teaspoon ginger, grated
- A handful basil, chopped
- A pinch of sea salt and black pepper

Directions:
In a blender, mix the water with the cream, walnuts and the other ingredients and pulse well.
Divide into bowls and serve.

Nutrition:
Calories: 112, Fat: 2 g, Fiber: 4 g, Carbs: 3 g, Protein: 3 g

567. Garlic Coconut and Avocado Soup

Preparation time: 10 minutes | **Cooking time:** 0 minutes | **Servings:** 2

Ingredients:

- 1 tablespoon olive oil
- 2 avocados, peeled, pitted and cubed
- A pinch of sea salt and white pepper
- 1 tablespoon coriander, chopped
- 1 and ½ cups low almond milk
- 3 garlic cloves, grated
- ½ teaspoon balsamic vinegar

Directions:
In a blender, mix the almond milk with the oil, avocados and eth other ingredients, blend and serve.

Nutrition:
Calories: 135, Fat: 3 g, Fiber: 5 g, Carbs: 2 g, Protein: 4 g

568. Cabbage Soup

Preparation time: 10 minutes | **Cooking time:** 30 minutes | **Servings:** 2

Ingredients:
- 1 green cabbage, shredded
- 1 tablespoon olive oil
- 1 yellow onion, chopped
- 1 teaspoon sweet paprika
- Juice of 1 lemon
- 1 tablespoon dill, chopped
- 1 red cabbage, shredded
- 2 spring onions, chopped
- 1 teaspoon chili powder
- A pinch of salt and black pepper
- 4 cups veggie stock

Directions:
Heat up a pot with the oil over medium heat, add the onion, spring onions, chili and paprika and cook for 5 minutes.
Add the cabbage and the other ingredients, stir and simmer the soup for 25 minutes.
Divide the soup into bowls and serve.

Nutrition:
Calories: 150, Fat: 3.9 g, Fiber: 3 g, Carbs: 5 g, Protein: 4.7 g

569. Quinoa Salad

Preparation time: 10 minutes | **Cooking time:** 0 minutes | **Servings:** 2

Ingredients:
- 2 cups hot water
- ½ cup almonds, roasted and chopped
- 1 cup cherry tomatoes, halved
- ½ cup parsley, chopped
- Juice of 1 lime
- 1 cup red quinoa
- ½ cup walnuts, chopped
- 1 teaspoon oregano, dried
- A pinch of sea salt and black pepper
- 2 tablespoons olive oil

Directions:
Put quinoa and hot water in a bowl, cover and leave aside for 10 minutes.
Transfer the quinoa to a bowl, fluff with a fork, add the rest of the ingredients, toss and serve.

Nutrition:
Calories: 150, Fat: 2 g, Fiber: 3 g, Carbs: 5 g, Protein: 2 g

570. Cream of Butter Squash

Preparation time: 5 minutes | **Cooking time:** 25 minutes | **Servings:** 2

Ingredients:
- 2 lbs. butter squash, peeled and cubed
- 1 onion, chopped
- ½-inch piece ginger, peeled and sliced
- ½ cup sour cream
- Salt and black pepper to taste
- 2 sprigs parsley, chopped
- ¼ tsp cumin
- 4 cups vegetable stock
- ½ cup pumpkin seeds toasted, for garnish
- 2 tbsp olive oil + some for drizzling

Directions:
Set your Instant Pot to Sauté and warm olive oil. Add in onion, parsley, salt, and pepper, and sauté until the onion is soft. Place in butter squash and brown for 5 minutes, stirring often. Put in ginger, cumin, and vegetable stock, and stir.
Seal the lid, select Manual/Pressure Cook, cook for 10 minutes on High. When done, perform a quick pressure release. Pour mixture in a blender and puree until smooth. Stir in sour cream. Serve garnished with pumpkin seeds, and a drizzle of olive oil.

Nutrition:
Calories: 276, Carbs: 25 g, Fat: 18 g, Protein: 9 g

571. Beef Stew with Potatoes & Mushrooms

Preparation time: 5 minutes | **Cooking time:** 65 minutes | **Servings:** 2

Ingredients:
- 2 tbsp olive oil
- 2 tbsp flour
- ½ tbsp paprika
- 1 lb. beef stew meat, cubed
- Salt and black pepper to taste
- 1 onion, chopped

1 carrot, chopped	1 celery stalk, chopped
1 garlic clove, minced	¼ cup red wine
1 bay leaf	1 tbsp dry thyme
4 potatoes, cubed	1 cup canned tomatoes
1 cup mushrooms, sliced	2 cups beef stock

Directions:
Set your Instant Pot to Sauté and heat olive oil. Toss the beef with flour, salt, and pepper until coated. Place into the pot and brown for 5-7 minutes per side until golden, set aside. Add in the onion, carrot, celery, garlic, mushrooms, salt, and pepper and cook for 5 minutes, until tender. Pour in the remaining ingredients and stir to combine.

Seal the lid, select Meat/Stew mode, and set the cooking time to 35 minutes on High. When done, perform a natural pressure release for 10 minutes, then a quick pressure release to let out the remaining steam. Unlock the lid and adjust the seasoning. Remove and discard the bay leaf. Ladle the stew into individual bowls to serve.

Nutrition:
Calories: 377, Carbs: 37 g, Fat: 12 g, Protein: 31 g

572. Beef & Butternut Squash Stew

Preparation time: 5 minutes | **Cooking time:** 40 minutes | **Servings:** 2

Ingredients:

2 tbsp olive oil	1 lb. beef stew meat, cubed
Salt and black pepper to taste	1 cup beef broth
1 tsp onion powder	1 tsp garlic powder
1 medium butternut squash, chopped	2 thyme sprigs, chopped
1 tsp cumin powder	1 tsp cornstarch

Directions:
Set your Instant Pot to Sauté mode.
Heat olive oil in inner pot, season beef with salt and pepper and fry in oil until brown on all sides, 4 minutes.
Pour in beef broth, add onion powder, garlic powder, butternut squash, thyme, and cumin powder.

Seal the lid, select Manual/Pressure Cook on High, and set cooking time to 15 minutes.
After cooking, perform natural pressure release for 10 minutes.
Unlock the lid and stir in cornstarch, adjust taste with salt and black pepper, and cook further for 1 minute on Sauté mode.
Serve with freshly baked bread.

Nutrition:
Calories: 315, Carbs: 17 g, Fat: 12 g, Protein: 26 g

573. Turkey with Tomatoes and Red Beans

Preparation time: 20 minutes | **Cooking time:** 18 minutes | **Servings:** 2

Ingredients:

1-lb. Turkey Breast, cut into bite-sized cubes	1 16 oz can Stewed Tomatoes
1 16 oz can Red Kidney Beans, drained	2 cups Chicken Stock
½ cup Sour Cream	Salt and Black Pepper, to taste
2 tbsp Parsley, freshly chopped	

Directions:
Place beans, tomatoes, turkey, stock, and sour cream in your pressure cooker.
Season to taste.
Seal the lid, set on soup/broth, cook for 20 minutes at high. Release the pressure quickly.
Sprinkle with parsley to serve.

Nutrition:
Calories: 212, Carbs: 12 g, Fat: 8 g, Protein: 23 g

574. Orange and Cranberry Turkey Wings

Preparation time: 40 minutes | **Cooking time:** 18 minutes | **Servings:** 2

Ingredients:

1 lb. Turkey Wings	¼ cup Orange Juice
1 stick Butter, softened	2 cups Cranberries
2 Onions, sliced	2 cups Vegetable Stock

½ tsp Cayenne Pepper	Salt and Pepper, to taste

Directions:
Melt the butter on sauté. Add the turkey wings, season with salt, pepper, and cayenne pepper, and cook until browned, for a few minutes. Stir in the remaining ingredients. Seal the lid. Cook for 25 minutes on poultry at high. Release the pressure naturally, for 10 minutes, and serve.

Nutrition:
Calories: 525, Carbs: 20 g, Fat: 38 g, Protein: 26 g

575. Chicken Cacciatore with Kale, Rice & Mushrooms

Preparation time: 10 minutes | **Cooking time:** 35 minutes | **Servings:** 2

Ingredients:

2 tbsp olive oil	4 chicken breasts
Salt and black pepper to taste	1 medium white onion, chopped
1 cup sliced white button mushrooms	¼ tsp ginger paste
½ cup short-grain rice	15 oz can diced tomatoes
½ cup chicken broth	1 tbsp Italian seasoning
¼ cup grated Parmesan cheese	2 cups kale, steamed

Directions:
Set your Instant Pot to Sauté and adjust to medium heat.
Heat olive oil in inner pot, season chicken with salt and black pepper, and sear in oil on both sides until golden brown, 4 minutes. Remove onto a plate and set aside.
Add onion and mushrooms to oil and cook until softened, 4 minutes.
Add ginger and allow releasing of fragrance, 1 minute. Stir in rice, tomatoes, chicken broth, and Italian seasoning.
Adjust taste with salt and black pepper and return chicken to pot.
Seal the lid, select Manual/Pressure Cook on High, and set cooking time to 10 minutes.
After cooking, perform natural pressure release for 10 minutes, then quick pressure release to let out the remaining steam.

Unlock the lid, adjust taste with salt and black pepper, and spoon cacciatore over a bed of steamed kale. Garnish with Parmesan cheese and serve warm.

Nutrition:
Calories: 534, Carbs: 30 g, Fat: 17 g, Protein: 55 g

576. Hot Chicken Dirty Rice

Preparation time: 10 minutes | **Cooking time:** 35 minutes | **Servings:** 2

Ingredients:
For the marinade:

½ tsp dried minced onion	½ tsp cayenne pepper
1 tsp salt	1 tsp garlic powder
1 ½ tsp paprika	½ tsp chili pepper
½ tsp dried basil	¼ tsp red pepper flakes
1 tsp lemon juice	1 tbsp olive oil
4 chicken thighs	

For the chicken and rice:

2 tbsp olive oil	1 link of andouille sausages, sliced
1 jalapeño pepper, deseeded and diced	1 medium yellow onion, diced
2 celery stalks, diced	A pinch red pepper flakes
¼ tsp cayenne pepper	1 cup basmati rice
2 ¼ cups chicken broth	Salt and black pepper to taste
2 tbsp scallions, for garnishing	2 tbsp chopped parsley

Directions:
In a medium bowl, combine onion, cayenne pepper, salt, garlic powder, paprika, chili pepper, basil, red pepper flakes, lemon juice, and olive oil. Place in chicken, coat in marinade, cover with plastic wrap and chill in the fridge for 1 hour.
Set your Instant Pot to Sauté mode. Heat olive oil in inner pot, remove chicken from marinade and sear in oil on both sides until golden brown, 6 minutes.
Place on a plate and set aside.
Brown sausages in the pot for 5 minutes and spoon to side of chicken.
To the pot, add jalapeño pepper, onion, celery, and sauté until softened, 3 minutes. Stir in red

pepper flakes, cayenne pepper, rice, chicken broth, salt, and pepper. Place chicken and sausages on top.

Seal the lid, select Manual/Pressure Cook on High, and set time to 5 minutes.

Allow sitting covered for 10 minutes and then perform a quick pressure release to let out remaining steam. Unlock the lid, stir rice, and spoon into serving plates.

Garnish with scallions and parsley, serve.

Nutrition:
Calories: 732, Carbs: 32 g, Fat: 52 g, Protein: 43 g

577. Spicy Mango-Glazed Chicken

Preparation time: 10 minutes | **Cooking time:** 25 minutes | **Servings:** 2

Ingredients:

1 tbsp butter	1 lb. chicken breasts, halved
Salt and black pepper to taste	1 medium mango, chopped
1 small red chili, minced	2 tbsp spicy mango chutney
½ cup chicken broth	2 scallions, thinly sliced

Directions:
Set your Instant Pot to Sauté mode and adjust to medium heat. Melt butter in inner pot, season chicken with salt and black pepper, and cook in fat until cooked through and golden brown, 6 to 8 minutes.

Plate chicken and set aside for serving.

To the pot, add mango, red chili, mango chutney, and broth.

Seal the lid, select Manual/Pressure Cook mode on High, and set cooking time to 1 minute.

After cooking, perform natural pressure release for 10 minutes, and then quick pressure release to let out remaining steam. Unlock the lid, stir sauce, and season to taste.

Spoon sauce over chicken, garnish with scallions and serve with steamed spinach.

Nutrition:
Calories: 345, Carbs: 16 g, Fat: 15 g, Protein: 32 g

578. Chicken Gruyere with Bell Peppers

Preparation time: 10 minutes | **Cooking time:** 40 minutes | **Servings:** 2

Ingredients:

1 tbsp olive oil	1 large white onion, chopped
2 red bell peppers, deseeded and chopped	2 green bell peppers, deseeded and chopped
Salt and black pepper to taste	2 garlic cloves, minced
¾ cup marinara sauce	2 tbsp basil pesto
4 chicken breasts, skinless and boneless	1 cup chicken broth
1 cup sliced baby Bella mushrooms	1 cup grated Gruyere cheese
4 flatbreads, warmed for serving	2 tbsp chopped parsley

Directions:
Set your Instant Pot to Sauté mode. Heat olive oil in inner pot and sauté onion, bell peppers, salt, and pepper until softened, 3 minutes.

Stir in garlic and cook until fragrant, 30 seconds. Add marinara sauce, basil pesto, chicken, and chicken broth.

Seal the lid, select Manual/Pressure Cook mode on High, and set cooking time to 12 minutes.

After cooking, perform a natural pressure release for 5 minutes, then a quick pressure release to let out remaining steam.

Unlock the lid and remove chicken onto a plate and shred into strands. Fetch out two-thirds cup of liquid in inner pot, making sure to leave in vegetables.

Select Sauté mode and mix in mushrooms. Cook until softened, 2 to 3 minutes.

Stir in chicken, adjust taste with salt, black pepper, and mix in Gruyere cheese to melt.

Spoon mixture onto flatbread, garnish with parsley, and serve.

Nutrition:
Calories: 613, Carbs: 26 g, Fat: 36 g, Protein: 43 g

579. Onion Chicken with Salsa Verde

Preparation time: 10 minutes | **Cooking time:** 35 minutes | **Servings:** 2

Ingredients:

- 1 large yellow onion, chopped
- ½ cup chicken broth
- 4 chicken breasts, cut into 1-inch cubes
- 1 cup salsa verde
- Salt and black pepper to taste

Directions:
In inner pot, combine onion, salsa verde, chicken broth, salt, black pepper, and chicken. Seal the lid, select Manual/Pressure Cook on High, and set cooking time to 12 minutes.
After cooking, perform a natural pressure release for 10 minutes, then a quick pressure release to let out remaining steam. Unlock the lid and remove chicken onto a plate and serve warm over salad.

Nutrition:
Calories: 422, Carbs: 8 g, Fat: 29 g, Protein: 32 g

580. Lime Squid and Capers Mix

Preparation time: 10 minutes | **Cooking time:** 20 minutes | **Servings:** 2

Ingredients:

- 1 lb. baby squid, cleaned, body and tentacles chopped
- 1 tablespoon lime juice
- 3 tablespoons olive oil
- 1 tablespoon parsley, chopped
- 1 shallot, chopped
- 1 cup chicken stock
- Salt and black pepper to the taste
- ½ teaspoon lime zest, grated
- ½ teaspoon orange zest, grated
- 1 teaspoon red pepper flakes, crushed
- 4 garlic cloves, minced
- 2 tablespoons capers, drained
- 2 tablespoons red wine vinegar

Directions:
Heat up a pan with the oil over medium-high heat, add the lime zest, lime juice, orange zest and the rest of the ingredients except the squid and the parsley, stir, bring to a simmer and cook over medium heat for 10 minutes.
Add the remaining ingredients, stir, cook everything for 10 minutes more, divide into bowls and serve.

Nutrition:
Calories: 302, Fat: 8.5 g, Fiber: 9.8 g, Carbs: 21.8 g, Protein: 11.3 g

581. Leeks and Calamari Mix

Preparation time: 10 minutes | **Cooking time:** 15 minutes | **Servings:** 2

Ingredients:

- 2 tablespoon avocado oil
- 1 red onion, chopped
- 1 lb. calamari rings
- 1 tablespoon chives, chopped
- 2 leeks, chopped
- Salt and black to the taste
- 1 tablespoon parsley, chopped
- 2 tablespoons tomato paste

Directions:
Heat up a pan with the avocado oil over medium heat, add the leeks and the onion, stir and sauté for 5 minutes.
Add the rest of the ingredients, toss, simmer over medium heat for 10 minutes, divide into bowls and serve.

Nutrition:
Calories: 238, Fat: 9 g, Fiber: 5.6 g, Carbs: 14.4 g, Protein: 8.4 g

582. Cod and Brussel s Sprouts

Preparation time: 10 minutes | **Cooking time:** 20 minutes | **Servings:** 2

Ingredients:

- 1 teaspoon garlic powder
- 2 tablespoons olive oil
- 4 cod fillets, boneless
- 1 teaspoon smoked paprika
- 2 lbs. Brussels sprouts, trimmed and halved
- ½ cup tomato sauce

1 teaspoon Italian seasoning

1 tablespoon chives, chopped

Directions:
In a roasting pan, combine the sprouts with the garlic powder and the other ingredients except the cod and toss.
Put the cod on top, cover the pan with tin foil and bake at 450°F for 20 minutes.
Divide the mix between plates and serve.

Nutrition:
Calories: 188, Fat: 12.8 g, Fiber: 9.2 g, Carbs: 22.2 g, Protein: 16.8 g

583. Cajun Shrimp

Preparation time: 10 minutes | **Cooking time:** 2 minutes | **Servings:** 2

Ingredients:
1 lb. shrimp, peeled and deveined
1 tbsp Cajun seasoning
15 asparagus spears
1 tsp olive oil

Directions:
Pour 1 cup of water in instant pot then place the steam rack inside the pot.
Arrange asparagus on a steam rack in a layer.
Place shrimp on the top of asparagus.
Sprinkle Cajun seasoning over shrimp and drizzle with olive oil.
Seal pot with lid and cook on steam mode for 2 minutes.
Once done then release pressure using the quick-release method than open the lid.
Serve and enjoy.

Nutrition:
Calories: 163, Fat: 3.2 g, Carbs: 5.2 g, Sugar: 1.7 g, Protein: 27.8 g, Cholesterol: 239 mg

584. Quick & Easy Shrimp

Preparation time: 10 minutes | **Cooking time:** 1 minute | **Servings:** 2

Ingredients:
30 oz frozen shrimp, deveined
½ cup apple cider vinegar
½ cup chicken stock

Directions:
Add all ingredients into the instant pot and stir well.
Seal pot with lid and cook on manual high pressure for 1 minute.
Once done then release pressure using the quick-release method than open the lid.
Serve and enjoy.

Nutrition:
Calories: 156, Fat: 2.6 g, Carbs: 1.5 g, Sugar: 0.1 g, Protein: 29 g, Cholesterol: 213 mg

585. Rosemary-Flavored Salmon

Preparation time: 5 minutes | **Cooking time:** 15 minutes | **Servings:** 2

Ingredients:
2 Salmon Fillets
1 tbsp Olive Oil
2 Rosemary Sprigs
1 cup Homemade Veggie Broth

Directions:
Pour the broth into the IP and place the rosemary sprigs inside.
Place the salmon fillets inside the steamer basket and drizzle with olive oil.
Lower the basket into the pot and put the lid on.
Close and seal and set the IP to MANUAL.
Cook on HIGH for 4 minutes.
Do a quick pressure release.
Serve and enjoy!

Nutrition:
Calories: 185, Fats: 8.5 g, Protein: 27 g

586. Tuna Steaks with Capers & Lemon

Preparation time: 5 minutes | **Cooking time:** 10 minutes | **Servings:** 2

Ingredients:
4 tbsp olive oil
Salt and black pepper to taste
2 tbsp chopped thyme + extra for garnishing
2 tuna steaks
1 lemon, zested and lemon juice
3 tbsp drained capers

Directions:
Pour 1 cup of water in inner pot and fit in trivet.
Season tuna with 1 tbsp of olive oil, salt, black

pepper, and arrange on trivet. Seal the lid, select Manual/Pressure Cook mode on High, and set cooking time to 6 minutes.

After cooking, do a quick pressure release. Remove fish to a serving platter. Empty and clean inner pot. Set the pot to Sauté and heat remaining olive oil. Sauté lemon zest, lemon juice, thyme, capers, and 2 tbsp of water. Cook for 3 minutes. Pour sauce over tuna and garnish with thyme.

Nutrition:
Calories: 437, Carbs: 8 g, Fat: 23 g, Protein: 48 g

587. Tuna Noodle One-Pot

Preparation time: 5 minutes | **Cooking time:** 25 minutes | **Servings:** 2

Ingredients:

16 oz egg noodles	Salt and black pepper to taste
3 tbsp unsalted butter	3 tbsp plain flour
1 ½ cups chicken broth	1 cup milk
2 3 oz. can tuna packed in oil, drained	5 oz frozen green peas
½ cup panko breadcrumbs	½ cup shredded Monterey Jack cheese

Directions:
In inner pot, add noodles, 3 cups of water, and salt. Seal the lid, select Manual/Pressure Cook on High, and set cooking time to 3 minutes.

After cooking, perform a quick pressure release, drain noodles and set aside.

Clean inner pot and select Sauté mode. Melt butter pot and stir in flour until lightly golden in color.

Mix in chicken broth gradually until a smooth liquid forms. Add milk and cook until thickened, 10 minutes. Season with salt and pepper. Mix in tuna and green peas.

Seal the lid, select Manual/Pressure Cook on High, and set time to 1 minute.

After cooking, perform a quick pressure release to let out steam, and unlock the lid. Stir in breadcrumbs, cheese, and cook further in Sauté mode until cheese melts.

Dish food into serving plates and serve warm.

Nutrition:
Calories: 854, Carbs: 46 g, Fat: 61 g, Protein: 31 g

588. Halibut & Butternut Squash Soup

Preparation time: 5 minutes | **Cooking time:** 30 minutes | **Servings:** 2

Ingredients:

3 tbsp butter	1 medium butternut squash, peeled and diced
1 medium Yukon gold potato, peeled and diced	1 medium yellow onion, chopped
2 garlic cloves, minced	1 tsp pureed ginger
1 tsp cumin powder	2 tsp turmeric powder
1 tsp chili powder or to taste	4 cups chicken broth
Salt and black pepper to taste	4 halibut fillets, cut into 1-inch cubes
4 tbsp heavy cream	1 lime, juiced
2 tbsp chopped cilantro to garnish	

Directions:
Set your Instant Pot to Sauté and melt butter. Sauté squash, potato, and onion until sweaty, 5 minutes.

Add garlic, ginger, cumin powder, turmeric, and chili powder. Stir-fry for 1 minute.

Pour in chicken broth, salt, pepper, and fish.

Seal the lid, select Manual/Pressure Cook on High, and set cooking time to 12 minutes.

After cooking, perform a quick pressure release to let out steam, and unlock the lid. Spoon out fish into a bowl and set aside.

Using an immersion blender, process ingredients until smooth and stir in heavy cream and lime juice.

Return fish to the soup, stir, and dish into serving bowls.

Garnish with cilantro and serve warm.

Nutrition:
Calories: 544, Carbs: 37 g, Fat: 32 g, Protein: 29 g

589. Fried Snapper in Orange-Ginger Sauce

Preparation time: 5 minutes | **Cooking time:** 25 minutes | **Servings:** 2

Ingredients:

- ½ cup plain flour
- Salt and black pepper to taste
- 2 green onions, chopped
- 1 ½ tsp pureed ginger
- ½ red scotch bonnet pepper, deseeded and minced
- 1 orange, zested and juiced
- 4 orange slices to garnish
- 4 red snapper fillets
- 3 tbsp olive oil, divided
- 3 sprigs thyme, leaves extracted
- 1 garlic clove, minced
- ½ cup chicken broth
- 1 tbsp honey
- 1 tbsp chopped parsley to garnish

Directions:

Pour flour onto a flat plate. Season fish with salt, black pepper, and dredge lightly in flour.
Set your Instant Pot to Sauté and adjust to medium heat. Heat 2 tbsp of olive oil in inner pot and fry fish on both sides until golden, 1 minute. Transfer to a plate and set aside. Empty, clean inner pot, and return to base.
Heat remaining oil in the pot and sauté green onions, thyme, ginger, garlic, and scotch bonnet pepper.
Cook for 1 minute. Mix in chicken broth, orange zest, orange juice, honey, allow heating for 1 minute and lay fish in sauce.
Seal the lid, select Manual/Pressure Cook on High, and set cooking time to 1 minute.
After cooking, perform a quick pressure release to let out remaining steam, and unlock the lid. Remove fish onto serving plates and top with orange sauce.
Garnish with orange slices, parsley, and serve warm.

Nutrition:
Calories: 417, Carbs: 25 g, Fat: 13 g, Protein: 47 g

590. Tangy Shrimp Asparagus

Preparation time: 5 minutes | **Cooking time:** 20 minutes | **Servings:** 2

Ingredients:

- 3 tbsp butter
- 4 garlic cloves, minced
- ½ cup chicken broth
- 1 lb shrimp, peeled and deveined
- ¼ tsp red chili flakes to garnish
- 1 lb. asparagus, trimmed, cut into 2-inch pieces
- ¼ tsp dried dill
- Salt and black pepper to taste
- ¼ cup lemon juice

Directions:

Set your Instant Pot to Sauté mode. Melt butter in inner pot and sauté asparagus until slightly softened, 5 minutes.
Add garlic, and dill, and keep sautéing until fragrant, 30 seconds. Pour in chicken broth, salt, pepper, and shrimp.
Seal the lid, select Manual/Pressure Cook on High, and set cooking time to 3 minutes.
After cooking, perform a quick pressure release to let out steam, and unlock the lid. Stir in lemon juice, adjust taste with salt, black pepper, and spoon food into serving bowls.
Garnish with chili flakes and serve warm.

Nutrition:
Calories: 213, Carbs: 8 g, Fat: 10 g, Protein: 19 g

591. Garlic Lemon Shrimp

Preparation time: 5 minutes | **Cooking time:** 20 minutes | **Servings:** 2

Ingredients:

- ½ cup butter, divided
- 1 lb jumbo shrimp, peeled and deveined
- ½ lemon, juiced
- 4 garlic cloves, minced
- Salt and black pepper to taste
- 2 tbsp chopped parsley, to garnish

Directions:

Set your Instant Pot to Sauté and adjust to medium heat. Melt 2 tbsp of butter in inner pot and sauté garlic until fragrant, 30 seconds.
Add shrimp, salt and black pepper, lemon juice, and 2 tbsp water.
Seal the lid, select Manual/Pressure Cook mode on High, and set cooking time to 2 minutes.

After cooking, do a quick pressure release to let out steam, and unlock the lid.
Stir in remaining butter until melted.
Spoon into serving plates and garnish with parsley.

Nutrition:
Calories: 172, Carbs: 2 g, Fat: 11 g, Protein: 16 g

592. Shrimp Creole

Preparation time: 5 Minutes | **Cooking time:** 10 Minutes | **Servings:** 2

Ingredients:
- 1-lb. frozen Jumbo Shrimp
- 2 tsp minced Garlic
- 2 Celery Stalks, diced
- 1 tbsp Tomato Paste
- 1 Bell Pepper, diced
- 1 Onion, chopped
- 28 oz. canned diced Tomatoes
- 1 tbsp Olive Oil
- ¼ tsp Thyme

Directions:
Heat the olive oil in the IP on SAUTE.
Add the onion, celery, and peppers, and cook for 3 minutes.
Add the garlic and cook for another minute.
Stir in the remaining ingredients and close the lid.
Set the IP to MANUAL.
Cook on HIGH for 1 minute or two.
Do a quick pressure release.
Serve and enjoy!

Nutrition:
Calories: 280, Fats: 17 g, Carbs: 3 g, Protein: 35 g, Fiber: 1 g

593. Crab Cakes

Preparation time: 5 minutes | **Cooking time:** 15 minutes | **Servings:** 2

Ingredients:
- 1 Carrot, shredded
- ½ cup boiled and mashed Potatoes
- ¼ cup chopped Black Olives
- 1 tbsp Olive Oil
- 1 cup Crab Meat
- ¼ Onion, grated
- ¼ cup Almond Flour
- 1 ½ cup canned diced Tomatoes
- ¼ cup Homemade Chicken Broth

Directions:
In a bowl, combine the carrots, crab meat, potatoes, onion, black olives, and almond flour.
Mix with your hands to combine and shape into 2 patties.
Heat the oil in the IP on SAUTE.
Add the crab cakes and cook for about a minute per side.
Pour the broth and tomatoes over and close the lid.
Set the IP to HIGH and cook for an additional minute or two.
Do a quick pressure release.
Serve the crab with the tomato sauce.
Enjoy!

Nutrition:
Calories: 300, Fats: 8 g, Carbs: 5 g, Protein: 18 g, Fiber: 2 g

594. Simple Broccoli Mackerel

Preparation time: 5 minutes | **Cooking time:** 10 minutes | **Servings:** 2

Ingredients:
- 4 Mackerel Fillets
- 1 tsp Garlic Powder
- 10 oz. Broccoli Florets
- 1 ½ cup Water

Directions:
Sprinkle the mackerel with garlic powder and arrange them inside the steamer basket.
Place the broccoli florets on top.
Pour the water into the IP.
Lower the steamer basket into the pot.
Close the lid and choose MANUAL.
Cook on HIGH for 2 minutes.
Do a quick pressure release.
Serve and enjoy!

Nutrition:
Calories: 130, Fats: 8 g, Carbs: 5 g, Protein: 16 g, Fiber: 2 g

595. Classic Shrimp Tomato Meal

Preparation time: 5-8 minutes | **Cooking time:** 5 minutes | **Servings:** 2

Ingredients:

- ¼ teaspoon oregano, dried
- 1 garlic clove, minced
- ⅓ cup water
- 10 oz. canned tomatoes, chopped
- 1 lb. shrimp, cooked, peeled and deveined
- 1 tablespoon parsley, chopped
- 2 tablespoons olive oil
- ⅓ cup tomato paste

Directions:

Take your instant pot, open the lid.
Press "SAUTE" setting, add the oil and heat it.
Add the garlic and stir gently. Cook while stirring until softened for 2-3 minutes.
Add the shrimp, tomato paste, tomatoes, water, oregano, and parsley, stir gently.
Seal the lid and put the valve in sealing position, press "MANUAL" setting. Cook for 3 minutes on "HIGH" pressure mode.
Press "CANCEL." Use the QPR function for quick pressure release.
Open the lid, transfer the recipe in serving plates. Serve warm.

Nutrition:

Calories: 216, Fat: 4 g, Carbs: 2 g, Sodium: 346 mg, Protein: 8 g

596. Hot Lemony Instant Pot Tilapia with Asparagus

Preparation time: 15 minutes | **Cooking time:** 2 hours and 15 minutes | **Servings:** 2

Ingredients:

- 6 tilapia filets
- 12 tbsp. lemon juice
- 3 tbsp. melted coconut oil
- 1 bundle of asparagus
- Lemon pepper seasoning

Directions:

Divide asparagus into equal amounts per each fillet.
Place each fillet in the center of a foil and sprinkle with about 1 tsp. of lemon pepper seasoning, drizzle with about 2 tbsp. of lemon juice and about ½ tbsp. melted coconut oil.
Top each filet with the asparagus and fold the foil to form a packet.
Repeat with the remaining ingredients and then place the packets into an instant pot.
Lock lid and cook on high for 15 minutes.

Nutrition:

Calories: 181, Fats: 11.5 g, Carbs: 1.8 g, Protein: 27.3 g, Fiber: 0.7 g

597. Instant Pot Thai Seafood Boil

Preparation time: 10 minutes | **Cooking time:** 4 hours and 10 minutes | **Servings:** 2

Ingredients:

- ½ lb. snow crab
- 1 stalk lemongrass, outer layer and top inch removed
- ¼ fresh mint, chopped
- 2 garlic cloves, minced
- 2 cups coconut milk
- ½ tsp. cumin
- 1 celery stalks, cut into 1-inch pieces
- 1 bell pepper, cut into 1-inch pieces
- ½ lb. shrimp in shells
- 2 tsp ginger
- 1 lime, cut in half
- 1 small onion, cut into quarters
- 32 oz. homemade broth
- 1 tsp. salt
- 1 lb. sweet potatoes, cut into quarters
- 1 ear of sweet corn, cut into 3-inch chunks

Directions:

Smash the end of lemongrass stalk with a rolling pin until soft,
Transfer to an instant pot along with ginger, mint, lime, garlic, onion, coconut milk, broth, cumin and salt.
Stir to combine well and then add in celery and sweet potatoes. Lock lid and cook on high for 10 minutes.
Quick release pressure and then corn, bell pepper and seafood, lock lid and continue cooking for 10 minutes.
Release pressure naturally. Strain the liquid and serve.

Nutrition:

Calories: 595, Fats: 31.5 g, Carbs: 52.6 g, Protein: 17.7 g, Fiber: 9.4 g

598. Cheesy Shrimp Grits

Preparation time: 10 minutes | **Cooking time:** 7 minutes | **Servings:** 2

Ingredients:

- 1 lb. shrimp, thawed
- ½ cup quick grits
- 1 ½ cups chicken broth
- ½ tsp paprika
- 1 tbsp coconut oil
- ½ cup cheddar cheese, shredded
- 1 tbsp butter
- ¼ tsp red pepper flakes
- 2 tbsp cilantro, chopped
- ½ tsp kosher salt

Directions:

Add oil into the instant pot and set the pot on sauté mode.
Add shrimp and cook until shrimp is no longer pink. Season with red pepper flakes and salt.
Remove shrimp from the pot and set aside.
Add remaining ingredients into the pot and stir well.
Seal pot with lid and cook on manual high pressure for 7 minutes.
Once done then allow to release pressure naturally then open the lid.
Stir in cheese and top with shrimp.

Nutrition:
Calories: 221, Fat: 9.1 g, Carbs: 12 g, Sugar: 0.3 g, Protein: 21.9 g, Cholesterol: 174 mg

599. Healthy Salmon Chowder

Preparation time: 10 minutes | **Cooking time:** 8 minutes | **Servings:** 2

Ingredients:

- 1 lb. frozen salmon
- 2 tbsp butter
- 1 onion, chopped
- 1 medium potato, cubed
- 4 cups chicken broth
- 2 garlic cloves, minced
- 2 celery stalks, chopped
- 1 cup corn
- 2 cups half and half

Directions:

Add butter into the instant pot and select sauté.
Add onion and garlic into the pot and sauté for 3-4 minutes.
Add remaining ingredients except for the half and a half and stir well.
Seal pot with lid and cook on manual high pressure for 5 minutes.
Once done then allow to release pressure naturally then open the lid.
Add half and half and stir well.
Serve and enjoy.

Nutrition:
Calories: 571, Fat: 35.1 g, Carbs: 26 g, Sugar: 3.9 g, Protein: 36.9 g, Cholesterol: 133 mg

600. Shrimp with Sausage

Preparation time: 10 minutes | **Cooking time:** 5 minutes | **Servings:** 2

Ingredients:

- 1 lb. frozen shrimp
- 3 ears corn, cut in thirds
- 2 cups chicken broth
- ¼ cup parsley, chopped
- 2 garlic cloves, minced
- 1 ½ cups sausage, sliced
- 1 lemon, wedges
- 1 ½ tbsp old bay seasoning
- 5 small potatoes, diced
- 1 onion, chopped

Directions:

Add all ingredients into the instant pot and stir well.
Seal pot with lid and cook on manual high pressure for 5 minutes.
Once done then release pressure using the quick-release method than open the lid.
Serve and enjoy.

Nutrition:
Calories: 290, Fat: 4.8 g, Carbs: 40.1 g, Sugar: 5.2 g, Protein: 23.6 g, Cholesterol: 119 mg

601. Nutritious Salmon

Preparation time: 10 minutes | **Cooking time:** 2 minutes | **Servings:** 2

Ingredients:

- 1 lb. salmon fillet, cut into pieces
- 1 tsp chili powder
- 1 tsp ground cumin
- 2 garlic cloves, minced

Pepper   Salt

Directions:
Pour 1 ½ cups of water into the instant pot then place the trivet in the pot.
In a small bowl, mix all ingredients except salmon.
Rub salmon with spice mixture and place on top of the trivet.
Seal pot with lid and cook on steam mode for 2 minutes.
Once done then release pressure using the quick-release method than open the lid.
Serve and enjoy.

Nutrition:
Calories: 211, Fat: 9.7 g, Carbs: 1.7 g, Protein: 29.7 g, Cholesterol: 67 mg

602. Tarragon Trout and Beets

Preparation time: 10 minutes | **Cooking time:** 35 minutes | **Servings:** 2

Ingredients:

1 lb. medium beets, peeled and cubed	3 tablespoons olive oil
4 trout fillets, boneless	Salt and black pepper to the taste
1 tablespoon chives, chopped	1 tablespoon tarragon, chopped
3 tablespoon spring onions, chopped	2 tablespoons lemon juice
½ cup chicken stock	

Directions:
Spread the beets on a baking sheet lined with parchment paper, add salt, pepper and 1 tablespoon oil, toss and bake at 450°F for 20 minutes.
Heat up a pan with the rest of the oil over medium-high heat, add the trout and the remaining ingredients, and cook for 4 minutes on each side.
Add the baked beets, cook the mix for 5 minutes more, divide everything between plates and serve.

Nutrition:
Calories: 232, Fat: 5.5 g, Fiber: 7.5 g, Carbs: 20.9 g, Protein: 16.8 g

603. Ginger Trout and Eggplant

Preparation time: 10 minutes | **Cooking time:** 22 minutes | **Servings:** 2

Ingredients:

4 trout fillets, boneless	1 eggplant, sliced
¼ cup tomato sauce	2 tablespoons olive oil
Salt and black pepper to the taste	2 teaspoons ginger, grated
2 tablespoons balsamic vinegar	2 tablespoons chives, chopped

Directions:
Heat up a pan with the oil over medium heat, add the eggplant and the rest of the ingredients except the trout and cook for 10 minutes.
Add the fish on top, introduce the pan in the oven and bake at 450°F for 12 minutes.
Divide everything between plates and serve.

Nutrition:
Calories: 282, Fat: 11.5 g, Fiber: 5.5 g, Carbs: 17.9 g, Protein: 14.8 g

604. Octopus Stew

Preparation time: 1 day | **Cooking time:** 8 minutes | **Servings:** 2

Ingredients:

1 octopus, cleaned, head removed, emptied, tentacles separated	1 cup red wine
½ cup vegetable oil	1 cup white wine
1 cup water	1 tablespoon paprika
½ cup extra virgin olive oil	2 tablespoons hot sauce
1 tablespoon tomato paste	2 garlic cloves, peeled and minced
1 yellow onion, peeled and chopped	4 potatoes, cut into quarters.
½ bunch fresh parsley, chopped	Salt and ground black pepper, to taste

Directions:
Place the octopus in a bowl and add white wine, red wine, water, vegetable oil, hot sauce, peppers, tomato paste, salt, pepper and parsley.

Stir to cover, cover and refrigerate for 1 day. Place the Instant Pot in the sauté mode, add the oil and heat. Add onion and potatoes, mix and cook for 3 minutes.

Add garlic, octopus and marinade, stir, cover and cook for 8 minutes in the Meat / Stew setting. Relieve the pressure, uncover the Instant Pot, divide the stew between the bowls and serve.

Nutrition:
Calories: 210, Fat: 9 g, Carbs: 4 g, Proteins: 32 g

605. Greek Octopus

Preparation time: 10 minutes | **Cooking time:** 16 minutes | **Servings:** 2

Ingredients:

1 octopus, cleaned, head removed, emptied, tentacles separated	2 rosemary sprigs
½ yellow onion, peeled and roughly chopped	4 thyme sprigs
2 teaspoons dried oregano	½ lemon
3 tablespoons extra virgin olive oil	1 teaspoon black peppercorns

For the Marinade:

¼ cup extra virgin olive oil Juice of	½ lemon
1 rosemary sprig	4 garlic cloves, peeled and minced
2 thyme sprigs	Salt and ground black pepper, to taste

Directions:
Place the octopus in the instant container. Add oregano, 2 sprigs of rosemary, 4 sprigs of thyme, onion, lemon, 3 spoons of olive oil, pepper and salt. Stir, cover and cook in manual mode for 10 minutes.

Relieve the pressure, uncover the Instant Pot, transfer the octopuses to a cutting board, cut the tentacles and place them in a bowl.

Add ¼ cup of olive oil, lemon juice, garlic, 1 sprig of rosemary, 2 sprigs of thyme, pepper and salt, blend well and set aside for 1 hour.

Heat the grill over medium heat, add the octopus, grill for 3 minutes on each side and divide between the plates. Sprinkle the marinade over the octopus and serve.

Nutrition:
Calories: 161, Fat: 1 g, Carbs: 1 g, Proteins: 9 g

606. Stuffed Squid

Preparation time: 10 minutes | **Cooking time:** 20 minutes | **Servings:** 2

Ingredients:

1 cup sticky rice	4 squid
4 tablespoons soy sauce	1 tablespoon mirin
14 oz. vegetable stock	2 tablespoons sake
2 tablespoons sugar	

Directions:
Chop the tentacles of a squid and mix with the rice. Fill each squid with rice and seal the ends with toothpicks.

Place the squid in the Instant Pot, add the broth, the soy sauce, the love, the sugar and the mirin. Cover and cook for 15 minutes. Release the pressure, uncover the instant pot, divide the stuffed squid between the plates and serve.

Nutrition:
Calories: 148, Fat: 2.4 g, Fiber: 1.1 g, Carbs: 7 g, Proteins: 11 g

607. Squid Masala

Preparation time: 10 minutes | **Cooking time:** 15 minutes | **Servings:** 2

Ingredients:

5 pieces coconut	17 oz. squid, cleaned and cut
1½ tablespoons chili powder	¼ teaspoon turmeric
2 cups water	3 tablespoons extra virgin olive oil
4 garlic cloves, peeled and minced	½ teaspoons cumin seeds
¼ teaspoon mustard seeds	1-inch ginger piece, peeled and chopped
Salt and ground black pepper, to taste	

Directions:
Place the squid in the instant pot. Add pepper powder, saffron, salt, pepper and water, mix, cover and cook in the manual for 15 minutes.
In a blender, mix the coconut with the ginger, garlic and cumin seeds and mix well.
Heat a pan of oil over medium-high heat, add the mustard seeds and grill for 2-3 minutes. Release the pressure from the Instant Pot and transfer the squid and water to the pan. Stir and mix with the coconut mixture. Cook until thick, divide between plates and serve.

Nutrition:
Calories: 255, Fiber: 1 g, Carbs: 7 g, Proteins: 9 g

608. Braised Squid

Preparation time: 10 minutes | **Cooking time:** 20 minutes | **Servings:** 2

Ingredients:

1 lb. fresh peas	1 lb. squid, cleaned and cut
White wine	½ lbs. canned crushed tomatoes
1 yellow onion, peeled and chopped	Salt and ground black pepper, to taste
Olive oil	

Directions:
Put the Instant Pot in the sauté mode, add the oil and heat. Add the onion, mix and cook for 3 minutes.
Add the squid, stir and cook for another 3 minutes.
Add wine, tomatoes and peas, mix, cover and cook 20minutes.
Release the pressure, uncover the Instant Pot, add salt and pepper, stir, divide between the dishes and serve.

Nutrition:
Calories: 145, Fat: 1 g, Carbs: 7 g, Proteins: 12 g

609. Squid Roast

Preparation time: 10 minutes | **Cooking time:** 25 minutes | **Servings:** 2

Ingredients:

2 inch ginger piece, peeled and grated	2 green chilies, chopped
1 of lb. squid, cleaned and also cut into pieces	10 garlic cloves, peeled and minced
2 yellow onions, peeled and chopped	1 bay leaf
¼ cup coconut, sliced	1 tablespoon coriander
½ tablespoon lemon juice	Salt and ground black pepper, to taste
¾ tablespoon chili powder	1 teaspoon garam masala
Turmeric	¾ cup water
1 teaspoon mustard seeds	3 tablespoons vegetable oil

Directions:
Put the Instant Pot in the sauté mode, add the oil and heat. Add the mustard seeds and fry for 1 minute. Add the coconut and cook for 2 minutes. Add the ginger, onion, garlic and peppers, stir and cook for 30 seconds. Add salt, pepper, bay leaf, coriander, chili powder, garam masala, saffron, water, lemon juice and squid. Stir, cover and steam for 25 minutes.
Release the pressure, uncover, divide between the plates and serve.

Nutrition:
Calories: 209, Fat: 10 g, Fiber: 0.5 g, Carbs: 9.3 g, Proteins: 20 g

610. Lemongrass Chicken

Preparation time: 10 minutes | **Cooking time:** 20 minutes | **Servings:** 2

Ingredients:

4 garlic cloves, peeled and crushed	2 tablespoons fish sauce
1 bunch lemongrass, bottom removed and trimmed	1-inch piece ginger root, peeled and chopped
3 tablespoons coconut aminos	1 cup coconut milk
1 teaspoon Chinese five spice powder	10 chicken drumsticks
Salt and ground black pepper, to taste	1 teaspoon butter
1 yellow onion, peeled and chopped	1 tablespoon lime juice
¼ cup cilantro, diced	

Directions:
In a food processor, mix the lemon grass with ginger, garlic, amines, fish sauce and the five powdered spices and mix well. Add the coconut milk and beat again. Put the Instant Pot in the sauté mode, add the butter and melt.
Add the onion, mix and cook for 5 minutes. Add the chicken, salt and pepper, mix and cook for 1 minute. Add the mixture of coconut milk and lemongrass, mix, cover, put in Poultry settings and cook for 15 minutes.
Release the pressure, uncover, add more salt and pepper and lemon juice, mix, divide between the dishes and serve with coriander sprinkled on top.

Nutrition:
Calories: 400, Fat: 18 g, Fiber: 2 g, Carbs: 6 g, Proteins: 20 g

611. Salsa Chicken

Preparation time: 10 minutes | **Cooking time:** 25 minutes | **Servings:** 2

Ingredients:

¾ teaspoon cumin	1 lb. chicken breast, skinless and boneless
1 cup chunky salsa	Salt and ground black pepper, to taste
Dried oregano	

Directions:
Add salt and pepper to the chicken to taste and add to the Instant Pot
Add the oregano, cumin and sauce, mix, cover, place the Instant Pot in Poultry mode and cook for 25 minutes.
Relieve the pressure, transfer the chicken and the sauce to a bowl, cut the meat into pieces with a fork and serve with tortillas on the side.

Nutrition:
Calories: 125, Fat: 3 g, Fiber: 1 g, Carbs: 3 g, Proteins: 22 g

612. Chicken and potatoes

Preparation time: 15 minutes | **Cooking time:** 15 minutes | **Servings:** 2

Ingredients:

2 lbs. chicken thighs, skinless and boneless	2 tablespoons extra virgin olive oil
¾ cup chicken stock	2 lbs. red potatoes, peeled, and slice into quarters
3 tablespoons Dijon mustard	¼ cup lemon juice
Salt and ground black pepper, to taste	2 tablespoons Italian seasoning

Directions:
Put the Instant Pot in the sauté mode, add the oil and heat. Add the chicken thighs, salt and pepper, mix and brown for 2 minutes.
In a bowl, mix the broth with mustard, Italian sauce, and lemon juice and mix well.
Pour over the chicken, add the potatoes, mix, cover the Instant Pot and cook for 15 minutes.
Release the pressure, uncover the Instant Pot, stir the chicken, divide between the plates and serve.

Nutrition:
Calories: 190, Fat: 6 g, Fiber: 3.3 g, Carbs: 23 g, Proteins: 18 g

613. Chicken Sandwiches

Preparation time: 10 minutes | **Cooking time:** 15 minutes | **Servings:** 2

Ingredients:

2 tablespoons lemon juice	6 chicken breasts, skinless and boneless
12 oz. orange juice	15 oz. canned peaches with juice
1 teaspoon soy sauce	¼ cup brown sugar
8 hamburger buns	20 oz. canned pineapple with juice, chopped
1 tablespoon cornstarch	8 grilled pineapple slices, for serving

Directions:
In a bowl, mix orange juice with soy sauce, lemon juice, canned pineapple, peach and sugar and mix well.
Pour half of this mixture into the Instant Pot, add the chicken and pour the rest of the sauce over the meat.
Cover the pan instantly and cook for 12 minutes in the poultry environment. Relieve the

pressure, remove the chicken and place it on a cutting board.

Shred the meat and reserve the dish. In a bowl, mix the cornstarch with 1 spoon the juice of cooking and mix well.

Transfer the sauce to a pan, add the cornstarch and chicken mixture, stir and cook for a few minutes. Divide this chicken mixture into hamburger buns, add the pieces of grilled pineapple and serve.

Nutrition:
Calories: 240, Fat: 4.6 g, Fiber: 4 g, Carbs: 21 g, Proteins: 14 g

614. Moroccan Chicken

Preparation time: 10 minutes | **Cooking time:** 25 minutes | **Servings:** 2

Ingredients:
- 2 tablespoons extra virgin olive oil
- 6 chicken thighs
- ½ teaspoon coriander
- ½ teaspoon ground ginger
- ½ teaspoon turmeric
- 1 teaspoon paprika
- 2 yellow onions, peeled and chopped
- ¼ cup white wine
- ¼ cup dried cranberries Juice of
- 1 cup chicken stock
- 10 cardamom pods
- 2 bay leaves
- 1 teaspoon cloves
- ½ teaspoon cumin
- ½ teaspoon ground cinnamon
- 5 garlic cloves, peeled and chopped
- 2 tablespoons tomato paste
- 1 cup green olives
- 1 lemon
- ½ cup parsley, diced

Directions:
In a bowl, mix the bay leaf with cardamom, cloves, coriander, ginger, cumin, cinnamon, turmeric and paprika and mix. Put the Instant Pot in the sauté mode, add the oil and heat.

Add the chicken thighs, brown them for a few minutes and transfer them to a plate. Add the onion to the Instant Pot, stir and cook for 4 minutes. Add the garlic, mix and cook for 1 minute.

Add wine, tomato paste, seasoning from the bowl, stock and chicken. Stir, cover and cook in the poultry dough for 15 minutes.

Relieve the pressure, discard the bay leaf, cardamom and cloves, add the olives, cranberries, lemon juice and parsley, mix, divide the chicken mixture between the dishes and serve.

Nutrition:
Calories: 381, Fat: 10.2 g, Fiber: 7.8 g, Carbs: 4 g, Fiber: 32 g

Chapter 4: Snacks And Desserts

615. Lemon Cake

Preparation time: 23 minutes | **Cooking time:** 25 minutes | **Servings:** 2

Ingredients:
- 3 ½ oz. Butter, liquefied
- 3 oz. Brown sugar
- 1 tsp. Dark chocolate, sliced
- 3 pcs. Eggs
- 3 oz. Flour
- ½ tsp. Lemon juice

Directions:
Blend all the ingredients in a container.
Put the mixture into an oiled cake pan and put in the fryer.
Heat at 360°F for 17 minutes.
Let the heat subside before eating.

Nutrition:
Calories: 220, Fat: 11 g, Fiber: 3 g, Carbs: 15 g, Protein: 7 g

616. Greek Creamy Vanilla Cake

Preparation time: 35 minutes | **Cooking time:** 25 minutes | **Servings:** 2

Ingredients:
- 1 ½ cups White flour
- ¾ cups Sugar
- ½ tsp. Baking powder
- 1 cup Greek yogurt
- Cooking spray
- ½ tsp. Vanilla extract
- 1 tsp. Baking soda
- 1 pc. Banana. crushed
- 2 tbsp. Vegetable oil
- 8 oz. Pumpkin puree
- 1 pc. Egg

Directions:
In a container, blend all ingredients - excluding the cooking spray - and mix carefully.
Put the blend into a cake pan oiled with cooking spray and place it in your air fryer's container.
Cook at 340°F for half an hour.
Let the heat subside, wedge, and enjoy.

Nutrition:
Calories: 192, Fat: 7 g, Fiber: 7 g, Carbs: 12 g, Protein: 4 g

617. Eggy Vanilla Bread

Preparation time: 50 minutes | **Cooking time:** 25 minutes | **Servings:** 2

Ingredients:

- 3 cups Zucchinis, sliced
- 1 tbsp. Vanilla
- 2 cups White flour
- 1 tbsp. Stick butter, liquefied
- 1 cup Sugar
- 2 pcs. Eggs, whipped
- 1 tbsp. Baking powder

Directions:

Place all of the ingredients in a container and blend carefully.
Transfer the blend into a arranged loaf pan and put in the fryer and heat at 360°F for 40 minutes.
Cut and enjoy.

Nutrition:

Calories: 132, Fat: 6 g, Fiber: 7 g, Carbs: 11 g, Protein: 7 g

618. Sugary Zucchini Bread

Preparation time: 50 minutes | **Cooking time:** 25 minutes | **Servings:** 2

Ingredients:

- ¾ cup Sugar
- 1 tsp. Vanilla extract
- 2 pcs. Zucchinis, sliced
- 1 ½ cups Flour
- ⅓ cup Milk
- ⅓ cup Butter
- 1 pc. Egg
- 1 tsp. Baking powder
- ½ tsp. Baking soda
- 1 ½ cup Tartar cream

Directions:

Put all ingredients in a container and blend carefully.
Transfer the blend into an organized loaf pan and put the pan in the air fryer.
Heat at 320°F for 40 minutes.
Let the heat subside, cut, and serve.

Nutrition:

Calories: 222, Fat: 7 g, Fiber: 8 g, Carbs: 14 g, Protein: 4 g

619. Citrus Cake

Preparation time: 30 minutes | **Cooking time:** 25 minutes | **Servings:** 2

Ingredients:

- 1 piece Egg
- 4 tbsp. Sugar
- 2 tbsp. Vegetable oil
- 2 tbsp. Orange juice
- 1 tbsp. Cocoa powder
- ½ tsp. Orange zest
- 4 tbsp. Milk
- 4 tbsp. Flour
- ½ tsp. Baking powder

Directions:

Put all the ingredients in a container and blend carefully.
Split the blend among 3 portions and set it in your air fryer.
Cook at 320°F for 20 minutes.
Eat and enjoy!

Nutrition:

Calories: 191, Fat: 7 g, Fiber: 3 g, Carbs: 14 g, Protein: 4 g

620. Cinnamon Apples

Preparation time: 20 minutes | **Cooking time:** 25 minutes | **Servings:** 2

Ingredients:

- 2 tsp. Cinnamon powder
- ½ tsp. Nutmeg powder
- 4 tbsp. Butter
- 5 pcs. Apples, sliced
- 1 tbsp. Maple syrup
- ¼ cup Brown sugar

Directions:

In a pot that suits your air fryer, blend the apples with the supplementary ingredients and flip.
Set the pan in the fryer and cook at 360°F for 10 minutes.
Separate it into cups and enjoy.

Nutrition:

Calories: 180, Fat: 6 g, Fiber: 8 g, Carbs: 19 g, Protein: 12 g

621. Yogurt Pine Carrot Cake

Preparation time: 55 minutes | **Cooking time:** 25 minutes | **Servings:** 2

Ingredients:

- 5 oz. Flour
- ½ tsp. Baking soda
- 1 pc. Egg, whipped
- ½ cup Sugar
- ¾ tsp. Baking powder
- ½ tsp. Cinnamon powder
- 3 tbsp. Yogurt
- ¼ cup Pineapple juice

4 tbsp. Vegetable oil
⅓ cup Coconut flakes, sliced
⅓ cup Carrots, sliced
Cooking spray

Directions:
Set all the ingredients - excluding the cooking spray - in a container, and blend carefully.
Transfer the mixture into a pan, oiled with cooking spray that suits your air fryer.
Set the pan in your air fryer and cook at 360°F for 45 minutes.
Let the heat subside before you wedge and eat it.

Nutrition:
Calories: 200, Fat: 6 g, Fiber: 7 g, Carbs: 12 g, Protein: 4 g

622. Ale Graham Cheesecake

Preparation time: 30 minutes | **Cooking time:** 25 minutes | **Servings:** 2

Ingredients:
2 tsp. Butter, liquefied
16 oz. Cream cheese, melted
½ cup Sugar
½ tsp. Vanilla extract
½ cup Graham cookies, crushed
2 pcs. Eggs
1 tsp. Rum

Directions:
Oil a pan with the butter and fill it with the crushed cookies on the beneath.
In a container, blend all the other ingredients and whip carefully, then put the crumbs all over.
Set the pan in your air fryer and heat at 370°F for 20 minutes.
Let the heat subside, put it in the fridge, and enjoy it cold.

Nutrition:
Calories: 212, Fat: 12 g, Fiber: 6 g, Carbs: 12 g, Protein: 7 g

623. Chinese Beef Bites

Preparation time: 10 minutes | **Cooking time:** 3 hours | **Servings:** 2

Ingredients:
2 lbs. beef stew meat, cubed
2 tablespoons olive oil
Salt and black pepper to the taste
3 tablespoons balsamic vinegar
1 teaspoon five spice
½ teaspoon allspice, ground
3 tablespoons balsamic vinegar
¼ cup scallions, chopped

Directions:
In a bowl, mix beef bites with the oil, vinegar and the other ingredients, toss, transfer to a sous vide bag, submerge in the preheated water oven and cook at 160°F for 3 hours.
Arrange on a platter and serve.

Nutrition:
Calories: 415 g, Fat: 23 g, Fiber: 3 g, Carbs: 8 g, Protein: 27 g

624. Shrimp Meatballs

Preparation time: 10 minutes | **Cooking time:** 1 hour | **Servings:** 2

Ingredients:
½ cup coconut flour
2 eggs, whisked
Salt and black pepper to the taste
1 tablespoon chives, chopped
½ teaspoon mustard powder
2 lbs. shrimp, peeled, deveined and chopped
4 scallions, chopped
3 teaspoons soy sauce
Cooking spray
¼ teaspoon sweet paprika

Directions:
In a bowl, mix the shrimp with the scallions, flour and the other ingredients except the cooking spray, stir well and shape medium meatballs out of this mix.
Divide the shrimp meatballs into sous vide bags, grease them with the cooking spray, seal the bags, submerge in the water oven and cook at 140°F for 1 hour.
Arrange them on a platter and serve as an appetizer

Nutrition:
Calories: 332, Fat: 18 g, Fiber: 1 g, Carbs: 7 g, Protein: 15 g

625. Sausage Bites

Preparation time: 10 minutes | **Cooking time:** 1 hour and 30 minutes | **Servings:** 2

Ingredients:
- 1 lb. beef sausages, sliced
- 1 tablespoon balsamic vinegar
- 1 teaspoon sweet paprika
- ¼ teaspoon red pepper flakes
- ½ teaspoon garlic powder
- 1 tablespoon olive oil
- Salt and black pepper to taste
- 3 tablespoons tomato sauce
- ¼ teaspoon onion powder

Directions:
In large sous vide bag, mix the sausage bites with the oil, vinegar and the other ingredients, toss, seal, submerge in the preheated water oven and cook them at 140°F for 1 hour and 30 minutes Divide the sausage bites into bowls and serve as a snack.

Nutrition:
Calories: 316, Fat: 35 g, Fiber: 3 g, Carbs: 4 g, Protein: 16 g

626. Vanilla and Apple Brownies

Preparation time: 10 minutes | **Cooking time:** 20 minutes | **Servings:** 2

Ingredients:
- 1 ½ cups apples, cored and cubed
- ½ cup quick oats
- ⅓ cup coconut cream
- ½ teaspoon baking powder
- Cooking spray
- 2 tablespoons stevia
- 2 tablespoons cocoa powder
- ¼ cup coconut oil, melted
- 2 teaspoons vanilla extract

Directions:
In your food processor, combine the apples with the stevia and the other ingredients except the cooking spray and blend well.
Grease a square pan with cooking spray, add the apples mix, spread, introduce in the oven, bake at 350°F for 20 minutes, leave aside to cool down, slice and serve.

Nutrition:
Calories: 200, Fat: 3 g, Fiber: 3 g, Carbs: 14 g, Protein: 4 g

627. Chocolate Zucchini Bundt Cake

Preparation time: 10 minutes | **Cooking time:** 30 minutes | **Servings:** 2

Ingredients:
- 3 cups of almond flour or coconut flour
- ½ cups of unsweetened cacao powder
- ½ teaspoon of fine sea salt
- ½ cup of unsalted butter, melted
- 2 teaspoons of pure vanilla extract
- 1 ½ cups of powdered erythritol or powdered swerve
- 2 teaspoons of baking powder
- 6 large organic eggs
- 2 medium zucchinis, peeled and pureed

For the Frosting:
- ¼ cup of coconut oil
- ½ cup of cacao powder

Directions:
Grease a half-size bundt cake pan with nonstick cooking spray.
In a large bowl, add all the cake ingredients and gently stir until well combined. Add the cake batter to the bundt pan and evenly smooth on top. Cover with aluminum foil.
Add 2 cups of water and a trivet inside your Instant Pot. Place the bundt cake pan on top of the trivet. Lock the lid and cook at high pressure for 30 minutes at high pressure.
When the cooking is done, naturally release the pressure for 10 minutes, then quick release the remaining pressure. Carefully remove the lid and remove the cake pan.
Allow the cake to cool and remove from the bundt pan.
To make the frosting, add the coconut oil and cacao powder and mix well. Spread the frosting over the cake. Serve and enjoy!

Nutrition:
Calories: 229, Fat: 21 g, Carbs: 4 g, Protein: 7.4 g

628. Molten Brownie Pudding

Preparation time: 10 minutes | **Cooking time:** 30 minutes | **Servings:** 2

Ingredients:

- 1 ½ cup of water
- 1 cup of erythritol or swerve sweetener
- ¼ cup of almond flour
- 1 teaspoon of pure vanilla extract
- A small pinch of fine sea salt
- 7 tablespoons of unsalted butter, melted
- 2 large organic eggs
- ¼ cup + 2 tablespoons of unsweetened cocoa powder
- ½ cup of unsweetened chocolate chips

Directions:

Add 1 ½ cup of water and a trivet inside your Instant Pot.

Spread 1 tablespoon of butter onto a baking or soufflé dish.

In a large bowl, add the 6 tablespoons of butter, erythritol, eggs, almond flour, cocoa powder, pure vanilla extract, fine sea salt. Beat until well combined.

Transfer the mixture to the dish and top with the unsweetened chocolate chips.

Place on top of the trivet and cover with aluminum foil.

Lock the lid and cook at high pressure for 30 minutes. When the cooking is done, manually release the pressure and remove the lid. Serve and enjoy!

Nutrition:
Calories: 349, Fat: 30.4 g, Carbs: 14 g, Protein: 6g

629. Nutella Lava Cakes

Preparation time: 10 minutes | **Cooking time:** 30 minutes | **Servings:** 2

Ingredients:

- 1 large organic egg
- 2 tablespoons of erythritol or swerve sweetener
- 2 tablespoons of almond flour
- 1 egg yolk
- ⅓ cup of Nutella spread

Directions:

In a medium bowl, add the egg and egg yolk. Whisk well until smooth.

Whisk in the erythritol or swerve sweetener. Add the Nutella spread and continue to whisk until smooth.

Whisk in the flour or until smooth.

Grease 2 ramekins with nonstick cooking spray and add the batter.

Pour 1 cup of water and add a trivet inside your Instant Pot. Place the ramekins on top of the trivet. Cover with aluminum foil.

Lock the lid and cook at high pressure for 9 minutes. When the cooking is done, quick release the pressure and remove the lid. Serve and enjoy!

Nutrition:
Calories: 154, Fat: 9 g, Carbs: 14 g, Protein: 3 g

630. Chocolate Peppermint Pudding

Preparation time: 2 hours | **Cooking time:** 2 minutes | **Servings:** 2

Ingredients:

- ½ cup coconut oil, melted
- 1 tablespoon cocoa powder
- 14 oz. canned coconut milk, unsweetened
- 10 drops stevia
- 13 stevia drops
- 1 teaspoon peppermint extract
- 1 avocado, pitted, peeled and chopped

Directions:

In a bowl, mix coconut oil with cocoa powder and 3 drops stevia, stir well, transfer to a lined container, keep in the fridge for 1 hour and chop into small pieces to use as chocolate chips.

In your instant pot, mix coconut milk with avocado, 10 drops stevia and peppermint oil, blend using an immersion blender, cover pot and cook on High pressure for 2 minutes.

Add 'chocolate chips', stir, divide pudding into bowls and keep in the fridge for 1 hour before serving.

Enjoy!

Nutrition:
Calories: 140, Fat: 3 g, Fiber: 2 g, Carbs: 3 g, Protein: 4 g

631. Coconut Pudding

Preparation time: 10 minutes | **Cooking time:** 3 minutes | **Servings:** 2

Ingredients:
- 1 ⅔ cups coconut milk, unsweetened
- 6 tablespoons swerve
- ½ teaspoon vanilla extract
- 1 tablespoon gelatin
- 3 egg yolks

Directions:
In a bowl, mix gelatin with 1 tablespoon coconut milk, stir well and leave aside for now.
Set your instant pot on saute mode, add milk and heat. Add swerve, egg yolks, vanilla extract and gelatin, stir well, cover pot and cook on High pressure for 2 minutes.
Divide everything into 4 ramekins and serve them cold.
Enjoy!

Nutrition:
Calories: 140, Fat: 2 g, Fiber: 1 g, Carbs: 3 g, Protein: 2 g

632. Orange Cake

Preparation time: 10 minutes | **Cooking time:** 25 minutes | **Servings:** 2

Ingredients:
- 6 eggs
- 1 ½ cups water
- 1 teaspoon baking powder
- 4 tablespoons swerve
- 2 oz. stevia
- 4 oz. coconut yogurt, unsweetened
- 1 orange, cut into quarters
- 1 teaspoon vanilla extract
- 9 oz. almond meal
- 2 tablespoons orange zest
- 4 oz. cream cheese

Directions:
In your food processor, mix orange with almond meal, swerve, eggs, baking powder and vanilla extract. Pulse well and transfer to a cake pan. Cover pan with foil.
Add the water to your instant pot, add steamer basket and place cake pan inside the basket. Cover and cook on High pressure for 25 minutes.
In a bowl, stir cream cheese with orange zest, coconut yogurt and stevia.
Spread this frosting over cake, slice and serve it. Enjoy!

Nutrition:
Calories: 170, Fat: 13 g, Fiber: 2 g, Carbs: 4 g, Protein: 4 g

633. Keto Orange Semolina Cake

Preparation time: 10 minutes | **Cooking time:** 30 minutes | **Servings:** 2

Ingredients:
For the Cake:
- 1 cup of fine semolina
- 1 teaspoon of cardamom powder
- ¾ cups of non-dairy milk
- ½ teaspoon of baking powder
- 1 tablespoon of almonds, sliced
- ¼ teaspoon of fresh orange zest
- ½ cup of erythritol or swerve sweetener
- ½ cup of non-dairy yogurt
- 3 tablespoons of unsalted butter, melted
- ½ teaspoon of baking soda
- 1 tablespoon of pistachios, sliced

For the Orange Syrup:
- 1 orange, juice and zest
- ½ cup of Swerve sweetener and erythritol
- ½ cup of water

Directions:
Grease a 6-inch cake pan with nonstick cooking spray.
Add 2 cups of water and a trivet inside your Instant Pot. Press the "Sauté" setting on your Instant Pot and allow the water to be heated.
In a large bowl, add the semolina, erythritol and cardamom powder. Stir until well combined. Stir in the non-dairy yogurt and non-dairy milk. Mix well. Finally, stir in the melted butter. Allow the cake batter to sit for 10 minutes.
Once the time is up, mix in the baking soda, baking powder and the orange zest.
Transfer the cake batter to the greased pan. Cover with aluminum foil. Place on top of the trivet.

Lock the lid and press the "Steam" setting and set the time to 22 minutes. When the timer beeps, remove the lid.

In a saucepan over medium heat, add the orange juice, orange zest, and swerve sweetener. Bring to a boil and stir until well combined. Reduce the heat and allow to cook for a couple more minutes, stirring frequently.

Pour the syrup over the cake. Serve and enjoy!

Nutrition:
Calories: 280, Fat: 13 g, Carbs: 14 g, Protein: 6 g

634. Banana Bread in a Jar

Preparation time: 10 minutes | **Cooking time:** 30 minutes | **Servings:** 2

Ingredients:
- 1 stick butter, at room temperature
- 3 eggs, whisked
- ¼ cup sour cream
- 1 teaspoon baking soda
- A pinch of nutmeg, preferably freshly grated
- ½ cup semisweet chocolate chips
- ¾ cup granulated sugar
- ½-lb. overripe bananas, mashed
- 2 ½ cups all-purpose flour
- A pinch of salt
- ½ teaspoon pumpkin pie spice

Directions:
Start by adding 1 ½ cups of water and a metal trivet to the base of your Instant Pot.

In a mixing bowl, thoroughly combine butter, sugar, eggs, banana, and sour cream. Then, in another mixing bowl, combine the flour, baking soda, salt, nutmeg, and pumpkin pie spice.

Then, add butter mixture to the flour mixture, mix to combine well. Fold in the chocolate chips. Divide the batter between mason jars. Lower the jars onto the trivet.

Secure the lid. Choose the "Multigrain" mode and cook for 55 minutes under High pressure. Once cooking is complete, use a natural pressure release, carefully remove the lid.

Let it sit for 5 to 10 minutes before serving.

Nutrition:
Calories: 453, Fat: 17.1 g, Carbs: 69.4 g, Protein: 7.9 g, Sugars: 26.3 g

635. Easy Cherry Cobbler

Preparation time: 10 minutes | **Cooking time:** 30 minutes | **Servings:** 2

Ingredients:
- 30 oz. cherry pie filling
- ½ cup coconut butter, melted
- ½ teaspoon ground cardamom
- 1 box yellow cake mix
- ½ teaspoon ground cinnamon
- ¼ teaspoon grated nutmeg

Directions:
Add 1 cup of water and metal rack to the Instant Pot. Place cherry pie filling in a pan.

Mix the remaining ingredients, spread the batter over the cherry pie filling evenly.

Secure the lid. Choose the "Manual" mode and cook for 10 minutes under High pressure. Once cooking is complete, use a natural pressure release, carefully remove the lid.

Serve with whipped topping. Enjoy!

Nutrition:
Calories: 499, Fat: 16.2 g, Carbs: 82 g, Protein: 4.5 g, Sugars: 24.3 g

636. Crack Chicken

Preparation time: 10 minutes | **Cooking time:** 30 minutes | **Servings:** 2

Ingredients:
- 4 boneless, skinless chicken breasts
- 1 packet of ranch seasoning
- 1 cup of cheddar cheese, shredded
- Fine sea salt and freshly cracked black pepper (to taste)
- 1 (8-oz.) package of cream cheese, softened
- ½ cup of homemade low-sodium chicken stock
- 6 medium slices of bacon, cooked and chopped

Directions:
Press the "Sauté" setting on your Instant Pot and add all the ingredients except for the cheddar cheese and bacon. Lock the lid and cook at high pressure for 15 minutes. When the cooking is

done, quick release the pressure and carefully remove the lid.

Transfer the chicken to a cutting board and use two forks to shred.

Press the "Sauté" feature on your Instant Pot and cook until the cheese has completely smoothened, stirring frequently.

Return the shredded chicken and add the bacon and cheddar cheese. Cover and allow the cheese to melt. Turn off the "Sauté" setting. Serve and enjoy!

Nutrition:
Calories: 742, Fat: 51.9 g, Carbs: 2.3 g, Protein: 64.1 g

637. Summer Pineapple Cake

Preparation time: 10 minutes | **Cooking time:** 30 minutes | **Servings:** 2

Ingredients:

1 lb. pineapple, sliced	1 tablespoon orange juice
½ cup cassava flour	½ cup almond flour
1 teaspoon baking powder	½ teaspoon baking soda
¼ teaspoon salt	½ cup margarine, melted
½ cup honey	½ teaspoon vanilla extract
½ teaspoon coconut extract	1 tablespoon gelatin powder

Directions:
Add 1 ½ cups of water and a metal rack to the Instant Pot. Cover the bottom of your cake pan with a parchment paper.

Then, spread pineapple slices evenly in the bottom of the cake pan, drizzle with orange juice. In a mixing bowl, thoroughly combine the flour, baking powder, baking soda, and salt.

In another bowl, combine the margarine, honey, vanilla, and coconut extract, add gelatin powder and whisk until well mixed.

Add the honey mixture to the flour mixture, mix until you've formed a ball of dough. Flatten your dough, place on the pineapple layer.

Cover the pan with foil, creating a foil sling.

Secure the lid. Choose the "Bean/Chili" mode and cook for 25 minutes under High pressure.

Once cooking is complete, use a natural pressure release, carefully remove the lid.

Lastly, turn the pan upside down and unmold it on a serving platter. Enjoy!

Nutrition:
Calories: 258, Fat: 14.4 g, Carbs: 33.2 g, Protein: 1.8 g, Sugars: 26.5 g

638. Favorite Almond Cheesecake

Preparation time: 10 minutes | **Cooking time:** 30 minutes | **Servings:** 2

Ingredients:

24 oz. Neufchâtel cheese	1 cup sour cream
5 eggs	¼ cup flour
½ teaspoon pure vanilla extract	½ teaspoon pure almond extract
1 ½ cups graham cracker crumbs	½ cup almonds, roughly chopped
½ stick butter, melted	

Directions:
In a mixing bowl, beat Neufchâtel cheese with sour cream. Now, fold in eggs, one at a time.

Stir in the flour, vanilla extract, and almond extract, mix to combine well.

In a separate mixing bowl, thoroughly combine graham cracker crumbs, almonds, and butter. Press this crust mixture into a baking pan.

Pour the egg/cheese mixture into the pan. Cover with a sheet of foil, make sure that foil fits tightly around sides and under the bottom of your baking pan.

Add 1 cup of water and a metal trivet to your Instant Pot. Secure the lid. Choose the "Bean/Chili" mode and bake for 40 minutes at High pressure.

Once cooking is complete, use a quick release, carefully remove the lid. Allow your cheesecake to cool completely before serving.

Nutrition:
Calories: 445, Fat: 33.2 g, Carbs: 15.3 g, Protein: 21.2 g, Sugars: 7.4 g

639. Fancy Buckwheat Pudding with Figs

Preparation time: 5 minutes | **Cooking time:** 25 minutes | **Servings:** 2

Ingredients:

1 ½ cups buckwheat	3 ½ cups milk
½ cup dried figs, chopped	⅓ cup honey
½ teaspoon ground cinnamon	1 teaspoon pure vanilla extract
½ teaspoon pure almond extract	

Directions:
Add all of the above ingredients to your Instant Pot.
Secure the lid. Choose the "Multigrain" mode and cook for 10 minutes under High pressure. Once cooking is complete, use a natural pressure release, carefully remove the lid.
Serve topped with fresh fruits, nuts or whipped topping.

Nutrition:
Calories: 320, Fat: 7.5 g, Carb: 57.7 g, Protein: 9.5 g, Sugars: 43.2 g

640. Vanilla cake with meringues

Preparation time: 30 Minutes | **Cooking time:** 1 hour and 20 Minutes | **Servings:** 2

Ingredients:

12 Calorie cooking spray	175 g White Self Raising Flour
½ tsp. Baking powder	150 g Caster Sugar
150 g Low Fat Spread	3 medium Egg, whole, raw
½ tsp. Vanilla Extract	4 tsp. Low Calorie Jam
150 g Strawberries	75 g Raspberries
1 individual Egg whites, raw	60 g Caster Sugar

Directions:
Preheat the broiler to 180°C/160°C fan. Shower two 18cm sandwich tins with cooking splash and line with preparing the paper.
Filter the flour and heating powder into a blending bowl and include the sugar, low-fat spread, eggs, and vanilla concentrate. Beat for around 3 minutes until velvety and pale, at that point separate between the tins and smooth the surface with a spatula.
Heat for 15-18 minutes until the wipes rise, brilliant and springy to the touch. Put aside to cool in their tins for 5 minutes, at that point turn out onto a wire rack, and suspend the covering papers and leave to cool totally.
To make the meringue kisses, decrease the broiler temperature to 120°C, fan 100°C, gas mark ½. Line a preparing sheet with heating paper. In a blending bowl, utilizing a handheld electric whisk, whisk the egg white until it's hardened and structures tops that hold their shape when the mixers are suspended.
Slowly rush in the sugar until the blend is smooth, firm and reflexive.
Shower the nourishment shading in 3 lines down within a funneling sack fitted with a 1.5cm spout, at that point spoon in the meringue blend.
Pipe little masses of the meringue onto the lined preparing plate, lifting the channeling pack up forcefully toward the conclusion to make focuses. Prepare for a 45-an hour until fresh and dry.
Put one of the wipes on a serving plate with the base confronting upwards and spread over the jam. Cut 100g of the strawberries at that point mastermind the cut natural product equally over the jam.
Top with the other wipe. Organize the quartered strawberries, raspberries and meringue kisses over the cake

Nutrition:
Calories: 198, Fat: 8 g, Carbs: 28 g, Sugars: 16 g, Protein: 2 g

641. Sweet Rice Pudding

Preparation time: 10 minutes | **Cooking time:** 15 minutes | **Servings:** 2

Ingredients:

1 ¼ cups milk	½ cup uncooked rice
½ cups brown sugar	½ cup raisin
1 teaspoon ground cinnamon	1 teaspoon butter, melted
2 eggs, beaten	1 teaspoon vanilla extract

¾ teaspoon lemon extract

1 cup heavy whipping cream

Directions:
Place all ingredients except the whipping cream in the Instant Pot.
Give a good stir to incorporate all ingredients.
Close the lid and press the Manual button.
Adjust the cooking time to 15 minutes
Allow to chill in the fridge before serving.
Serve with whipping cream

Nutrition:
Calories: 437, Carbs: 63 g, Protein: 8 g, Fat:17 g, Fiber: 1 g

642. Coconut, Cranberry, And Quinoa Crockpot Breakfast

Preparation time: 5 minutes | **Cooking time:** 20 minutes | **Servings:** 2

Ingredients:
- 2 ½ cups coconut water
- ½ cup coconut meat
- ½ cup dried cranberries
- ¼ cup honey
- ¼ cup slivered almonds
- 1 cup quinoa, rinsed
- 1 tablespoon vanilla

Directions:
Place all ingredients except the whipping cream in the Instant Pot.
Give a good stir to incorporate all ingredients.
Close the lid and press the Manual button.
Adjust the cooking time to 20 minutes
Allow to chill in the fridge before serving.

Nutrition:
Calories: 278, Carbs: 66.1 g, Protein: 6.4 g, Fat: 25.8 g, Fiber: 8.1 g

643. Caramel and Pear Pudding

Preparation time: 10 minutes | **Cooking time:** 15 minutes | **Servings:** 2

Ingredients:
- ½ cup sugar
- 1 ½ teaspoons baking powder
- ¼ teaspoon salt
- ½ teaspoon ground cinnamon
- ⅛ teaspoon ground cloves
- ¾ cup milk
- 4 medium pears, peeled and cubed
- ¾ cup brown sugar
- ½ cup pecans, chopped
- ¼ cup softened butter

Directions:
Place all ingredients in the Instant Pot.
Give a good stir to incorporate all ingredients.
Close the lid and press the Manual button.
Adjust the cooking time to 15 minutes
Allow to chill in the fridge before serving.

Nutrition:
Calories: 274, Carbs: 47 g, Protein: 3 g, Fat: 9 g, Fiber: 3 g

644. Cardamom and Banana Tapioca Pudding

Preparation time: 20 minutes | **Cooking time:** 25 minutes | **Servings:** 2

Ingredients:
- 1 cup small pearl tapioca, soaked and well-rinsed
- 4 cups coconut milk
- ½ cup coconut sugar
- 4 peaches, diced
- 1 teaspoon cardamom
- 1 teaspoon vanilla extract
- 2 bananas, peeled and sliced

Directions:
Start by adding 1½ cups of water and a metal trivet to the base of your Instant Pot.
Mix tapioca, cardamom, coconut milk, vanilla, and sugar in a baking dish. Lower the dish onto the trivet.
Secure the lid. Choose the "Multigrain" mode and cook for 10 minutes under High pressure.
Once cooking is complete, use a quick pressure release, carefully remove the lid.
Add banana and peaches, gently stir to combine and serve.

Nutrition:
Calories: 449, Fat: 8.5 g, Carbs: 86.1 g, Protein: 9.8 g, Sugars: 45.7 g

645. Carrot Almond Cake

Preparation time: 10 minutes | **Cooking time:** 15 minutes | **Servings:** 2

Ingredients:

- 2 eggs
- 1 ½ tsp apple pie spice
- ½ cup Swerve
- ½ cup walnuts, chopped
- ½ cup heavy whipping cream
- ¼ cup coconut oil
- 1 tsp baking powder
- 1 cup almond flour
- 1 cup carrot, shredded

Directions:
Spray 6-inch baking dish with cooking spray and set aside.
Add all ingredients into the large mixing bowl and mix with electric mixer until well combined.
Pour batter into the prepared dish and cover dish with foil.
Pour 2 cups of water into the instant pot then place a trivet in the pot.
Place baking dish on top of the trivet.
Seal pot with lid and cook on high for 40 minutes.
Allow to release pressure naturally for 10 minutes then release using quick release method.
Remove dish from the pot and set aside to cool completely.
Serve and enjoy.

Nutrition:
Calories: 184, Carbs: 3.9 g, Protein: 5 g, Fat: 17.6 g, Sugar: 1.1 g, Sodium: 38 mg

646. Indian Rice Pudding

Preparation time: 10 minutes | **Cooking time:** 15 minutes | **Servings:** 2

Ingredients:

- 1 cup basmati rice, rinsed and drained
- ½ cup walnuts
- 3 cups milk
- 1 cups sugar
- 1 cup water

Directions:
Add rice, 2 cups milk, and half sugar into the instant pot and stir well.
Seal pot with lid and cook on manual mode for 30 minutes.
Meanwhile, Soak walnut into the water for 15 minutes.
Add walnuts and ½ cup water into the food processor and process until a coarse paste.
Release pressure using quick release method than open the lid.
Mash rice with a ladle.
Set instant pot on sauté mode. Add remaining milk, walnut paste, and sugar.
Stir well and simmer for 3 minutes.
Serve and enjoy.

Nutrition:
Calorie: 466, Carbs: 85.7 g, Protein: 11.4 g, Fat: 10.5 g, Sugar: 59.3 g, Sodium: 99 mg

647. Raspberry Parfait

Preparation time: 10 minutes | **Cooking time:** 30 minutes | **Servings:** 2

Ingredients:

- Raspberry chia seeds
- 1 cup frozen raspberries, reserve some for garnish
- ½ c. unsweetened almond milk
- Chocolate tapioca
- 1 cup unsweetened almond milk
- ½ Tbsp. cocoa powder
- 3 tbsps. chia seeds
- ¼ tsp. white sugar
- ⅛ tsp. lemon juice
- ⅛ cup seed tapioca
- 1 bar chopped dark chocolate, reserve some for garnish
- 1 cup water

Directions:
For the raspberry chia seeds, put together raspberries, chia seeds, almond milk, white sugar, and lemon juice. Mix until all ingredients are well combined. Make sure to mash berries. Cover with saran wrap. Place inside the fridge for 2 hours or until ready to use.
For the chocolate tapioca, put together tapioca, dark chocolate, almond milk, cocoa powder, and water.
Close the lid. Lock in place and make sure to seal the valve. Press the "pressure" button and cook for 8 minutes on high.
When the timer beeps, choose the quick pressure release. This would take 1–2 minutes. Remove the lid.
To serve, spoon an equal amount of chocolate tapioca in glasses. Put raspberry–chia mixture. Garnish with fresh raspberries and chocolate.

Nutrition:
Calories: 100, Fat: 1 g, Carbs: 21 g, Protein: 2 g

648. Greek Hosafi (Stewed Dried Fruits)

Preparation time: 10 minutes | **Cooking time:** 30 minutes | **Servings:** 2

Ingredients:

2 oz. dried figs	2 oz. dried apricots
1 oz. sultana raisins	1 oz. prunes, pitted
1 oz. almonds	¼ cup sugar
1 cinnamon stick	1 vanilla bean
¼ teaspoon whole cloves	¼ teaspoon whole star anise
1 cup water	1 tablespoon Greek honey

Directions:

Place all ingredients in the inner pot of your Instant Pot.

Secure the lid. Choose the "Manual" mode and cook for 2 minutes at High pressure. Once cooking is complete, use a natural pressure release for 10 minutes, carefully remove the lid. Serve with Greek yogurt or ice cream, if desired.

Nutrition:

Calories: 227, Fat: 7.3 g, Carbs: 66.4 g, Protein: 4.8 g, Sugars: 45.8 g, Fiber: 4.7 g

649. Nut Butter Brownies

Preparation time: 10 minutes | **Cooking time:** 30 minutes | **Servings:** 2

Ingredients:

¼ cup walnut butter	2 tablespoons sunflower seed butter
¼ cup coconut sugar	2 tablespoons cocoa powder
1 egg	A pinch of grated nutmeg
A pinch of salt	¼ cardamom powder
¼ teaspoon cinnamon powder	½ teaspoon baking soda
½ teaspoon vanilla extract	¼ cup dark chocolate, cut into chunks

Directions:

Place a metal trivet and 1 cup of water in your Instant Pot. Spritz a baking pan with nonstick cooking spray.

In a mixing bowl, combine all ingredients, except for the chocolate, stir well to create a thick batter.

Spoon the batter into the prepared pan. Sprinkle the chocolate chunks over the top, gently press the chocolate chunks into the batter.

Lower the baking pan onto the trivet.

Secure the lid. Choose the "Manual" mode and cook for 20 minutes at High pressure. Once cooking is complete, use a natural pressure release for 10 minutes, carefully remove the lid. Place your brownies on a cooling rack before slicing and serving.

Nutrition:

Calories: 256, Fat: 38.1 g, Carbs: 25.1 g, Protein: 7.5 g, Sugars: 17.9 g, Fiber: 3.5 g

650. Hot Mulled Apple Cider

Preparation time: 10 minutes | **Cooking time:** 30 minutes | **Servings:** 2

Ingredients:

1 ½ cups apple cider	½-inch piece fresh ginger, peeled and sliced
1 cinnamon stick	1 vanilla bean
½ teaspoon whole cloves	½ teaspoon allspice berries
¼ orange, sliced into thin rounds	¼ cups brandy

Directions:

Place all ingredients, except for the brandy, in the inner pot of your Instant Pot.

Secure the lid. Choose the "Slow Cook" mode and cook for 1 hour 30 minutes at the lowest temperature.

Strain the cider mixture and stir in the brandy. Serve immediately.

Nutrition:

Calories: 239, Fat: 0.4 g, Carbs: 26.2 g, Protein: 0.5 g, Sugars: 18.9 g, Fiber: 1.9 g

651. Hungarian Golden Dumpling Cake

Preparation time: 10 minutes | **Cooking time:** 30 minutes | **Servings:** 2

Ingredients:
- ¼ cup granulated sugar
- ½ teaspoon grated lemon peel
- 1 teaspoon fresh lemon juice
- 1 tablespoon cream cheese, at room temperature
- ½ teaspoon vanilla extract
- 1 oz. walnuts, ground
- 1 tablespoon butter, at room temperature
- 4 oz. refrigerated buttermilk biscuits
- 4 tablespoons powdered sugar

Directions:
Place 1 cup of water and a metal trivet in the inner pot of your Instant Pot. Lightly grease a loaf pan with shortening of choice.
In a shallow bowl mix the granulated sugar, walnuts, and lemon peel. Mix the melted butter and lemon juice in another shallow bowl.
Cut each biscuit in half. Dip your biscuits into the butter mixture, then, roll them in the walnut/sugar mixture.
Arrange them in the loaf pan.
Secure the lid. Choose the "Manual" mode and cook for 25 minutes at High pressure. Once cooking is complete, use a natural pressure release for 5 minutes, carefully remove the lid.
In the meantime, whip the cream cheese with the powdered sugar, and vanilla extract. Drizzle over the hot cake and serve.

Nutrition:
Calories: 264, Fat: 23.5 g, Carbs: 58.8 g, Protein: 6.6 g, Sugars: 33.3 g, Fiber: 2.6 g

652. Walnut Cream

Preparation time: 10 minutes | **Cooking time:** 1 minute | **Servings:** 2

Ingredients:
- 2 oz. coconut oil
- 1 teaspoon vanilla extract
- 4 tablespoons stevia
- 4 tablespoons cocoa powder
- 1 cup chopped walnuts

Directions:
In your instant pot, mix cocoa powder with oil, vanilla, walnuts and stevia. Blend using an immersion blender, cover pot and cook on High pressure for 1 minute.
Transfer to a bowl, leave in the fridge for a couple of hours and serve.
Enjoy!

Nutrition:
Calories: 100, Fat: 5 g, Fiber: 1 g, Carbs: 3 g, Protein: 4 g

653. Chocolate Cream

Preparation time: 1 minute | **Cooking time:** 3 minutes | **Servings:** 2

Ingredients:
- ½ cup coconut cream, unsweetened
- 4 oz. dark chocolate, unsweetened and chopped

Directions:
In your instant pot, mix cream with dark chocolate, cover pot and cook on High pressure for 3 minutes.
Stir your cream well, divide into dessert cups and serve cold.
Enjoy!

Nutrition:
Calories: 78 g, Fat: 2 g, Fiber: 1 g, Carbs: 3 g, Protein: 1 g

654. Skinny Blueberry Lemon Loaf or Muffins

Preparation time: 10 minutes | **Cooking time:** 16 minutes | **Servings:** 2

Ingredients:
- 1 egg
- ¾ cup fresh or frozen blueberries
- 1 Tbsp fresh lemon juice
- 3 Tbsp. sugar substitute
- 1 tsp. baking soda
- Dash of lemon extract
- ½ -¾ cup water
- 2 Tbsp. brown sugar
- 1 ¼ cup self-rising flour
- 1 tsp. baking powder

Directions:
Preheat broiler to 350°F and splash portion dish (9x5 or 8x4) or biscuit tin with nonstick cooking shower.
In a medium bowl include egg, water, lemon juice, lemon concentrate, and dark colored sugar substitute. Blend well.
In a different bowl consolidate flour, preparing soft drink and powder, and sugar substitute.
Include dry fixings into the wet gradually as you mix.
Before the two are fused include solidified blueberries and dissolved spread. Mix just until scarcely joined.
Don't over blend. The main tip is to not over blend.
Empty player into container or biscuit tin. Heat for 30-45 minutes or until an embedded blade or toothpick tells the truth. If created into biscuits, decrease the cooking time to 14-16 minutes.

Nutrition:
Calories: 180, Fat: 7 g, Carbs: 29 g, Sugars: 20 g, Protein: 1 g

655. Banana Cake

Preparation time: 10 minutes | **Cooking time:** 25 minutes | **Servings:** 2

Ingredients:
- 2 cups almond flour
- 1 banana, peeled and mashed
- ½ cup coconut sugar
- ¼ cup coconut oil, melted
- 1 teaspoon vanilla extract
- Cooking spray
- ¼ cup cocoa powder
- ½ teaspoon baking soda
- ¾ cup almond milk
- 2 tablespoons flaxseed mixed with 3 tablespoons water
- 1 tablespoon lemon juice

Directions:
In a bowl, combine the flour with the cocoa powder, banana and the other ingredients except the cooking spray and stir well.
Grease a cake pan with cooking spray, pour the cake mix, spread, bake in the oven at 350°F for 25 minutes, cool down, slice and serve.

Nutrition:
Calories: 245, Fat: 5.6 g, Fiber: 4 g, Carbs: 17 g, Protein: 4 g

656. Chia Pudding

Preparation time: 10 minutes | **Cooking time:** 10 minutes | **Servings:** 2

Ingredients:
- 2 tablespoons stevia
- 2 tablespoons cocoa powder
- ⅓ cup chia seeds
- 3 tablespoons almond flour
- 2 cups almond milk
- ½ teaspoon vanilla extract

Directions:
In a pan, mix the stevia with the flour and the other ingredients, stir, cook over medium heat for 10 minutes pour into small cups and serve cold.

Nutrition:
Calories: 182, Fat: 5 g, Fiber: 3 g, Carbs: 16 g, Protein: 6 g

657. Coconut Mousse

Preparation time: 10 minutes | **Cooking time:** 0 minutes | **Servings:** 2

Ingredients:
- 2 and ¾ cup almond milk
- 1 teaspoon coconut extract
- 4 teaspoons stevia
- 2 tablespoons cocoa powder
- 1 teaspoon vanilla extract
- 1 cup coconut, toasted

Directions:
In a bowl, combine the almond milk with cocoa powder and the other ingredients, whisk well, divide into small cups and serve cold.

Nutrition:
Calories: 352, Fat: 5.4 g, Fiber: 5.4 g, Carbs: 11 g, Protein: 3 g

658. Mango Coconut Pudding

Preparation time: 10 minutes | **Cooking time:** 50 minutes | **Servings:** 2

Ingredients:
- 1 cup coconut, shredded
- 1 cup coconut cream

1 mango, peeled and chopped
2 tablespoons coconut sugar
½ teaspoon cinnamon powder
1 cup coconut milk
1 teaspoon vanilla extract

Directions:
In a pan, mix the coconut with the cream and the other ingredients, stir, simmer for 50 minutes over medium heat, divide into bowls and serve cold.

Nutrition:
Calories: 251, Fat: 3.6 g, Fiber: 4 g, Carbs: 16 g, Protein: 7.1 g

659. Rhubarb and Berries Pie

Preparation time: 10 minutes | **Cooking time:** 25 minutes | **Servings:** 2

Ingredients:
2 cups coconut flour
1 cup pecans, chopped
4 cups rhubarb, chopped
8 oz. coconut cream
1 cup coconut butter, soft
1 and ¼ cup coconut sugar
1 cup strawberries, sliced

Directions:
In a bowl, combine the flour with the butter, pecans and ¼ cup sugar and stir well.
Transfer this to a pie pan, press well into the pan, introduce in the oven and bake at 350°F for 20 minutes.
In a pan, combine the strawberries with the remaining ingredients, stir well and cook over medium heat for 4 minutes.
Spread this over the pie crust and keep in the fridge for a few hours before slicing and serving.

Nutrition:
Calories: 332, Fat: 5 g, Fiber: 5 g, Carbs: 15 g, Protein: 6.3 g

660. Banana Salad

Preparation time: 10 minutes | **Cooking time:** 0 minutes | **Servings:** 2

Ingredients:
¼ cantaloupe, cubed
1 apple, cored and cut into chunks
1 teaspoon vanilla extract
3 bananas, cut into chunks
1 tablespoon stevia
Juice of 1 lime

Directions:
In a bowl, mix the cantaloupe with the bananas and the other ingredients, toss and serve.

Nutrition:
Calories: 126, Fat: 3.3 g, Fiber: 1 g, Carbs: 1.2 g, Protein: 2 g

661. Lemon Berries

Preparation time: 10 minutes | **Cooking time:** 10 minutes | **Servings:** 2

Ingredients:
2 teaspoons lemon juice
Juice of 1 apple
1 lb. blackberries
4 tablespoons stevia
2 teaspoons lemon zest, grated
1 teaspoon vanilla extract
1 lb. strawberries

Directions:
In a pan, mix the berries with the stevia and the other ingredients, stir and cook over medium heat for 10 minutes.
Divide into cups and serve cold.

Nutrition:
Calories: 170, Fat: 3.4 g, Fiber: 3 g, Carbs: 4 g, Protein: 4 g

662. Orange Compote

Preparation time: 10 minutes | **Cooking time:** 15 minutes | **Servings:** 2

Ingredients:
5 tablespoons stevia
1 lb. oranges, peeled and sliced
1-oz. orange juice

Directions:
In a pot, combine the oranges with the stevia and the other ingredients, toss, bring to a boil over medium heat, cook for 15 minutes, divide into bowls and serve cold.

Nutrition:
Calories: 120, Fat: 2 g, Fiber: 3 g, Carbs: 6 g, Protein: 9 g

663. Vanilla Yolk Ice Cream

Preparation time: 30 minutes | **Cooking time:** 1 hour plus freezing | **Servings:** 2

Ingredients:

1 teaspoon vanilla	2 cups half-and-half
½ cup sugar	6 egg yolks

Directions:
Prepare your Sous-vide water bath to a temperature of 181°F.
Put all the ingredients in a cooking pouch and vacuum seal it.
Immerse the pouch in water bath and cook for 60 minutes.
Once done, remove the pouch from the water bath.
Filter the ice cream through a strainer to remove clumps.
Transfer and chill in a fridge.
Spoon the ice cream in a churn machine.
Freeze.
Serve and enjoy!

Nutrition:
Calories: 291, Fat: 268 g, Carb: 1.72 g, Protein: 63 g

664. Rum Bananas

Preparation time: 10 minutes | **Cooking time:** 30 minutes | **Servings:** 2

Ingredients:

1 cup brown sugar	1 tablespoon dark rum
4 large bananas, sliced	1 tablespoon pineapple juice

Directions:
Prepare your Sous-vide water bath to a temperature of 176°F.
Put the pineapple juice, bananas, sugar, and rum in a cooking pouch and seal it using a vacuum sealer.
Shake the pouch to combine well.
Lower the pouch in the water bath and cook for 31 minutes.
Once done, remove the pouch from the water bath and transfer the contents to a bowl.
Serve and enjoy!

Nutrition:
Calories: 269, Fat: 5 g, Carbs: 61 g, Fiber: 6 g, Protein: 5 g

665. Pistachio Almond Milk Ice Cream

Preparation time: 20 minutes + inactive time | **Cooking time:** 1 hour | **Servings:** 2

Ingredients:

¾ cup heavy cream	½ cup brown sugar
1 cup shelled pistachios	¼ teaspoon pistachio extract
5 medium egg yolks	1 cup almond milk

Directions:
Prepare your Sous-vide water bath to a temperature of 180°F.
Put the sugar and pistachios into a food blender and blend until mixture turns powdery.
Mix the pistachios mixture with heavy cream and milk in a pan.
Simmer the contents and remove from heat.
Keep aside to steep for 60 minutes.
Strain the milk using a fine mesh strainer and do away with the solids.
Transfer the milk into a food blender and blend alongside the eggs and pistachio.
Blend the mixture until frothy.
Pour the milk into a cooking pouch and seal using a vacuum sealer.
Place the pouch into the preheated water bath and let it cook for 60 minutes. Shake the pouch every 10 minutes.
Once done, remove the pouch from the water bath and transfer it to an ice water bath to cool.
Churn in an ice cream maker.
Serve and enjoy!

Nutrition:
Calories: 356, Fat: 27 g, Carb: 27 g, Fiber: 1 g, Protein: 8 g

666. Citrus Confit

Preparation time: 10 minutes | **Cooking time:** 1 hour | **Servings:** 2

Ingredients:
- 2 lemons, sliced and cut into quarters
- 1 lime, sliced and cut into quarters
- ½ cup salt
- 1 orange, sliced and cut into quarters
- ½ cup sugar

Directions:
In a big bowl, combine all ingredients and mix well, making sure that fruits are evenly covered with salt and sugar.
Carefully put the mixture into the vacuum bag and seal it.
Cook for 1 hour in the water bath, previously preheated to 185°F.
This confit is very rich in vitamins and can be stored in the fridge for at least 1 month.

Nutrition:
Calories: 90, Protein: 1 g, Fats: 2 g, Carbs: 17 g

667. Raspberry Compote

Preparation time: 10 minutes | **Cooking time:** 1 hour | **Servings:** 2

Ingredients:
- 1 cups raspberry
- 1 orange zest
- 1 lemon zest
- 1 tbsp white sugar

Directions:
Put the ingredients into the vacuum bag and seal it.
Cook for 1 hour in the water bath, previously preheated to 185°F.
Serve over ice cream or cake.

Nutrition:
Calories: 106, Protein: 2 g, Fats: 1 g, Carbs: 25 g

668. Strawberry Jam

Preparation time: 10 minutes | **Cooking time:** 1 hour and 30 minutes | **Servings:** 2

Ingredients:
- 2 cups strawberries, coarsely chopped
- 2 tbsp orange juice
- 1 cup white sugar

Directions:
Put the ingredients into the vacuum bag and seal it.
Cook for 1 hour 30 min in the water bath, previously preheated to 180°F.
Serve over ice cream or cheesecake, or store in the fridge in an airtight container.

Nutrition:
Calories: 50, Carbs: 13 g

669. Peach and Orange Jam

Preparation time: 10 minutes | **Cooking time:** 2 hours | **Servings:** 2

Ingredients:
- 2 cups peaches, coarsely chopped
- 1 cup water
- 1 ½ cup white sugar
- Zest and juice of 1 orange

Directions:
Put the ingredients into the vacuum bag and seal it.
Cook for 2 hours in the water bath, previously preheated to 190°F.
Serve over ice cream or cake, or store in the fridge in an airtight container.

Nutrition:
Calories: 50, Carbs: 14 g

670. Blueberry Jam

Preparation time: 10 minutes | **Cooking time:** 1 hour and 30 minutes | **Servings:** 2

Ingredients:
- 2 cups blueberries
- 2 tbsp lemon juice
- 1 cup white sugar

Directions:
Preheat the water bath to 180°F.
Put the ingredients into the vacuum bag and seal it.
Cook for 1 hour 30 min in the water bath.
Serve over ice cream or cake, or store in the fridge in an airtight container.

Nutrition:
Calories: 50 Carbs: 13 g

671. Coconut and Date Pudding

Preparation time: 15 minutes | **Cooking time:** 15 minutes | **Servings:** 2

Ingredients:

- ½ cup Medjool dates, finely chopped
- ½ teaspoon ground cardamom
- ½ teaspoon ground cinnamon
- 1 ½ cups water
- 1 14-oz. can coconut milk
- 1 ½ cups millet

Directions:

Add all the above ingredients to your Instant Pot, stir to combine well.
Secure the lid. Choose the "Manual" mode and cook for 1 minute at High pressure. Once cooking is complete, use a natural pressure release for 10 minutes, carefully remove the lid. Serve warm or at room temperature.

Nutrition:

Calories: 320, Fat: 3.3 g, Carbs: 63.1 g, Protein: 9.3 g, Sugars: 6.7 g

672. Chocolate Mousse

Preparation time: 10 minutes | **Cooking time:** 6 minutes | **Servings:** 2

Ingredients:

- 4 egg yolks
- ½ cup sugar
- 1 cup heavy cream
- ½ cup milk
- ¼ cup water
- 1 tsp vanilla
- ½ cup cocoa powder
- ¼ tsp sea salt

Directions:

Whisk egg yolk in a bowl until combined.
In a saucepan, add cocoa, water, and sugar and whisk over medium heat until sugar is melted.
Add milk and cream to the saucepan and whisk to combine. Do not boil.
Add vanilla and salt and stir well.
Pour 1 ½ cups water into the instant pot then place a trivet in the pot.
Pour mixture into the ramekins and place on top of the trivet.
Seal pot with lid and cook on manual mode for 6 minutes.
Once done then release pressure using the quick-release method than open the lid.
Serve and enjoy.

Nutrition:

Calories: 235, Fat: 14.1 g, Carbs: 27.2 g, Sugar: 21.5 g, Protein: 5 g, Cholesterol: 203 mg

673. Chocolate Chip Oat Cookies

Preparation time: 5 minutes | **Cooking time:** 30 minutes | **Servings:** 2

Ingredients:

- ¼ cup Oats
- 1 tbsp Honey
- 2 tsp Coconut Oil
- 2 tbsp Chocolate Chips
- Pinch of Salt
- 2 tbsp Milk
- 2 tbsp Sugar
- ½ tsp Vanilla Extract
- ¼ cup Flour
- 1 ½ cups Water

Directions:

Pour the water into the Instant Pot. Lower the trivet.
Combine all the cookie ingredients in a bowl.
Line a baking dish with parchment paper.
With a cookie scoop, drop the cookies onto the paper.
Make sure to flatten them slightly.
Place the dish on the trivet and close the lid.
Set the IP to MANUAL.
Cook on HIGH for 8 minutes.
Do a quick pressure release.
If they are not crispy for your liking.
Cook them on SAUTE for a few extra minutes.
Serve and enjoy!

Nutrition:

Calories: 410, Fats: 20 g, Carbs: 58 g, Protein: 6 g, Fiber: 1 g

674. Banana Chocolate Chip Muffins

Preparation time: 5 minutes | **Cooking time:** 30 minutes | **Servings:** 2

Ingredients:

- ⅓ cup Buttermilk
- 2 tbsp Chocolate Chips
- ½ cup Flour
- 1 tbsp Honey
- 3 tbsp Butter, melted
- ⅓ tsp Baking Soda
- 1 Banana, mashed
- 1 cup Water
- Pinch of Cinnamon
- 1 tbsp Flaxseeds

Directions:

Pour the water into the Instant Pot. Lower the trivet.
Whisk together all the ingredients.
Make sure to get rid of all the lumps.

Divide the mixture between two silicone muffin cups.
Place the muffin cups on the trivet.
Close the lid and set the IP to MANUAL.
Cook on HIGH for 15 minutes.
Do a quick pressure release.
Serve and enjoy!

Nutrition:
Calories: 230, Fats: 13 g, Carbs: 30 g, Protein: 3 g, Fiber: 3 g

675. Simple Vanilla Egg Custard

Preparation time: 5 minutes | **Cooking time:** 25 minutes | **Servings:** 2

Ingredients:
- 2 Eggs
- ¼ tsp Vanilla Extract
- 1 ½ cups Water
- Pinch of Cinnamon
- 1 ⅓ cup Milk
- ¼ cup Sugar

Directions:
Pour the water into the Instant Pot. Lower the trivet.
In a bowl, beat the eggs.
Add the rest of the ingredients and whisk to combine.
Grease 2 ramekins and divide the mixture between them.
Place the ramekins on the trivet and close the lid.
Cook on HIGH for 7 minutes.
Release the pressure naturally.
Serve and enjoy!

676. Chocolate Fondue

Preparation time: 5 minutes | **Cooking time:** 15 minutes | **Servings:** 2

Ingredients:
- 5 oz. Chocolate
- 4 oz. Heavy Cream
- Pinch of Salt
- Pinch of Cinnamon
- 1 tsp Coconut Liqueur
- ½ cup Lukewarm Water

Directions:
Pour the water into the Instant Pot. Lower the trivet.
Melt the chocolate in a microwave, in a heatproof bowl.
Add the rest of the ingredients, except the liqueur, and stir to combine.
Place the dish on the trivet.
Close and seal the lid and set the IP to STEAM.
Cook for 4 minutes.
Add the liqueur, stir to incorporate.
Serve and enjoy!

Nutrition:
Calories: 215, Fats: 20 g, Carbs: 12 g, Protein: 2 g

677. Pressure Cooked Brownies

Preparation time: 5 minutes | **Cooking time:** 45 minutes | **Servings:** 2

Ingredients:
- 1 tbsp Honey
- ½ cup Sugar
- 2 tbsp Cocoa Powder
- ¼ cup melted Butter
- ⅓ cup Baking Powder
- 2 cups Water
- 1 Egg
- Pinch of Salt
- ⅔ cup Flour

Directions:
Pour the water into the Instant Pot. Lower the trivet.
Whisk the wet ingredients in one bowl.
Stir together the dry ones in another.
Combine the two mixtures gently.
Grease a baking dish with some cooking spray.
Pour the batter into it.
Place the dish on the trivet and close the lid.
Cook on HIGH for 25 minutes.
Do a quick pressure release.
Serve and enjoy!

Nutrition:
Calories: 525, Fats: 25 g, Carbs: 75 g, Protein: 8 g, Fiber: 3 g

678. Almond Tapioca Pudding

Preparation time: 5 minutes | **Cooking time:** 30 minutes | **Servings:** 2

Ingredients:
- ⅔ cup Almond Milk
- 2 tbsp Sugar
- ½ cup Water
- ¼ cup Tapioca Pearls
- ½ tsp Almond Extract
- Pinch of Cinnamon

Directions:
Pour the water into the Instant Pot. Lower the trivet.
Take a heat –proof bowl and place all of the ingredients into it.
Stir well to combine.
Cover with a foil and place the bowl on the trivet.
Close the lid and set the IP to MANUAL.
Cook on HIGH for 7-8 minutes.
Do a natural pressure release.
Serve and enjoy!

Nutrition:
Calories: 190, Fats: 2.5 g Carbs: 39 g Protein: 2.5 g, Fiber: 5.2 g

679. Spiced Rum Apple Cider

Preparation time: 55 minutes | **Cooking time:** 30 minutes | **Servings:** 2

Ingredients:
- 4 tablespoons rum
- 1 vanilla bean
- 4 cups water
- 2 cinnamon sticks
- 1 small naval orange
- 1 teaspoon whole cloves
- ¾ cup brown sugar
- 6 apples, cored and diced

Directions:
Place the ingredients in the inner pot of your Instant Pot.
Secure the lid. Choose the "Manual" mode and cook for 50 minutes at High pressure. Once cooking is complete, use a quick pressure release, carefully remove the lid.
Mash the apples with a fork or a potato masher.
Pour the mixture over a mesh strainer and serve hot.

Nutrition:
Calories: 173, Fat: 0.4 g, Carbs: 39.5 g, Protein: 0.6 g, Sugars: 32.6 g

680. Fancy Creamed Fruit Salad

Preparation time: 15 minutes | **Cooking time:** 30 minutes | **Servings:** 2

Ingredients:
- 2 cups water
- ⅓ cup dried figs, chopped
- ¼ teaspoon ground nutmeg
- ½ teaspoon ground cinnamon
- 1 stick butter, at room temperature
- ½ cup granulated sugar
- 20 oz. peaches, pitted and sliced
- 10 oz. canned pineapple
- ⅓ cup dried raisins, chopped
- 1 cup pineapple juice

Directions:
Add all of the above ingredients to your Instant Pot.
Secure the lid. Choose the "Manual" mode. Cook for 8 minutes at High pressure. Once cooking is complete, use a natural release, carefully remove the lid.
Ladle into individual bowls and serve with yogurt.

Nutrition:
Calories: 276, Fat: 11.6 g, Carbs: 45 g, Protein: 1.2 g, Sugars: 42.2 g

681. Perfect Strawberry Souffle

Preparation time: 10 minutes | **Cooking time:** 15 minutes | **Servings:** 2

Ingredients:
- 3 egg whites
- 1 tbsp sugar
- ½ tsp vanilla
- 2 cups strawberries

Directions:
Spray four ramekins with cooking spray and set aside.
Add strawberries, vanilla, and sugar into the blender and blend until smooth.
In a large bowl, beat egg whites until medium peaks form. Add strawberry mixture and fold well.
Pour batter into the prepared ramekins.
Place the dehydrating tray in a multi-level air fryer basket and place basket in the instant pot.
Place ramekins on a dehydrating tray.
Seal pot with air fryer lid and select bake mode then set the temperature to 350 F and timer for 15 minutes.
Serve and enjoy.

Nutrition:
Calories: 49, Fat: 0.3 g, Carbs: 8.8 g, Sugar: 6.8 g, Protein: 3.2 g

682. Fudgy Brownie Pots

Preparation time: 10 minutes | **Cooking time:** 25 minutes | **Servings:** 2

Ingredients:
- 1 egg
- 1/3 cup cocoa powder
- 1/4 tsp vanilla
- 4 tbsp butter, melted
- 1/4 tsp baking powder
- 1/3 cup all-purpose flour
- 1/2 cup sugar
- 1/8 tsp salt

Directions:
In a small bowl, whisk together melted butter and sugar until well combined.
Add egg and vanilla and stir until combined.
In a medium bowl, mix together flour, cocoa powder, baking powder, and salt.
Add egg mixture into the flour mixture and mix until combined.
Pour batter into the two ramekins.
Place the dehydrating tray in a multi-level air fryer basket and place basket in the instant pot.
Place ramekins on a dehydrating tray.
Seal pot with air fryer lid and select bake mode then set the temperature to 350 F and timer for 25 minutes.
Serve and enjoy.

Nutrition:
Calories: 532, Fat: 27.3 g, Carbs: 74.3 g, Sugar: 50.6 g, Protein: 7.8 g, Cholesterol: 143 mg

683. Peanut Butter Cookies

Preparation time: 10 minutes | **Cooking time:** 10 minutes | **Servings:** 2

Ingredients:
- 1 egg
- 1/2 cup erythritol
- 1 cup peanut butter

Directions:
In a mixing bowl, mix together egg, peanut butter, and sweetener until soft mixture is formed.
Place the dehydrating tray in a multi-level air fryer basket and place basket in the instant pot.
Line dehydrating tray with parchment paper.
Make cookies from the mixture and place some cookies on the dehydrating tray.
Seal pot with air fryer lid and select bake mode then set the temperature to 350 F and timer for 12 minutes.
Bake remaining cookies using the same method.
Serve and enjoy.

Nutrition:
Calories: 132, Fat: 11.2 g, Carbs: 14.3 g, Sugar: 12.1 g, Protein: 5.8 g, Cholesterol: 14 mg

684. Chewy Brownies

Preparation time: 10 minutes | **Cooking time:** 30 minutes | **Servings:** 2

Ingredients:
- 2 eggs
- 1/4 cup all-purpose flour
- 2 tsp vanilla
- 1/2 cup butter, melted
- 1/2 cup walnuts, chopped
- 1 cup brown sugar
- 1/4 cup cocoa powder
- 1/8 tsp salt

Directions:
Spray a baking dish with cooking spray and set aside.
In a bowl, whisk eggs with vanilla, butter, and cocoa powder.
Add flour, walnuts, sugar, and salt and stir until well combined.
Pour batter into the prepared baking dish.
Place steam rack into the instant pot then place baking dish on top of the rack.
Seal pot with air fryer lid and select air fry mode then set the temperature to 320 F and timer for 30 minutes.
Serve and enjoy.

Nutrition:
Calories: 344, Fat: 23.5 g, Carbs: 31 g, Sugar: 23.9 g, Protein: 5.7 g, Cholesterol: 95 mg

685. Lemon Lb. Cake

Preparation time: 10 minutes | **Cooking time:** 30 minutes | **Servings:** 2

Ingredients:
- 4 eggs
- 1 tsp vanilla
- 1 tbsp lemon zest, grated
- 2/3 cup yogurt
- 2 tbsp fresh lemon juice
- 1 cup Swerve

½ cup butter, softened
1 ½ cups all-purpose flour
1 tsp baking powder
½ tsp salt

Directions:
Spray bundt cake pan with cooking spray and set aside.
In a medium bowl, mix together flour, baking powder, and salt.
In a mixing bowl, beat together butter and sweetener until creamy.
Add eggs and beat until well combined.
Add flour mixture, vanilla, yogurt, lemon juice, and lemon zest and blend until smooth.
Pour batter in prepared cake pan.
Place steam rack into the instant pot then place the cake pan on top of the rack.
Seal pot with air fryer lid and select air fry mode then set the temperature to 320 F and timer for 30 minutes.
Serve and enjoy.

Nutrition:
Calories: 316, Fat: 19 g, Carbs: 27.1 g, Sugar: 2.5 g, Protein: 8.7 g, Cholesterol: 151 mg

686. Perfect Limoncello

Preparation time: 15 minutes | **Cooking time:** 3 hours | **Servings:** 2

Ingredients:
- 2 cups vodka
- 3 limes
- 4 tablespoons granulated sugar
- Sparkling water, to serve with

Directions:
Preheat your Sous Vide cooker to 130°F.
Remove the zest from limes, using a vegetable peeler. This is the easiest method. If you get too much white part stuck on your peel, remove it with a knife.
Combine vodka, sugar, and lime peel in a Sous Vide bag.
Seal the bag using a water immersion method and clip the bag at the edge of your pot.
Cook the limoncello 3 hours.

Finishing steps:
Remove the bag from the cooker.
Strain the limoncello in a sterilized glass bottle.
To serve, add few ice cubes in a glass. Pour the limoncello over ice.
Finish off with sparkling water.
Serve.

Nutrition:
Calories: 127, Carb: 9 g, Fiber: 6 g, Protein: 1 g

687. Lime-Ginger Gin Tonic

Preparation time: 20 minutes | **Cooking time:** 2 hours | **Servings:** 2

Ingredients:
- 1 cup gin
- 1-inch ginger, peeled
- 1 cup ice
- 1 lime, cut into wedges
- 1 ¼ cup tonic water

Directions:
Preheat the water bath to 125°F.
Pour gin, ginger, and half the lime into a bag. Seal and place in water bath. Cook 2 hours. After 2 hours, remove to the refrigerator and cool completely.
When gin infusion is cool, divide ice between 4 glasses. Strain solids from gin. Pour an equal amount of the gin infusion into each glass. Garnish with lime wedge.

Nutrition:
Calories: 630, Carb: 39 g, Fiber: 2 g, Protein: 22 g

688. "Barrel-Aged" Negroni

Preparation time: 20 minutes | **Cooking time:** 24 hours | **Servings:** 2

Ingredients:
- ½ cup gin
- ½ cup Campari
- 1 orange, cut into wedges
- ½ cup vermouth
- ½ cup water
- ½ cup winemaking toasted oak chips

Directions:
Preheat the water bath to 120°F.
Combine all ingredients in a bag. Seal and place in water bath. Cook 24 hours.
Strain solids from liquid using a coffee filter or cheesecloth. Serve over ice.

Nutrition:
Calories: 216, Fat: 9 g, Carb: 13 g, Protein: 7 g

689. Lemon Cupcakes

Preparation time: 10 minutes | **Cooking time:** 15 minutes | **Servings:** 2

Ingredients:
- 2 eggs
- 1 tbsp lemon zest, grated
- 1 tsp vanilla
- ¼ cup butter
- 1 ¼ cups all-purpose flour
- 1 tbsp fresh lemon juice
- ¼ cup milk
- ¾ cup sugar
- 1 ½ tsp baking powder
- ¼ tsp salt

Directions:
In a small bowl, mix together flour, baking powder, and salt and set aside.
In a mixing bowl, beat together sugar and butter until well combined.
Add eggs, lemon juice, lemon zest, milk, and vanilla and beat until combined.
Add flour mixture and stir to combine.
Pour batter into the 12 silicone muffin molds.
Place the dehydrating tray in a multi-level air fryer basket and place basket in the instant pot.
Place 6 silicone muffin molds on dehydrating tray.
Seal pot with air fryer lid and select bake mode then set the temperature to 350 F and timer for 15 minutes.
Bake remaining cupcakes using the same method.
Serve and enjoy.

Nutrition:
Calories: 143, Fat: 4.8 g, Carbs: 23.2 g, Sugar: 12.9 g, Protein: 2.5 g, Cholesterol: 38 mg

690. Apple Crisp

Preparation time: 10 minutes | **Cooking time:** 9 minutes | **Servings:** 2

Ingredients:
- 4 large apples, cored and sliced
- ¼ cup water

For topping:
- ¼ cup butter, melted
- 1 ½ tsp ground cinnamon
- ½ tsp nutmeg
- ½ cup all-purpose flour
- ½ cup brown sugar
- ½ tsp salt
- 1 cup old fashioned oats

Directions:
Add water and apple slices into the instant pot.
Mix all topping ingredients and sprinkle over apple mixture.
Seal the pot with pressure cooking lid and cook on high pressure for 5 minutes.
Once done, allow to release pressure naturally for 5 minutes then release remaining pressure using quick release. Remove lid.
Seal pot with air fryer lid and select broil mode and set timer for 4 minutes.
Serve and enjoy.

Nutrition:
Calories: 671, Fat: 19.7 g, Carbs: 117.6 g, Sugar: 56 g, Protein: 9.9 g, Cholesterol: 41 mg

691. Moist Chocolate Cake

Preparation time: 10 minutes | **Cooking time:** 25 minutes | **Servings:** 2

Ingredients:
- 1 egg
- 1 tsp baking powder
- 1 cup of sugar
- 1 tsp vanilla
- 1 cup boiling water
- 1 tsp baking soda
- 3 tbsp cocoa powder
- 1 cup all-purpose flour
- ¼ cup butter
- ¼ tsp salt

Directions:
Spray a baking dish with cooking spray and set aside.
Add butter and boiling water in a mixing bowl and beat until butter is melted.
Add vanilla and egg and beat until well combined.
In a medium bowl, mix flour, baking soda, baking powder, cocoa powder, sugar, and salt.
Add egg mixture into the flour mixture and beat until well combined.
Pour batter in prepared baking dish.
Place steam rack in the instant pot then places a baking dish on top of the rack.
Seal pot with air fryer lid and select bake mode then set the temperature to 350 °F and timer for 25 minutes.
Serve and enjoy.

Nutrition:
Calories: 216, Fat: 6.7 g, Carbs: 38.5 g, Sugar: 25.2 g, Protein: 2.7 g, Cholesterol: 36 mg

692. Key Lime Pie

Preparation time: 10 minutes | **Cooking time:** 30 minutes | **Servings:** 2

Ingredients:
For the Filling:
- 2 eggs
- ¼ cup condensed milk
- 2 tbsp fresh lime juice

For the Crust:
- 1 tbsp butter, melted
- ¼ cup crushed cracker crumbs

Directions:
Mix crushed cracker crumbs and melted butter.
Add crushed cracker mixture into the ramekin and press down with the back of the spoon.
Place the dehydrating tray in a multi-level air fryer basket and place basket in the instant pot.
Place ramekin on a dehydrating tray.
Seal pot with air fryer lid and select bake mode then set the temperature to 350 F and timer for 15 minutes.
Once done then remove ramekin from the pot and set aside to cool.
For the filling, in a small bowl whisk eggs with condensed milk and lime juice until smooth.
Pour egg mixture into baked crust.
Again, place the ramekin on a dehydrating tray.
Seal pot with air fryer lid and select bake mode then set the temperature to 350 F and timer for 15 minutes.
Serve and enjoy.

Nutrition:
Calories: 589, Fat: 29 g, Carbs: 67 g, Sugar: 47.8 g, Protein: 18.9 g, Cholesterol: 384 mg

693. Lemon Broccoli

Preparation time: 5 minutes | **Cooking time:** 7 minutes | **Servings:** 2

Ingredients:
- 1 cup water
- 900 g broccoli, tough parts removed and ends scored
- 4 tablespoons lemon juice
- Salt and pepper

Directions:
Add water to your instant pot and add in broccoli, drizzle with lemon juice and season with salt and pepper.
Lock lid and cook on high for 2 minutes and then release pressure naturally. Serve.

Nutrition:
Calories: 126, Fats: 4.3 g, Carbs: 21.6 g, Protein: 4.3 g, Fiber: 8.4 g

694. Baked Potato

Preparation time: 10 minutes | **Cooking time:** 40 minutes | **Servings:** 2

Ingredients:
- 2 medium potatoes, well-scrubbed
- 1 tablespoon olive oil
- 2 sheets aluminum foil
- ¼ cup sour cream
- Salt, to taste

Directions:
Arrange the trivet in the Instant Pot.
Rub the potatoes with olive oil and salt.
Wrap the potatoes tightly in the aluminum foil.
Transfer the potatoes on the trivet.
Set the instant pot to "Manual" and cook for 30 minutes at low pressure.
Release the pressure naturally and fill in the sour cream.

Nutrition:
Calories: 269, Fat: 13.2 g, Carbs: 34.7 g, Sugars: 2.5 g, Protein: 4.5 g

695. Cajun Spiced Pecans

Preparation time: 10 minutes | **Cooking time:** 30 minutes | **Servings:** 2

Ingredients:
- ½ lb. pecan halves
- 1 teaspoon dried basil
- 1 teaspoon dried thyme
- ½ tablespoon chili powder
- ¼ teaspoon garlic powder
- ¼ teaspoon cayenne pepper
- 1 tablespoon olive oil
- 1 teaspoon dried oregano

Salt, to taste

Directions:
Put all the ingredients in the Instant Pot.
Set the instant pot to "Manual" and cook for 20 minutes at low pressure.
Release the pressure naturally and serve.

Nutrition:
Calories: 345, Fat: 33.1 g, Carbs: 7.2 g, Sugars: 0.1 g, Protein: 4.4 g

696. Easy Instant Pot Cheesecake

Preparation time: 10 minutes | **Cooking time:** 30 minutes | **Servings:** 2

Ingredients:
- 3 8-oz. cream cheese, room temperature
- 3 eggs
- 1 cup white sugar
- ½ tablespoon vanilla extract

Directions:
Place a steamer in the Instant Pot and pour a cup of water.
In a bowl, mix all the ingredients until well combined.
Pour the batter into a springform pan that will fit inside the Instant Pot.
Put aluminum foil on top.
Place on the steamer and close the lid.
Press the Manual button and adjust the cooking time for 30 minutes.
Do natural pressure release.

Nutrition:
Calories: 264, Carbs: 3 g, Protein: 9.1 g, Fat: 15.8 g

697. Apple Streusel Dessert

Preparation time: 10 minutes | **Cooking time:** 30 minutes | **Servings:** 2

Ingredients:
- 6 cups sliced, peeled, and cored tart apples
- ¼ teaspoon ground allspice
- ¼ teaspoon ground nutmeg
- 2 tablespoons butter, softened
- ½ cup all-purpose flour
- 1 ¼ teaspoon ground cinnamon
- ¾ cup milk
- ¾ cup brown sugar
- 2 large eggs, beaten
- ⅓ cup packed brown sugar
- ½ cup sliced almonds
- 1 teaspoon vanilla extract
- 3 tablespoons cold butter

Directions:
Place a steamer rack in the Instant Pot and pour a cup of water.
Place the apples in a baking dish that will fit in the Instant Pot.
In a mixing bowl, combine flour, allspice, cinnamon, nutmeg, milk, butter, ¾ cup brown sugar, eggs, and vanilla extract. Mix until well combined.
Pour over the apples and toss to coat.
In another bowl, combine the brown sugar, butter, and almonds.
Sprinkle the mixture on top of the apples.
Cover the baking dish with aluminum foil.
Close the lid and press the Steam button.
Adjust the cooking time to 30 minutes.
Do natural pressure release.

Nutrition:
Calories: 378, Carbs: 57 g, Protein: 5 g, Fat: 16 g, Fiber: 3 g

698. Hot Fudge Sundae Cake

Preparation time: 10 minutes | **Cooking time:** 30 minutes | **Servings:** 2

Ingredients:
- 1 ¾ cups packed brown sugar, divided
- 5 tablespoons baking cocoa, divided
- ½ teaspoon salt
- ½ cup milk
- ⅛ teaspoon almond extract
- 4 teaspoon instant coffee granules
- 1 cup whole wheat flour
- 2 teaspoons baking powder
- 2 tablespoons butter, melted
- ½ teaspoon vanilla extract
- ½ cup boiling water

Directions:
Place a steamer in the Instant Pot and pour a cup of water.
In a bowl, mix all the ingredients until well combined.

Pour the batter into a dish that will fit inside the Instant Pot.
Put aluminum foil on top.
Place on the steamer and close the lid.
Press the Manual button and adjust the cooking time for 30 minutes.
Do natural pressure release.

Nutrition:
Calories: 255, Carbs: 48 g, Protein: 3 g, Fat: 7 g, Fiber: 1 g

699. American-Style Cheesecake

Preparation time: 45 minutes | **Cooking time:** 15 minutes | **Servings:** 2

Ingredients:

- 2 tablespoons golden caster sugar
- 3 tablespoons almonds, ground
- 1 cup creme fraiche
- 1 teaspoon vanilla extract
- 1 tablespoon arrowroot powder
- 12 oz. Philadelphia cheese
- 4 tablespoons granulated sugar
- 10 large graham crackers, crumbled
- ½ cup golden caster sugar
- ⅓ teaspoon cinnamon
- 1 tablespoon lemon zest
- 3 eggs
- 4 tablespoons butter

Directions:
Place a metal trivet and 1 cup of water in your Instant Pot. Spritz a baking pan with nonstick cooking spray.
Next, mix 4 tablespoons of granulated sugar, butter, crackers, almonds, and cinnamon into a sticky crust. Press the crust into the prepared baking pan.
In a mixing bowl, combine the Philadelphia cheese, vanilla extract, lemon zest, arrowroot powder, ½ cup of golden caster sugar, and eggs. Pour the filling mixture over the crust and cover it with a piece of foil.
Lower the baking pan onto the trivet.
Secure the lid. Choose the "Manual" mode and cook for 25 minutes at High pressure. Once cooking is complete, use a natural pressure release for 15 minutes, carefully remove the lid.

Lastly, beat the creme fraiche with 2 tablespoons of golden caster sugar. Spread this topping over the cheesecake right to the edges. Cover loosely with foil and refrigerate overnight.

Nutrition:
Calories: 340, Fat: 20.1 g, Carbs: 29.7 g, Protein: 10.7 g, Sugars: 18.1 g

700. Lemon and Blueberry Mousse

Preparation time: 35 minutes | **Cooking time:** 15 minutes | **Servings:** 2

Ingredients:

- ½ cup fresh lemon juice
- 1 ¼ cups sugar
- 1 large egg yolks
- 2 teaspoons cornstarch
- ¼ cup heavy whipping cream
- 1 stick butter, softened
- 1 tablespoon lemon zest, finely grated
- Mint leaves, for garnish
- A pinch of salt
- 3 eggs
- 6 tablespoons blueberries

Directions:
Beat the butter and sugar with an electric mixer. Gradually, add the eggs and yolks, mix until pale and smooth.
Add the lemon juice and lemon zest, add salt and cornstarch, mix to combine well. Pour the mixture into four jars, cover your jars with the lids.
Add 1 cup of water and a trivet to the Instant Pot. Lower the jars onto the trivet, secure the lid. Select "Manual" mode, High pressure and 15 minutes.
Once cooking is complete, use a natural release for 15 minutes, carefully remove the lid. Serve well-chilled, garnished with heavy whipping cream, blueberries, and mint leaves.

Nutrition:
Calories: 445, Fat: 30.1 g, Carbs: 40.6 g, Protein: 5.4 g, Sugars: 36.7 g

701. Grandma's Stuffed Apples

Preparation time: 25 minutes | **Cooking time:** 15 minutes | **Servings:** 2

Ingredients:
4 tablespoons currants
2 tablespoons coconut oil
⅓ cup granulated sugar
½ teaspoon cinnamon
⅓ cup walnuts, chopped
4 baking apples
½ teaspoon cardamom

Directions:
Add 1 ½ cups of water and a metal rack to the bottom of the inner pot.
Core the apples and use a melon baller to scoop out a bit of the flesh. Mix the remaining Ingredients. Divide the filling between your apples.
Secure the lid. Choose the "Steam" mode and cook for 15 minutes at High pressure. Once cooking is complete, use a quick pressure release, carefully remove the lid.
Serve with ice cream, if desired.

Nutrition:
Calories: 266, Fat: 11.5 g, Carbs: 43.9 g, Protein: 1.6 g, Sugars: 36 g

702. Cinnamon Cherry Crumble

Preparation time: 20 minutes | **Cooking time:** 15 minutes | **Servings:** 2

Ingredients:

1 box yellow cake mix	¼ teaspoon grated nutmeg
½ teaspoon ground cinnamon	½ teaspoon ground cardamom
½ cup coconut butter, melted	30 oz. cherry pie filling

Directions:
Add 1 cup of water and metal rack to the Instant Pot. Place the cherry pie filling in a pan.
Mix the remaining ingredients, spread the batter over the cherry pie filling evenly.
Secure the lid. Choose the "Manual" mode and cook for 10 minutes under High pressure. Once cooking is complete, use a natural pressure release, carefully remove the lid.
Serve with whipped topping. Enjoy!

Nutrition:
Calories: 499, Fat: 16.2 g, Carbs: 82 g, Protein: 4.5 g, Sugars: 24.3 g

703. Cranberry Sweet Risotto

Preparation time: 20 minutes | **Cooking time:** 15 minutes | **Servings:** 2

Ingredients:

½ cup dried cranberries	A pinch of salt
A pinch of grated nutmeg	2 eggs, beaten
1 teaspoon vanilla extract	¼ teaspoon cardamom
2 cups milk	⅓ cup maple syrup
1 cup white rice	1 ½ cups water

Directions:
Place the rice, water, and salt in the inner pot of your Instant Pot.
Secure the lid. Choose the "Manual" mode and cook for 3 minutes at High pressure. Once cooking is complete, use a natural pressure release for 10 minutes, carefully remove the lid. Add in the milk, maple syrup, eggs, vanilla extract, cardamom, and nutmeg, stir to combine well.
Press the "Sauté" button and cook, stirring frequently, until your pudding starts to boil. Press the "Cancel' button. Stir in the dried cranberries.
Pudding will thicken as it cools.

Nutrition:
Calories: 403, Fat: 6.6 g, Carbs: 75.6 g, Protein: 9.8 g, Sugars: 31.9 g

704. Brown Rice Pudding

Preparation time: 10 minutes | **Cooking time:** 20 minutes | **Servings:** 2

Ingredients:

1 ½ cups almond milk	½ tsp vanilla
¾ cup brown rice	1 cup of water
1 ½ tsp ground cinnamon	Pinch of salt

Directions:
Add rice, cinnamon, vanilla, water, almond milk, and salt into the instant pot and stir well.
Seal pot with lid and cook on porridge mode for 20 minutes.

Once done then allow to release pressure naturally then open the lid.
Stir well and serve.

Nutrition:
Calories: 340, Fat: 22.4 g, Carbs: 32.9 g, Sugar: 3.1 g, Protein: 4.8 g

705. Cranberry Stuffed Apples

Preparation time: 10 minutes | **Cooking time:** 30 minutes | **Servings:** 2

Ingredients:
- 5 medium apples, cored
- 2 tablespoons walnuts, chopped
- ¼ teaspoon ground cinnamon
- ⅓ cup fresh cranberries, chopped
- ¼ cup packed brown sugar
- ⅛ teaspoon ground nutmeg

Directions:
Place a steamer basket in the Instant Pot and pour a cup of water
Place the cored apples in a baking dish that will fit in the Instant Pot.
In a mixing bowl, combine the cranberries, walnuts, sugar, cinnamon, and nutmeg.
Spoon the mixture into the hollowed center of the apples.
Place an aluminum foil on top of the baking dish.
Place on the steamer rack.
Close the lid and press the Steam button.
Adjust the cooking time to 30 minutes.
Do natural pressure release.

Nutrition:
Calories: 136, Carbs: 31 g, Protein: 1 g, Fat: 2 g, Fiber: 4 g

706. Gingerbread Pudding Cake

Preparation time: 15 minutes | **Cooking time:** 30 minutes | **Servings:** 2

Ingredients:
- 1 cup water
- ¼ cup butter, softened
- 1 large egg white
- 1 ¼ cups whole wheat flour
- ½ cup molasses
- ¼ cup granulated sugar
- 1 teaspoon vanilla extract
- ¾ teaspoon baking soda
- ¼ teaspoon salt
- ½ teaspoon ground cinnamon
- ¼ teaspoon ground allspice
- ½ teaspoon ground ginger
- ⅛ teaspoon ground nutmeg
- ½ cup chopped pecans

Directions:
Place a steamer in the Instant Pot and pour a cup of water.
Combine water and molasses in a mixing bowl. Stir in the softened butter, granulated sugar, egg white, and vanilla. Mix until fluffy.
In another bowl, combine the flour, baking soda, and salt. Add the ginger, cinnamon, nutmeg, and allspice.
Mix the wet ingredients to the dry ingredients until well combined.
Fold in the pecans.
Pour into a baking dish that will fit inside the Instant Pot and sprinkle with top brown sugar.
Put aluminum foil on top of the baking dish.
Place on the steamer rack and press the Steam button.
Adjust the cooking time to 30 minutes.
Do natural pressure release.
Allow to cool before slicing.

Nutrition:
Calories: 431, Carbs: 48 g, Protein: 3 g, Fat: 25 g, Fiber: 1 g

707. Tom Collins Cocktail

Preparation time: 10 minutes | **Cooking time:** 1 hour | **Servings:** 2

Ingredients:
- 7 cups gin
- 2 cups lemon rind
- Soda water, to serve with
- 1 cup lemon juice
- 1 ½ cups granulated sugar

Directions:
Preheat Sous Vide to 131°F.
In a large Sous vide bag, combine gin, lemon juice, lemon rind, and sugar.
Fold the edges of the bag few times and clip to the side of your pot.
Cook the cocktail 1 hour.
Finishing steps:
Strain the cocktail into a large glass jug.

Place aside to cool completely before use.
Serve over ice and finish off with a soda water.
Garnish the cocktail with lemon rind or fresh thyme.

Nutrition:
Calories: 270, Fat: 2 g, Carb: 12 g, Fiber: 6 g, Protein: 3 g

708. Cherry Manhattan

Preparation time: 10 minutes | **Cooking time:** 1 hour | **Servings:** 2

Ingredients:
For the Bourbon Infusion:
- 2 cups bourbon
- ¼ cup raw cacao nibs
- 1 cup dried cherries
- 4oz. sweet vermouth
- Chocolate bitters, as desired

Directions:
Make the infusion, preheat Sous Vide to 122°F.
In a Sous Vide bag combine bourbon, cacao nibs, and cherries.
Seal the bag, and cook 1 hour
Remove the bag from the water bath and let cool.
Strain the content into a jar.
Fill the tall glasses with ice.
Add chocolate bitters (3 dashes per serving) and ⅛ of the infused bourbon.
Skewer the Sous vide cherries and garnish.

Nutrition:
Calories 163, Fat 3 g, Carb 2 g, Fiber 6 g, Protein 4 g

709. Caramel Macchiato Cake

Preparation time: 10 minutes | **Cooking time:** 30 minutes | **Servings:** 2

Ingredients:
- 15-oz. of yellow cake mix
- ½ cup vegetable oil
- Pinch of salt
- 2 tablespoons of butter
- 3 eggs
- ¾ cup of brown sugar
- 1 cup of international delight mix (caramel macchiato
- 1 ½ cups of boiling water

Directions:
Combine the cake mix with oil, caramel macchiato, and eggs in mixing bowl. Mix until smooth. Pour the batter into a greased baking pan, and cover top of pan with foil. Add 1 cup of water into instant pot, and place trivet in pot. Place the baking pan on top of trivet and set to Manual on high for a cook time of 50-minutes. When the cook time is completed, release the pressure naturally for 15-minutes. Remove the cake and allow to sit for 30-minutes on wire rack to cool. Serve cake with some warm caramel sauce.

Nutrition:
Calories: 321, Fat: 2.5 g, Carbs: 36 g, Protein: 6.2 g

710. Apple Peach Cobbler

Preparation time: 10 minutes | **Cooking time:** 30 minutes | **Servings:** 2

Ingredients:
- ¾ cup cornmeal
- 1 cup granulated sugar, divided
- 1 ¼ cups milk
- 1 ½ cups almond flour
- 3 lbs. peaches, sliced
- ¾ cup apple butter
- Pinch of salt
- ¼ cup of bourbon
- ½ cup butter, melted

Directions:
To make the filling, toss ¼ cup of sugar, peach, bourbon, apple butter and pinch of salt into a mixing bowl. Spread the filling on the bottom of the baking pan. Mix the flour with ¾ cup sugar, cornmeal, and pinch of salt in mixing bowl. Add milk, followed by melted butter, mixing continuously. Spread the flour mix over the peach filling. Close the pot lid and set to Manual on high for a cook time of 45minutes. When the cook time is completed, release the pressure naturally for 15-minutes. Serve warm.

Nutrition:
Calories: 311, Fat: 2.8 g, Carbs: 32 g, Protein: 6.4g

711. Cheesy Asparagus

Preparation time: 8-10 minutes | **Cooking time:** 3 minutes | **Servings:** 2

Ingredients:
½ lb. asparagus spears
5-oz. sliced prosciutto

Directions:
Wrap the prosciutto slices around the asparagus. Switch on the pot after placing it on a clean and dry platform.
Pour 2 cups water into the pot. Arrange the trivet inside it, arrange the asparagus over the trivet.
Close the pot by closing the top lid. Also, ensure to seal the valve.
Press "Manual" cooking function and set cooking time to 3 minutes. It will start cooking after a few minutes. Let the pot mix cook under pressure until the timer reads zero.
Press "Cancel" cooking function and press "Natural release (NPR)" setting. It will take 8-10 minutes for natural pressure release.
Open the pot and serve warm. Enjoy it with your loved one!

Nutrition:
Calories: 124, Fat: 4 g, Carbs: 5.5 g, Fiber: 2 g, Protein: 17 g

712. Oregano Black Bean

Preparation time: 5-8 minutes | **Cooking time:** 20 minutes | **Servings:** 2

Ingredients:

15 cherry tomatoes, sliced in half	1 teaspoon coriander
1 teaspoon oregano	½ teaspoon chili flakes
1 teaspoon cumin	1 teaspoon sea salt
2 tablespoons vegetable oil	1 teaspoon paprika
1 ½ cups dry black beans	3 garlic cloves, minced
1 large yellow onion	2 cubes vegetable bouillon

Directions:
Take Instant Pot and carefully arrange it over a clean, dry kitchen platform. Turn on the appliance.
In the cooking pot area, add beans and water to the pressure cooker and dissolve in bouillon cubes.
Close the pot lid and seal the valve to avoid any leakage. Find and press "Manual" cooking setting and set cooking time to 15 minutes.
Allow the recipe ingredients to cook for the set time and after that, the timer reads "zero".
Press "Cancel" and press "NPR" setting for natural pressure release. It takes 8-10 times for all inside pressure to release.
Open the pot and remove beans from the pot.
Place oil in the pot and using sauté setting, cook onion 3 minutes. Add garlic and cook 1 minute.
Put all remaining ingredients including the beans in the pot. Stir gently.
Close the pot lid and seal the valve to avoid any leakage. Find and press "Manual" cooking setting and set cooking time to 1 minutes.
Allow the recipe ingredients to cook for the set time, and after that, the timer reads "zero".
Press "Cancel" and press "NPR" setting for natural pressure release. It takes 8-10 times for all inside pressure to release.
Open the pot and arrange the cooked recipe in serving plates. Enjoy the vegan recipe!

Nutrition:
Calories: 356, Fat: 11 g, Carbs: 41.5 g, Fiber: 12 g, Protein: 28 g

713. Coconut Pudding

Preparation time: 10 minutes | **Cooking time:** 3 minutes | **Servings:** 2

Ingredients:

1 ⅔ cups coconut milk, unsweetened	1 tablespoon gelatin
6 tablespoons swerve	3 egg yolks
½ teaspoon vanilla extract	

Directions:
In a bowl, mix gelatin with 1 tablespoon coconut milk, stir well and leave aside for now.
Set your instant pot on saute mode, add milk and heat. Add swerve, egg yolks, vanilla extract and gelatin, stir well, cover pot and cook on High pressure for 2 minutes.
Divide everything into 4 ramekins and serve them cold.
Enjoy!

Nutrition:
Calories: 140, Fat: 2 g, Fiber: 1 g, Carbs: 3 g, Protein: 2 g

714. Sriracha Turkey Bites

Preparation time: 10 minutes | **Cooking time:** 2 hours | **Servings:** 2

Ingredients:

- 2 lbs. turkey breast, skinless, boneless and cubed
- 1 tablespoon soy sauce
- 2 teaspoons sriracha sauce
- ½ teaspoon chili powder
- 1 tablespoon olive oil
- 2 tablespoons tomato sauce
- ¼ cup chives, chopped
- Salt and black pepper to the taste

Directions:
In a sous vide bag, combine the turkey with the oil, sriracha sauce and the other ingredients, toss, seal the bag, submerge in the preheated water oven, cook at 146°F for 2 hours, arrange on a platter and serve as an appetizer.

Nutrition:
Calories: 320, Fat: 23 g, Carbs: 12 g, Protein: 37 g

715. Beet Salsa

Preparation time: 10 minutes | **Cooking time:** 1 hour | **Servings:** 2

Ingredients:

- 1 lb. red beets, peeled and cubed
- 1 cup cherry tomatoes, halved
- 2 tablespoons olive oil
- ½ teaspoon herbs de Provence
- 1 tablespoon chives, chopped
- 1 cup green olives, pitted and halved
- Juice of 1 lime
- Salt and black pepper to the taste
- 2 red onions, chopped

Directions:
In a large sous vide bag, combine the beets with the olives and the other ingredients, toss, seal the bag, introduce in the preheated water oven and cook at 185°F for 1 hour.
Serve as a snack.

Nutrition:
Calories: 320, Fat: 8 g, Fiber: 4 g, Carbs: 12 g, Protein: 10 g

716. Balsamic Salmon Bites

Preparation time: 10 minutes | **Cooking time:** 20 minutes | **Servings:** 2

Ingredients:

- 1 lb. salmon fillets, boneless and cubed
- ½ tablespoon honey
- 1 tablespoon parsley, chopped
- 2 tablespoons olive oil
- 2 tablespoons balsamic vinegar

Directions:
In a sous vide bag, mix the salmon with the oil and the other ingredients, toss, seal the bag and cook in the water oven at 170°F for 20 minutes. Arrange the bites on a platter and serve as an appetizer.

Nutrition:
Calories: 222, Fat: 2 g, Fiber: 5 g, Carbs: 4 g, Protein: 6 g

717. Lemon Gelatin Cream

Preparation time: 5 minutes | **Cooking time:** 15 minutes | **Servings:** 2

Ingredients:

- 1 tsp. Gelatin
- 4 oz. Strawberries
- ½ tbsp. Lemon juice
- ½ cup Heavy cream
- 8 oz. Cream cheese
- 2 tbsp. Water
- ¼ tsp. Sugar

Directions:
Set all ingredients in your blender and start blending.
Split the blend into 6 portions and set them in your air fryer.
Cook at 360°F for 15 minutes.
Put it on the fridge and eat it until it is cold.

Nutrition:
Calories: 202, Fat: 8 g, Fiber: 2 g, Carbs: 6 g, Protein: 7 g

718. Caramel Cream

Preparation time: 15 minutes | **Cooking time:** 20 minutes | **Servings:** 2

Ingredients:
- 2 tbsp. Butter
- 3 tbsp. Coffee
- 1/3 cup Sugar
- 8 oz. Cream cheese
- 3 pcs. Eggs
- 1 tbsp. Caramel syrup

Directions:
Set all ingredients in your blender and start blending.
Split the mixture among 6 portions and put it in the fryer.
Cook at 370°F
Bake for 10 minutes.
Let the heat subside and then put in the fridge prior to eating.

Nutrition:
Calories: 234, Fat: 12 g, Fiber: 4 g, Carbs: 11 g, Protein: 5 g

719. Chocolate Pudding

Preparation time: 20 minutes | **Cooking time:** 14 minutes | **Servings:** 2

Ingredients:
- 1/2 cup butter
- 1/4 cup caster sugar
- 2 teaspoons fresh orange rind, finely grated
- 2 tablespoons self-rising flour
- 2/3 cup dark chocolate, chopped
- 2 medium eggs
- 1/4 cup fresh orange juice

Directions:
In a microwave-safe bowl, add the butter, and chocolate. Microwave on high heat for about 2 minutes or until melted completely, stirring after every 30 seconds.
Remove from microwave and stir the mixture until smooth.
Add the sugar, and eggs and whisk until frothy.
Add the orange rind and juice, followed by flour and mix until well combined.
Set the temperature of air fryer to 355°F. Grease 4 ramekins.
Divide mixture into the prepared ramekins about 3/4 full.
Air fry for about 12 minutes.
Remove from the air fryer and set aside to completely cool before serving.
Serve warm.

Nutrition:
Calories: 454, Carbs: 34.2 g, Protein: 5.7 g, Fat: 33.6 g, Sugar: 28.4 g, Sodium: 217 mg

720. Vanilla Soufflé

Preparation time: 15 minutes | **Cooking time:** 39 minutes | **Servings:** 2

Ingredients:
- 1/4 cup butter, softened
- 1/2 cup plus 2 tablespoons sugar, divided
- 3 teaspoons vanilla extract, divided
- 5 egg whites
- 2 tablespoons powdered sugar plus extra for dusting
- 1/4 cup all-purpose flour
- 1 cup milk
- 4 egg yolks
- 1 teaspoon cream of tartar

Directions:
In a bowl, add the butter, and flour and mix until a smooth paste forms.
In a medium pan, mix 1/2 cup of sugar and milk over medium-low heat and cook for about 3 minutes or until the sugar is dissolved, stirring continuously.
Add the flour mixture, whisking continuously and simmer for about 3-4 minutes or until mixture becomes thick.
Remove from the heat and stir in 1 teaspoon of vanilla extract.
Set aside for about 10 minutes to cool.
In a bowl, mix the egg yolks and 1 teaspoon of vanilla extract.
Add the egg yolk mixture into milk mixture and mix until well combined.
In another bowl, add the egg whites, cream of tartar, remaining sugar, and vanilla extract and whisk until stiff peaks form.
Fold the egg whites mixture into milk mixture.

Set the temperature of air fryer to 330°F. Grease 6 ramekins and sprinkle each with a pinch of sugar.
Place mixture evenly into the prepared ramekins and with the back of a spoon, smooth the top surface.
Arrange the ramekins into an air fryer basket in 2 batches.
Air fry for about 14-16 minutes.
Remove from air fryer and set aside to cool slightly.
Sprinkle with the powdered sugar and serve warm.

Nutrition:
Calories: 250, Carbs: 29.8 g, Protein: 6.8 g, Fat: 11.6 g, Sugar: 25 g, Sodium: 107 mg

721. Chocolate Soufflé

Preparation time: 15 minutes | **Cooking time:** 16 minutes | **Servings:** 2

Ingredients:

3 oz. semi-sweet chocolate, chopped	¼ cup butter
2 eggs, egg yolks and whites separated	3 tablespoons sugar
½ teaspoon pure vanilla extract	2 tablespoons all-purpose flour
1 teaspoon powdered sugar plus extra for dusting	

Directions:
In a microwave-safe bowl, put the butter, and chocolate. Microwave on high heat for about 2 minutes or until melted completely, stirring after every 30 seconds.
Remove from microwave and stir the mixture until smooth.
In another bowl, add the egg yolks and whisk well.
Add the sugar, and vanilla extract and whisk well.
Add the chocolate mixture and mix until well combined.
Add the flour and mix well.
In a clean glass bowl, add the egg whites and whisk until soft peaks form.
Fold the whipped egg whites in 3 portions into the chocolate mixture.

Set the temperature of air fryer to 330 °F. Grease 2 ramekins and sprinkle each with a pinch of sugar.
Place mixture evenly into the prepared ramekins and with the back of a spoon, smooth the top surface.
Arrange the ramekins into an air fryer basket.
Air fry for about 14 minutes.
Remove from air fryer and set aside to cool slightly.
Sprinkle with the powdered sugar and serve warm.

Nutrition:
Calories: 569, Carbs: 54.1 g, Protein: 6.9 g, Fat: 38.8 g, Sugar: 42.2 g, Sodium: 225 mg

722. Chili Cake Chocolate

Preparation time: 20 minutes | **Cooking time:** 1 hour 15 minutes | **Servings:** 2

Ingredients:

½ lb. chocolate chips	4oz. unsalted butter
2 tablespoons cocoa powder	4 large eggs
¼ cup brown sugar	½ teaspoon chili powder

Directions:
Prepare your Sous-vide water bath to a temperature of 115 °F.
Put the butter and the chocolate chips in a cooking pouch and seal the pouch.
Place the pouch in the preheated water bath and let it cook for 15 minutes.
Once done, remove the pouch from the water bath.
Increase the sous vide temperature to 170°F.
Apply cooking spray to 6 4ox mason jars.
In a bowl, whisk the eggs and brown sugar together with cocoa powder, chili powder and chocolate.
Pour the egg mixture into the jars and seal it.
Lower the jars into the water bath and cook for 1 hour.
Once done, place the jars on a wire rack to cool.
Serve in a bowl with raspberry ice cream.

Nutrition:
Calories: 413, Fat: 31 g, Carb: 28 g, Fiber: 9 g, Protein: 6 g

723. Chip Cookies Chocolate

Preparation time: 30 minutes | **Cooking time:** 30 minutes | **Servings:** 2 cookies

Ingredients:

- 3 tablespoons unsalted softened butter
- 1 pinch salt
- 1 teaspoon vanilla paste
- ½ cup mini chocolate chips
- ½ teaspoon baking powder
- ½ cup flour
- ⅓ cup granulated sugar
- 1 small egg

Directions:
Prepare your Sous-vide water bath to a temperature of 195 °F.
Mix the flour with salt and baking powder in a bowl.
Add vanilla paste and egg and beat until smooth.
Combine the egg mixture with the flour mixture and stir thoroughly.
Fold the mini chocolate chips.
On a clean surface, roll the dough in a baking paper.
Cut with a cookie cutter.
Put the cookies in 2 sous vide bags and seal the bags after removing the excess air.
Immerse the bags in the water bath and cook for 30 minutes.
When ready, remove the bags from the water and remove the cookies.
Serve!

Nutrition:
Calories: 44, Fat: 4 g, Carb: 7 g, Fiber: 1 g, Protein: 9 g

724. Mousse Strawberry

Preparation time: 10 minutes | **Cooking time:** 45 minutes | **Servings:** 2

Ingredients:

- 1 ½ tablespoons lemon juice
- 3 tablespoons fine sugar
- ½ cup heavy cream
- ½ lb. strawberries
- ½ teaspoon vanilla paste

Directions:
Prepare your Sous-vide water bath to a temperature of 180°F.
Mix the lemon juice, sugar and strawberries in a bowl and transfer the mixture in a cooking pouch.
Vacuum seal the pouch and immerse it in the preheated water bath.
Cook for 45 minutes.
When ready, remove the pouch and remove the strawberries from the cooking pouch.
In a food processor, blend the mixture until it becomes smooth.
In a bowl, thoroughly mix the vanilla and the heavy cream.
Add the puree into the vanilla mixture and stir to mix.
Distribute the mouse amongst 4 bowl and refrigerate for one hour.
Serve!

Nutrition:
Calories: 105, Fat: 8 g, Carb: 19 g, Fiber: 2 g, Protein: 7 g

725. Creme Chocolate de Pots

Preparation time: 30 minutes | **Cooking time:** 6 hours | **Servings:** 2

Ingredients:

- 3 cups half-and-half
- ½ lb. semisweet chocolate, melted
- ¼ cup sugar
- 6 egg yolks
- ¼ teaspoon salt

Directions:
Prepare your Sous-vide water bath to a temperature of 195 °F.
Put all the ingredients into a mason jars and seal the lids such that air can escape during cooking.
Gently lower the jar into the water bath and cook for 6 hours.
Once cooked, remove the jars from the water bath.
Serve the contents on a serving bowl either chilled or warm.

Nutrition:
Calories: 615, Fat: 465 g, Carb: 519 g, Fiber: 3 g, Protein: 18 g

726. Cookie Caramel Dough

Preparation time: 10 minutes | **Cooking time:** 10 minutes | **Servings:** 2

Ingredients:
- ¾ cup brown sugar
- ½ cup softened butter
- 1 ¼ cups almond flour
- 1 teaspoon molasses
- ½ cup salted caramel chips
- 1 medium egg

Directions:
Prepare your Sous-vide water bath to a temperature of 171°F.
Whisk the butter, egg, molasses, sugar, and almonds in a bowl until smooth and well mixed.
Put the caramel chips and thoroughly mix.
Refrigerate the mixture for 60 minutes.
Once cooked, remove the dough from the refrigerator and form into 12 balls.
Put the balls into cooking pouches and immerse into the preheated water.
Cook for 10 minutes.
Remove the pouch from the water bath and refrigerate for 10 minutes.
Serve and enjoy.

Nutrition:
Calories: 253, Fat: 19 g, Carb: 19 g, Fiber: 6 g, Protein: 4 g

727. Rice Pudding

Preparation time: 30 minutes | **Cooking time:** 2 hours | **Servings:** 2

Ingredients:
- 3 cups milk
- ½ cup brown or raw sugar
- 2 teaspoons cinnamon
- ½ cup dark rum
- ½ cup raisins
- 2 cups uncooked rice

Directions:
Prepare your Sous-vide water bath to a temperature of 140°F.
Leave the raisins in water over night. Do away with the rum.
Put the milk, raisins, cinnamon, rice and sugar in a cooking pouch and vacuum seal the pouch.
Immerse the pouch in the water bath and cook for 2 hours.
Once cooked, remove the pouch from the bath and stir the contents.
Serve and enjoy chilled or warm.

Nutrition:
Calories: 465, Fat: 41 g, Carb: 803 g, Fiber: 8 g, Protein: 62 g

728. Banoffee Sweeten Pie

Preparation time: 40 minutes | **Cooking time:** 20 hours | **Servings:** 2

Ingredients:
- 1 can sweeten condensed milk
- 1 prepared graham cracker crust
- 6 bananas, sliced
- Whipped cream for serving
- ¼ cup butter
- ½ cup brown sugar

Directions:
Prepare your Sous-vide water bath to a temperature of 185°F.
In a large bowl, mix the butter, condensed milk and sugar.
Pour the mixture into a mason jar and attach the lid and seal it such that steam can still pass through it during cooking.
Lower the jar gently into the preheated water bath and let it cook for 20 hours.
Remove the jar from the water bath once cooked.
To prepare the pie, spread all the slices of banana on the toffee.
Drizzle with whipped cream.
Serve and enjoy!

Nutrition:
Calories: 433, Fat: 160 g, Carb: 755 g, Fiber: 7 g, Protein: 57 g

729. Frozen Yogurt Spiced

Preparation time: 10 minutes | **Cooking time:** 24 hours | **Servings:** 2

Ingredients:
- ½ cup light honey
- 3 tablespoons yogurt
- 4 cups milk
- 1 teaspoon vanilla paste
- ¼ cup fine sugar
- ¼ teaspoon nutmeg
- ½ teaspoon cinnamon

Directions:
Prepare your Sous-vide water bath to a temperature of 115°F.
Put the milk in a pan and heat to 180°F.
Transfer the milk into a canning jar and chill to 120°F.
Once chilled, add the vanilla paste, yogurt and spices.
Attach the lid and seal it such that steam can escape during cooking period.
Immerse the jars in the water bath and let it cook for 24 hours.
Once cooked, remove the jar from the water bath and churn in ice cream machine.
Serve and enjoy with fresh fruits.

Nutrition:
Calories: 154, Fat: 6 g, Carb: 33 g, Fiber: 1 g, Protein: 4 g

730. Vanilla Brownies

Preparation time: 20 minutes | **Cooking time:** 3 hours | **Servings:** 2

Ingredients:
- ½ cup cocoa powder
- 1 teaspoon vanilla paste
- 4 large eggs
- 1 teaspoon espresso coffee granules
- 1 teaspoon baking powder
- 1 ¼ cup flour
- 1 ½ cups granulated sugar
- ½ cup butter
- 10oz. quality dark chocolate, melted

Directions:
Prepare your Sous-vide water bath to a temperature of 186°F.
Get a bowl, add the butter and sugar and combine well.
Add the vanilla paste, eggs and melted chocolate.
Add the coco powder, baking powder and cocoa powder and stir well.
Distribute the batter amongst the half pint jars.
Attach the lids and seal properly.
Immerse the jars into the water bath and cook for 3 hours.
Once done, remove the jars from the water bath.
Keep the brownies to cool.
Run a knife in the jars to remove the content to a platter.
Serve and enjoy!

Nutrition:
Calories: 303, Fat: 11 g, Carb: 49 g, Fiber: 5 g, Protein: 9 g

731. Pomegranate Fudge

Preparation time: 2 hours | **Cooking time:** 5 minutes | **Servings:** 2

Ingredients:
- ½ cup almond milk
- 5 tablespoons cocoa powder
- ½ cup pomegranate seeds
- 1 teaspoon almond extract
- ½ cup chopped almonds

Directions:
Heat up the milk in a pan over medium-low heat then add the cocoa, stir and cook for 5 minutes.
Add the rest of the ingredients, stir and pour this into a lined baking pan, spread and sprinkle with the rest of the nuts.
Cover and keep in the fridge for a few hours before serving.

Nutrition:
Calories: 178, Fat: 4.4 g, Fiber: 4 g, Carbs: 6 g, Protein: 7.1 g

732. Dates and Almonds Cake

Preparation time: 5 hours | **Cooking time:** 0 minutes | **Servings:** 2

Ingredients:
For the crust:
- ½ cup dates, pitted
- ½ teaspoon vanilla extract
- 1 tablespoon water
- ½ cup almonds

For the cake:
- 3 cups almonds, soaked for 8 hours
- 4 tablespoons stevia
- 1 cup blueberries
- 1 tablespoon coconut oil, melted

Directions:
In your food processor, mix dates with water, vanilla and almonds and pulse well. Transfer the dough to a work surface and roll it out then transfer to a lined cake pan.
In your blender, mix the almonds and the other ingredients for the cake and blend well.

Spread evenly on the crust and place cake in the freezer for 5 hours, slice and serve.

Nutrition:
Calories: 330, Fat: 7.2 g, Fiber: 5 g, Carbs: 12 g, Protein: 4 g

733. Grape Cream

Preparation time: 10 minutes | **Cooking time:** 0 minutes | **Servings:** 2

Ingredients:
- 1 lbs. grapes
- 1 teaspoon vanilla extract
- ½ lb. coconut cream
- 1 tablespoon stevia

Directions:
In your food processor, puree the grapes with the cream and the other ingredients, divide into small cups and serve.

Nutrition:
Calories: 120, Fat: 9 g, Fiber: 3 g, Carbs: 10 g, Protein: 3 g

734. Lime Parfait

Preparation time: 10 minutes | **Cooking time:** 0 minutes | **Servings:** 2

Ingredients:
- 4 cups coconut cream
- 2 tablespoons lime juice
- 2 avocados, peeled and chopped
- 3 tablespoons stevia
- 2 teaspoons lime zest, grated
- 1 tablespoon mint, chopped

Directions:
In a bowl, combine the cream with stevia and the other ingredients except the avocados and stir.
Divide the avocado pieces into small cups, add the coconut mix in each and serve.

Nutrition:
Calories: 200, Fat: 3 g, Fiber: 4 g, Carbs: 15 g, Protein: 10 g

735. Peach Pie

Preparation time: 10 minutes | **Cooking time:** 20 minutes | **Servings:** 2

Ingredients:
- 4 peaches, peeled and sliced
- 2 tablespoons flaxseed mixed with 3 tablespoons water
- ½ cup almond milk
- ¼ cup coconut cream
- ½ teaspoon coconut sugar
- 1 tablespoon avocado oil
- ½ cup almond flour

Directions:
In a bowl, mix peaches with sugar and stir. In another bowl, mix the rest of the ingredients stir well and pour into a greased pie plate. Add the peaches mix on top, spread, bake in the oven at 400°F for 20 minutes, slice and serve.

Nutrition:
Calories: 199, Fat: 4 g, Fiber: 3 g, Carbs: 12 g, Protein: 9 g

736. Coconut and Cocoa Brownies

Preparation time: 10 minutes | **Cooking time:** 30 minutes | **Servings:** 2

Ingredients:
- 4 tablespoons cocoa powder
- ½ cup hot water
- ⅔ cup coconut sugar
- ½ cup walnuts, chopped
- 1 teaspoon baking soda
- 2 tablespoons flaxseed mixed with 3 tablespoons water
- 1 teaspoon vanilla extract
- 1 and ½ cups almond flour
- Cooking spray

Directions:
In a bowl, mix the cocoa with the flaxseed and the other ingredients stir well, pour this into a cake pan greased with cooking spray, spread well, bake in the oven for 30 minutes, cool down, slice and serve.

Nutrition:
Calories: 244, Fat: 5.5 g, Fiber: 4 g, Carbs: 9 g, Protein: 8.2 g

737. Mango and Cranberries Tart

Preparation time: 10 minutes | **Cooking time:** 25 minutes | **Servings:** 2

Ingredients:
- 2 mangoes, peeled and cubed
- ½ cup cranberries, dried
- 1 teaspoon vanilla extract
- ¼ cup natural apple juice
- 2 teaspoons coconut sugar
- ¼ teaspoon almond extract

For the crust:
- 1 and ¼ cup almond flour
- 3 tablespoons coconut oil, melted
- 2 teaspoons stevia
- ¼ cup cold water

Directions:
In a bowl, mix the flour with stevia and the other ingredients for the crust, stir and knead until you obtain a dough, flatten it, roll into a circle and transfer to a tart pan.
In a separate bowl, combine the mangoes with the apple juice and rest of the ingredients for the filling stir and spread over the crust.
Introduce the pan in the oven, bake at 375°F for 25 minutes, cool it down, slice and serve.

Nutrition:
Calories: 182, Fat: 5 g, Fiber: 4 g, Carbs: 15 g, Protein: 5.7 g

738. Avocado Cake

Preparation time: 10 minutes | **Cooking time:** 25 minutes | **Servings:** 2

Ingredients:
- 3 cups almond flour
- 1 tablespoon vanilla extract
- 1 cup avocado, peeled, pitted and mashed
- 2 cups coconut cream
- 4 tablespoons stevia
- 3 tablespoons cocoa powder
- 2 and ½ teaspoons baking soda
- ½ cup coconut oil, melted

Directions:
In a bowl, combine the flour with the stevia and the other ingredients, stir well and pour into a cake pan.
Introduce in the oven at 350 °F, bake for 25 minutes, leave the cake to cool down, slice and serve.

Nutrition:
Calories: 200, Fat: 47.1 g, Fiber: 2.7 g, Carbs: 12 g, Protein: 6 g

739. Blueberry Pancakes

Preparation time: 10 minutes | **Cooking time:** 10 minutes | **Servings:** 2

Ingredients:
- 1 cup coconut flour
- 1 teaspoon baking soda
- 2 tablespoons flaxseeds
- 2 tablespoons stevia
- ½ cup blueberries
- Cooking spray
- ¼ cup almond flour
- 1 teaspoon baking powder
- ½ teaspoon nutmeg, ground
- ½ cup natural orange juice
- ¼ cup water

Directions:
In a bowl, combine the flour with the baking soda, powder and the other ingredients except the cooking spray and stir well.
Heat up a pan over medium-high heat, grease with cooking spray, drop some of the batter, spread, cook the pancake until it's golden on both sides and transfer to a plate.
Repeat with the rest of the batter and serve your pancakes warm.

Nutrition:
Calories: 232, Fat: 5.1 g, Fiber: 6 g, Carbs: 5.2 g, Protein: 4 g

740. Avocado Fudge

Preparation time: 2 hours | **Cooking time:** 7 minutes | **Servings:** 2

Ingredients:
- 1 cup almond milk
- 2 cups coconut sugar
- 1 teaspoon vanilla extract
- ½ cup coconut butter, soft
- 2 cups avocado, peeled, pitted and mashed

Directions:
Heat up a pan with the milk over medium heat, add the coconut butter and the other ingredients, stir and cook for 7 minutes.
Pour this into a lined square pan, spread well, keep in the fridge for 2 hours, cut into small squares and serve.

Nutrition:
Calories: 214, Fat: 5.3 g, Fiber: 5 g, Carbs: 16 g, Protein: 3 g

741. Orange Cake

Preparation time: 10 minutes | **Cooking time:** 25 minutes | **Servings:** 2

Ingredients:
- 6 eggs
- 1 ½ cups water
- 1 teaspoon baking powder
- 4 tablespoons swerve
- 2 oz. stevia
- 4 oz. coconut yogurt, unsweetened
- 1 orange, cut into quarters
- 1 teaspoon vanilla extract
- 9 oz. almond meal
- 2 tablespoons orange zest
- 4 oz. cream cheese

Directions:
In your food processor, mix orange with almond meal, swerve, eggs, baking powder and vanilla extract. Pulse well and transfer to a cake pan. Cover pan with foil.
Add the water to your instant pot, add steamer basket and place cake pan inside the basket. Cover and cook on High pressure for 25 minutes.
In a bowl, stir cream cheese with orange zest, coconut yogurt and stevia.
Spread this frosting over cake, slice and serve it. Enjoy!

Nutrition:
Calories: 170, Fat: 13 g, Fiber: 2 g, Carbs: 4 g, Protein: 4 g

742. Watermelon Mint Vodka Infusion

Preparation time: 20 minutes | **Cooking time:** 2 hours | **Servings:** 2

Ingredients:
- 1 cup vodka
- 2-3 sprigs fresh mint
- 1 cup watermelon, cubed

Directions:
Preheat the water bath to 140°F.
Seal all ingredients in a bag. Place in water bath and cook 2 hours.
Strain solids from the infusion. Use in your favorite martini recipe.

Nutrition:
Calories: 140, Fat: 6 g, Carb: 91 g, Fiber: 2 g, Protein: 23 g

743. Rummy Eggnog

Preparation time: 30 minutes | **Cooking time:** 1 hour | **Servings:** 2

Ingredients:
- 4 eggs
- 1 cup heavy cream
- ¾ cup sugar
- ½ cup rum
- 2 cups whole milk
- ½ tablespoon vanilla
- 2 cinnamon sticks
- Freshly grated nutmeg for garnish

Directions:
Preheat the water bath to 140°F.
Beat eggs until pale and fluffy. Beat in milk, cream, vanilla, and sugar. Pour into bag with the cinnamon stick and seal using water immersion method.
Place bag in water bath and cook 1 hour.
Strain solids from the bag using a coffee filter or cheesecloth. Chill completely.
To serve, pour into glasses and top with freshly grated nutmeg.

Nutrition:
Calories: 551, Fat :354 g, Carb: 242 g, Fiber: 6 g, Protein: 14 g

744. Caramel Sauce

Preparation time: 5 minutes | **Cooking time:** 2 hours
Servings 2

Ingredients:
- 1 cup coconut milk.
- Vanilla extract.
- 5 pitted dates.
- Pinch of salt.

Directions:
Put all the ingredients in a cooking pouch and vacuum seal it.
Prepare your Sous-vide water bath to a temperature of 58°F.
Immerse the pouch in the water bath and cook for 120 hours.
Remove and transfer the contents to a blender.
Once blended, transfer the mixture to your refrigerator to chill.
Serve and enjoy!

Nutrition:
Calories: 77, Carbs: 8 g, Fats: 5 g, Proteins: 3 g

745. Coconut Milk Cardamom

Preparation time: 30 minutes
Cooking time 3 hours
Servings 2

Ingredients:
- Granulated sugar.
- 30ml basmati rice
- 1 cup water
- Cardamom pods.
- 1 cup coconut milk whole.

Directions:
Put all the ingredients in a bowl and combine.
Divide the mixture into 2 canning jars.
Seal and submerge the jars in the water bath.
Cook for 2 hours and remove once done.
Transfer it to a serving platter.
Add pudding as topping.
Serve and enjoy.

Nutrition:
Calories: 552, Fats: 57 g, Carbs: 13 g, Protein: 5 g

746. Vanilla Cake with Chocolate Topping

Preparation time 30 minutes | **Cooking time:** 3 hours
Servings 2

Ingredients:
- Granulated sugar
- Cake mix. 50g butter
- Cocoa powder

Directions:
Prepare your Sous-vide water bath to a temperature of 91°F.
Get the cake mix poured into a jar.
Seal the jars and immerse it into the preheated water bath.
Cook underwater for 3 hours.
Remove the jar from the water bath and keep to cool.
To make the topping, add the coco powder and butter and mix until well combined.
Refrigerate the mixture for a while.
Add chocolate as toping to the cake and serve.

Nutrition:
Calories: 234, Carbs: 23g, Protein: 19 g, Fat: 10 g

747. Vanilla Caramel Ice Cream

Preparation time: 1 hour | **Cooking time:** 30 minutes | **Servings:** 2

Ingredients:
- 50g heavy cream
- 50g sugar
- 1 cup whole milk
- 1tbsp vanilla extract.
- 2 egg yolks Kosher salt.

Directions:
Put the sugar in a pan and heat it until it melts.
Add the heavy cream to pan and combine well.
Transfer the mixture to the fridge to chill.
In a bowl, add the remaining ingredients and refrigerate.
Once chilled, combine the caramel in ice cream maker.
Serve and enjoy!

Nutrition:
Calories: 152, Protein: 7 g, Carbs: 12 g, Fat: 10 g

748. Creamy Eggy Berry Blend

Preparation time: 5 minutes. | **Cooking time:** 30 minutes | **Servings:** 2

Ingredients:
- 1 cup Blackberries
- ½ cup Heavy cream
- 5 tbsp. Sugar
- 2 tsp. Baking powder
- 2 pcs. Eggs
- ½ cup Butter, liquefied
- 2 tsp. Vanilla extract

Directions:
Put all of the ingredients in a container and whip carefully.
Split the blend among 4 portions and set the portions in the fryer.

Heat at 370 o F for 12 minutes.
Put it in the fridge and eat while it is cold.

Nutrition:
Calories: 230, Fat: 2 g, Fiber: 2 g, Carbs: 14 g, Protein: 7 g

749. Milky Cacao Brownies

Preparation time: 30 minutes | **Cooking time:** 30 minutes | **Servings:** 2

Ingredients:
- 1 tsp. Vanilla extract
- 1 pc. Egg
- 2 cups White flour
- ½ cup Butter, liquefied
- 4 tbsp. Sugar
- ½ cup Chocolate chips

Directions:
Set all the ingredients in a container and blend carefully.
Put the blend into a pan religiously that suits your air fryer.
Set the pan in the fryer and heat at 185 o F for 25 minutes.
Let the heat subside, wedge, and eat.

Nutrition:
Calories: 230, Fat: 12 g, Fiber: 2 g, Carbs: 12 g, Protein: 5 g

750. Yogurt and Cream Cheesecake

Preparation time: 40 minutes | **Cooking time:** 30 minutes | **Servings:** 2

Ingredients:
- 6 pcs. Eggs, whipped
- 1 tsp. Vanilla
- 9 oz. White flour
- 4 oz. Cream cheese, melted
- 1 pc. Mandarin orange, skinless
- 1 tsp. Baking powder
- 6 tbsp. Sugar
- 4 oz. Yogurt

Directions:
In a blender, put the mandarin, flour, 2 tbsp. of sugar, vanilla, eggs, and baking powder then start the blender.
Split the blend among 2 cake pans organized with parchment paper cook each in the air fryer at 370 °F for 15 minutes.
In a container, mix the yogurt, cream cheese, and 4 tbsp. sugar, whip carefully.
Put one layer of the cake on a platter and set with half of the yogurt blend then put it thoroughly in equal amounts.
Put the remaining cake layer on the upper portion of the first with the yogurt blend, and put the yogurt blend on the upper portion, scattering it excellently.
Wedge, eat, and enjoy!

Nutrition:
Calories: 231, Fat: 12 g, Fiber: 2 g, Carbs: 11 g, Protein: 5 g

Conclusion

Home-cooked meals have a huge effect on your health, especially because there are increasing rates of healthcare difficulties in our time today. Having a healthy diet would prove to be beneficial, especially because we are surrounded by processed and manufactured goods. We are living in a polluted world taken over by smoke from factories and cars, so it should be our main priority to take better care of our health. A healthy diet can help strengthen our immunity and reduce weight loss, as well as improve our overall mental health and energy level. Making home-cooked meals are not only good for losing weight and dieting; it is also a great past time and stress reliever from our busy lives filled with paper works and city noises. Cooking is seen as a creative outlet and will allow you to express your feelings more clearly.

With the many recipes provided in this book, as well the comprehensive guideline, you now know the capability of every ingredient, as well as how to properly use them to enjoy a range of flavorsome meals. I genuinely hope that you have enjoyed the various recipes from every cultural background as you experience new and exotic flavors without having to spend the extra money.

Because this book includes a step-by-step method in cooking a variety of meals ranging from breakfast, lunch, dinner, dessert, and even healthy snacks – even a beginner can one day master cooking. With the use of various ingredients such as meat, vegetables, seafoods, and dairy, cooking at home will be a breeze from now on. These ingredients will not take up much time from your busy lives as they can be done in the time span of 10 minutes up to a few hours if you are feeling more productive.

This recipe book was created with the thought of couples who may be running out of ways to spend time and learn new things about each other. I hope that you were able to create delicious food and have romantic dates with your significant other with the use of recipes provided in this book.

Cooking and eating together will be an experience that you and your partner would love as this will allow deeper bonds to be formed between you and your loved one. It is very important to spend time with your partner as this will allow you to communicate about your relationship, as well as avoid any conflict. Taking time to have a date night should not be something to be guilty about, instead you should be looking forward to taking a break from the chaos of the world. I hope that this recipe book will allow you to form new memories that you and your loved one can one day look back to and remember happy times.

I am dedicating this book to all the couples who are beginners at cooking but have taken a giant leap to achieve a healthier lifestyle, as well as a healthier relationship. With the help of this recipe book, I hope that you and your partner can effortlessly prepare the various recipes included with no challenge, as well as to have the opportunity to increase feelings of intimacy and build attachment.

Thank you for allowing me to be a part of your journey!

CPSIA information can be obtained
at www.ICGtesting.com
Printed in the USA
LVHW061035280621
691334LV00020B/311